ANTI-CATHOLICISM IN NORTHERN IRELAND, 1600–1998

Also by John D. Brewer

AFTER SOWETO: An Unfinished Journey

BLACK AND BLUE: Policing in South Africa

CAN SOUTH AFRICA SURVIVE? (*editor*)

CRIME IN IRELAND 1945–95: 'Here be Dragons'
(*with Bill Lockhart and Paula Rodgers*)

INSIDE THE RUC: Routine Policing in a Divided Society
(*with Kathleen Magee*)

MOSLEY'S MEN: The BUF in the West Midlands

THE POLICE, PUBLIC ORDER AND THE STATE (*with Adrian Guelke, Ian Hume, Edward Moxon-Browne and Rick Wilford*)

RESTRUCTURING SOUTH AFRICA (*editor*)

THE ROYAL IRISH CONSTABULARY: An Oral History

Anti-Catholicism in Northern Ireland, 1600–1998

The Mote and the Beam

John D. Brewer
Professor of Sociology
The Queen's University of Belfast

with

Gareth I. Higgins
Researcher
The Queen's University of Belfast

First published in Great Britain 1998 by
MACMILLAN PRESS LTD
Houndmills, Basingstoke, Hampshire RG21 6XS and London
Companies and representatives throughout the world

A catalogue record for this book is available from the British Library.

ISBN 0–333–74634–1 hardcover
ISBN 0–333–74635–X paperback

First published in the United States of America 1998 by
ST. MARTIN'S PRESS, INC.,
Scholarly and Reference Division,
175 Fifth Avenue, New York, N.Y. 10010

ISBN 0–312–21738–2

Library of Congress Cataloging-in-Publication Data
Brewer, John D.
Anti-Catholicism in Northern Ireland, 1600–1998 : the mote and the
beam / John D. Brewer, with Gareth I. Higgins.
p.   cm.
Includes bibliographical references and index.
ISBN 0–312–21738–2
1. Anti-Catholicism—Northern Ireland—History.   2. Northern
Ireland—Religion.   3. Northern Ireland—Politics and government.
I. Higgins, Gareth I.   II. Title.
BX1766.B74   1998
305.6'20416—dc21   98–28305
                                                        CIP

This book is printed on paper suitable for recycling and made from fully managed and
sustained forest sources.

10   9   8   7   6   5
07   06   05   04   03   02   01   00

Printed and bound in Great Britain by
Antony Rowe Ltd, Chippenham, Wiltshire

To my children, Bronwen and Gwyn

Why beholdest thou the mote that is in thy brother's eye but considerest not the beam that is in thine own eye? Wilt thou say to thy brother, 'let me pull out the mote out of thine eye'; and behold, a beam is in thine own eye. Thou hypocrite, first cast out the beam out of thine own eye: and then shalt thou see clearly to cast out the mote out of thy brother's eye.

(Matthew 7:3–5)

eface and Acknowledgements

nan Swift, the well-known eighteenth-century satirist and Irishman, once said
reland had enough religion to make its citizens hate, but not enough to make
love one another. On a day in April 1997, when the Irish Republican Army
) shot a woman, with three young children, in the back in a deliberate and cold-
led attempt to kill her, I realised then, if I had not before, the extent of the hatred
people in Ireland feel for those with whom they disagree politically. Critics
e IRA understandably made much of shooting. That she was a policewoman
ot alter the principle, as these critics saw it, that the IRA believe that political
es are progressed by shooting women, and in the back at that. The incident further
ared the hatred some people feel toward the IRA. The following month a
ceman was kicked to death by a frenzied mob, egged on by women in the crowd
se sense and reason was consumed by hatred for the victim – a father of three
ag children, one of whom is disabled – because he helped to deny them what
saw as their right to march in orange sashes and bowler hats through a Catholic
ict. This book is about such contempt and hatred, but exclusively that shown
ard Catholics and the Catholic Church by some of the very Protestants who
lemn the IRA and yet who themselves kill policemen. It is no surprise that the
hatred feeds on the other, and the book is written in the hope that exploring the
ological processes and historical dynamics of one set of hatreds will make
ryone examine the beam in their own eye, as Christ put it, before judging the
e in their neighbour's.

he Biblical reference to motes and beams in the title is deliberate. Many
testants allege that Catholics have beams in their eyes in the way they are
posed to look at Protestants, as reflected in the allegations, for example, that
holics are anti-Protestant, and in claims about Protestant ethnic cleansing, and
supposed extirpation of Protestants on the island of Ireland. However, what many
in the eyes of their Catholic neighbours is shaped by the beam in their own eyes,
resented by anti-Catholicism. The purpose of this book, therefore, is not to give
h sides of a story — the tragedy of Northern Ireland has been told many times –
t to challenge the Protestant community about anti-Catholicism. It is not motivated
anti-Protestantism; I am a Christian and believe in salvation through faith in Jesus
d that justification comes through grace. I do not believe that the Reformation
ıs a mistake; nor do I claim that all Protestants are anti-Catholic or that anti-
otestantism does not exist, but that its scale and intensity are different and it has
t permeated the social and cultural structures of Northern Ireland so systemati-
lly, or to anywhere near the same level, or for as long. Anti-Protestantism exists
a negative discourse and a set of pejorative beliefs amongst some Catholics, but
has not defined a type of society. Anti-Catholicism, however, is one (and only

viii

Contents

one) of the tap-roots of sectarianism and has shaped a whole social structure for centuries.

There are other motivations to the study which also have nothing to do with any alleged anti-Protestantism. As a Christian sociologist I am puzzled to understand the processes which make some believers in Jesus treat and perceive other human beings so unjustly and inhumanely. Perhaps above all, the book is motivated by the wish to apply to Northern Ireland one of the truths spoken by Nelson Mandela. Mandela was a man who had every reason to hate after a quarter of a century spent in prison – much the same length of time as the current period of civil unrest in Ulster – but he emerged to work tirelessly for peace and reconciliation. One of his remarks is telling for Northern Ireland. He once said that if one genuinely wished to negotiate an end to violence with one's opponent, it is necessary to place oneself in their position, to understand how they think and what locates their attitudes and beliefs. This book is intended to convey to Protestants what it is like to be subjected to anti-Catholicism, so that they can better understand what motivates many Catholics to want to change society, and to convey to Catholics the social and political processes which cause some Protestants to be anti-Catholic, so that they can better understand Protestant fears and anxieties.

The research on which the book is based was originally suggested to me over lunch by the Rev. Ken Newell, a good friend, pastor and counsellor, who has long sought to ensure that people in Northern Ireland see each other clearly, with eyes free from all beams and motes. The book is a dedication to his tirelessness and passion for reconcilation between Catholics and Protestants. The research on which it is based was funded by the Central Community Relations Unit in Northern Ireland and the European Union's Physical and Social Environment Programme, where Marguerite Eagan acted as a kind and helpful intercessor. I am grateful for their permission to publish the findings of the research, the small report on which was entitled 'The Roots of Sectarianism'. The Rev. John Dunlop kindly read the report and we are grateful for his comments. The views expressed are our own, not those of the Central Community Relations Unit. Gareth Higgins was employed as Research Assistant on the project and he collected some of the data. Both of us are Christians and sociologists, and much enjoyed our collaboration in applying both sets of principles to an understanding of an aspect of Northern Irish society. Gareth wrote a draft of the Postscript and while I wrote the rest of this volume, I am happy to acknowledge Gareth's positive contribution throughout by co-authorship of the book.

Several people and organisations helped us in the research – by agreeing to be interviewed, by helping to establish contacts and set up interviews, and by commenting on written work and assisting in numerous other ways – and we acknowledge their contribution with very grateful thanks: Cecil Andrews, Dr Esmond Birnie, Professor Paul Bew, Professor Steve Bruce, Jimmy Drumm, David Ervine, Dr Bernie Hayes, Professor David Hempton, Rev. Professor Finlay Holmes, Dr Liam Kennedy, the Linenhall Library, Pastor Kenny McClinton, Cyril McMaster, Gary McMichael, Sharon McMullan, Rev. Ken Newell, Fr. Eddie O'Donnell SJ, Professor Liam

O'Dowd, Fr. Gerry O'Hanlon SJ, Fr. Myles O'Reilly SJ, Sr. Geraldine Smyth, Take Heed Ministries, Francis Teeney, Rev. Professor John Thompson and Dr Nicola Yeates. The tireless efforts of Francis Teeney on our behalf need recording with very special thanks. We are also grateful to those ordinary Christian believers whom we interviewed as part of the research, whose desire for anonymity permits only this brief record of thanks. Gareth Higgins wishes to acknowledge the love and support of his family, Fay, Iain, Brian and Caryll.

John D. Brewer
February 1998

List of Figures

Introduction

Racism has a deterministic belief system to reinforce racial divisions based on claims about biological science rooted in the nineteenth century; sectarianism on claims about Scripture based in the sixteenth century. Despite the passage of time, claims about biological science are still common-sensically used today in folk notions of 'race', and anti-Catholicism is still claimed to be scriptural as we enter the third millennium. These claims about Scripture are particularly important in Northern Ireland, where they form part of the dynamics to Northern Ireland's conflict. The belief that anti-Catholicism is scriptural is part of the self-defining identity of certain Protestants and inhibits reconciliation between the two communities by suggesting that divisions are immutably upheld by theological doctrine. The roots of sectarianism thus lie partly in claims about theology four centuries ago.

Anti-Catholicism, however, needs to be approached sociologically rather than theologically, for anti-Catholicism was given a scriptural underpinning in the history of Protestant–Catholic relations in Northern Ireland in order to reinforce divisions between the religious communities and to offer a deterministic belief system to justify them. It has been mobilised in this way at particular historical junctures in Protestant–Catholic relations in Ireland and as a result of specific socio-economic and political processes. Anti-Catholicism is thus a powerful resource and can be located sociologically by identifying the socio-economic and political processes that lead to theology being mobilised in the protection and justification of social stratification and social closure.[1]

But the sociological features of anti-Catholicism do not rest solely on its role in social inequality and stratification. Anti-Catholicism is not a resource with a monolithic character and form. Four types of anti-Catholicism in Northern Ireland can be distinguished – the passive, covenantal, secular and Pharisaic modes – which articulate claims about Catholicism and Catholics quite differently. Each mode or type is distinguished by the foundational ideas on which it is premised, the form of rhetoric used, the constituency within Protestantism to which it primarily appeals, and in terms of its consequences for reconciliation and relationship with Catholics. Moreover, describing the various types of anti-Catholicism illustrates some general sociological features about religion and identity in modern Northern Ireland, as well as illustrating the sociological role of language in both representing and reproducing sectarian experiences in Northern Irish society. Talk about Catholics in typical derogatory terms is simultaneously a way of perceiving them. Finally, an analysis of anti-Catholicism forces enquiry about the sociological processes which explain why certain theological claims still resonate in Northern Ireland today when they do not have the same saliency elsewhere.

What is Anti-Catholicism?

Anti-Catholicism is one of the tap roots of sectarianism and can be defined in the same terms as I once defined sectarianism (Brewer, 1992): the determination of actions, attitudes and practices by negative beliefs about individual Catholics, the Catholic Church as an institution or Catholic doctrine, which results in these negative beliefs being invoked as an ethnic boundary marker, which can be used, in some settings, to represent social stratification and conflict. It occurs at three levels – that of ideas, individual behaviour and the social structure. In terms of ideas, anti-Catholicism is expressed in negative stereotypes and pejorative beliefs, notions and language about Catholics and the Catholic Church. At the level of individual action, it shows itself in various forms of direct discrimination, intimidation, harassment and sectarianism against Catholics or the Catholic Church because of their Catholicism. At the level of the social structure, anti-Catholicism expresses itself in patterns of indirect and institutional discrimination and social disadvantage experienced by Catholics because they are Catholics.[2] Anti-Catholicism is thus a small sub-type of sectarianism, which is itself a sub-type of ethnocentrism, and has some parallels with racism (on which, see Brewer, 1992; Hickman, 1995; McVeigh, 1995) and anti-Semitism.

There is nothing inevitable about the progression through these levels, for anti-Catholicism can remain as a set of ideas without affecting behaviour or having implications at the social structural level. In its worst manifestations however, such as Northern Ireland, it occurs at all three levels. In its most developed form, anti-Catholicism ranges over ideas, language and behaviour, and is involved in the determination and rationalisation of social closure, affecting individual Catholics and the group membership as a whole. Thus, while sixteenth-century theological disputes may be the source, anti-Catholicism in some settings is mobilised as a resource for critical socio-economic and political reasons, using processes that are recognisably sociological rather than theological.

Disputes over theology are thus sometimes the least of the conflicts anti-Catholicism is mobilised to fight. Nor is theology the only source of belief and claim that infuses anti-Catholic ideas, although some are theologically derived. The Pope is alleged to be the antiChrist predicted in the Book of Revelation. The Catholic Church is also alleged to be the Beast, Harlot, Whore and Mystery Babylon written of in Scripture. Aspects of Catholic practice and doctrine are objected to on theological grounds in that they allegedly either breach Scripture or are unscriptural, such as devotion to Mary, the Saints and icons; the intermediary role of the priest and the Pope; the value placed on Church tradition alongside Scripture; the practice of penance; and the belief in such things as papal infallibility, salvation by works rather than grace alone, confession, venial and mortal sins, purgatory and transubstantiation (belief in the real presence of Christ in the Eucharist during mass). Some anti-Catholics claim on theological grounds therefore that Catholicism is unChristian; some claim even that it is pagan, while others contend merely that it is in need of reform. These theological disputes evince considerable historical continuity, being raised first at the time of the Reformation and articulated ever since. Thus, a pamphlet in 1716 echoes down the ages in the theological complaints made against Catholicism:

> a Papist is an idolater, who worships images, pictures, stocks and stones, the works of men's hands; calls upon the virgin Mary, saints and angels to pray for them; adores relics ... He prefers traditions before the Holy Scriptures; thinks good works alone merit heaven; eats his God by the cunning trick of transubstantiation and swears the Pope is infallible.[3]   (quoted in Haydon, 1993: 22)

The political content of some anti-Catholic ideas, however, is very high and these show less historical continuity. Many of the anti-Catholic ideas that abound have no root in theology but various political conspiracies, which vary with the time and context. It was popular to believe in the seventeenth century, for example, that King Charles had been executed as a result of a Jesuit plot (while others contended that the King was himself proto-Catholic). What changes with the day is the substance of the conspiracy. Thus, some people claim that the Catholic Church today acts in order to realise a single world-wide government, run by the Pope from Rome. The Catholic Church is alleged to have been involved in several conspiracies across the years: the growth of communism, the fall of communism, the rise of Nazism, the assassination of Abraham Lincoln, the overthrow of Third World dictatorships, the development of the European Union (whose flag is said to represent evil images of the antiChrist predicted in Scripture), both world wars (whose point was to set Protestant nations against one another), and the divorce between the Prince and Princess of Wales, amongst other things. Catholics are said to have infiltrated senior positions in Western governments, national security agencies, the media, the military and the British monarchy for evil political design. Sometimes the evil intent is theologically understood, as with the claim that it is all done in order to abolish Protestantism (M. Farrell, n.d.) or to advance ecumenism (de Semlyen, 1993: 138), but it is also rendered political, reflecting the supposed ambitions of the Catholic Church for political power. Under these conspiracies, the confessional is simply a mechanism by which information is collected for transmission to Rome, and the Catholic Church nothing but a device for spying (lo Bello, 1982): it is claimed to be better at spying than professional organisations, comparing favourably, apparently, with the former KGB, with two and a half million trained agents. Others allege that the Catholic Church is simply a device for making money for the Vatican (de Semlyen, 1993: 124). That it is difficult to detect evidence for these conspiracies only proves the point, because 'Papists' are so well concealed and the Catholic Church so secretive.

Another prominent feature of anti-Catholicism which has no basis in theology is the alleged sexual perversion of believers, especially celibates. As Bruce shows (1985a), allegations of sexual perversion are plausible because everyone is capable of sexual activity and thus it *might* have happened, and allegations of sexual activity against celibates threaten the very legitimacy of the Catholic ethos of a sacrificial life for priests and nuns. Allegations against celibates often involve projection of the accuser's own sexual fantasies and realisation of being unable to contemplate life without sexual activity: priests and nuns *must* therefore be sexually active. Nuns serve priests sexually; priests abuse women in the confessional. One allegation concerning members of Opus Dei is worth repeating. Numenaries apparently self-flagellate with the cat-o'-nine-tails and wear a metal chain in their genital area that inflicts pain when they walk. People as young as fourteen have supposedly been recruited into doing this (reflecting the projection of yet more sexual fantasies). Haydon's analysis of anti-Catholicism in eighteenth-century England discusses the extent to which people projected their sexual fantasies on to the Catholic Church (Haydon, 1993: 254–5), suggesting that the fantasies represented their own repressed desires and feared temptations. And public revelations concerning sexual abuse of young children by priests only confirm the suspicion of the sexual degradation of the Catholic Church.

It is clear at this juncture that the beliefs, notions, stereotypes and behaviours which comprise anti-Catholicism can be placed along two axes, describing the extent of theological content and the degree of political content, as represented in Figure 1. Anti-Catholic beliefs, which can be high or low in theological content, can have a high or low level of political content, in that they can be used by some people to mobilise against a wide variety of issues locally and they can also be used to support allegations of several international political conspiracies. Although there are theological differences in the teachings of Catholics and Protestants, the interesting

low ←   **theological content**   → **high**

high

↑

political content

↓

low

Figure 1   The two axes of anti-Catholicism

sociological question is why the theological differences can become associated with socio-economic and political conflicts and circumstances to an extent that, in some settings, theology is almost absent or long-forgotten. Anti-Catholicism in Northern Ireland is such a case; Britain generally was also once a good case.

Anti-Catholicism in Britain

We know a great deal about anti-Catholicism in Britain, covering twentieth-century Scotland (Bruce, 1985b, 1985c; Hickman, 1995), and England for the seventeenth (Hill, 1971; Millar, 1973), eighteenth (Colley, 1992; Haydon, 1993), nineteenth (Norman, 1968; Arnstein, 1982; Wolffe, 1991; Paz, 1992), and twentieth centuries (Hickman, 1995). Anti-Catholicism was once very common, evident even in liberal thinkers in eighteenth-century England such as Locke, and radical satirists like Defoe, who said that Catholicism was the spectre with which nurses frighten naughty children. It circulated amongst the intelligensia and in popular culture. Thus, Paz (1992), for example, contrasts organised and popular anti-Catholicism in England. There was anti-Catholicism disseminated in organised fashion through petitions, lobbying of Parliament and pressure groups, public meetings and demonstrations, and numerous forms of printed propaganda; and anti-Catholicism at the level of everyday life and popular culture, expressed through festivals, bonfires, street and pub brawls and communal riots. It was articulated by means of classic literature appealing to the elite, such as Bunyan's *Pilgrim's Progress*, and popular literature for the masses, like comics and almanacs (almanacs are discussed by Colley, 1992), as well as the narratives and oral traditions passed around on deprived city-streets (on oral traditions amongst the poor see Haydon, 1993: 42). Anti-Catholicism was also enshrined in law. From the seventeenth to early nineteenth centuries, Catholics were not allowed the vote and excluded from Parliament and all other state offices. They were subjected to punitive taxation and to social restrictions on access to weaponry, education, property and worship. And while it was true after the eighteenth century that the negative stereotypes could be suspended by personal contact with individual Catholics (ibid.: 11) and that, locally, relations with Catholics could be good (Colley, 1992: 22), the anti-Catholic Gordon Riots were the worst communal violence in Britain's history (see Wolffe, 1991: 12) and in times of political conflict, national danger or war with Catholic powers, Catholics in Britain were – like witches centuries before – made scapegoats and easy targets for attack and abuse (Colley, 1992: 23).

This work on anti-Catholicism in Britain associates it with a variety of processes lying outside theological disputes. In the seventeenth century, for example, anti-Catholicism was particularly associated with attacks on absolutism in government and the monarchy, and a defence of political liberty and parliamentary democracy. Absolutism was Catholic; Protestantism was associated with liberty, won in hardship by the English Civil War and the Glorious Revolution of 1688, which saw Protestant William of Orange defeat Catholic James II. Thus, Parliament swept away considerations of heredity when it ensured a Protestant successor to the throne in 1701 by declaring that a Catholic was incapable of governing the realm (an Act which remains in force). Queen Anne was required to make a declaration at her coronation in 1702 against the doctrine of transubstantiation and Colley shows that Parliament passed over more than fifty people who were closer as blood relations to Queen Anne but were ineligible for the Crown after her death because they were Catholic, opting instead for a German, with a smattering of English, whose only advantage was that he was Lutheran (ibid.: 46).

A related process is the association of Protestantism with nationhood in Britain, and thus of anti-Catholicism with the development of a British identity (argued by Colley, 1992; Wolffe, 1994; Hickman, 1995; Hempton, 1996). As part of their nation-making after the travails of the defeat of the Catholic Jacobites and the incorporation of Scotland into Union, Britons were encouraged to believe they were God's elect, watched over because they were defending Protestantism against the antiChrist and the Whore, represented by the Pope and the Catholic Church. As Hempton shows (1996: 143), British anti-Catholicism was different from its continental expressions because it became part of the ideological project of the state. It contributed to the creation of national myths and the dissolution of lingering fissures within society. Protestantism was British, it preserved freedom, and it defined in part the nation's identity. In so far as Britain was free, democratic and economically prosperous, it was because it was not Catholic (ibid.: 146). As Britain prospered, its superiority was attributed to its election by God and thus, in this mind-set, to its Protestantism.

Notions of cultural superiority are often associated with xenophobia, and anti-Catholicism in Britain was also originally linked with negative attitudes towards foreigners who challenged or threatened it, most of whom were Catholic, like the French, Spanish or Portuguese. By the nineteenth century, however, anti-Catholicism in Britain had become more narrowly linked with xenophobia toward the Irish, as Hickman (1995) emphasises. Anti-Irishness was also much of the animus for anti-Catholicism in Scotland well into the 1930s (Bruce, 1985c: 25). The political problem posed by Home Rule for Ireland, and the influx of Irish immigrants to Britain's cities, were processes at the heart of Victorian anti-Catholicism. Hempton argues that sixteenth- and seventeenth-century anti-Catholic ideas, without root in Ireland, were mobilised in nineteenth-century England against Irish nationalism and the Irish people generally (Hempton, 1996: 145), although the campaign against Catholic Ireland also mobilised popular ideas drawn from Victorian 'scientific racism', which claimed that the Irish were racially inferior to the British (on the use of scientific racism to marginalise the Irish, see Curtis, 1971; Miles, 1982). However, because anti-Catholicism was a general cultural tenet in Victorian England, its expression did not necessarily correlate with the presence of Irish migrants locally.

Two other processes, with greater connection to theology, were also associated with anti-Catholicism in Britain, the emergence of evangelistic Protestantism and militant Catholicism. A confident, assertive and developing Catholic Church invariably provoked reaction, in which Protestant senses of threat and fear combined to reproduce anti-Catholicism (Paz, 1992: 81ff.). Any proselytising by Catholics or missionary zeal by priests often lead to anti-Catholic rhetoric or behaviour. Additions to Catholic numbers were seen as strengthening the forces of the antiChrist, as well as further threatening the Crown, liberty, prosperity and all other virtues associated with Protestantism in national myth. The Catholic Church did grow in nineteenth-century Britain but quite often Catholic expansion bore little relation to Protestant fears (Haydon, 1993: 8). None the less, the growth was alleged to be pervasive. Linked to this was the influence of evangelistic Protestantism. In its Methodist guise, evangelism was politically radical, but Wolffe has shown that by the mid-nineteenth century, evangelistic enterprise was linked to Toryism (Wolffe 1991: 300) and the transmission of values of civility and prosperity linked fundamentally to notions of Empire and the Protestant religion. Aggressive evangelism by Protestant churches and evangelistic societies fostered dispute as much over the cultural, political and economic backwardness of Catholic countries as the theological weaknesses of Catholicism. Empire, economics and evangelism were a familiar alliteration: Jesus Christ was free trade, and free trade was Jesus Christ, declared the Governor of Hong Kong (quoted in Hempton, 1996: 159), and, of course, Jesus was in many a Music Hall joke both Protestant and an Englishman. Evangelism, Empire and anti-Catholicism were thus closely related.

Anti-Catholicism in Ireland

In the midst of all that we now know about anti-Catholicism in Britain and the processes which underlay it, it is remarkable that there have been no studies of similar processes in Ireland, the one overwhelmingly Catholic country in the British Isles and, in the North at least, the only place where it has survived in its virulent and extreme form. Well-known and authoritative studies of the churches in Ireland are conspicuous for failing for mention anti-Catholicism (on the Church of Ireland, see Akenson, 1971; on the Catholic Church, see Keenan, 1983, and Corish, 1985; on the Presbyterian Church, see Barkley, 1959; on the Reformed Presbyterian Church, see Loughridge, 1984). It is touched on briefly in Hempton's study of evangelism in nineteenth-century Ulster (Hempton, 1996: 93–116; Hempton and Hill, 1992), and is implicit in historical and contemporary accounts of Protestant–Catholic relations in Ireland, North and South, and any reference to sectarianism. This gap in knowledge is unfortunate, for an explicit and detailed focus on anti-Catholicism for the whole of Ireland historically and for Northern Ireland in the present day, is important for three reasons. First, it fills the one omission from the literature on anti-Catholicism in the British Isles. Second, it permits an explanation of why its saliency and public resonance have not declined in Northern Ireland when they have done so elsewhere in Britain and Ireland. Third, this second issue highlights the sociological dynamics of anti-Catholicism and the array of socio-economic and political processes it is linked to beyond theology.

A large amount of anti-Catholic literature circulates in Northern Ireland today, and it is clearly problematic because this material, while perhaps of marginal appeal elsewhere, has resonance in the North for sociological reasons. Some of the claims made in this literature are worth listing. The theological claims include the claim that the early Christians in the Book of Acts were Protestant; that Catholicism is anti-Christian, pagan, and even satanic and that the Pope is the antiChrist predicted in the Book of Revelation; that Catholics are cannibals; that they worship Mary above Jesus, and even that they reject Jesus; that the Pope sells masses for money, is carried on the shoulders of servants in splendour, and that he claims authority in Heaven; and that the mass is absurd and a pantomime. Claims involving international conspiracies include the notion that both Nazism and communism were Catholic-inspired, that the Second World War was a Jesuit plot, and that the European Union is directed from the Vatican as part of its ambitions for political power and a single world government. Local conspiracies include the idea that the boycott of Protestant businesses by local Catholics arising from contentious Orange Order marches is predicted in the Book of Revelation and is part of the unfolding of the antiChrist; that the Catholic Church supports terrorism and aids the IRA; and that it seeks to ethnically cleanse Protestants by annihilating them. This literature warns people off from making friendships with Catholics because social mixing leads to marriage, and mixed marriages dilute Protestantism. Were such claims to feature racial minorities, most would be illegal under race relations legislation, but Catholics have no similar legal protection.

Messages like this are disseminated by every possible modern means, including books, pamphlets, magazines, newspapers, tracts, videos, tapes and comics. The comics come from the US and are printed in forty-three languages, including Zulu, Creole, pidgin and Swahili. Northern Ireland is integrated into an international network of printers and publishers, exporting material into Britain and Ireland. Anti-Catholic material is obtainable from the Internet, and there is a computer database, run from Louisville, containing information on the Catholic Church which can be accessed by those interested in evangelising them (in book form, see Jackson, 1988), known ironically as the 'Vatican Bank'. Much of this information is exported directly to local bookshops and churches in Northern Ireland as well as imported by local distributors for relay onwards. A lot of literature is also locally produced, connected with several organisations and individuals in the North who are hostile to Catholicism, such as Inheritance Ministries, Take Heed Ministries, the Evangelical Protestant Society, the Free Presbyterians and the Orange Order. A summary of the connections is presented in Figure 2.

Although some of this material is global, it resonates in Northern Ireland and is appropriated into local circumstances; some of the international literature even makes reference to Ireland. For example, de Semlyen (1993: 102) claims that Protestants in Ireland are under siege and that the IRA is supported by the Vatican and local priests (ibid.: 110–11), which are familiar themes amongst local publishers and authors. Claims like these are important because they affect people's ideas and behaviour. Anti-Catholicism in Northern Ireland is different from many of the other countries or regions which produce and export similar material (such as the Southern

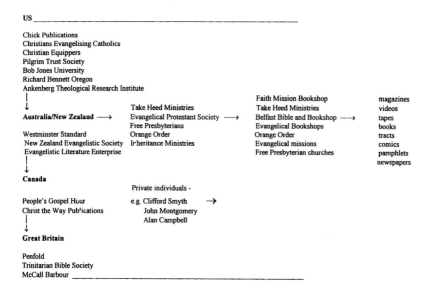

US

Chick Publications
Christians Evangelising Catholics
Christian Equippers
Pilgrim Trust Society
Bob Jones University
Richard Bennett Oregon
Ankenberg Theological Research Institute

		Faith Mission Bookshop	magazines
↓	Take Heed Ministries	Take Heed Ministries	videos
Australia/New Zealand ⟶	Evangelical Protestant Society ⟶	Belfast Bible and Bookshop ⟶	tapes
	Free Presbyterians	Evangelical Bookshops	books
Westminster Standard	Orange Order	Orange Order	tracts
New Zealand Evangelistic Society	Inheritance Ministries	Evangelical missions	comics
Evangelistic Literature Enterprise		Free Presbyterian churches	pamphlets
↓			newspapers

Canada

Private individuals -

People's Gospel Hour   e.g. Clifford Smyth   ⟶
Christ the Way Publications   John Montgomery
↓   Alan Campbell

Great Britain

Penfold
Trinitarian Bible Society
McCall Barbour

Figure 2   Sources and distribution of anti-Catholic literature in Northern Ireland

states of the US, Canada, and the Antipodes) because it does not just remain at the level of ideas in Northern Ireland but influences hostile behaviour toward Catholics and acts as a rationalisation of the social structural disadvantage and discrimination experienced by Catholics. It is integrally wrapped up in a conflict that has long historical roots and is bitter and violent. Anti-Catholicism fits seamlessly into the zero-sum quality of this conflict (on the zero-sum nature of the conflict in Northern Ireland, see Nelson, 1984; Bruce, 1986; Ruane and Todd, 1996), where conflict is polarised around what are presented ideologically as two mutually exclusive groups, which lack a developed sense of the general good capable of transcending their particular interests. As Ruane and Todd argue (1996: 106–7), the persistence of this zero-sum quality is not a result of the refusal of people in Northern Ireland to contemplate new interests because they are trapped in the past, but is a result of the continuity in the ways the conflict is structured and ideologically defined. Anti-Catholicism is part of the ideological apparatus that constructs two mutually exclusive groups with opposed sets of interests and identities, and it forms part of the symbolic myths, rituals and language which reproduce and represent polarised and sectarian experiences and behaviour, even though in reality the differences between Catholics and Protestants might be small (on which, see Akenson, 1988).

Outline of the Book

The study falls into two parts. The first seeks to illustrate from Irish history the use of anti-Catholicism as a resource in social stratification and social closure, thus showing it to be a sociological process. Sociological processes in their technical sense do important functional work in society and this historical account of anti-Catholicism in Ireland across three centuries examines the various articulations of anti-Catholicism, the issues around which it was mobilised historically and the purpose to which it was put throughout Irish history. It is not intended as a chronological history of Ireland, North and South, which is admirably done elsewhere (see, for recent examples, Foster, 1988; Bardon, 1992; Kee, 1995), nor to be exhaustive in historical detail. The focus is on the emergence and development of anti-Catholicism set against two relationships into which anti-Catholicism must be located as a sociological process, that between Protestant and Catholics in Ireland and between Britain and Ireland generally. Part I is divided into three historical periods: plantation to the United Irishmen, Union to partition, and the period covering the formation of Northern Ireland to the present.

Part II presents a sociological description and analysis of contemporary articulations of anti-Catholicism in Northern Ireland, focusing on the four modes or types which exist, and the sociological processes which help to sustain them. Various challenges are made to the foundational ideas on which each mode is based. The study ends by identifying some sociological features involved in anti-Catholicism and its theological misunderstandings and distortions. The common-sense 'cognitive map' underpinning anti-Catholicism is identified, along with its common-sense reasoning processes. The characteristic language used to express anti-Catholicism is analysed as a 'discursive formation', where it is portrayed as representing a language of power reflecting the past reality of power in Northern Ireland. The link between language and identity is addressed with respect to anti-Catholicism, showing that talk about Catholics is simultaneously talk about identity, and that anti-Catholic language is constitutive of the identity of a certain kind of Protestant. The Conclusion summarises the arguments and identifies what a sociological account of anti-Catholicism needs to contain. In the process it answers sociologically the question of why anti-Catholicism has survived in Northern Ireland when it has diminished elsewhere. Comparisons are made with anti-Catholicism in Britain and the US. A Postscript suggests a better way for people in Northern Ireland to deal with theological and doctrinal differences.

Part I

Anti-Catholicism as a Sociological Process in Irish History

Anti-Catholicism is more than a theological debate about the doctrine and practice of the Roman Catholic Church concerning salvational truth, for it can also be understood as a sociological process. Describing something as a 'sociological process' is vacuous unless the phrase itself is defined. A sociological process is a method of doing or producing something that is identifiably social in character. Thus, for example, gender is a sociological process for producing the division of labour in the family; socialisation the sociological process for producing the transmission of culture across the generations, and social class the process for producing strata in a modern industrial society. In this way, sociological processes are resources which achieve some purpose in society, and one or more sociological processes might function simultaneously to achieve this end. In common-sense discourse, the term 'resource' has three meanings. The dictionary definition of the term describes a resource as a means used to expedite an end, a source of support in times of need, and as a supply of material aid or prosperity. Resources can be concrete items, such as physical objects like weapons, cars or buildings; or be more abstract, such as beauty, power or intelligence; and any particular resource can serve one or more of these functions. Money, for example, is a very concrete object, and acts as a resource in all three ways: it is a means to expedite goals, it is a support in times of need, and supplies material wealth and prosperity. Power is another resource, although more abstract, which operates in all three ways.

Anti-Catholicism in Northern Ireland is a resource in the same way and with the same features: it is used to expedite goals, forms a source of support, and supplies material benefits. It operates in this way only in a definite social context, where it develops a distinctive profile. In limited social contexts it can thus be termed a sociological process – a method for producing something social. To locate a sociological process is to render its origins and use in terms of the 'social item' it produces, describing its character and form as they help to produce this social item. The social item can be anything from the transmission of culture between the generations, the allocation of people into economic strata or the creation of a division of labour between family members. Following this argument, anti-Catholicism in Northern Ireland is a sociological process for the production of different

11

rights, opportunities and material rewards between people in a society where religious labels are used to define group boundaries. It has distinct modes or types in the way it operates, and not all function as resources in this manner, but the main modes of the covenantal and secular types produce social stratification and social closure in a distinct type of society. Anti-Catholicism does not operate as a resource to produce this social item in every society, for its function to this end is demarcated by a cultural milieu in which theology can stand for and represent other sorts of differences and conflict between people.

In her account of anti-Catholicism in nineteenth-century Britain, Hickman (1995) provides the only sociological profile of anti-Catholicism. Briefly put, Hickman's argument is that the sociological base of anti-Catholicism in nineteenth-century Britain lay in the need in the nineteenth century to differentiate Irish migrants from native Britons, in which it merged with anti-Irish racism; and the need to create a British national identity, where it merged with cultural nationalism, or what Hickman calls 'cultural racism' (ibid.: 2), which helped to reinforce the cultural superiority of the British by identifying excluded and outsider groups like the Irish Catholics. This sociological base fits nineteenth-century anti-Catholicism in Britain very well, but is not particularly fruitful for explaining sixteenth- or seventeenth-century anti-Catholicism in England, whose roots lie in political conflicts around monarchical versus parliamentary power rather than the need for social closure. But Hickman's argument usefully illustrates that the genesis, nature and purpose of anti-Catholicism can change over time, and that as a sociological process the social item it helps to produce can evolve, becoming larger or narrower as time changes, and more or less the same as in earlier times. Historians of nineteenth-century anti-Catholicism in Britain support the view that while it drew on earlier notions and ideas, its purpose in the nineteenth century was conditioned by the changed social circumstances of the time, notably the influx of Irish migrants competing for scarce socio-economic resources with the native working class and the distorted ideas about the Irish in nineteenth-century 'scientific racism' (see Hempton, 1996: 145).

What is characteristic about anti-Catholicism in Ireland compared to Britain, as Part I will demonstrate, is its timelessness. There has been continuity in its genesis, nature and purpose from plantation to partition and beyond. In Northern Ireland today, as in the whole of Ireland between plantation and partition, anti-Catholicism is used as a resource in a two-fold manner: as a mobilisation to defend the socio-economic and political position of Protestants against opposition that threatens it; and as a rationalisation to justify and legitimise both that privileged position and any conflict with those who challenge or weaken it. The 'social item' produced by this sociological process was, and is, social stratification and social closure. Anti-Catholicism in Ireland has been timeless because the patterns and structure of the conflict in Ireland have remained the same, resulting in a continuity of function for anti-Catholicism as a resource. The lines of differentiation in Ireland have always coalesced, so that theology has always accurately represented differences of race, culture, national origin, power, political participation, and economic wealth and prosperity. Exceptions to this exist, as we shall see, especially in the sixteenth and seventeenth centuries, through the existence, for example, of large Catholic landowners and discrimination against Presbyterian dissenters, but these exceptions were minor and eventually obliterated. The Catholic landowners had political power, and eventually the land itself, wrested from them by the Anglicisation of politics, and Presbyterians were incorporated into a Protestant hegemony after the debacle of the United Irishmen. As Jenkins notes in his recent analysis of Northern Ireland (Jenkins, 1997: 93), whatever confessional differences existed amongst Protestants, they were subsumed under the more significant differences with Irish Catholics. The timelessness of anti-Catholicism in Ireland resides in this timelessness of the patterns of differentiation. Down the centuries Catholicism has stood for defeat in the colonial conflict, equating Catholicism with Irishness and thus cultural barbarity, economic dispossession and political disempowerment. Accordingly, anti-Catholicism has been a resource constantly used to mobilise and rationalise this social stratification and social closure. It has expedited the goal of sectarian inequality, supplied material aid and prosperity in upholding and justifying sectarian inequality to the advantage of Protestants, and been a source of support when Protestant privilege seemed to be threatened by Catholic advances or interfering British governments.

Part I will demonstrate that anti-Catholicism has been deployed as a resource to defend Protestant interests in a variety of different historical circumstances and events, of a theological, political and economic kind. Some of these circumstances and events have been theological, such as when the Roman Catholic Church seemed to progress and prosper as a church, becoming assertive and self-confident, and growing in membership. Anti-Catholic tirades at the level of ideas, or sectarian harassment of Catholics at the level of behaviour, have been provoked, for example, by Cardinal Cullen's strategy in the mid-nineteenth century of transforming Catholicism into a more 'foreign' ultramontanist version, the 'devotional revolution' following the great famine, and the activities of an untrammelled Catholic Church in the newly independent Irish Free State. It has been provoked by political circumstances, when anti-Catholicism has been mobilised as a resource to defend Protestant political interests when these seemed threatened by political events, such as an active and assertive Irish nationalism, or during the events surrounding Home Rule, partition, and civil unrest since 1969. Protestant political interests have not only been threatened by Irish nationalism but also by external forces like Irish and British governments, when anti-Catholicism merged with anti-Irishness and anti-Britishness in an attempt to defend the Union or give voice to opposition against Catholic reform, whether this be Catholic emancipation during the nineteenth century or the 'talks process' in 1997. The demand by Catholics for the full political rights of citizenship within the United Kingdom, let alone for a united Ireland, has always provoked anti-Catholicism. This is not just true for political citizenship; the British government had to force the Stormont government to introduce some welfare state measures in the 1950s because local Unionists thought they advantaged Catholics. Anti-Catholicism is also mobilised in response to economic events, when changed economic circumstances seem to threaten the privileged access Protestants have to scarce socio-economic resources. Anti-Catholicism, for example, was used openly and blatantly by government ministers to rally co-religionists to protect the rights of Protestant unemployed in the 1930s when the economic crisis restricted the ability of the government to deploy preferential employment practices. And anti-Catholicism was used to stymie attempts to mobilise the working class on non-sectarian grounds, such as during the dock strike in 1907 and the poor law relief riots in the 1930s.

Anti-Catholicism has not only functioned as a resource to categorise 'the other', those people excluded by means of social closure from the privileges accorded the rest; it has also helped to define the boundaries of privilege by identifying 'the insider' and the bounds of similarity between them. Ethnic labels as a whole do this, and anti-Catholicism has worked to this end along with other ethnic categorisation processes in Northern Ireland, such as everyday language and political behaviour. But as Jenkins (1997: 93) notes, religion is not a residue of all that remains of the original ethnic-national conflict at the time of plantation, but *is* the boundary marker used in ethnic categorisation. Religious difference draws the boundary lines, and when ethnicity is unpacked in Northern Ireland it dissolves into religion (see ibid.). Anti-Catholicism is one way of drawing the lines of group identity and of reinforcing feelings of unity and similarity amongst 'the insider'. It is used as part of the hegemonic process by which a sacred canopy is thrown around Protestants when their unity is essential to their interests. It has helped to overcome divisions between Protestants and to heal past conflicts between them, such as those arising from the Presbyterian involvement in the United Irishmen, or when the campaign to disestablish the Church of Ireland was presented as an attack on Protestantism generally. The Rev. Henry Cooke's use of conservative evangelicalism as the sacred canopy first occurred in response to Catholic emancipation in 1829, and this helped to sustain the cross-class alliance within Protestantism for generations.

The three chapters that follow attempt to illustrate the timeless use of anti-Catholicism as a resource in social stratification and social closure, making it, in the case of Ireland at least, an important sociological process.

1 Plantation to the United Irishmen: 1600–1799

Introduction

Anti-Catholicism in Ireland has its genesis in the social structure of Irish society, which was itself conditioned by the colonial relationship between Britain and Ireland.[1] The final colonisation of Ireland in the sixteenth and seventeenth centuries was achieved in large measure by an alliance between England and loyal Protestants in Ireland, all of whom had recent origins in England or Scotland, many in the plantation. English, and later, British control of Ireland required Protestant control in Ireland, and Ireland's social structure reflected the dominance of Protestants. Theological differences in Ireland obtained their saliency therefore because they corresponded to all the major patterns of structural differentiation in society, such as ethnic and cultural status, social class, ownership of property and land, economic wealth, employment, education and political power. Colonisation proceeded on the basis of neutering the remnants of Gaelic and Catholic wealth and power by the ascendancy of Protestantism, linking this form of theology forever after with political loyalty, economic privilege and cultural superiority. Anti-Catholicism played a major part in this process. It was a key resource in the ideological construction of Irish society into two groups in a zero-sum competition, which begins with the plantation but was not finally accomplished until the nineteenth century. It was also an important rationalisation for the flagrant structural inequalities between the protagonists in the zero-sum game. The alliance between Britain and Irish Protestants thus became a 'holy' alliance because theology played its part in both constructing and legitimising it.

But unlike those instances of colonisation where the indigenous population was annihilated, the Gaelic and Catholic people in Ireland remained in subservient positions within the social structure. They were never entirely powerless. They possessed political resources in the form of Irish nationalism, economic resources by means of their labour power, and cultural resources by the legitimacy, internationally if not locally, of their Catholic faith. At various junctures in British–Irish relations, Irish Catholics were able to place immense pressure on British governments. Attempts to improve Catholic access to scarce socio-economic and political resources from the eighteenth century onwards, whether made as a result of pressure by Catholics in Ireland or the political self-interests of English governments, disturbed well-established patterns of dominance in Ireland and threatened Protestant interests. In the zero-sum game, Catholic gains became seen by Protestants as their losses. The Protestant alliance with Britain thus occasionally became an unholy alliance as far as Britain was concerned when its interests in Ireland changed as a result of Catholic grievances.[2] It became increasingly 'unholy' by the end of the nineteenth century. By then, however, the structure of dominance could not be easily altered without provoking major Protestant resistance. Hence the familiar chain in Irish politics from the eighteenth century to near the twenty-first: Catholic protest, British reform, Protestant reaction, partial British retraction, renewed Catholic protest (this is emphasised by Ruane and Todd, 1996: 12).

Anti-Catholicism played a major role in mobilising Protestant opposition in Ireland, giving shape and form to the reaction and spreading its appeal amongst the masses; Protestant politics in Ireland has always had a high theological content and focus. The Protestant political cleric is thus a familiar type in Ireland going back to the sixteenth century, skilfully weaving together, from pulpit and election platform, theological vilification of Catholicism and defence of Protestant political and economic interests. The political priest, long established in Protestant mythology as a disloyal rebel, does not exist in the Catholic tradition to anywhere near the same degree, not really emerging until the nineteenth century.

English Policy in Ireland

After the initial military conquest of Ireland in the early medieval period, English control was ceded to the Norman lords, known as the 'Old English', who were Catholic but loyal to the English Crown, and the Gaelic lords, who were no less Catholic but more autonomous of English control. The Tudors, however, tried to reassert tighter control. In part the motivation was theological as Henry VIII tried to extend the Reformation to Ireland. But even in England the Reformation was as much about political control as doctrine. Henry assumed the title of King of Ireland, and the power of the Pope in Ireland was replaced with that of the King. Any attempt at theological reform was stymied under Catholic Queen Mary. It was she who began the plantation of English people in Ireland, but they were Catholics, established in Leix and Offaly in 1556 (Liechty, 1993: 13). It was with Elizabeth that the Tudors began anew the task of establishing Protestantism in Ireland. On this occasion, theological reform took a higher profile. An ecclesiastical commission was established to reform the Church, attendance at Anglican worship was made compulsory on pain of a fine, use of the Common Book of Prayer was required and no preaching could be done in Irish (Ford, 1986: 51). English Puritans also moved to Ireland during Elizabeth's reign in large numbers. Trinity College at this time was dominated by staff who were Scottish Calvinists or English Puritans influenced by Thomas Cartwright (Barkley, 1959: 2). The dominant subject at Trinity was theology, and the sole substance of doctrinal debate was the vilification of Catholicism (Ford, 1986: 64).

Tudor motives were not always theological however. The Protestantisation of Ireland was moved by strategic concerns to protect England's western lands, to raise income for the Crown from property and land, and to quell troublesome rebels who challenged Tudor authority in Ireland. The object of Tudor policy was not just to transfer Church wealth and power to the Crown, but also to establish control over independent lords by undermining their economic and political power base. The resources and income of the Church therefore declined substantially during the sixteenth century in those areas under government control (ibid.: 52), as did the authority of the Old English and Gaelic lords, who became more rebellious. Increasing levels of coercion needed to be applied in pursuit of this policy; Elizabeth's 'Irish wars' occurred on and off from the beginning of her reign. When Elizabeth eventually died, at the beginning of the seventeenth century, so finally did attempts to conciliate Irish rebels: Hugh O'Neill, the leader of Gaelic Ireland, went into exile after military defeat, leaving a legacy of massacre and mendacity on both sides.

The defeat of the rebels encouraged Protestant clergymen to urge on the new King James that he continue apace the Reformation of Ireland. Priests and Jesuits should be banished, clergymen from England sent to preach locally, and the legislation enforcing Protestant worship rigorously applied (ibid.: 58). Thus, priests were banished in 1605 and a fine of one shilling imposed for failure to attend Protestant worship. But James quickly relaxed these impositions once England's more domestic problems over the gunpowder plot had diminished, and Protestants in Ireland objected vociferously to the failure of the English authorities to support them. Anxieties amongst Protestants about the reliability of the English thus have early roots. According to Ford (ibid.: 50), Irish Church leaders demanded coercion of local Catholics. They were being motivated by fears of Protestant decline and Catholic resistance to conversion. Church leaders were disappointed that the Reformation was not succeeding. The Bishop of Cork wrote in 1595, for example, that attendance at Protestant churches was declining: 'where I have had a thousand or more in a church sermon, I now have not five' (quoted in ibid.: 58). By 1604 he was complaining of the dark forces of Catholic idolatry spreading again. In his diocese there had apparently been no Protestant marriages, christenings or burials for eleven years. Resistance by Catholics to the new faith remained strong. There was a popular distaste for Protestantism amongst Catholic laity because it was the religion of the conqueror and coloniser, and many preferred to go to prison than attend Protestant worship. Catholic landlords and traders also used their economic power to prevent conversion to the new religion. A letter from the Protestant Bishop of Ferns circulated in 1612 complaining on behalf of citizens that 'no popish merchant would employ them ... no popish landlord would let them any lands, nor set them houses in tenantry', if 'they should be of our religion' (quoted in C. Smyth, 1996: 9).

Thus, contemporary reports vary on how harshly Catholics were treated at the beginning of the seventeenth century. A report from the Pope's internuncio in 1613 was optimistic, with Catholics able to practise their religion (see Rafferty, 1994: 11), although this might be an understatement because Catholic bishops sought to avoid giving offence to the English government, on whose good terms they tried to get. On the other hand, a report to the King of Spain in the same year was pessimistic. Spain was Catholic, and thus the report is likely to contain some exaggeration for strategic effect. It explained that fines were being imposed for non-attendance at Anglican worship, Catholic schoolmasters were forbidden and children forced to be taught by Protestants, and penalties imposed for hearing mass, ranging from 200 crowns for a first offence and life imprisonment for the third. What is confirmed is the level of atrocity against Catholic priests, many of whom were put to death – some drawn and quartered in the fashion of the day; one of whom was an eighty-year-old bishop. All this was before 1625, when a plot was discovered amongst Catholic priests to persuade Spain to invade Ireland during its war with England.

The accession of Charles I in 1625 began a period of concession to Irish Catholics, in part because his Queen was Catholic but also because the loyalty of potential rebels in Ireland needed to be purchased to avoid an alliance with Spain during the war. Concessions were also made in return for more taxation. Local Protestants objected. The English-born Dean of Limerick warned against toleration, reminding the government that in Deuteronomy, God told the Israelites to destroy the nations who shared the promised land: an injunction he called for in Ireland's case. Neither covenant nor marriage must be made with idol worshippers; worse still for local Catholics, they should be smitten and utterly destroyed. Archbishop Ussher of Armagh issued a statement in 1625 calling for continued coercion on theological grounds: 'the religion of the papists is superstitious and idolatrous, their faith erroneous and heretical, their church, in respect to both, apostatical. To give them therefore a toleration, or to consent that they may freely exercise and profess their faith and doctrine, is a grievous sin' (quoted in Rafferty, 1994: 23). Thus it was in 1629 that local Protestants made the English government fully aware that the policy of 'planting civility and Protestantism ... hath not had the good effect which was expected of it' (quoted in Ford, 1986: 64). A more vigorous policy of social closure was thus necessary, which came in the wake of the 1641 massacre of Protestants and Cromwell's extirpations.

Gaelic Ireland in the Early Seventeenth Century

Gaelic Catholicism was a folk religion, almost unrecognisable to the Vatican after its post-Council of Trent reform, which modernised the Catholic Church in Europe. The orthodox Counter-Reformation theology and practice of the post-Tridentine Catholic Church appealed to the educated classes in Ireland, but the rural masses were very traditional. There were married priests and divorce was permitted amongst the laity. While the Pope congratulated the Irish in 1606 for their perseverance in adhering to Catholicism, assuring them of a 'heavenly crown' as a result of their devotion (Rafferty, 1994: 13), the Catholic Church in Ireland set about internal reform based on implementing the decrees of the Council of Trent, and aggressive Counter-Reformation based on hostility to Protestantism.

The Synod of Drogheda in 1614 began to promulgate the decrees of Trent, formulated more than half a century before, in order to steel Irish Catholics for the Counter-Reformation. Amongst other things, priests were reminded to be pious, warned off drink and clandestine marriages, told to ensure parishioners kept the sabbath, and informed that the Church believed inviolably in transubstantiation (a major Protestant objection to Catholic teaching). They were told to avoid contact with 'heretics', except to convert them, but also to avoid confrontation with the civil authorities. Thus, they were warned to keep from meddling in politics. To further reform and assist in the Counter-Reformation, seminarians were increasingly sent abroad to study. This also tended to cut the Protestant Church off from potential local recruits to the Protestant clergy, who found themselves having to rely on English and Scottish clergy. Archbishop Jones bemoaned in 1615 that: 'we cannot possibly get ministers, for the natives, generally addicted to popery, do train up their children in superstition and idolatry, so they send them beyond the seas whence they return either as priests, Jesuits or seminaries (*sic*), enemies of the religion established' (quoted in Ford, 1986: 55). The tendency to recruit clergy from Oxbridge and the major Scottish universities, culturally distant from poor Irish peasants and educationally worlds apart, sometimes with little or no experience of Ireland, only reinforced the social and ethnic exclusiveness of the Protestant clergy from the very people they were supposed to convert. The unsuitability of clergy was the major reason used by Protestant leaders at the time, like Archbishop Ussher, to explain the failure of the Reformation in Ireland.

Avoidance of Protestants and their faith was the second Counter-Reformation strategy of the Catholic Church. Catholic separatism as a survival strategy thus begins very early in Protestant–Catholic relations. The Pope forbade Catholics from attending any divine service in a Protestant church, even for the sake of outward obedience to the law. Anti-Protestantism was strong amongst priests, causing many to find it difficult to avoid confrontation. At open-air mass, many priests urged resistance, in politics and theology. A Friar McCrudden, at an open-air mass one Sunday in May 1613, drew down the wrath of Heaven on this 'English service' which had replaced the mass, arguing that it 'proceeded from the sediment of the devil' (quoted in Rafferty, 1994: 20).

The post-Trent reforms were very slow to bear fruit in Ireland, however. In 1631, for example, one Catholic bishop was still complaining that his clergy swaggered from house to house 'playing or drinking or vagabonding' (quoted in Foster, 1988: 46). The truth was that Catholicism was split between its Gaelic-Celtic form and its Tridentine version. Some priests and orders were pro-Gaelic, favouring Celtic Christianity, others Tridentine, preferring modern European Catholicism. The Jesuits, for example, were Tridentine and favoured the elimination of 'barbarous customs [and] bestial rites', and wished to convert 'detestable intercourse into polite manners' (quoted in ibid.: 47). The contrast between these two versions of Catholicism extended beyond the virtue of the clergy, for it was fundamentally a conflict over authority within the Catholic Church, with the Tridentine clergy accepting the authority of the Pope and the Gaelic Catholics wishing to maintain local autonomy. Counter-Reformation reform of the Church thus became a battle over power within it. Because reform along Tridentine lines was slow, the Pope later sent a nuncio to ensure that the Irish 'subject themselves to the mild yoke of the Pontiff, at least in all spiritual affairs', but the Catholic primate at the time disliked interference from Rome, favouring the settlement of ecclesiastical issues locally (Rafferty, 1994: 81).

Conflicts between the two versions of Catholicism manifested themselves politically as well. Celtic Christians within the Catholic Church desired an accommodation with the English and adjustment to Protestant control, while the Pontiff in Rome often had an agenda which conflicted with this. Thus, for example, the nuncio recommended rejection of a peace treaty negotiated by King Charles I and local Catholics during the English Civil War, because it did not challenge the ascendancy of Protestants but merely helped Charles better to fight the Puritans, but the treaty was supported by most Irish Catholics, save, ironically, those in Ulster, because O'Neill, whose power base was Ulster, needed the Pope's money and soldiers. The nuncio recommended withdrawal of all sacraments and ceremonies from those towns which supported the treaty. Ulster Catholics, however, were not necessarily Tridentine, for they later objected to Rome foisting bishops on them and parishes often asserted their autonomy by selecting their own priest (ibid.). In fact, the conflicts between the Tridentine and Gaelic versions of Catholicism continued until the middle of the nineteenth century, when Rome was finally able to impose a standardised and continental form of Catholicism on Ireland, two centuries after trying.

Pope Paul V's stipulations to avoid confrontation with the English powers came in 1606, after the defeat of the Gaelic-Irish lords, but his predecessor, Pope Clement VIII, had urged war in 1600. All those who fought with O'Neill were given the same spiritual status as Crusaders battling against the Turks. Ulster was their base, for it was resolutely Catholic and Gaelic at this time. O'Neill referred to his troops as the Catholic army of Ulster, and used Catholicism as the means by which to mobilise opposition to the Tudor expropriation of his land, wealth and power. Ulster responded. Foster described the province in 1600 as synonymous with wildness and untamed Gaelicism: separate by nature and geography, least inhabited and least developed (Foster, 1988: 7). It was the rebels' stronghold. Thus a contemporary pamphlet, written by someone newly arrived in 1615 from Norfolk, described the place as 'depopulated Ulster, dispoyled, ragged, sad sabled ... there remayneth nothing but ruynes and desolation, with a very little showe of any humanitie' (quoted in Bardon, 1992: 126). It was here that O'Neill's greatest strength had lain, and here where the effects of his defeat were most felt, giving rise to that variant of colonialism known as the Ulster plantation.

The Plantation

Elizabeth I had planted people in Munster from 1586 and there had been a plan to extend this to the eastern part of Ulster. James brought it to fruition. In 1606, Scots were allowed by private treaty to settle in Ulster. Two years later, the major plantation of Ulster began as a matter of state policy, starting with the city of Derry and extending to all the counties in the province. The planters were English or Scottish, Protestant, and conquerors. Some were members of the English Army given lands when the spoils were divided; most were migrants searching for better prospects and profit. Most detested and feared Catholicism. Stewart (1977: 95) poses the question of why these planters did not assimilate into Gaelic-Catholic culture, like earlier medieval land-seekers and adventurers. He suggests that the Reformation precluded it. By now theology was being used in the ideological construction of Irish society into mutually exclusive groups in a zero-sum competition. All the modes of differentiation in Irish society after the plantation, such as religion, ethnic status, social class and levels of cultural civility, began to coalesce around two polarities. The vanquished were Catholic, Gaelic-Irish, seen as savage and uncivilised, and were now economically dispossessed if not already poor; the planters were Protestant, Scots-English, saw themselves as culturally civilised, and were now economically privileged (see Ruane and Todd, 1996: 10–11).

Anti-Catholicism thus easily stood as a representation of other conflicts and sets of interest. The Protestantisation of the uncivilised Gaelic-Irish native, however, came with its own internal logic and justification, for in as much as the planters had privileges it was because they had the true religion: Catholics were dispossessed and poor because they were not elect ('unsaved' in modern parlance), being kept in bondage by their priests (Bruce, 1994: 26–7). It was because theology helped to define the groups, with their mutually exclusive sets of interest, that it remained important in seventeenth-century Ireland, whereas in seventeenth-century England, anti-Catholicism was fed primarily by anxiety over the monarchy and political power. As Hempton argues (1996: 93), Catholicism in Ireland was the creed of the defeated 'race', ensuring that theology played its troublesome part in signifying future differences with the victors.

But there was more than theological doctrine on the agenda during plantation. Foster shows the political realism behind English policy, for more Protestants were needed by the government in rebellious Ulster, and later Ireland generally, so that it did not continually have to cajole the Gaelic-Irish landed class (Foster, 1988: 59). The plantation was thus about political control of Ireland. The last vestiges of power and influence were wrested away from the Gaelic-Irish and Old English by means of the Anglicanisation of power (Ford, 1986: 69; Foster, 1988: 51), in which administrative reins and political office were in the hands of the English state or local Anglicans, although they did not lose most of their land until later in the century. The plantation was also about access to wealth. Land appropriation was a chief intent, and no Irish tenant was allowed on land taken over by the major undertakers who arranged the settlement (although some ignored this because they needed the labour power). Access to trade was restricted by forms of territorial segregation, which often prevented Catholics from living and trading within the city walls. It was also about imposing English values and culture on a 'barbarous' and 'savage' nation, the 'civilising mission' behind much of English colonialism. The Anglicanisation of Ireland by means of the plantation was not just based on a sense of theological superiority from having the 'pure Gospel'; it was fed by ideas of cultural superiority.

There were, however, theological grounds to the different development the plantation took in Ulster compared to elsewhere; right from the beginning Ulster was set a place apart in Ireland (on the plantation in County Longford, see Kennedy, 1996: 1–34). Outside Ulster, the planters did assimilate into Irish culture quite quickly. Anglicanisation in Munster, for example, did not involve the replacement of place-names by English forms, intermarriage was common even in the seventeenth century, and Irish natives were still leased land (Foster, 1988: 70). While it is true that even in Ulster the planters still needed the labour power of Irish Catholic farm workers, and employed them on the land, planters in Munster did not see themselves as an embattled minority and their future in Ireland did not involve hanging on to the Englishness associated with their past. Ulster was different, for several reasons.[3] Planters did see themselves as embattled, in part because Ulster kept its rebels who preyed on the settlers. The planters in Ulster came more from Scotland than England, bringing with them Presbyterianism and its tendency to separatism. And to begin with, Presbyterians experienced their own exclusion by Anglicans, but their covenantal theology precluded any assimilation or empathy with the Catholic Irish.

The Plantation in Ulster

Settlers are frontiers-people with frontier attitudes (emphasised by Stewart, 1977: 47), but the siege mentality that developed in Ulster was initially forged both by conflict with the enemy outside the gates and by separatism within it. Both distinguished Ulster from Munster. The former O'Neill rebels and soldiers, with Ulster as their stronghold, disappeared into the hills and forests of the province after O'Neill's defeat and exile, harassing settlers as robbers, thieves and murderers. Ulster was as much like Virginia in the hostility facing the settlers. Fear of attack was heavy. Sir Thomas Philips warned the English government in 1628, for example, that the bands of dispossessed bandits would have no hesitation in killing planters: 'it is fered that they will rise upon a sudden and cutt the throts of the poor dispersed Brittish' (quoted in Bardon, 1992: 132). The planters contributed to the sense of foreboding, as defensiveness and aggression combined. Bardon quotes the death-bed prophecy of a Presbyterian minister from Antrim in 1634, in which he predicted the slaughter of many Irish Catholics: 'the dead bodies of many thousands, who this day despise the glorious gospel, shall lie upon the earth as dung unburied' (ibid.). Looking on from Cork in 1630, the first Earl of Cork described Ulster as a 'rude and remote kingdom', the 'first likely to be wasted ... if any trouble or insurrection should arise' (quoted in Foster, 1988: 78). Thus, Roy Foster, one of the foremost historians of Ireland, claims that Ulster's planters believed they lived permanently on the edge of persecution, an attitude that has not moderated with time.

Separatism added to this mentality. Many of Ulster's planters were Scottish Presbyterians, marked off from other planters by their non-Englishness and by their religion. It was not just the Irish 'natives' who were unreliable to these people, few people inside the laager could be trusted because they were either not 'elect' or engaged in their own persecution of Scots Presbyterians. The Scottish presence in Ulster, especially east-coast Ulster, predated the plantation, as people traversed the narrow sea between the two. Scottish lairds began their own private plantation after James assumed the English Crown, and there were many Scots who travelled with the English as part of the Crown's formal settlements in Ulster. The Scots outnumbered the English in Ulster by a ratio of five to one in 1640 (Akenson, 1992: 108), and the cultural legacy of these Scots is manifest today in many facets of popular culture and in place-names (Gailey, 1975).[4] The Scots were, by terms of the original plantation settlement, lowland and Presbyterian (Barkley, 1959: 5–6), bringing with them their covenantal theology and loyalty to Scotland and the Scottish Kirk. This was also a lasting legacy.

Presbyterianism was as much feared by Anglicans as Catholicism, although persecution of Presbyterians took on a different form to that of Catholics and was less severe; it primarily consisted of limitations on worship. Anglican churchmen objected to the Presbyterian view of the Established Church as similar in apostasy, superstition and idolatry to the Catholic Church. Looking back to this time from 1715, in an enquiry into the 'state of religion and the causes of its present decay', the General Synod of Ulster wrote that the High Church at this time 'plainly inclined to Popery' and 'with the utmost violence persecuted all that differed from them' (General Synod of Ulster, n.d.: 375). King Charles I objected to dissenters on political grounds, fearing their disloyalty. The Scottish Kirk, to which Irish Presbyterians owed their affiliation, opposed Charles for his attempts to impose Anglicanism on dissenters and supported rebellion in Scotland. In 1634, Charles sent an aide to Ireland to expropriate money and to enforce conformity to Anglicanism as much on dissenters as Catholics. The former involved fines and increased rents, the latter the enforcement of the 'Black Oath', which required all Scots in Ulster aged sixteen and above to pledge allegiance to Charles and to abjure the Scottish covenant through which the Kirk had professed only conditional loyalty to the King. When dissenting worship was forbidden in Ireland, Ulster congregations would row over to Scotland and back again to attend kirk; when ministers could not be trained in Ireland, they came from Scotland. Separatism was therefore, not unnaturally, an integral part of the siege mentality of Ulster Presbyterians. Their isolationism appeared to Anglicans at the time as false claims to superiority. As one Antrim man said: 'the Presbyterians are very bigoted in their religious and political ideas, warmly attached to their own and hostile to any other form of worship' (quoted in Akenson, 1992: 124).

This separatism extended to having their own systems of social control based around the presbytery to the point where Hempton and Hill describe Ulster Presbyterians as a self-contained and regulating community organised according to its own principles and virtually independent of the wider structures of the English state and Established Church (Hempton and Hill, 1992: 16). Although Presbyterian ministers came originally from Scotland, as the community developed, ministers were local men serving the farming areas from which they themselves came. Presbyterians were thus self-sufficient and separatist. As many others have argued, Ulster Presbyterians saw their task as keeping themselves true to the reformed tradition, searching out apostates within their community rather than evangelising amongst Anglicans or Catholics (Miller, 1978a, 1978b; Wallis and Bruce, 1986: 272–3; Hempton and Hill, 1992: 18), although, as Holmes (1985: 45, 57) shows, Irish Presbyterians were also prevented from establishing new congregations (some early attempts at out-reach by Presbyterians are discussed by Blaney, 1996: 20–40). The notion that they were, in terms of Calvinist theology, God's covenanted 'elect', only reinforced the tendency to differentiate themselves from Irish Catholics. While English planters in Ireland from the Established Church referred to themselves in biblical terms as Israelites, entering a land covenanted by God (a point greatly emphasised by Ford, 1986), this idea was no more than a convenient rationalisation momentarily seized upon and not sustained for long, and quite alien to normal Anglican doctrine. To the Presbyterians, however, it was fundamental both to their theology and to their politics, and has remained so ever since (the covenantal nature of Ulster Protestant politics is emphasised by Miller, 1978a).

Covenantal Theology

The Established Church in Ireland made an early statement of its doctrinal principles in the 'Irish Articles'. As Foster explains (1988: 49), the Church of Ireland evolved its own identity in the early seventeenth century, with Archbishop Ussher, Professor of Divinity at Trinity College, drawing up its doctrinal principles in 1615. The Irish Articles were the first distinctly Irish Protestant statement, and although its 104 Articles drew in part on the 'Thirty Nine Articles' formed by the Church of England in 1562, the fuller Irish principles were more anti-Catholic and stricter in interpretation of predestination (Liechty, 1993: 14), reflecting the influence of local circumstance in drawing sharper boundaries between Irish Protestants and Catholics. Ford has shown that the Irish Articles took a more aggressive stance than the English Articles in identifying the Pope with the antiChrist (Ford, 1986: 65) – that 'man of sin foretold in the holy Scriptures', 'the Babylonish beast of Rome' (quoted in Barkley, 1967: 18). Liechty argues that it was from the Irish Articles in 1615 that people in Ireland began to define themselves in terms of opposition to each other and for two polarities to emerge (Liechty, 1993: 15).[5] The Catholic Church was described in the Articles as having erred, 'Romish doctrine' was 'repugnant to the word of God', and priests peddled 'blasphemous fables and dangerous deceits'. Presbyterians made their statements of faith slightly later, but they were equally anti-Catholic: Barkley claims that the Westminster Confession's identification of the Pope as the antiChrist was borrowed straight from the Established Church (Barkley, 1967: 18).

Calvinism came to Ireland via Scotland and John Knox. However, Knox gave Calvinist notions of predestination by divine election a twist by being linked to domestic Scottish issues of the mid-sixteenth century. Only the righteous should rule, according to Calvin, which for Knox meant the overthrow of the Scottish monarchy and all forms of absolutism: Knox favoured democracy in Church governance via the local presbytery and in politics via Parliament. A further twist was to link Calvinism with covenants. McManners (1990: 289) argues that the idea of the covenant became popular as an alternative to the notion of predestination, which was falling out of popularity for its ambiguity, and it allowed the notion of predestination to be linked to the issue of land as well as politics. Covenants replicated the Old Testament covenant which God formed with Abraham, in which He gave a promised land so long as His people remained loyal. Covenants are by their nature conditional, requiring that parties keep to the terms of the agreement or else it is justifiably abrogated, and while the template was the sacred covenant between God and His children, the principle was applied politically to the contract between political ruler and citizen. The feature of covenants which is highlighted most often is the conditional loyalty to rulers they imply, which commentators argue presages contemporary Loyalism (Miller, 1978a). However, they also drew God into politics, and they did so in several ways. Covenants see the citizen–ruler bond as secondary to the bond with God and they also see the former relationship as needing to be underwritten and blessed by God if it is to work. This imposes obligations of loyalty on rulers and ruled alike, because the terms of the agreement are watched over by The Almighty, and can only be breached if one of the parties abrogates the terms of the covenant, whereupon God Himself releases the injured party from any obligations. Covenants thus give a sacred gloss to politics and reinforce the tendency for theology to represent political conflicts.

The first Scottish covenant was entirely theological. In 1557, Knox and other Scottish reformed theologians formed a covenant between themselves and God to make the Reformed Church the established religion in Scotland, something that was achieved only two years later. By 1581, however, the so-called King's Covenant became political, binding King James of Scotland to uphold both the 'true' Presbyterian religion and political liberty, for which the signatories agreed to support the King's authority. James came later to renege, so that in 1638 the Scots signed what is called the 'national covenant', although by now it was his son, Charles I, who upheld neither Parliament nor Presbyterianism. The Scots had common cause with the English Parliament in this, and by 1643, the Solemn League and Covenant was signed by Scottish Presbyterians and the English Parliament, through which the parties pledged to preserve the reformed religion in Scotland, and to work for its introduction in England and Ireland. From this year until 1649, the Assembly of Divines met in Westminster to promulgate reformed doctrine, resulting in the Westminster Confession (on this see Barkley, 1959; Thompson, 1981; Loughridge, 1984), which became the final statement of Presbyterian covenantal theology and politics. The 1715 review of the state of Presbyterianism in Ulster by the General Synod described the purposes of the Westminster Confession, which superseded all earlier covenants as follows: 'to extirpate Popery, prelacy, schism and prophaness;

to maintain the privileges of Parliament and the rights and prerogatives of the King' (General Synod of Ulster, n.d.: 376).

Earlier covenants had been replete with anti-Catholicism when describing in contrast the nature of the 'true' religion. The Pope was the antiChrist, and the Catholic Church idolatrous and its practices blasphemous. The covenants had an explicitly anti-Catholic agenda. The 1643 Solemn League and Covenant, for example, bound Scottish Presbyterians and the English Parliament to 'root out of the empire all heretics and enemies of the true worship of God'. The Pope was condemned as the 'Roman anti-Christ', and abuse was laid against Catholic practice and worship, which was described as the Pope's 'five bastard sacraments, his devilish mass, his blasphemous priesthood'. The Westminster Confession gave full expression to this anti-Catholicism. The Pope was 'that anti-Christ, that man of sin and son of perdition, who glorifies himself as opposed to Christ'. Criticism of the Pope's absolutism was incorporated into an attack on Anglicanism, which was supposedly Romanism in disguise, and on the English Crown, which had supposedly moved its theological loyalty to Rome and advocated political absolutism in the form of 'the divine right of kings', for which Charles eventually went to the axe. That the English Civil War was raging at the time, and Cromwell had landed in Ireland, sharpened any criticism of political and theological absolutism. Thus, although the Irish Articles of the Church of Ireland were similar to the Westminster Confession in their anti-Catholicism and support for the Reformation (Thompson, 1981: 9), Ussher preached against the covenant because he was Royalist and could not subscribe to criticism of King Charles.

The covenants were popularly endorsed amongst the Ulster Scots, who by 1642 had established formally the first presbyteries in Ireland, although the Presbyterian Church in Ireland was still closely allied to the Scottish Kirk, being required to act 'in exact conformity to the parent establishment in Scotland' (Barkley, 1959: 10). The covenants were popular, and the number of presbyteries grew so quickly in Ulster in the 1640s, because they meshed with local issues. Miller argues that the immediate meaning of the covenants to local Protestants was that they became a public band against the danger from Irish Catholic natives (Miller, 1978a: 15). Some Anglicans in Ulster found convenantal theology and politics attractive for the same reason, although such people were banished from the established church; there was what Barkley calls a 'Presbyterian party' within the Established Church in Ireland in 1642, although its fortunes waned (Barkley, 1959: 11). Public banding in this way became so attractive because of the rebellion and massacre of Protestants the year before.

The 1641 Massacre

At the time, the representation of the 1641 massacre and rebellion by the Catholic Church raised it to a holy war, justifiable on moral grounds. The Catholic Bishop of Armagh declared the rebellion a just war to defend the Catholic faith, waged against those who plotted 'the destruction of Catholics, the slavery of the Irish and the abolition of the King's prerogative' (quoted in Rafferty, 1994: 29). Some modern-day writers ennoble the event by referring to Catholics as being under siege, bereft of political power and economic security, with their culture under erosion (see ibid.: 1). In fact, the position of Catholics in Ireland had improved considerably since the initial plantation. Under King Charles, the Catholic Church was given latitude to worship, and while it is true that in some parts of the country, mass had to be said in the open air, in woods, hills and private houses, the companies responsible for plantation had built several mass houses on their properties by 1631. Local Protestants recognised this. Thus, the Protestant Bishop of Kilmore complained in 1634 that: 'the popish clergy is double to us in number, and having the advantage of tongue, the love of the people, of the very hatred of subdued people to their conquerors, they hold them still in blindness and superstition' (quoted in Ford, 1986: 73). Catholics received favourable treatment before the courts (even priests; see Rafferty, 1994: 22), and they occupied a great deal more land than they were originally allowed after the plantation (Kee, 1995: 41).

The rebellion and massacre of 1641 have to be located in the context of Catholic fear that Protestants were coming to annihilate them as a result of the claim of such in the covenants, which Protestants everywhere were signing up to; a letter to this effect circulated in Ulster in 1641, claiming that a Scottish covenanting army was about to arrive to make the Ulster Scots the sole possessors of the land. It was also rooted in a base anti-Protestantism. Irish Catholics were urged by an Irish Jesuit, exiled in Portugal, to 'kill your heretic adversaries', to 'kill the heretics or expel them from the territory of Ireland' (quoted in Liechty, 1993: 16). While this may have appealed to the landless masses, the Catholic landed class, hanging on to dwindling estates, had the book which extolled them thus burned by the hangman. The rebellion and resulting massacre, however, have more to do with the interests of the declining Catholic gentry than popular anti-Protestantism. Those who led the revolt were not the landless and dispossessed, driven by hatred to rebel, but the Catholic gentry with estates, primarily in Ulster, which they were seeking to retain. That Catholics held more land than was allotted to them under plantation did not matter, for they considered all of it theirs in the first place (Kee, 1995: 41).

In September 1641, the Gaelic Catholic lords rose in rebellion, led by one of the younger O'Neills. They supported Charles against Parliament and sought to overthrow the Puritan administration in Ireland. Their defiance was complexly mixed with loyalty to the English Crown, which was pro-Catholic, the throne to which the covenanters also pledged allegiance but which the King had supposedly abrogated by his tolerance of Catholicism. While Sir Phelim O'Neill declared in October 1641 that the rising intended no hurt to those of the English and Scottish nations resident in Ireland, many thousand Protestants were massacred in November. Just how many is under dispute: Protestant mythology puts it as 150,000, but historical evidence suggests only 2,000 (Foster, 1988: 85); others 12,000 (Bardon, 1992: 185), although this number was added to by retaliatory deaths of Catholics. The level of atrocity was high, as women, children and the aged were slaughtered without hesitation or compunction. Protestant towns which surrendered to the rebels under promise of mercy were put to the sword none the less. Protestants were run off a bridge into the sea and left to drown; those making back to the shore were bludgeoned. Depositions were collected from survivors some years later during Puritan governance in Ireland following Cromwell's victory, and the accounts stress the anti-Protestantism of the rebels: but they would anyway by this time. These depositions were collected together in a two-volume, vehemently anti-Catholic tome in the late-nineteenth century (Hickson, 1884), for their political effect during Home Rule debates. This gives a hint to the real meaning of the massacre.

Many of the claims contained in the depositions are open to dispute, and by some counts as many Catholics died in retaliation as in the original massacre, and with equal atrocity towards women and children (see Bardon, 1992: 139), but the event has entered the pantheon of Protestant mythology, commemorated and kept alive today in its distorted form. Its immediate effects on Protestants were more real, however. It convinced the settlers of the innate untrustworthiness and savagery of Catholics and that there was no limit to the horrors these idolaters would inflict on believers of the 'true' religion. It intensified their conviction that Protestants needed to be vigilant both in self-defence and loyalty to the reformed tradition. Both commitments reflected in the covenant, which articulated antipathy to Catholicism and resulted in public banding. The massacre fitted well into covenantal theology, because Protestants drew the obvious apocalyptic moral that their divine election was challenged by the idolaters and heathens, making them like the Israelites who needed to war with the Canaanites before the promised land could be theirs (Ford, 1986: 72), and, as Wallis and Bruce (1986: 273) point out, what better proof could there be of their own salvation if the damned were disposed to attack and repel them? Protestant churchmen ensured that the government in England were reminded often that God's assistance to the Israelites was to exterminate the Canaanites. Hence the popularity of the Old Testament amongst Northern Irish Calvinists which has survived to this day (the tendency of early settlers to see themselves as Irish Israelites, planted on land by God, is emphasised by Miller, 1978a; Ford, 1986; Akenson, 1992). In this sense, the assistance of The Almighty came in the form of Oliver Cromwell.

The Civil War and Cromwell in Ireland

Catholics and Protestants occasionally found themselves in alliance in their support for Charles during the English Civil War, which began in 1642. The Established Church was Royalist; its Presbyterian wing and the Ulster Scottish Presbyterians were Puritan and for Cromwell. The Catholic landed class, the so-called Old English, were engaged in their own rebellion against the Crown at this time, although pledging fealty to the King, but they later came to pursue peace with Charles when it appeared that he was losing to Cromwell and they risked worse under the Puritans, although the treaty was opposed by the Pope's representative who even provided arms by which the fight could be continued. The nuncio set himself up as the new leader of Irish Catholics, after becoming dissatisfied with the lack of fighting spirit in O'Neill's younger kin, urging the Irish to war with Protestants, Royalists and par-liamentarians alike (Bardon, 1992: 140). The execution of Charles in 1649 ended such notions, and Cromwell took revenge for even contemplating it; he also avenged the massacre of 1641.

Oliver Cromwell came to Ireland within months of the execution of the King, declaring himself commander-in-chief and Lord Lieutenant. His purpose was to enforce the control of the English Parliament. This initially involved the subjugation of the remaining military opposition, whether Royalist or rebel; it later came to involve further plantation by Protestants and land appropriation from Catholics. The military campaign was bloody. He stormed Drogheda and Wexford and massacred many. By the time his forces arrived in Ulster, towns surrendered but many hundreds were killed in a battle outside Lisburn. Skirmishes continued until 1653, but parliamentary forces had essentially won by Christmas 1649. The slaughter seemed not to be simple anti-Irishness: English Royalists defending the garrison in Drogheda were killed; one elderly gentlemen being beaten to death with his own wooden leg. The agenda was clearly driven by English politics. There was, however, a strong current of anti-Catholicism. By his own admission later in the House of Commons, no priest was left alive in Drogheda and Catholic churches were torched. The rationalisation for the violence was explicitly theological. It was all done by the spirit of God and 'it is therefore right that God alone should have the glory' (quoted in Kee, 1995: 46). To the Speaker of the House, Cromwell later explained that his conduct had been a 'righteous judgement of God upon these barbarous wretches who have imbrued their hands in so much innocent blood'. The victims in the 1641 massacre were thus finally avenged, no matter that it involved other victims of a different hue.

Under the Protectorate, Catholics also faced assault on the worship of their religion. Worship was outlawed, priests were hunted and killed, church buildings were demolished, and the laity were deprived of the sacraments. People who sheltered priests were imprisoned and mass took place, if at all, illegally in remote places – 'in the mountains, forests and inaccessible bogs, where the trooper cannot reach us', as someone said at the time (quoted in Rafferty, 1994: 43). By the time of the Restoration of the monarchy in 1660, there were three Catholic bishops left in Ireland, all based in the old Gaelic core of Ulster.

Cromwell's Commonwealth not only strengthened the association of theology with politics, it reinforced its connection with economic privilege. The 1662 Act of Settlement deprived Catholics of land in three provinces, leaving them barren Connaught, and even there the holdings were smaller. Ten years before, Catholics owned 59 per cent of the land in Ireland; at the end of Cromwell's Protectorate they owned 10 per cent (Liechty, 1993: 18). Transportation of Catholic landowning families to new lands in the west in many ways finally completed the Irish policy of English governments pursued since the Tudors. It was not just the Gaelic landowners from Ulster who lost wealth, but the Old English – also Catholic – from more settled areas of Ireland. They were replaced by English Protestants, some of whom had financed Cromwell's campaign, and ex-soldiers, who had been given the promise of land in lieu of wages: 'land was allocated regiment by regiment, company by company, on the lands they had conquered' (Barkley, 1959: 15). On the whole these people were English Puritans, rather than Scottish Presbyterians, and received considerably more favourable treatment from the English government than the Ulster Scots.

The position of the covenanters under Cromwell was ambiguous. They were Protestant and puritan, but the covenant had implied loyalty to the King, however conditional: some had even condemned his execution. Thus, Presbyterians were required to sign a covenantal oath pledging loyalty to Cromwell's Commonwealth. Ministers to new Puritan communities in Ireland were brought in from England rather than from Ulster or Scotland. Ulster's Presbyterians refused to sign the oath, in most part because of an objection at being forced to do so, and in 1653 they were banished from the island. By the following year, however, Cromwell's son and his father's Lord Deputy, cancelled the banishment scheme and even granted some Presbyterian ministers a state stipend. He was less affected than his father by pique at the Presbyterians' show of independence. Within a few years, most Presbyterian ministers had accepted the stipend, despite their preference for independence: division within Protestant ranks was unappealing to the Protectorate and Presbyterians alike, since it appeared that the pro-Catholic Stuarts could well resume kingly authority again.

The Restoration

Irish Protestants feared the Restoration because, in zero-sum terms, they anticipated Catholic gains. But in a sense it was a double restoration, for Charles II resumed kingly authority and Anglicanism theological authority. Both risked losses by Protestant dissenters and Presbyterians. The 1662 Act of Settlement gave some Catholics – the 'innocent Papists' who had remained loyal to the Crown – the right to appeal land appropriation and dispossession. Appeals favoured the Old English rather than Gaelic Catholics, particularly the landed gentry with influence at Court, and only about half of the petitions were accepted (Foster, 1988: 115). Later the Cromwell soldiers were required to give up half their land to accommodate Catholic repossession. After Restoration, the proportion of Irish land in Catholic ownership doubled, but was still only a third of what it had been in 1641. In the most Gaelic part of Ireland, Ulster, very little land was repossessed by Catholics (Bardon, 1992: 142), and the province once again became the stronghold of landless outlaws and robbers, most of whom were Gaelic small landowners who had lost everything in 'Cromwell's curse' (known as 'tories', a term of abuse subsequently applied to the British Conservative Party). Tory-hunting was as much a sport as hawks and hounds for country gentlemen. They were also opposed by the Catholic hierarchy which issued a decree against disorder to avoid alienating the new King; triumphant and exaggerated calls to war had long gone from Catholic bishops, who sought accommodation with England rather than conquest.

However, Charles II did restore legal public worship, if not land, to Catholics, illustrating to the bishops that accommodation worked. Churches were built and members of religious orders returned, all to the chagrin of Irish Protestants, who conspired to allege that Irish Catholics were involved in a plot to encourage France to invade. This eventually led to the Catholic Archbishop and Primate of Ireland, Oliver Plunkett, being hung, drawn and quartered at Tyburn, even though he was the chief supporter of accommodation with England and chief critic of disorder. Anglicanism, however, remained the Established Church. Presbyterians were subject to this as much as Catholics, even though they avoided the economic exclusion enforced on Catholics (see Allen, 1994: 125). People within positions of authority locally were required to be Anglicans, including schoolmasters. Public banding was made unlawful, whether in the form of public meetings of five people or more, or signatory to new covenants; no person could abjure the unlawfulness of taking up arms against the King. Ulster Scots were thus forced to make their covenantal oaths of loyalty less conditional, at least in the King's eyes if not God's, and the King rejected an attempt by the Presbyterian Church in Ireland to declare a new covenant in which Charles affirmed his grandfather's loyalty to Presbyterianism (on which, see Loughridge, 1984: 10). The Solemn League and Covenant, which enshrined this pledge, was burned and condemned as 'schismatical, seditious and treasonable'. The King withdrew the stipend to Presbyterian ministers, at least until 1672, and most were deprived of their livings for refusing to conform to episcopalianism.[6] Marriages performed by them were said to the illegitimate; so were any children born of the union. It was now the Presbyterians who took refuge in the remoter places for worship, some to Scotland. Those members who strongly supported the idea of covenanting formed themselves into groups and societies and established links with the covenanting societies in Scotland. Presbyterians with a less strong commitment to covenantal theology and politics, preferred a lower profile, theologically and politically. The divisions between these two strains were to solidify, later leading to a formal split, but they have their roots in disagreements over how best to accommodate to English policy in Ireland.

Ironically, it was the most Catholic of the Stuarts, James II, succeeding his brother in 1685, who ended the persecution of dissenters, but only because it was part of a suspension of all limitations on worship designed primarily to benefit Catholics. Catholic fortunes in Ireland improved immediately. A Catholic former landowner, dispossessed by Cromwell, was made James's agent in Ireland and subsequently made an earl. He changed the dynamics of power and office in Ireland, with the Catholicisation of local government, the judiciary, the military and town corporations. James would not overturn previous land settlements however (not even later when desperate to raise a Catholic army in his war with William and Mary), but priests were allowed salaries and Jesuits were put in charge of government-controlled schools. Catholic judges and army officers were a shock to local Protestants (Foster, 1988: 140); key resources of power and patronage passed into the hands of Catholics. It was no surprise, therefore, that James was interpreted by Protestants as seeking to establish 'Romanism', as it was being described still in the mid-twentieth century (Barkley, 1959: 18). Local Protestants feared the loss of power and privilege, and a massacre in the mould of 1641. 'The menace of Romanism', Professor Barkley wrote, 'proved a unifying factor and the entire Protestant population united in its opposition to James' (ibid.). Anti-Catholicism was an important factor in promoting Protestant mobilisation against James: an anonymous letter circulated in Ulster during 1688 claiming that the Papists were 'sworn to fall on to kill and murder man, wife and child' (quoted in Bardon, 1992: 152).[7] But it was the Protestant magnates in England who ousted him, by inviting his Protestant daughter, Mary, and her husband, William of Orange, in 1688 to assume the throne – an act precipitated by the birth of James's son and Catholic heir that year.

While James's problems originated in English politics, they were played out in Ireland. His support amongst Catholics in Ireland was high; he was detested by local Protestants. Covenantal oaths were made in Ulster swearing loyalty to William and to Presbyterianism. Miller argues that Ulster Presbyterians hoped to extract from William a commitment to make Presbyterianism the Established Church in Ulster (Miller, 1978a: 22), as he did in Scotland in 1690. Even the Anglicans in Ireland, who had bound themselves 'under no pretence to take up arms against the King', supported William, as they did in England. James's only support was amongst Catholics in Ireland, hence it was to the island that he fled when William landed in England, hoping to raise a Catholic army. William quickly followed him. A European dynastic war was thus set to be fought on Irish soil.

The Williamite Wars in Ireland

James sent a regiment to Ireland in 1689 to secure his position. To local Protestants this meant an invasion by Catholics. With anti-Catholicism prevalent, nurtured by fears roused by rumours about a massacre on the scale of 1641, the attempt by the army to obtain quarters in the walled towns of Derry and Enniskillen, entirely Protestant, was repelled since they were 'Papist' and thus without restraint or civility (see the terms of the declaration in Miller, 1978a: 23). Leading bishops in the Church of Ireland declared that it was unlawful to refuse the King's soldiers, but the covenanters and Presbyterians who dominated in the towns refused entry. Thus began the Siege of Derry. Both towns had a massive influx of Protestants from all over Ulster seeking refuge; Derry had up to 30,000 people crammed within it (Bardon, 1992: 154). The siege lasted over 100 days and people resorted to eating candles, leather, cats, dogs and vermin to survive, but they did not surrender, as modern-day Ulster Protestantism continually reminds us. A victory was achieved in Enniskillen and Derry was eventually relieved by William's men, and while it appears that hereafter the battles have been celebrated annually by proud Protestants, the 'deliverance from Popery' only began to be commemorated on the centenary of the event during renewed sectarian tensions.

The end of the siege was not the end of the war. William landed in Carrickfergus in 1690, and was lauded by the Protestants he passed on his march to Dublin. The Presbyterian Church presented an Address to him in Belfast, and received news that they were to be given an annual stipend from him. The Battle of the Boyne saw his triumph, and that of Protestantism. Leaving aside that the Pope supported William, the victory was seen as one over Catholicism. The Pope's support for William caused him to be conciliatory to Irish Catholics. The peace treaty signed at Limerick said that Romanists could retain such privileges as they exercised under the Restoration (not much, but better at least than under Cromwell), and those who took an oath recognising William's government could secure their property and possessions. But all this would have been a battle lost to local Protestants, and the Irish Parliament which William called in 1692 objected vociferously and they annulled his provisions, arguing that they would free themselves from the 'yoke of England' rather than permit Catholics freedom of worship and property.[8] A long-standing culture of anti-Catholicism was vented. The Protestant Bishop of Meath preached in such violent terms against William's tolerance of Catholicism in the Treaty of Limerick that the English government removed him from the Irish Privy Council (Liechty, 1993: 22). One of the Presbyterians welcoming William in Belfast in 1690 urged upon him that he 'pull the stiff kneck of every Papist down' (quoted in Bardon, 1992: 161). Thus, there was further land confiscation from Catholics. In 1703, Catholics held only a third of the land they held in 1688; in a place like Ulster they had little left to lose, although the Catholic Earl of Antrim kept his estate, and more Catholics took refuge in Ulster's wilderness as robbers and outlaws, harassing the local population and further reinforcing Protestant fears and hostility towards the vanquished Jacobites. The capacity of the Irish Parliament to overrule William's toleration of Catholicism was a portent for the Protestant ascendancy and the deprivations to be faced by Catholics during the eighteenth century.

The Establishment of the Ascendancy in the Eighteenth Century

The seventeenth century began with the plantation of tentative, insecure and uncertain Protestants, encircled by a threatening, hostile and dispossessed Catholic population. It ended with the defeat of Gaelic-Irish political power, and the erosion of Catholic economic and cultural status. A confident and aggressive Protestant population, still a minority, now faced a humiliated and subjugated people who had lost land, power, wealth and status within the span of a century. What had not been achieved was the Irish Reformation, for the Irish Gaels remained defiantly Catholic. Religion thus retained its potency in the eighteenth century in marking group boundaries in Ireland. In fact, as third-and fourth-generation English and Scots planters became increasingly Irish in identity – Irish enough in the early eighteenth century to assert their wish for legislative independence from England and to be thoroughly anti-English – religion remained the sole marker of the original differentiation between settler and native. Anti-Catholicism was ensured a continued social role because Catholics remained a political problem – at least in Europe if not in Ireland any more; Catholicism posed a threat as the embodiment of the antiChrist and the Whore of Babylon, and Protestant ascendancy needed to be legally established and further secured.

The penal laws were fundamental to the ascendancy. The 1695 Irish Parliament began the passage of legislation but the 1704 Popery Act symbolised it. Property ownership – and thus class position and wealth – was the key resource closed off from 'Papists'. Catholic tenants could not lease land for more than thirty-one years, a Catholic landowner was deprived of all rights of testament over his estate, and Catholics were barred from acquiring land from a Protestant by purchase, gift, inheritance or dowry (see Allen, 1994: 82–3). In order to reduce the size of Catholic landholdings, owners were required to pass on land in equal portions to sons. But if the eldest son converted to the Church of Ireland, he gained all the property and his father retained the land as tenant for life (Liechty, 1993: 22). It is thus erroneous to claim that the penal laws saw Irishness rather than Catholicism as the threat (McVeigh, 1995: 625). Social closure to protect Protestants was the object, recognised and admitted at the time. Chief Justice Robinson declared of the penal laws: 'the law does not suppose any such person to exist as an Irish Roman Catholic' (quoted in Bardon, 1992: 170). Access to the bourgeois and commercial professions was closed off to Catholics. Catholics could not practice law, enter the armed forces, hold any position of authority, teach schoolchildren, serve on juries, or have the freedom of cities or town corporations (Allen, 1994: 84). Civil and political rights were addressed as well. A series of laws forbade 'Papists' from possessing arms or gunpowder, from owning a horse above the value of £5, and from serving in Parliament, or voting in an election, whether to Parliament or a town corporation. Freedom of worship was also addressed. Parish priests were allowed to celebrate mass, but all other orders were banished. Nor were new seminarians allowed to be trained, with the intention for the priesthood thus to die out naturally. Priests had to be registered, the requirement for which was that they abjure the authority of the Pope. Only thirty-three took such an oath (Bardon, 1992: 169). The English Parliament threw out a recommendation from the Irish Parliament that unregistered priests be castrated, preferring instead that they be branded with the letter 'P' on the forehead. Pilgrimages were outlawed (Lecky's monumental study of Ireland rightly points out that persecution in Ireland never approached that of Louis XIV and was insignificant compared to that against Protestants and Jews in Spain –see Lecky, 1892: 38).

The impulse to the penal laws, however, was social closure and the protection of Protestant access to wealth and power. Catholicism was the boundary marker which represented the closed-off group, but as ascendancy made Protestant access secure, most Protestants outside the covenanting tradition were indifferent to, rather than vehemently opposed to, the religion itself. Thus, many of the restrictions on worship were not enforced and the practice of Catholic worship was tolerated. Hence the Catholic Church survived. Officials required to enforce the restrictions on worship could easily be bribed (for one such documented case, see Kee, 1995: 55). A report in 1731 on 'the state of Popery', shows numerous mass-houses and by 1750 there was a full parochial structure in place, with schools (Foster, 1988: 208). Wholesale conversions to Protestantism were thus unnecessary, and by 1800 only 5,800 had done so (Allen, 1994: 77), although there was little evangelistic enthusiasm amongst the Protestant churches to promote conversions from Catholics since the point behind the penal laws was economic self-interest rather than theology (Hempton, 1996: 73). They were content to keep Catholics, as Archbishop Synge admitted, in 'slavish subjugation [rather] than have them made Protestants and thereby entitled to the same liberties and privileges with the rest of their fellow subjects' (quoted in Allen, 1994: 78). Hempton is thus correct to argue that the penal laws reinforced rather than eroded religious boundaries (Hempton, 1996: 74), but they did more than that, for they strengthened the association between religion and other sources of differentiation and further assisted in constructing a zero-sum conflict in which Catholic gains were Protestant losses. As William King, Protestant Bishop of Derry, explained, 'either they or we must be ruined' (quoted in Bardon, 1992: 168).

The penal laws focused most severely on property rights because it was assumed that land was the source of wealth. However, society was in transition during the eighteenth century with the growth of a commercial economy and proto-industrialisation, and those Catholics who were able to trade outside the professions and invest in commerce often received better return than from farming. The penal laws thus did not prohibit the development of a successful Catholic middle class; Bardon even claims that this class grew because of the penal laws, for commerce was all Catholics had (ibid.: 169). The rapid economic growth in Ireland in the mid-eighteenth century and after benefited Catholics too, although Protestants still dominated. By 1775, for example, only a third of Dublin's merchants were Catholic, only a quarter of Cork's (Dickson, 1987: 121). The greatest measure of Catholic economic progress and class mobility was not realised until the nineteenth century when it added power to their grievances and provoked Protestant fears of a loss of privilege, but its roots lay in the period of the penal laws.[9]

The Churches in the Early Eighteenth Century

The Church of Ireland represented the ascendancy at prayer linked to the Church of England, the English government and the Irish landowning class. It trusted neither Catholics nor Presbyterians. Dissenters were thought of as politically disloyal and theologically suspect. Covenants were a corruption of politics and theology; Swift, after all, alleged that the covenanters even bore a basic affinity to 'popishness in their corruption of religion'. The penal laws limited their rights to some public offices although their right to worship was unaffected. The 1704 Popery Act enforced a sacramental test, obliging holders of public offices to take sacraments according to the Church of Ireland, which excluded Presbyterians from town corporations and from positions of authority in the military. As otherwise eager supporters of the Act, protests by Presbyterians were muted (Bardon, 1992: 172), and Presbyterians showed their continued commitment to the ascendancy by flocking to join the militia during rumours of a Jacobite invasion in 1715.

It is commonplace amongst Irish historians to argue that, ultimately, the government knew it could rely on Presbyterians because they were Protestants before being dissenters; that is, the Presbyterians' own anti-Catholicism overrode the government's anti-Presbyterianism. Daniel Defoe, no dissenter himself, defended the Presbyterians, arguing from his prison cell in Newgate that Protestant unity was the only guarantee against 'Popery': imposing the sacramental test on Presbyterians was like cutting off the foot to cure the corns, he said. The 1715 report of the state of religion by the Presbyterian General Synod of the Ulster was very critical of harassment from the episcopalians, but it also recognised the need for a pan-Protestantism. 'The great schism among Protestants in Britain and Ireland', the report argued, 'may be justly numbered among the principal causes of the decay of religion ... Divisions have been extremely prejudicial to the Church'; such schism had allowed 'Popery' to be revived and led to all manner of profanities and corruption (General Synod of Ulster, n.d.: 375, 378). Dissenters were encouraged to pray for the Established Church because theirs was a 'common Christianity'. Four years later, Presbyterianism was given official recognition in Ireland and various indemnity acts were passed permitting dissenters access to public offices, although pan-Protestantism did not emerge for another hundred years because the theological divisions within Protestantism remained important.[10] Although socio-economic and political privilege for Protestants was secured, theological disputes within the Protestant churches were as lively as with Catholicism, but not as vituperative.

Within Presbyterianism, anti-Catholicism took third or fourth place to internecine conflicts over its own doctrine. The task was not to defeat or enervate Catholicism but to keep the reformed tradition true, and factions outbid each another in pledging loyalty to sixteenth- and seventeenth-century covenants. While the covenanting tradition within Presbyterianism separated them from Anglicans and Catholics, it also divided them from each other. Given that covenants had theological and political dimensions, covenantal disputes were more than theological debates. Scottish conflicts over subscription to the Westminster Confession, which some had seen as dominated by the English, led to factionalism between supporters and detractors of the Confession, which spread to Ireland. The Irish Presbyterians originally signed up to the 1557 Scottish covenant formulated by Knox but the pressure of local circumstance influenced support for the English Westminster Confession. The Church insisted in 1698 that a licence to preach required subscription to the Westminster Confession as a statement of faith. Many presbyteries did not enforce this, however, and the 'Belfast Society' emerged in 1705 to co-ordinate the activities of several churchmen in Antrim who objected to subscription of a 'man-made confession' as a test of orthodoxy. Known as 'New Light', these churchmen felt that interpretation of Scripture should be left to individual conscience and religious obedience should be founded on personal persuasion, not fealty to covenants. New Light theology came to represent the more enlightened and unorthodox wing of

Presbyterianism; 'Old Light' were traditional Calvinists who remained covenantal, but were divided over loyalty to Scottish or English covenants. Scottish 'Seceders' travelled to Ulster in the first part of the eighteenth century seeking converts. Covenanters objected to acceptance of any English monarch who was non-covenanting and non-Presbyterian and thus rejected accommodation to episcopalian theology or politics. Tolerance and modernism was denounced, remaining loyal to the 1643 Solemn League and Covenant: purity and truth lay in the past. This tradition was represented in Scotland by the Reformed Presbyterian Church. The Seceders in Scotland were themselves divided between the Burghers and Anti-Burghers, the latter seeing themselves as yet more strict in their loyalty to the 1643 covenant. This fissure also came to Ireland (on the Scottish background to these theological disputes in Ireland, see Stewart, 1977: 96–9). The covenanting societies which formed in Ireland during the eighteenth century made explicit their loyalty to the seventeenth-century covenants, both in their theological antipathy to Catholicism and political loyalty to the old Constitution. For example, applicants to membership were asked if they abjured Popery and Prelacy, if they supported the extirpation of Catholicism, recognised the sinfulness of the present constitution and government, and wished for the Reformation of Ireland (see Loughridge, 1984: 136–8). However, Irish churchmen sought to avoid a formal split and in 1726 the Presbyterian Church in Ireland divided into the General Synod and the non-subscribing New Light presbytery of Antrim, between whom there was 'friendly relations for another eighty years' (Barkley, 1959: 29), and it was able to contain the various covenantal disputes throughout the eighteenth century.

The disputes within covenantal theology were infused by a further influx of Scottish migrants to Ulster at the beginning of the eighteenth century, often known as the second plantation, who brought with them the internal disputes of the Scottish Kirk. In 1714, the Catholic Bishop of Clogher wrote a report to the Pope's internuncio in which he said: 'Calvinists are coming over here daily in large groups of families, occupying the towns and villages, seizing the farms in the richer part of the country and expelling the natives' (quoted in Rafferty, 1994: 66). The opportunity was taken during the penal laws to grab more land, but they were also escaping harvest failure and famine in Scotland. Either way, Presbyterian congregations doubled in size in the first two decades of the eighteenth century. Of course, just as many Presbyterians left Ulster to emigrate to America, reaching a peak in 1728–9. Protestant leaders were concerned about its effects on the population dynamics. William King, now Archbishop of Dublin and a commissioner for the Irish government, expressed his anxieties in 1718, believing that emigration could drain Ireland of its Protestant settlers: 'The papists, being already five or six to one, and being a breeding people, you can imagine in what condition we are like to be in' (quoted in Bardon, 1992: 176). The lesson was not lost on the government, which recognised the Presbyterian Church the following year and rarely applied the sacramental test rigorously, although the outflowing tide could not be easily stemmed.[11] Protestant churchmen blamed the exodus on landlords, some of whom, apparently, would evict Protestant tenants and give the farms 'to Papists for the sake of a little increase in rent' (quoted in ibid.: 178). This illustrates the extent of toleration permitted under the penal laws. There is also considerable evidence that at a local level, relations between Catholic and Protestant neighbours could be good. Mixed marriages still occurred in Wexford for example (Foster, 1988: 154), and people in Loughinisland shared a church for a time (Rafferty, 1994: 68). Toleration did not always extend to the Catholic clergy, however.

The Catholic Church showed the effects of its subordinate position within eighteenth-century Irish society in several ways. It had a siege mentality (something it shared with Calvinists but for different reasons), suffering under a fear of loss of souls to Protestantism, a shortage of priests and poor parochial structure, as well as all the privations arising from the penal laws themselves. It was torn between isolation from and accommodation with the ascendancy politically, and Calvinist notions and practice began to creep into its theology and worship, causing further division.

The Catholic Church in a sense had its own Calvin, Bishop Cornelius Jansen, a theologian at the University of Louvain, who reacted to the force of the Reformation by establishing a case for the reform of the Church. Jansenism borrowed the Calvinist notion of salvation by grace alone to argue that only the elect would enter the Kingdom of Heaven. While Reformed theologians were tranforming Calvin's ideas about predestination into the notion of the covenant, Jansen sought to appropriate them for Catholicism. Catholicism had also, he claimed, alienated Christians from Jesus because it had lost sight of the simple and humble. Official Church doctrine was that everyone is free to earn salvation by their merits alone; good works rather than God's grace are one's passport. Jansenism was Calvinism in purple robes and resoundly criticised by the Catholic Church. The Jesuits in Louvain opposed him and the Pope issued a bull in 1642 forbidding anyone to read Jansen's work. Successive Popes condemned him as heretical. The bishops of France were required to make all clergy and members of religious orders sign a declaration of authority to official Catholic doctrine. While an autonomous Jansenist church was established at Utrecht in 1723, Jansen's ideas were taken up by many Catholics elsewhere in their battles with pontifical authority. They did so in Ireland. By the end of the seventeenth century, Jansenism was popular in Ireland (Rafferty, 1994: 72) and in 1714 the hierarchy refused to promulgate another anti-Jansen papal bull, although local bishops were split in their support for Jansenist theology. In part this support reflected an assertion of Gaelic independence from papal authority but it was also a measure of the dominance of Calvinist ideas in Ulster. Rafferty shows that there is evidence that the penal laws were applied more strictly in Ulster (ibid.: 74), and a report to the Irish House of Lords in 1731 on the state of Catholicism revealed the Church in Ulster to be operating under the greatest difficulties. Jansenism ensured some accommodation with Calvinists theologically, if not politically. The impression of non-conformism was also manifest in Irish Catholic churches, which, Miller shows (1978a: 39), had the austerity and simplicity of Presbyterian meeting houses – some to the point of adopting the fashion of arranging the seating so that the congregation and priest faced each other. The need to avoid creating offence locally with non-conformist neighbours was critical, and the continental fashion of ornate buildings and devotion was not adopted until the mid-nineteenth century when the post-Tridentine reform project was finally completed.

Accommodation with the ascendancy was reflected in other ways. Some local Catholic bishops did not wish to alienate the civil authorities for risk of greater penalisation, and priests were urged periodically to stress on the laity the need to desist from disorder, whether politically inspired or simple drunkenness. The penal laws were not always strictly adhered to but anti-Catholicism was ever-present, and the Church was too powerless to risk challenging the small measure of toleration that the Catholic Church obtained under the penal laws. Thus, during the putative Jacobite invasion of 1745, when the Church of Ireland Archbishop of Armagh instructed his clergy to 'raise in your people a religious abhorrence of the Popish government and polity (for I can never be brought to call Popery a religion)' (quoted in Rafferty, 1994: 75), the Catholic bishops urged on the laity loyalty to the civil authorities. The Church recognised the benefits of being used by the state as a means of social control, and during the Jacobite rising by the Young Pretender in 1745, Irish Catholics supported the Hanoverians at least by failing to heed the Stuarts (see McFlynn, 1981). Many historians note that by this time, middle-class Catholics established in trade had little wish to see the restoration of the Stuarts (for a different view see Liechty, who argues that Irish Catholics did look to the Young Pretender for political salvation – Liechty, 1993: 23): some Catholics had worked a niche for themselves under the penal laws which led to accommodation rather than rebellion. This quiescence is true even in Ulster, where the Catholic middle class was less well developed because of the dominance of trade by Presbyterians, which the sacramental test did not affect.

Liberalisation of the Penal Laws

By the mid-eighteenth century, there was more freedom of action than the letter of the law suggested (on which, see Foster, 1988: 211). But although winning for themselves a connivance, Catholics wished the penal laws gone because they represented their formal subjugation. However, the penal laws were symbolic of the ascendancy and they permitted Protestants to control the terms and the extent to which Catholicism was tolerated. Thus, despite good relations with Catholics locally, even to the point of attending funerals in Catholic churches and the provision of financial support to build churches, Protestants overwhelmingly objected to the repeal of the penal laws.

In 1778, the English Parliament restored full property rights to Catholics, although by that time short leases had become the norm anyway and the penal laws had worked their effect, for Catholics held but 5 per cent of the land in spite of comprising three-quarters of the total population (ibid.: 211). In subsequent legislation, various restrictions on worship were withdrawn (although Catholic churches could still not have steeples and bells), priests were allowed formally to live in Ireland and to provide schooling, intermarriage was permitted, and Catholic seminaries were established to offer training for the priesthood locally.[12] Catholics were allowed to practise at the Bar and, as the last concession in 1793, given back the franchise.

For permitting such, the English government received fulsome praise from Catholic clergy and fury from Irish Protestants, who felt, once more, that England had let them down. Hugh O'Donnell, a priest in Belfast, preached a sermon in 1782 applauding the government for its enlightened policies, encouraging members of his parish to make themselves useful 'to king and country' (Rafferty, 1994: 89). He noted, regretfully, that most Protestants seemed not to share his view. Protestants responded with bitterness, seeing themselves as jettisoned at the whim of English politics. The liberalisation and eventual repeal of the penal laws was an attempt by the English government to curry Catholic favour in order to establish political stability in Ireland, to stave off a possible invasion by France, to encourage Catholic recruits to the armed forces (Ruane and Todd, 1996: 38), and to prevent an alliance with the United Irishmen. Allen expresses this idea more pungently: wanting cannon-fodder, Protestant privilege in Ireland was sacrificed so that Catholics could die in military service to the Crown (1994: 92). The government also had a vested interest in encouraging Catholic middle-class support for the status quo (Foster, 1988: 207).

Protestants also responded with insecurity and fear. The ascendancy had been prey throughout the eighteenth century to fears that England would break their monopoly (ibid.: 173). These fears resulted in a measure of anti-Englishness, whether manifest in objections to English imports to Ireland or general governmental interference, and in the claim for parliamentary independence from England. The ascendancy gave Ireland Swift, Defoe, Sheridan, Goldsmith and Burke, who articulated the demand to be treated equally to Britain: a Protestant version of Irish nationalism (Kee, 1995: 56). It was Swift who had urged on his fellow Irishmen in the 1720s that they burn everything English except English coal. There was also annoyance at the number of English people sent over to take up key posts in the public administration of the ascendancy (Foster, 1988: 174). Protestant opposition to English penal law policy only delayed reform; the principle was lost on English expediency: the draft bill of the 1778 legislation was initially very sweeping, removing all restrictions save parliamentary representation and access to Crown offices, but these reforms were reinstated over the next ten years. While legislative independence from England was granted in 1782, perhaps as a sop to compensate for the erosion of the Protestant monopoly, anti-Englishness became as prevalent as anti-Catholicism in the last part of the eighteenth century, as the United Irishmen were to demonstrate.

Anti-Catholicism played a significant part in mobilising Protestant opposition to the repeal of the penal laws. The Rev. John Rodgers preached a sermon in 1782, the same year as legislative independence was achieved, extolling his congregation to see through the ruse. Do 'not consent to the repeal of the penal laws', he told them, 'or allow a legal toleration of the Popish religion. Popery is of a persecuting spirit and has always marked her steps, wherever she trod, with blood. Protestants must not expect to have any security for their religious liberty from her' (quoted in Bardon, 1992: 217). Three themes in Protestant mythology were woven from Rodgers's pulpit – the view that Catholic gains are Protestant losses, that any erosion of the position of Protestants sullies the memory of those innocents who died defending the true religion, and that Catholicism would annihilate Protestants and Protestantism. All that the Protestant martyrs had died for – from 1641 onwards – appeared to be risked in any generosity to Catholics and their Church. Even John Wesley, in one of his evangelical missions in Ireland in 1780, defended the penal laws out of the outrageous fear that Catholics needed to be hindered from doing harm or else they would 'cut the throats of their quiet neighbours'. His diary on one of his visits to Ireland notes how Catholics still seem to thirst for blood (see Haydon, 1993: 65).[13] Catholics, in short, were ideologically constructed still as barbarians and savages, and their relations with Protestants understood in zero-sum terms. Confessional labels had their saliency reinforced, therefore, when reform threatened the capacity of Protestants to engage in social closure.

Only when under external attack do Protestants find unity and overcome the schism and factionalism inherent in their theology; and sometimes attacks are manufactured or exaggerated for this very purpose (on the tendency to schism within Protestantism, see Bruce, 1985b). That the English Methodist joined with the Ulster Scots Presbyterian shows that an unintended consequence of the repeal debate was to force unity of purpose on the Protestant denominations in Ireland. Presbyterians and Anglicans found common cause under the repeal debate, allowing them to put aside the theological disputes that divided them at the beginning of the century. Over most of Ireland, Protestants of any denomination were a small minority, and churchmen united in defending their position out of fear of doing otherwise. Church of Ireland clergy, for example, fanned public feeling by claiming that land reform assisted Catholic attempts to undermine Protestantism through an attack on tithes. By directing attention away from tithes to the maintenance of the ascendancy generally, Anglican clergy were able to win the support of many Presbyterians, who also objected to paying tithes. The Anglican Bishop of Cloyne, for example, warned his Presbyterian colleagues in 1785 that the two churches were aligned and 'the subversion of one must necessarily overthrow the other' (quoted in Bailie, 1981: 79). Only Presbyterians in eastern Ulster were in a majority situation, and their relations with Catholics were entirely different. It was in Belfast, for example, that leading Presbyterians attended mass in St Mary's chapel in 1784 to commemorate its opening, because they had largely paid the costs to build it (Bardon, 1992: 218). Presbyteries in Antrim and Bangor passed resolutions supporting universal toleration in religious matters. Support for the United Irishmen a few years later would show how different these Presbyterians were from their kinspeople in other presbyteries, let alone Protestants in different denominations.

Sectarian Violence in Ulster in the Late Eighteenth Century

It was in the context of government reform and Protestant resistance that a new form of sectarian violence erupted in Ireland, with Ulster as its epicentre, which has lasted to the present day. Agrarian unrest was a typical feature of eighteenth-century Ireland, focused on opposition to tithes, rents and enclosures. Protestants were often as badly affected by landlordism as Catholics, and Presbyterians resented paying tithes to the Church of Ireland as much as did Catholics. The peasant conflicts were structured on denominational lines, since this was the reality in which people lived their lives giving meaning to the whole Irish social structure, and secret societies articulating peasant interests reflected this, but poor tenants and the landless were in similar structural positions against the landlord regardless of confessional label. What distinguished sectarian violence in County Armagh from the 1780s was its increasingly sophisticated organisational form, the effect of proto-industrialisation in both dividing the Catholic and Protestant working class and intensifying the hostility between them, and the use of anti-Catholicism as a resource to overcome fissures in Protestant hegemony rather than solely to mobilise opposition to Catholics.

Protestant resistance to the liberalisation of the penal laws was not the only feature of the Irish landscape into which this new form of anti-Catholic violence must be located. The last quarter of the eighteenth century saw several processes merge to make anti-Catholicism unusually problematic. The first was zealous evangelism by conservative Protestants. By the end of the eighteenth century, evangelism of the heathen had become a major priority for English-based Protestant organisations and evangelical societies as part of the great missionary movement to the wider world, and they vented their anti-Catholicism in Ireland (see Hempton and Hill, 1992), sometimes influenced by events in England rather than Ireland (Haydon, 1993). The antics of Gideon Ouseley testify to this. His preaching was unashamedly emotional and he vividly argued his case that Catholicism was superstition, unChristian and pagan; audiences were regaled with details of alleged attacks by Catholic mobs on Protestants, some of which were real, and base prejudices and fears amongst Protestants were played on (on Ouseley, see Hempton and Hill, 1992: 41–3). What made preaching like this disturbing was the political climate in which it resonated, because events in English politics and internationally had their effect on destabilising Ireland and exposing Catholics to increasingly virulent opposition. The 'three revolutions' – French, American and Industrial – were processes which fundamentally affected the saliency of anti-Catholicism in late eighteenth-century Ireland.

The American War of Independence forced Catholics to emphasise their own loyalty to the British Crown. The government trusted Catholics enough to allow them to be armed to protect the Crown's interests, since the American colonists had supporters amongst Northern Presbyterians, and an American ship had actually engaged the Royal Navy in Belfast Lough in 1778. The prospect of armed Catholics defending Ireland, perhaps against Protestants, set fears raging, and by the time France entered the war in support of the Americans, Protestants knew they could not support anyone in alliance with a Catholic state (France had earlier invaded Carrickfergus during the Seven Years War). The French Revolution, the second of the great revolutions in the eighteenth century, while steeling local Protestants in their own demand for independence, was mythologised as an attack on a Catholic-dominated government and the Catholic Church by erstwhile French Catholics and taken as a portent for local events (Hempton, 1996: 98). The Industrial Revolution was also to increase the resonance for anti-Catholicism in Ireland and effect new forms of sectarian violence. The early industrialisation of Ireland was restricted to Ulster because of linen production, one of the first industries to mechanise and experience the benefits of the modern division of labour, allowing Ulster's economy to interact with the Industrial Revolution occurring in England (Foster, 1988: 213). The port of Belfast also added economic strength, allowing Belfast to emerge economically by the end of the seventeenth century (Bardon, 1992: 146); French Protestants were given land around Lisburn in 1698 to encourage weaving, which gave trade to the port. The growth of a proto-industrial sector based around linen in eighteenth-century County Armagh, which had become used to being avowedly ascendant, Protestant and Presbyterian, attracted poor Catholic farmers, tenants and landless Catholics to the area to an extent that its population balance was disturbed. Armagh became the most populous county in Ireland, and Catholics now competed with Protestants for land, market pitches, weaving contracts and other forms of employment associated with linen, and economic position and wealth generally. Moreover, Hempton and Hill (1992: 43) show that evangelical fervour by conservative groups was particularly enthusiastic in the linen districts of County Armagh, where there had also been a revivalistic growth of Methodism (see Hempton, 1980, 1986), which Hempton takes as a sign of social disruption (Hempton, 1996: 95) but which also contributed to anti-Catholicism.

Concessions to Catholics in the context of this volatility transformed the nature of sectarian violence. But as a commentator at the time noted, the repeal of the penal laws was only the precipitation for the violence, its nature and extent had broader structural features: 'much offence had lately been taken because the catholics, in the general increase in wealth, had raised the price of land. This was the cause of our ill-humour: the relaxation of the popery laws but the pretense' (quoted in Bardon, 1992: 224). The organisational forms, and level of anti-Catholic hostility, of the 'ill-humour' merit examination.

There were two sorts of impulse to the new organisational forms through which anti-Catholic violence was orchestrated: the first formal paramilitary activity; the second the tradition of forming secret societies to agitate on agrarian issues. One feature of all colonial situations is that settlers develop a tradition of being citizens and soldiers, and, whether under the name of the Antrim Association in 1689, the militia in 1715, 1719, 1745, 1756, 1760 and 1793, the Volunteers in 1778, or the Yeomanry in 1796, the Protestant tenantry, under the leadership of their landlords, were accustomed to the paramilitary role to defend property and life (Miller, 1978a:

25). Under the invasion crisis of the late 1770s, when the French were expected to land in support of the Americans fighting for independence, corps of volunteers were even formed on occupational lines, one being formed amongst hairdressers (Foster, 1988: 245). These were composed of middle-class Protestants in trade, many of whom were Presbyterian (see Barkley, 1959: 25; Holmes, 1973: 9–10). The Volunteers had within them, therefore, all the strains of Protestant politics. Some were generous in supporting Catholic reform as part of a more general process of independence for Ireland. The Dungannon Convention of Volunteers in 1782, composed almost entirely of dissenters (Barkley, 1959: 35), passed a resolution calling for legislative independence for Ireland and 'the relaxation of the laws against our Roman Catholic fellow subjects'. A corps of Volunteers formed the honour guard when the first Catholic chapel to be built in Belfast was opened, paid for largely by local Protestants. Most were less generous and did not extend to Catholics the reforms they advocated for themselves. Some clergy warned against liberalisation of the penal laws and urged the Volunteers be used to 'keep the Papists in order', as John Wesley noted in his diary. The Belfast delegates to the Dungannon Convention had argued for Catholics to be given the vote, but this was too much for the Volunteers, who accepted a weaker declaration. Most wanted voting and procedural reform to apply to Protestants only (Foster, 1988: 256).

Protestants also formed new secret societies, with groups emerging such as the Peep O'Day Boys in 1786 and the Orange Order in 1795. Older secret societies amongst Protestants, like the Steelboys, were also anti-Catholic. The Steelboys, for example, resented land being given to 'Papists' prepared to pay higher rents (ibid.: 223). The new organisations were more openly sectarian and violent, and linked to the proto-industrial circumstances in County Armagh. The Peep O'Day Boys was set up, its members said, to enforce the penal laws which the civil authorities were reneging on. It appealed to poorer Protestants connected to linen and weaving who feared they were losing out in competition with Catholics, and was a regrouping and consolidation of smaller secret societies like the Nappach Fleet, Bawn Fleet and the Bunkerhill Defenders (Bardon, 1992: 223). The Orange Order was similar in origin. Thus, at first it had little appeal to Presbyterians, most of whom worked in trade rather than linen, and Barkley notes that those Presbyterians who did support the Order from the beginning 'belonged to the class of agricultural labourers or country tradesmen' (Barkley, 1959: 36). It was vehemently anti-Catholic. Its original oath enjoined members to 'support the King and his heirs as long as he or they support the Protestant Ascendancy' (quoted in Foster, 1988: 275). An early Orange Toast was franker, referring to the Pope as the Devil. It even attacked Protestant mill owners and linen manufacturers in Armagh who continued to employ Catholics (Gibbon, 1975: 39–40). When the Yeomanary was formed in 1796, members of the Orange Order flooded to the ranks. It was overwhelmingly Protestant and anti-Catholic, but open to infiltration from Catholics and radical United Irishmen. Let loose, it struck terror in its attempts to impose order, although the largely Catholic militia, formed in 1793, also developed a reputation for violence.

Catholics developed new organisational forms too. Agrarian unrest in the mid-eighteenth century saw Catholics form secret societies like the Rightboys, whose name shows their platform was to claim their original rights, and Oakboys. Generally they were localised and agitated on issues of land reform, an economic interest they shared with many poor Protestant tenants, which is why some Protestants joined these organisations as well. But in the 1780s an organisation known as the Defenders absorbed and consolidated these societies and transformed the focus to support the interests of the rural and proto-industrial Catholic workforce, mostly in County Armagh. Its name suggests that members saw themselves as reacting to Protestant violence and protecting Catholic interests in self-defence, but it was very anti-Protestant and anti-English, with a capacity for spectacular violence (Foster, 1988: 272; Rafferty, 1994: 90).

These new organisational forms were simultaneously both a product of intense sectarian violence and its cause. The new form of sectarian violence broke out in County Armagh in the 1780s. Anger at increased rents, Catholic incursion on to land and competition within the linen industry, was translated in two directions: opposition against wealthier Protestants who seemed willing to undermine the privileges of the labouring class of Protestants, and the Catholics who dared encroach. Organisations like the Peep O'Day Boys emerged to take the battle to Catholics and their Protestant friends. Numerous sectarian incidents occurred. The homes of Catholic tenants and weavers were burned, and Protestant landowners had homes barricaded. The wealthy Protestant landowners sometimes supported their Catholic tenants and employees, loaning them arms (Bardon, 1992: 223), but Protestants had better access to arms because of their soldier-citizen background. Some landowners described the Peep O'Day Boys as 'fanatick madmen' and 'holy crusados' but they could do little to stop the violence. Violent incursions into Catholic districts transformed the Defenders from an interdenominational organisation agitating on land reform for all, into an organisation for defending the life and property of Catholic labourers. They retaliated in kind and attacked Protestant homes and settlements. The Volunteers and the Yeomanry policed the Defenders. A magistrate in 1798 said he had no hesitation in giving arms to 'the Protestant boys that have none' because the Defenders 'are now beginning their night depredations and lye in wait behind ditches to murder and destroy every protestant that appears' (quoted in ibid.). By 1792, there is evidence that the Defenders had moved beyond violence to revolution, secretly negotiating with the French over possible assistance in Ireland. Members of the ascendancy became alarmed at the threat. Growing Catholic strength was interpreted as a direct assault on Protestant ascendancy (Rafferty, 1994: 91).

In the autumn of 1795, Defenders faced Peep O'Day Boys for battle at a place in County Armagh known as the Diamond. Shots were fired at Catholics and a contemporary report mentions a death toll of thirty. The victorious Peep O'Day Boys went that night to the house of James Sloan and formed the Orange Order. They, too, saw themselves as merely defensive. It modelled itself on the Defenders, with oaths, passwords, signs, and lodges, but their aim, as a contemporary report noted, was proactive, to 'drive from this quarter of the county the entire of its Roman Catholic population. A written notice was thrown into or posted upon the door of a house warning the inmates, in the words of Oliver Cromwell, to betake themselves "to hell or Connaught"' (quoted in Bardon, 1992: 226). They broke up homes, smashed looms, drove Catholics from the land, and killed many 'without mercy', as Lord Gosford noted at the time. He continued: 'the only crime which the wretched objects of this ruthless persecution are charged with, is a crime of easy proof; it is simply a profession of the Roman Catholic faith, or an intimate connection with a person professing this faith' (quoted in ibid.: 227). He went on to complain of the lack of protection Catholics were given from magistrates in Armagh.

The sectarian violence in County Armagh bequeathed the North of Ireland the phenomenon of Orangeism, and it was in the context of this violence that the first commemoration took place of the Battle of the Boyne, 100 years after the event, as a celebration of the ascendancy that working-class Protestants now feared they were losing. The roots of Orangeism lay in proto-industrial competition rather than agrarian unrest, and it intensified the level of anti-Catholic hatred as a resource to re-establish the social closure it benefited from and feared was now over. But Orangeism also highlighted the divisions within Protestant politics. Protestant landowners initially attacked the Orange Order and its fellow paramilitary groups like the Peep O'Day Boys. In part they were driving off their employees and tenants, and bringing chaos and disorder which disrupted trade and civil life. Fissures within Protestantism were marked as liberal Protestants stood against Orangeism. Many within the United Irishmen chose to support Catholics (but not all), but anti-Catholicism was successfully mobilised in the 1790s to heal these fissures and reunite Protestants – at least those outside the United Irishmen.

Gentry and tenant, mill owner and labourer, began an alliance under Orangeism which gave it its distinctive character and strength (Holmes, 1973: 12), in which political stability and profit in Ulster were married with privilege for the Protestant working class, with the bond between them cemented by the panoply of Orangeism, including anti-Catholicism. Gentry and mill owners very quickly endorsed lodges amongst their tenants and labourers and used Orangeism as both a means of social control of Catholics (see Allen, 1994: 126–7) and for the defence of their economic and political interests (Holmes, 1973: 12). Protestants in the United Irishmen claimed that Orangeism sought to extend beyond the plantation and exterminate all Catholics (ibid.); it was little surprise therefore that Orangemen viciously attacked fellow Protestants in the interdenominational and republican United Irishmen who sought common cause with Catholics. It was this danger that set the alliance with Orangeism in motion for wealthy Protestants, giving the Orange Order licence for their anti-Catholicism. Hence, a British General wrote in a report on violence in mid-Ulster in the 1790s that he had 'arranged to increase the animosity between the Orange men and the United Irish. Upon that animosity depends the safety of the centre counties of the North' (quoted in Allen, 1994: 127). The United Irishmen posed a serious threat to the Protestant ascendancy by their republican ideas and

advocacy of equality for Catholics, although the movement failed because it was split by these twin claims and many potential supporters were alienated by the notion of equality for Catholics.

The United Irishmen

The Society of United Irishmen was formed in Belfast in 1791 by Wolfe Tone, a Dublin lawyer, and William Drennan, the son of a non-covenantal New Light Presbyterian minister, plus other Presbyterians. It appealed to young, articulate, middle-class Protestant businessmen and professionals (Bardon, 1992: 220) determined to challenge the ascendancy in politics, economics and theology. The Society's declarations demanded political independence for Ireland and full political citizenship for Catholics, economic reallocation and the erosion of the dominance of landlordism, and union between Catholics and Protestants as Irish people. Such a platform won them some Catholic support; if they were to overthrow the ascendancy Catholic support was vital. The Society directed its appeal to middle-class Catholics ('the rich Catholic') offering them incorporation into full citizenship, but support did not come in sufficient levels and later the hierarchy of the Catholic Church in Ireland would threaten to excommunicate anyone who joined in rebellion. Catholic support was also problematic for those Protestant United Irishmen who wanted a Protestant Republic which excluded Catholics.

The leading members of the Society were Presbyterians, and they called for 'the common name of Irishmen' in place of 'the denominations of protestant, catholic and dissenter'. In 1793, the General Synod of Ulster called for parliamentary reform and Catholic emancipation, saying that it prayed 'that the time may never more return when religious distinctions shall be used as a pretext for disturbing society or arming man against his neighbour' (General Synod of Ulster, n.d.: 157). These were, however, New Light Presbyterians – unorthodox, non-covenantal and politically radical – whose base was restricted to Belfast and Antrim. Even here, some Belfast ministers warned against Catholic emancipation (see Holmes, 1973: 10), and this view was endorsed by Conservative and orthodox elements in the Synod – the Old Light covenantal Presbyterians, who saw the Catholic Church as the Whore and the Beast, and who feared politically a strident Catholicism. By 1798, the covenanters in the Synod were dominant, strengthened by what they saw as the disturbing events of the rebellion that year and by the talk of alliances with Catholic France. They reaffirmed the covenantal oath of loyalty to the Crown and Constitution, condemning the 'few unworthy members of our body whose conduct we can only view with grief and indignation' (General Synod of Ulster, n.d.: 208). As Hempton shows, political events (both domestic and international, with the French Revolution) reacted with the covenanters' millenarianism, in which the end-time predicted in the Bible was thought to be upon them (Hempton, 1996: 98–9; see also Miller, 1978b: 80–1). The defeat of the antiChrist, as part of the end-time, meant the downfall of Catholicism (and episcopalianism), which they saw as being achieved in France by the Revolution. God's chosen nation, Ulster, could thus not but assist in the downfall, and there was a dramatic religious revival amongst reformed churches in Ulster in 1799 (perhaps related to the failure of the rebellion), although New Light Presbyterians tended to see the struggle between Christ and the antiChrist politically, represented by the conflict between liberty and despotism (Hempton and Hill, 1992: 28).

Tone believed that all Presbyterians were United Irishmen (quoted in Holmes, 1973: 7), and there was a tradition of political radicalism and unorthodox theology amongst some Presbyterians which made them sympathetic to the claims for Catholic emancipation. But this was restricted on the whole to presbyteries in Antrim and Down where there were fewer Catholics and no history of sectarian fighting. Presbyteries elsewhere were less radical and had deep reservations about Catholic emancipation. Presbyterians in Antrim became United Irishmen (for a case study of one such minister, see Bailie, 1981), but Orangemen in Armagh. The former was dominated by New Light theology, political radicalism and secure middle-class Protestantism, the latter by insecure Protestant labourers competing with Catholics for work, and a desire for orthodoxy in theology and politics, preferring Old Light covenanting and the Protestant ascendancy (Miller (1978b: 77–9) suggests, however, that there is no simple link between New Light theology and radicalism). But within a few years, support was falling away for the United Irishmen amongst Presbyterians even in Antrim and Down. Ten years earlier Ulster Protestants had met in Dungannon to declare their support for Catholic emancipation, but in 1793 few turned out again, there were no delegates from Armagh, and the Convention was split over support for emancipation (Holmes, 1973: 11). Presbyterian ministers who had formerly been United Irishmen, like Bruce from Belfast and Black from Derry, shifted toward conservatism and preached against 'seditious spirits who wished to overturn the constitution' (quoted in ibid.). The violent course of events in France, with the execution of the King and Queen, disillusioned erstwhile Presbyterian United Irishmen. Orangeism also grew rapidly from the mid-1790s, and once the Protestant landowners had resumed alliance with Protestant tenants, weavers and linen workers, the base for radical Presbyterianism was narrowed in Ulster. Anti-Catholicism was a unifying force which undercut support for the United Irishmen in most of Ulster, and most Presbyterians had, anyway, been reformers rather than real revolutionaries (Holmes, 1982: 538).

When the rising by United Irishmen occurred therefore, it was an essentially Southern Irish event. According to Bardon (1992: 236), 20,000 people died in the rebellion, most in Leinster. The only counties affected in Ulster were Antrim and Down (on the rising in Ulster, see ibid.: 232–7). In Antrim and Down, 'thousands of United Irishmen, mostly Presbyterian farmers armed with pike and musket, rose in rebellion' (Barkley, 1959: 38) but were killed or suppressed. Support diminished further as a result of anti-Protestant massacres in Wexford which reinforced sectarian attitudes (recent historical research has disputed that the Wexford incident was anti-Protestant, although this was how it was perceived at the time – see Whelan, 1996); some Northern Presbyterians executed for their part in the rebellion renounced the massacres as they were hanged. Two Presbyterian ministers were eventually executed for taking part, eighteen were imprisoned and several were banished to America. Catholics in Ulster on the whole stayed clear of the warfare. The Catholic Church, preferring accommodation with the civil authorities and English government, did not support the rebellion; Catholics who supported the Defenders were threatened with excommunication. Bishop McDevit belied most Protestant stereotypes of politically meddlesome Catholic bishops when he urged on the laity during the rebellion 'not to be misled from the loyalty due to your sovereign and to obedience to the laws of your country' (quoted in Rafferty, 1994: 95), and some local priests warned against participating in the United Irishmen. This shows the extent of the successful co-option of the Catholic hierarchy, but the fact that fourteen priests were implicated in the rebellion shows the problems bishops had in asserting political control over the clergy: both would become motifs of Catholicism in the nineteenth century.

2 Union to Partition: 1800–1920

Introduction

Nineteenth-century Ireland showed great continuity with its past. All its old conflicts continued, its lines of differentiation remained, and the social structure kept its familiar pattern. Developments in Protestant–Catholic relations throughout the century were conditioned by the past, so that progress, in some ways, always went backwards, back to the plantation and the sort of society it helped to shape, back to old battles and events, returning to the same zero-sum notions and anti-Catholic ideas that existed in the sixteenth century. However, as time evolved Ireland was increasingly unable to live with its past because the old conflicts and fissures caused tremendous strain in its social structure. Protestant and Catholic people emerged in the nineteenth century as solidaristic communities, transcending fault-lines within each as they confronted the other as a separate community in a zero-sum conflict in which it seemed that they did not have mutually compatible sets of interests. Political and economic developments in the nineteenth century divided the island of Ireland into two identities, mutually sculpted in opposition to each other, and it became increasingly difficult to contain both in the one territory. Social structural strains eventually developed to the point that the colonial society planted in the sixteenth century was overturned – at least in twenty-six of its counties. Union to partition was a journey to nationhood in which anti-Catholicism lost its power as a resource to shape economics, politics and society, but the journey for some Catholics took a route to the new state of Northern Ireland, where old and familiar anti-Catholicism played a critical sociological role in Ulster's own version of the ascendancy.

Union with Britain

The English government's response to the republican violence by Protestants in Ireland was to incorporate the country into Union with Britain in 1800. The Irish Parliament was initially dissolved but many members of the elite within the Protestant ascendancy were absorbed into the metropolitan core to maintain access to office and power; a local administration also remained in Dublin Castle. The Orange lobby was against Union because management of Catholics locally, with its implications for the maintenance of Protestant privileges, was taken over by London and they feared the consequences of this for Catholic emancipation. Some radicals from the United Irishmen also opposed Union because it was seen as a means of reinforcing English control on Irish matters. A radical strain in Protestantism survived – New Light in theological terms and liberal politically – which later supported Catholic emancipation. In other words, Union was not yet seen as the guarantor of Protestant position and privilege and had not become the single cleavage around which Protestant and Catholic political differences were fought (for a critique of Union, see Kennedy, 1996: 37–48). This did not occur until the 1830s. By then, however, Protestantism and Unionism became inseparable to all but the most liberal Protestant, with reformed theology providing what sociologists call a 'sacred canopy'. The Protestant religion overarched Unionist politics, Protestant privilege, and the shared communal identity which bonded Protestants together in a class alliance; Unionism was distinguished by this class alliance and Protestantism was its 'sacred canopy'. An Orange song gave voice to the alliance guarded by Protestantism: 'Let not the poor man hate the rich/nor rich on poor look down/But each join each true Protestant/for God and for the Crown' (quoted in Devlin, 1981: 18).

The hierarchy within the Catholic Church initially supported Union. Political accommodation with the English government and civil authorities in Ireland had developed to the point where the Church accepted the monarch's right to veto nominations for bishoprics in Ireland and it accepted a salary from the state for its priests in return for support for Union. The leading bishops were led to believe that Union would result in more favourable treatment for Catholics in relation to tithes and parliamentary representation; Catholics were still required to abjure certain Catholic doctrines and beliefs before they could sit in Parliament, and the government promised repeal of such an oath. England seemed to offer a more tolerant Protestant majority than Ireland, and some Catholic bishops were liberal and ecumenical by temperament. The Bishop of Derry between 1798 and 1823 earned the nickname 'Orange Charlie' for his friendliness to local Protestants; he suspended one of his priests for radical remarks about Catholic emancipation (Rafferty, 1994: 114).[1] The majority of Northern bishops favoured Union (ibid.: 127). But emancipation was delayed for another thirty years. English duplicity in the past had led some Catholics, like Daniel O'Connell, to criticise the Union from the beginning. O'Connell later began the Catholic Association to fight for Catholic emancipation, with the support of the Catholic Church. While it is popular to see the Catholic Association as a form of Irish nationalism, O'Connell did politicise Ireland's Catholic population and opposition to Union was part of Catholic political maturation. Union, in other words, did not achieve what English policy makers intended, for the old fissures and modes of differentiation in Ireland continued. Rather than obliterating the conflicts by incorporating them into Britain's wider social structure, Union ensured that Ireland's fissures now affected the core of British society, and British governments proved more willing to respond to Catholic grievances than local Protestants.

In his campaign against Union, Daniel O'Connell is reputed to have said that Ireland's Protestants were political Protestants only; that is, they were Protestants by reason of their participation in political power rather than in commitment to reformed theology, and once they were put on an equal plane with Catholics the religious bigotry and opposition would wither away. This was not an unreasonable belief. Protestants in Ireland had been divided theologically ever since the seventeenth century. In relating to each other, these divisions proved very important to Protestants; it was only in their relationship to Catholics that Protestants showed any kind of unity politically. However, the first half of the nineteenth century saw Protestantism furnish the sacred canopy which bound Protestants together for the first time, and it did so when Protestants felt under most threat. At the beginning of the nineteenth century, the majority of Protestants were not self-confident or triumphant, but defensive, protective and under siege, sensing untrustworthiness in the British and local Catholics alike. It was in their defensiveness, and while believing themselves under siege, that unity was found around a common Protestantism. This was to become a recurring motif of Protestantism in the nineteenth and twentieth centuries: in times of crisis, Protestantism was stressed as the common denominator. But Protestantism came to symbolise more than a religion, for the sacred canopy extended over society, politics and economics. Eventually Protestants became a solidaristic community where theological differences counted for less than their shared Protestantism; they became a cohesive political entity with a common interest in the Union, and Protestants developed a class alliance which transcended economic differences between them. Anti-Catholicism was integral to the sacred canopy by identifying those entitled to its protective covering and those left outside.[2] Religious bigotry and opposition thus did not wither away in the nineteenth century but intensified, remaining part of a process of social closure which was constructed around confessional labels and justified theologically.

The Sacred Canopy of Protestantism

Protestant unity did not emerge immediately with Union and was a response to several circumstances in the first half of the nineteenth century, which helped to shape their identity. A common identity emerged in response to a sense of threat, in which Catholic advances were seen as a challenge to the position of Protestants. The crisis in Protestant–Catholic relations was often affected by the broader relation between Britain and Ireland, for British governments occasionally responded to Catholic grievances because Ireland now threatened Britain's social structure. The contingencies which contributed to Protestants' siege mentality and around which Protestantism threw a sacred canopy uniting Protestants together included the mobilisation of opposition against Catholic emancipation (at least opposition from amongst Old Light Presbyterians like Henry Cooke); anxiety about Catholic self-confidence and assertiveness, especially in politics, which prompted fear of 'political Popery'; anti-Protestant sectarian violence, and widespread evangelism by conservative Protestants, with accompanying shifts in Presbyterianism toward the covenanting tradition and theological conservatism generally in Irish Protestantism.

One of the continuities between eighteenth- and nineteenth-century Ireland was sectarian violence. Union did little to stop the warring bands of peasants and artisans. Defenderism amongst Catholics was perpetuated in a proliferation of agrarian protest movements and secret societies. The best known and most popular were the Ribbonmen. Ribbonism was proto-nationalist in its aspirations but markedly anti-Protestant and sectarian (Foster, 1988: 293). Its base was Ulster (Bardon, 1992: 243), because Protestants were in a majority there, and conflicts with Orangemen were often bloody and violent. This anti-Protestantism became volatile when mixed with the millenarian prophecies of Pastorini, espoused by some Catholic clergy, which predicted the destruction of the Reformation and the British government in 1825; when this year passed quietly 1844 was the new nemesis. Ribbonmen pledged themselves to assist its coming to pass, as their oath shows: 'I do swear in the presence of my brethren and by the cross of St. Peter and Our Blessed Lady that I will aid and support our holy religion by destroying the heretics, so help me God' (quoted in ibid.). Orangeism flourished under attacks from Ribbonmen in the early nineteenth century, and the violence encouraged a siege mentality amongst Protestants in which, in their defensiveness, they would look to each other for unity and support.

The siege mentality was reinforced by the sense that Protestants confronted a confident, assertive and politically astute Catholic Church, whose flock had emerged from subjugation, with the tacit assistance of the British. British governments were seen as unreliable in their commitment to the ascendancy. Even Tories gave various reassurances to Catholics about tithes and the possible ending of all legal restrictions on Catholics, including standing for Parliament. The powers of various paramilitary Protestant forces, like the Yeomanry, were severely curtailed in the development of impartial police forces, the administration of justice was improved by reform of magistrates, and Orange marches were banned. At one point it appeared as if the Orange Order would become extinct (ibid.). Defensiveness amongst Protestants was not just a response to concessions, or the promise of concessions, to Catholics, but the sense that the Catholic Church was engaged in 'political Popery', manipulating British governments by mobilising the Catholic laity as a powerful political force and by profusions of loyalty from the bishops. Political Popery was perceived in the campaign by the Catholic Church against tithes, which Catholics saw as a form of religious persecution (Akenson, 1971: 95), but the opposition to which Protestants saw as not just a threat to the Church of Ireland but Protestantism generally (Rafferty, 1994: 115). It was also thought to be evident in the education debate of the early nineteenth century. The British government established a non-sectarian and non-denominational system of national schools in Ireland long before it did so in England, which the Catholic Church supported. Protestants in the North objected. The population dynamics in the North resulted in many schools where Protestants were the majority, and all Protestant churches objected to Catholic clergy being given access to such schools to teach religious instruction to Catholic pupils. They also wanted formal Bible readings for all pupils to expose Catholics to Holy Scripture. To agree to the national school system, said one Protestant clergyman, was 'to favour the claims and advance the designs of Roman Catholics, to afford encouragement to the teaching of the dogmas of Rome' (Porter, 1871: 240). While the 1832 Synod only narrowly voted against the new system, some Presbyterians described it thus:

'the most cunning, the most daring, and the most specious attempt that has been made against Protestantism' (ibid.: 241). They detected the 'evil' influence of the Catholic Church over the British government's refusal to depart from the principle of non-denominationalism, since this really meant, in a distorted mind-set, that Catholic dogma went unchallenged.[3]

The summit of so-called political Popery came with the development of political self-confidence and assertiveness amongst Catholics in the debate over emancipation. Historians have noted that it was in the struggle for emancipation that Catholicism and Irish consciousness were associated and became a national movement. Catholics felt confident enough to challenge the existing order politically, and in doing so gave themselves, for the first time, a single political identity (Ruane and Todd, 1996: 35). The effects of Catholic emancipation on Protestants were equally profound. Allen interprets the passing of the 1829 Catholic Emancipation Act as a rubicon in which the British government signalled to Protestants that it was no longer committed to the ascendancy (Allen, 1994: 100). It meant a recognition by the state that social control in Ireland was best served by religious parity rather than Protestant ascendancy – parity in the courts, policing, government employment, education, and in parliamentary representation. Government appointments favoured Catholics; some Protestants resigned in protest against the government's 'surrender to popery' (ibid.: 111). Orangemen protested against emancipation. Riots broke out when the Bill became law; the Orange Order was banned at the time and the annual 12 July parade in Belfast was banned, which added to the rioting in the city. Anti-Catholic Brunswick Clubs were set up to replace the Orange Order lodges, and they organised massive demonstrations, marches and protests. There was rioting right across the North (Bardon, 1992: 247). The General Synod of the Presbyterian Church supported Catholic emancipation in 1813, calling for the 'abolition of political distinctions on account of religious profession', reflecting the afterglow of the United Irishmen. But the conservative shift towards the covenanting tradition, which the Church was soon to undergo under Henry Cooke's period of leadership, resulted in support for 'limited' emancipation (Holmes, 1981: 125). Cooke later defined this as emancipation for Catholics everywhere in Ireland except the North (Porter, 1871: 77), allowing Protestants their ascendancy in Ulster, a portent of how Ulster's Protestants would respond later in the century to the demand for Home Rule. When O'Connell dared even entertain a visit to Belfast, Cooke made allusions back to the 1641 massacre, weaving ideas of emancipation with rebellion and massacre (see ibid.: 411).

A liberal Protestant tradition remained based around New Light theology and Whig politics but it was continually undercut by circumstances which encouraged most Protestants into believing themselves beleaguered. The position of liberals was further undermined by the shift towards evangelical theology which affected Protestantism during the first part of the nineteenth century, arising from successful evangelistic crusades and the revival of the covenanting tradition. If Protestantism spread a sacred canopy around most Protestants, it was conservative in theology. Theological conservatism was matched equally with political conservatism, such that Presbyterians lost their radical tradition (on which demise, see Holmes, 1973, 1982). Bardon describes the outcome of evangelistic revival in nineteenth-century Ireland as a resurgence of Puritanism amongst Anglicans and Presbyterians alike (Bardon, 1992: 251) and the ethos of Irish Protestantism by mid-century was evangelical (Liechty, 1993: 35; see also Hempton and Hill, 1992). Evangelicalism drew Presbyterian and episcopalian together in a common Protestantism (Holmes, 1973: 13). Although the original intention had been to convert Catholics, the missions revitalised Protestantism but in an anti-Catholic direction. This was an irony. The crusades intended to leave future generations a legacy of 'peace' by converting Catholics in large numbers, but the conservative theology they imparted encouraged anti-Catholicism, leaving a greater legacy of sectarian animosity (a similar point is made by Liechty, 1993: 32).

Bruce (1986: 11; see also Wallis and Bruce, 1986: 275) argues that the attempt to convert Catholics only began seriously in the nineteenth century when the theological lines of demarcation became firm, so that the possibility of large numbers of Catholics converting was remote and conversion would have entailed political realignment as well. Akenson interprets this to mean that they evangelised only once their Protestant identity became secure (1992: 147). However, evangelicalism began at a time when Protestants felt most under threat and a common identity as Protestants emerged *inter alia* from the evangelical revival rather than its cause. Moreover, the initial push to evangelism came from England rather than local Protestants. The evangelical awakening in Ireland began with the activities of the English Methodists, but went apace in the nineteenth century with the formation of the Hibernian Bible Society in 1806 and the Religious Tract and Book Society in 1810. There were countless smaller organisations, gathered later under the auspices of the Irish Evangelical Society. Many were Anglican, backed by wealthy benefactors and organisations from England where, by the mid-1830s, evangelicalism had also merged with Toryism (Wolffe, 1991: 300).

The evangelicals sought to create what they called the 'Second Reformation' in Ireland, even though there had not been a first, hailed in torrents of pamphlets, tracts, Bibles translated into Irish, sermons, four-hour-long daily debates in the Dublin Institute, numerous missions, Sunday Schools, and multifarious activities by temperance movements. Akenson describes these activities as the creation of a pan-Protestantism which did not convert Roman Catholics but shored up the faith of Protestants (Akenson 1992: 147). The revivals also reinforced humble Calvinists' (who lacked worldly success) belief of their salvation (Miller, 1978b: 70) and re-recruited lapsed Protestants (Wallis and Bruce, 1986: 274). Hempton and Hill show how the Sunday Schools helped to effect the class alliance within Unionism by stressing 'mutual kindness and affection between rich and poor' (Hempton and Hill, 1992: 114). The evangelistic impulse was also anti-Catholic in its style and rhetoric; 'winning souls from Popery' was how Lord Farnham put it as founder of the Association for Promoting the Second Reformation. The tendency to parade publicly the anti-Catholic views of converts dates from Farnham's activities. Some landlords evicted Catholic tenants who failed to convert (Bardon, 1992: 252), and missionaries made much of the supposed link between Catholicism and poverty, indolence, and ignorance. Nineteenth-century evangelicalism inherited the style and rhetoric of older forms of 'No Popery' (Hempton and Hill, 1992: xiii), but gave new fervency to anti-Catholicism by employing it in already volatile sectarian situations where Protestants felt beleaguered and embattled. Evangelicalism, and its associated anti-Catholicism, therefore helped to resolve insecurities and shape Protestant identity when it felt most under threat.[4]

The emergence of conservative evangelicalism amongst Protestants occurred simultaneously with the revival of the covenanting, Old Light tradition in Presbyterianism. The roots of this lay partly in a political shift towards Toryism. The demise of the radicalism of the United Irishmen was obvious to commentators even in 1803, when Alexander Knox informed Lord Castlereagh that Presbyterians had become disillusioned with radicalism: 'they are in a humour for acquiescing in the views of the government beyond which they ever were' (quoted in Holmes, 1982: 540).[5] The much-quoted views of Mrs McTier in 1801 reveal her perception that preachers in Belfast were now 'extremely zealous and loyal, a zealous religion, very judiciously blended with loyalty' – and she was the sister of William Drennan, one of the original ideologues of the United Irishmen. The 1835 Ordnance Survey Memoir for a district in County Armagh comments that men who had been in the 1798 rebellion were now changed 'and seem indifferent or careless' in politics (quoted in Bardon, 1992: 240). Some of these declarations of loyalty were for political effect and could be overdone, and a Whig tradition remained in Presbyterianism which supported Catholic emancipation (see Foster, 1988: 297),[6] but Toryism was the most popular political affection amongst Presbyterians.

Liberalism was not permitted in local matters but it was fine abroad. Thus, in 1846, when the Presbyterian Church in the US contacted the Irish General Synod seeking support for the position taken by American Presbyterians in favour of slavery, appealing to their common anti-Catholicism and being replete with references to the antiChrist and the Beast of Rome, which they hoped would resonate locally, the Irish Church rebuked them for supporting slavery. In reply the General Assembly reiterated its anti-Catholicism – 'Popery is the deadly enemy of civil liberty, as well as of divine truth' – but declared against slavery: 'whatever may be the law, no Christian ought to hold in forcible servitude anyone obtained by the crime of man-stealing; no professor of the Gospel should hold his brother man in bondage' (for the correspondence see Presbyterian Church in Ireland, 1846: 507–11). This from a general assembly that a year earlier had passed a resolution opposing the establishment of Maynooth College because it was 'Popish', announcing that it 'detests the dark, tyrannical and soul-destroying system of Popery which enslaves; Popery is most injurious to the true interests of all its adherents' (ibid., 1845: 414–15).

Political conservatism like this was matched by theological conservatism. The Ulster Synod was split apart in the 1820s when the new evangelicalism sweeping Ireland led to the dominance of the Old Light covenanting theology within the Church against liberal New Light Presbyterians (for excellent accounts of the split see Holmes, 1981; Hempton and Hill, 1992: 70–6). Old Light covenanters took over positions of authority within the Synod and were influential in determining teaching posts for the training of new ministers, by which they came to influence generations. The apostle of Old Light theology and political conservatism was the Rev. Henry Cooke.

The Rev. Henry Cooke DD LL.D

Henry Cooke's life stands as a template for the processes affecting Presbyterianism in the first half of the nineteenth century. It was Cooke who, according to some historians, forged the link in the public's mind between evangelicalism, doctrinal orthodoxy and anti-Catholicism (Hempton and Hill, 1992: 73). His son-in-law and biographer, J.L. Porter, a Presbyterian theologian himself, describes him as connecting 'purity of religious principles with respect for law and order, and with the development of true national greatness' (Porter, 1871: x). Toryism, Empire and Union were his political motifs; orthodoxy, evangelicalism and anti-Catholicism his theological ones. He was a prolific writer and charismatic preacher – he once spent three and a half hours preaching a sermon on the evils of 'Popery' – and he had a domineering influence on Protestantism from the late 1820s (a more charitable reading of Cooke is provided by Holmes, 1983).

His theological motifs were ingrained from childhood and family. His ancestors were Calvinist; some had fought in the Siege of Derry. They had taken a firm stand against the United Irishmen and watching the rebellion as a small boy left an indelible impression on Cooke, later influencing his commitment to law and order, political conservatism and patriotism. His stern and narrow Calvinist upbringing inclined him to theological orthodoxy. His resigned his first post as minister after two years because his orthodoxy offended the congregation, and within a few years he was attacking supporters of Arianism, a theological movement which denied the Trinity. Cooke advocated discipline and conformity within the Presbyterian Church (Boyd, 1969: 5), and insisted on loyalty to the covenantal tradition. All new ministers and clerical students should be required to subscribe to the Westminster Confession. The New Light Presbyterians, based around the Belfast Society, formed in 1705, vigorously opposed such orthodoxy. The New Light Presbyterians were led by Henry Montgomery, a liberal in politics and theology, whose kith and kin were closely involved with the United Irishmen. He later said that 'I have found my best, my clearest-minded and my warmest-hearted friends among the United Irishmen' (quoted in ibid.). He had also campaigned for Catholic emancipation, standing alongside Catholic bishops in Catholic churches declaring his opposition to ascendancy. Montgomery objected to the outdated anti-Catholicism of the Westminster Confession and its covenantal theology, and opposed subscription.

When Cooke became moderator of the Ulster Synod in 1824, the opportunity arose to inveigh his ideas on the Church. He became well-known for his evangelistic tours of Ulster and Scotland, and took a prominent position on the education debate defending Protestant interests. He was not afraid to identify himself as a narrow partisan in defending Protestantism. On once being accused of being illiberal, he said: 'I rejoice in the epitaph; I glory in the accusation. I was born the subject of a Protestant government, the original liberty of which my Presbyterian forefathers chiefly contributed to establish and maintain' (quoted in Porter, 1871: 78). He was proud of his anti-Catholicism: 'I confess I am a party man. If it be a party man to be a party to Presbyterianism, I am one. If it be a party man to belong to the anti-Popery party, then I am a Protestant-Presbyterian party man' (quoted in ibid.: 387). These were the views he wished the Church as a whole to extol. In 1829 Montgomery and the New Light Presbyterians left to form their own church, later to become the Non-Subscribing Presbyterian Church, principally believing that members should not subscribe to the Westminster Confession or any man-made profession of faith, with Holy Scripture itself being sufficient. By 1835, the Presbyterian Church was imposing subscription to the Westminster Confession on all its members. Presbyterianism had thus in its mainstream shifted back to covenantal theology, such that the differences disappeared between the Ulster Synod and the old eighteenth-century Seceders, who were remnants of former theological battles over subscription. The two joined together in 1840 to form one united church.[7]

Covenants were both theological and political pledges, and the shift to covenantal theology within mainstream Presbyterianism carried with it political implications, for the Presbyterian Church under Cooke took a great leap to the right politically. Montgomery was left to lament that 'our church is now in a melancholy condition. Political and religious bigotry have mingled together. Scarce an individual is now held orthodox who is not also an enemy to the civil or religious rights of his fellow men' (quoted in Boyd, 1969: 8). Cooke, however, believed that his God was Protestant, there to defend Protestant political interests exclusively:

> we will maintain with the indomitable spirit of our fathers in the perennial fee-simple that lies in 'No Surrender'. We have sound Protestant principles, we have true Protestant hearts; above all, we have humble and secure dependence upon the mighty God of Protestantism.   (quoted in Porter, 1871: 336)

God underwrote the British Empire and Ulster. Of the former Cooke once said that 'Protestant Christianity is the law of the empire' (quoted in ibid.: 381); of Ulster he said that God's blessing on its Protestantism was evident by its material and industrial progress. By these notions, Cooke tried to draw Ulster Presbyterianism increasingly to the Tories: the sacred canopy was thrown around nation and Empire as well as Ulster. Indeed, Ulster's future blessing by God depended on being able to serve the expanding markets of Britain's Empire (Bardon, 1992: 257). He was friend and confidante of the large Tory landowners, and said on one occasion: 'I decidedly avow myself a Conservative ... I am conservative of the rights of property. I am conservative of abstract and general Protestantism ... I am conservative of the Bible' (quoted in Porter, 1871: 265). He was conservative in politics too. He opposed Catholic emancipation, education reform, and the 1832 Reform Act. Parliamentary reform, he once asserted, was 'just a discreet word for Romanish ascendancy and Protestant extermination' (quoted in Bardon, 1992: 254). Cooke's politics, in other words, were typical of the Church of Ireland, which had long supported the interests of the Anglo-Irish landowning class, and perhaps his greatest contribution to Protestantism was to create the rapprochement between Presbyterianism and prelacy, although the liberal tradition within Presbyterianism always opposed him (see Holmes, 1997; Holmes argues that Ulster Presbyterianism did not become Tory until the Home Rule debates later in the century).

At a great protest rally in Hillsborough in 1834, called by landowners who opposed Catholic emancipation and parliamentary reform, Cooke announced that he came to declare publicly the banns of marriage between Presbyterianism and the Church of Ireland. It was a pledge, he said, of Protestant union and co-operation. In crisis, when the ascendancy had been formally renounced by the Whig government's reforms, Protestants should unite in 'a sacred marriage'. Lord Roden, one of the organisers, said that Protestants of all sects should unite because their privileges were under 'imminent peril', just like in 1688. Cooke took up the theme. The priesthood and laity of Rome, along with the infidel, were at Ulster's door, and a common platform of Protestantism was needed as a bulwark against Catholicism (the speech is contained in Porter, 1871: 172–8). As a Presbyterian standing before prelacy Cooke did not betray his charge, for, he said, 'I cheer forward another column of our noble Protestant army who wield the same weapons of truth and serve under the same banners' (quoted in ibid.: 273). The prelates in the Church of Ireland were now part of the same company in the great Protestant army. Later he would say that Protestantism came before loyalty to denomination: 'while you are Presbyterians you are Protestants; one is your Christian name, the other your surname' (quoted in ibid.: 364). To the accusation that he was involving Presbyterianism in politics he said from the platform as Hillsborough: 'a minister must interfere in politics whenever politics interferes with religion. Such a crisis has now arisen. Never in the history of Ireland was Protestantism in greater danger than at this hour' (quoted in ibid.: 272–3). He once likened himself to the Old Testament prophet Ezekiel, appointed by God to be the watchman, to give warning of the signs of the times. It was thus his obligation to involve himself in public events. Without seeing the contradiction, Cooke later complained often that Catholicism was being political. In fact, politics was its point: 'Rome is a huge monarchy guided by politics, not by religion. It can mould itself to any form of religion – its politics alone do never change' (quoted in ibid.: 342).[8] Some Presbyterians later objected to his association of their church with prelacy, but their strict Calvinism none the less predisposed them to anti-Catholicism and Cooke gave his critics plenty of that to cheer about. Concessions to Catholics meant the extermination of Protestantism; the survival of their faith required there be no concessions to Catholics: God, to many of his supporters, was, after all, a Protestant (although Cooke himself might have ridiculed this idea).

Presbyterians in the South of Ireland found these arguments objectionable. The Synod of Munster wrote to him in 1828 complaining of his 'unChristian temper', which they felt must have been engrafted on his character 'by some external influence or the operation of some sinister motive'. He was asked to examine his heart in the presence of God. A lengthy correspondence ensued (for correspondence see ibid.: 141–50) in which Cooke railed against Presbyterians who lacked the spirit of the covenanters, accusing the people from Munster of being 'narrow, bigoted and exclusive'.

> The union of church fellowship can never be established between the believer in Jesus and those who deny Him or know Him not ... Gentlemen you wish to be called Presbyterians. Oh that you were like the Hamiltons, the Knoxes, those genuine Presbyterians ... I disavow connexion with you. That God may direct you to see the light and flee from error is [my] earnest prayer. (quoted in ibid.: 144–5)

Northern Presbyterians had a political agenda that was clear to Southern co-religionists, which separated Southerners even at the beginning of the century. This made the leaving of them behind at partition all the easier. Cooke's message was to Ulster alone. On his death-bed, he wrote a plea to the 'Protestant electors of Ireland', but its contents were primarily directed to the North. 'All the Protestant institutions in the land are now in danger. I call upon you, as you value your faith, as you love your country, be faithful to your country, to your religion, and to your God. Be watchful against the insidious advances of Popish error and despotism. Farewell' (quoted in ibid.: 493). But if Protestants lost their champion of anti-Catholicism, Catholics were about to gain their champion of anti-Protestantism, in the person of Cardinal Paul Cullen. The opportunity now arose, as the *Northern Whig* was later to lament, for confrontation between 'ultra-Protestantism, which [runs] riot on the one side, and ultramontane Catholicism, which [goes] fanatically crazy on the other'.

Cardinal Cullen and the Catholic Church

The Tridentine reform project, begun in the sixteenth century as a response to the Reformation, had not been successful in Ireland. When Cullen returned to Ireland to assume a bishopric after a long period on the continent, he found a Church that was still Gallican. There was little of the ornate continental style in worship or architecture. Crosses were simple, often of plain wood without the crucifix (D. Bowen, 1983: 124–5). The anti-Catholic stereotype of Irish Catholics is that they are docile, devout, faithful mass-goers, with rosaries always ready, and respectful of the priest (Nic Ghiolla Phadraig, 1995: 595), but the pre-famine Irish Catholic was different. Mass was attended by a minority, mostly the wealthy and urban, and rural Ireland subscribed to a number of beliefs that were characteristic of the Celtic church rather than Tridentine. These included superstitious interpretations of historic Christian festivals; a wide range of magical practices from calendar customs to charms, including belief in fairies, and particularly enthusiastic and drunken wakes and festivals

(Hempton, 1996: 89; see also Rafferty, 1994: 99–103; on marriage rite superstitions see Corish, 1985: 135). Faith and fancy mixed in equal measure and Keenan likens these 'unofficial Christian beliefs' in nineteenth-century Ireland to those which pertained in Elizabethan England (Keenan, 1983: 23). It was not just the laity that caused Cullen anxiety. Some Catholic clergy drank and pleasured themselves; some were found too drunk to preach. The ratio of priests to population was high, and mass attendance low.

But immorality and indifference were not the chief problems with the Church. The Gallican tradition in Irish Catholicism asserted its independence from the Pope, preferring local autonomy in religious matters, and tried to accommodate to Protestantism locally. While there were some priests who supported proto-nationalist causes, the bishops were overwhelmingly in favour of keeping Catholics out of politics. During O'Connell's Repeal movement, the hierarchy disciplined priests who supported him and church premises were not allowed to be used for Repeal meetings. The British government made considerable use of Irish Catholic bishops to urge restraint and order on their flock (Rafferty, 1994: 135). Cullen, however, was an ultramontanist, in favour of papal authority and the continental Roman-style in liturgy, worship and architecture. He was also anti-Protestant and anti-British and the assertion of papal authority meant distancing the local Catholic hierarchy from Dublin Castle. But neither was Cullen a nationalist (see Steele, 1975), and papal authority was imposed on clergy who were abusing local autonomy to engage politically.

Reform was a mammoth task but it was made easier for Cullen by the famine. The 'great hunger' had a powerful effect on Ireland and no less on the Catholic Church. Cullen thought that the actions of the government during the famine were intended to eliminate the Catholic faith in Ireland by genocide while profligate members of every bankrupt Orange family were protected, a view now fashionable in nationalist historiography. Cullen particularly objected to the proselytising which evangelical Protestants attempted while distributing food and famine relief, although many Protestant church groups and individual ministers acted without malice or sectarianism in supporting the starving. But the coincidence of the famine with the Second Reformation in Ireland, with its renewed evangelistic spirit, has ensured that proselytism has become the dominant interpretation of Protestant actions during the famine (Liechty, 1993: 33). The Baptist Irish Society wrote in its 1847 Annual Report that evangelism of the starving was the primary task not famine relief, but there is equal evidence of great work done by Protestants to alleviate hunger. Some landlords were cruel to their starving tenants, others sympathetic. Some Protestants became extremely critical of the landlords and government for failing to act more proactively to support the starving (see, for example, Bardon, 1992: 241; Kee, 1995: 100).

Yet there is evidence of considerable anti-Catholicism during the famine. The popular *Fraser's Magazine* wrote in March 1847 that the starving were idle and fickle, unwilling to work. Leading Orangemen in Lurgan, for example, objected to the 'industrious' people of Ulster being forced to pay taxes to relieve the lazy in Munster and Connacht (see MacAtasney, 1997: 85). The hunger was a result of mismanagement by Catholics and only confirmed some Orangemen's view that Ulster was prosperous and spared by the famine because it was Protestant (a view supported by the General Assembly of the Presbyterian Church in Ireland: see Annual Report 1847: 699), although MacAtasney shows that parts of Lurgan and Portadown did suffer but that Lord Lurgan was very supportive of his Catholic tenants (1997: 100). This moral critique of the starving was nurtured in part by notions of scientific racism which became popular in Victorian England, by which the Irish were racialised and given many undesirable traits, including laziness and sloth; and by traditional anti-Catholicism, which drew on the idea that Catholicism as a religion was given to pleasure, consumption, indolence and antipathy to work.[9]

Cullen was in the bishopric of Armagh at the end of the famine and it left a legacy of resentfulness and bitterness with him, which reinforced his anti-Protestantism and anti-Britishness. Yet, ironically, it allowed him to complete the Tridentine reform project first begun three centuries before. Ultramontanist Catholicism is a post-famine innovation in Ireland. The collective trauma suffered by Catholics during the famine and subsequent emigration, which split up families and uprooted them from the land, made them turn to the Catholic Church both for solace and for ethnic identity. Mass attendance increased dramatically after the famine, coinciding with what is called the 'devotional revolution' amongst Irish Catholics, and along with it came an increase in the ability of the Catholic Church to impose ideological control (see Larkin, 1972; Nic Ghiolla Phadraig, 1995). The proportion of priests and nuns increased after the famine (see Foster, 1988: 338), in part because the population declined but the number of priests also increased by a quarter (Larkin, 1972: 644), and more people started attending mass. Foster claims that attendance rose three-fold (Foster, 1988: 339) and it spread from the urban middle classes to the poor in rural areas and the towns (Corish, 1985: 167). During the 1850s, missions were held in every parish in order to encourage the faithful (Larkin, 1972: 644). Missions were also part of the effort devoted to evangelising the landless Catholic labourers who migrated to Belfast in search of work. The Catholic hierarchy noted that 30,000 people attended confession in Belfast during one mission (Bardon, 1992: 346).

The ideological control which the Catholic Church attempted to exert was heavily influenced in content by Cullen's ultramontanism. The devotional revolution which occurred adopted Roman-style liturgy and worship, and the laity were encouraged into their devotions by new forms of worship, such as novenas, the rosary, perpetual adorations, blessed altars, benedictions, devotions to the Sacred Heart and to the Immaculate Conception (promulgated in 1854), and processions and retreats. Devotional tools were used, such as beads, scapulars, medals, missals, catechisms and holy pictures (Larkin, 1972: 645). These were of Roman origin rather than Celtic, and Cullen placed Ireland under the patronage of the Blessed Virgin rather than St Patrick, a fact bemoaned by the Protestant *Dublin Evening Mail*, which remarked that 'absurdities suited to the latitude of Rome and Naples are sadly out of place in Ireland' (quoted in D. Bowen, 1983: 130). It later announced, with a hypocritical hint of regret, that the 'Papal church in Ireland is no longer Irish but Roman, the Irish Catholic Church of forty years ago has vanished'. Rafferty describes 'a craze for church building' after the famine to accommodate the devotional revolution (Rafferty, 1994: 150), but Cullen insisted that they be in the ornate Roman style in order to demonstrate Catholic self-confidence. He wished to equal 'many of the Roman churches ... we are determined to be very grand' (quoted in D. Bowen, 1983: 146). Schools, hospitals and asylums were built in large numbers after 1850, all staffed by clergy and members of religious orders. The numbers within religious orders increased, as did the variety in the orders permitted to work in Ireland. They brought with them continental fashions in worship and building style.[10] One of the orders was the Irish Christian Brothers, which concentrated on the education of poor Catholics by means of a specifically Catholic curriculum, and this control over education intensified the influence of an ultramontanist form of Catholicism.[11]

If the famine gave the laity a devotional need and an ethnic identity crisis, which Larkin argues, persuasively, were met by Catholicism (1972: 650; see also Brown, 1981: 28–9), Cullen's success over the Gallicans ensured it was ultramontanist – that is, *Roman* – Catholicism. He marked his success as early as the 1850 Thurles conference of Irish Catholic bishops, the first national conference since 1666, when Cullen imposed his order on the Catholic Church. The bishops agreed to strengthen themselves as a collective unit and to begin to assert their collectively authority; they accepted the authority of the Pope and opposed local autonomy. Celtic practices and beliefs were to be rooted out, and a new discipline imposed on laity and clergy alike. Opposition was declared against Protestant missionary work amongst Catholics, and no accommodation with Protestants was permitted. Mixed marriages were permissible only if the Protestant partner agreed to bring all children up as Catholics, which anticipated the Vatican's ruling on this by more than half a century, and the non-denominational Queen's Colleges were denounced. Bishops were instructed to do what they could to ensure Catholics did not attend. By means of new appointments, Cullen was able to maintain the decisions taken at Thurles. By 1869, three years after Cullen had been made Ireland's first cardinal, all the bishops in post were now Cullen's appointees, and the ultramontanist spirit in the Catholic Church was cemented in following year by the Vatican Council's declaration of papal infallibility. After Archbishop McHale left, all the Irish bishops were infallibilist; only in some parish clergy did notions of liberalism and local autonomy survive. Bishop Denvir, an ecumenist with good relations with Presbyterians, was the last Gallican bishop to succumb after being called to Rome to explain himself to the Pope; he resigned office in 1865 (on the conflict between Cullen and Denvir, see Rafferty, 1994: 153–5). Denvir's funeral was attended by no less a Presbyterian than Henry Cooke.

The victory of ultramontanist Catholicism had political implications as well as ecclesiastical ones. Cullen has been described as a zealot, whose sole purpose was to advance the position of the Catholic Church in Ireland. Considerations of the socio-economic well-being of the Irish Catholic people, the political benefits of accommodation with the state, or the interests of Irish nationalism were subservient to the relentless advance of ultramontanist Catholicism (D. Bowen, 1983: 20). One of his first acts was to curtail the activities of those bishops who were too friendly with Dublin Castle and those clergy who sought to accommodate with Protestant neighbours. He took a view on this similar to his arch opponent, Henry Cooke. As Rafferty (1994: 137) explains, the state existed for the benefit of religion – by which he meant Roman Catholicism – but if it opposed the Church, then the state itself should be resisted. Gallican Catholics were resisting papal authority and failing to resist a state that opposed the Catholic Church. The 'throne and altar' alliance between Gallican Catholics and the British did nothing to advance ultramontanist Catholicism, despite its claims as a political strategy. They were derided as 'hacks of the Castle' or 'Castle Catholics', and government men. In his correspondence, Cullen used these terms interchangeably with Jansenism (D. Bowen, 1983: 44), which was another resistance to the Pope's authority and had once been strong in Ireland. Jansenists like Thaddeus O'Malley, were described as in the pay of the government. Earlier bishops, like Crolly and Murray, who were Gallican, were said to be Jansenists, with too little respect for Rome and too much for the British, with the Castle in Dublin rather than the Vatican as the object of their veneration. By 1858, Gallican Catholics were writing that they now feared visiting Dublin Castle because of Cullen's reaction (see, for example, Thomas McGivern, quoted in ibid.: 188).

Cullen was politically paranoiac about the Maynooth seminary for its supposed tendency to produce independent thinkers, and about the Catholic Church in Belfast under Denvir's leadership, which was supposedly too close to Orangeism. Denvir had been known to refuse to hold missions if they provoked Orangemen, and sometimes avoided celebrating mass for this reason, but Cullen described him, on his death, as a man 'utterly unfit' to administer the Church in Belfast (quoted in ibid.: 189). Cullen placed his own man there in 1865, when Denvir was forced to resign. The new bishop, Dorrian, set out to convert Protestants rather than accommodate the Catholic Church to them; of accommodation he said it was the 'evil genius of Ireland – a few offices for traitors and starvation and oppression for the rest of the Catholic people' (quoted in ibid.). Protestants were heretics, even infidels – Belfast the 'stronghold of heresy', 'the capital of Orangeism' – and the Catholic Church was to set itself in opposition to Protestantism rather than find a workable relationship.

Cardinal Cullen's anti-Protestantism was thus another feature which he impressed on the Catholic Church in Ireland. The only true church was the Catholic Church; the Pope was the Bishop of Rome, Peter's successor. Catholics may well show charity to Protestants 'but at the same time we should let them know that there is but one true church and that they are strayed sheep in the fold' (quoted in ibid.: 82). But sometimes even the charity was missing in Cullen. He objected on one occasion to one of his clergy saying mass in English, to another for 'basing his sermons from a Protestant version of scripture', and to another who attended a funeral of a 'brutal Protestant bishop'. He considered mixing with Protestants dangerous and warned that only unavoidable communication with them was permissible. 'Catholics who mix with Protestants', he once wrote, 'are hostile to us', and he went on to declare proudly that he had never even dined with a Protestant (although in later life he dined with the Prince of Wales). Such religious apartheid was partly the result of Cullen's own bigotry but also a response to the evangelistic activities of Protestants during the nineteenth century. He objected to Catholic soldiers attending mass in mixed churches, urging instead separate chapels at the Curragh. The English, as Protestants, were also vilified as infidels who had 'never heard of Christ and scarcely knew there was a God'. Not unsurprisingly, Cullen was treated unmercilessly in the Protestant press, but this only confirmed him in his prejudices.[12]

However, Cullen was also against Irish nationalism and worked as tirelessly to ensure his clergy avoided fraternisation with Fenianism. His opposition to Maynooth was that its independent thinkers sometimes emerged as nationalists rather than ultramontanists. Radical priests like Fr. Lavelle (on whom, see Foster, 1988: 387) and bishops like Higgins (on whom, see D. Bowen, 1983: 65ff.)[13] were as much a focus of Cullen's wrath as 'Castle Catholics'. Romanticised notions of Ireland were secondary to Cullen's wish for Ireland to be a *Roman* and ultramontanist Catholic country. Radical politics were a danger to this ambition because they risked anti-Catholic pogroms. Thus, Cullen was critical of young Catholics who abused government figures, he opposed violence of any kind, and was firmly against Ribbonism and Fenianism, persuading Pope Pius IX in 1870, himself recently declared infallible, to denounce Fenianism by name as evil. Catholic clergy were instructed to condemn radical and clandestine movements, to urge on laity peace, order and obedience, and to desist from giving support or succour to radicals. Fr. Lavelle was threatened with excommunication for his activities in support of Fenianism, and pastoral letters used strong language attacking radicalism.

The failure of the Catholic Church to impose political control over some of the laity is shown by the fact that Fenians, also known as the Irish Republican Brotherhood, had between 50,000 and 80,000 supporters (Foster, 1988: 394) in the mid-1860s. Such a level of support forced Cullen to establish an O'Connell-like 'National Association' to rival the Fenians as an expression of protest amongst ordinary Catholics. When Fenians declared an Irish Republic in March 1867, marking the Fenian Rising, Bishop Dorrian, Cullen's man in Belfast, wrote a pastoral letter describing the declaration as the 'blindest folly', made by men who were 'selfish and sordid apostles of a false and odious liberty' (quoted in Bardon, 1992: 353). Therefore, it is as far back as the time of Cullen's leadership, that the Catholic Church in Ireland has condemned the 'physical force' tradition within Irish nationalism and separated itself from Catholics who advocate violence. Knowing its condemnation from the pulpit and in pastorals, Fenianism attacked the Catholic Church vociferously, leading Cullen once to describe it as 'more Protestant than Catholic', obviously dominated by outsiders (whom he identified as Americans). Cullen suggested that Fenianism was being used by Protestants as a ruse to finally realise the Reformation in Ireland, and in a pastoral letter in 1865 he announced that Fenianism was created by Orangeism, for they are 'reckless madmen who would rob us of the only treasure we have, our religion'. Fenians were like 'ultra-Protestants' in their anti-Catholicism. Cullen thus praised the British when the Fenian Rising was crushed. Policemen in the Irish Constabulary, soon to be given the prefix 'Royal' for their efforts in the uprising, won praise from Cullen (see letters in D. Bowen, 1983: 270).

Anti-Catholic Violence in Mid-Nineteenth-Century Belfast

Anti-Catholic violence had continued throughout the first part of the nineteenth century associated with Catholic emancipation and local incidents by Orangemen. Old animosities continued even during the famine. The Orange march from Rathfriland to Tollymore Park in 1849, particularly long and taking in many Catholic villages, was designed to provoke the Ribbonmen, for the marchers proceeded 'all armed to the teeth' as a contemporary report described it. They met Ribbonmen with pitchforks, pikes and muskets at Dolly's Brae in Magheramayo, whereupon Orangemen opened fire, leaving fifty Catholics dead or injured with no Orangeman even wounded; a government report on the violence placed the number of Catholic dead at thirty (see Bardon, 1992: 302–5). Their deaths are today still applauded in an Orange song, 'Dolly's Brae'.

But the nature and extent of anti-Catholic violence was transformed in mid-century by a number of factors. The growth of a strident, ultramontanist Roman Catholicism, which was triumphalist, self-confident and anti-Protestant, coincided with vigorous evangelistic campaigns by Protestants, who had found an encompassing 'sacred canopy' in a conservative evangelicalism which was particularly anti-Catholic, as reflected in the attitudes and comments of people like Henry Cooke. Moreover, the disestablishment of the Church of Ireland and the failure of the government to shed the Anglican Prayer Book of its alleged Catholic overtones was perceived by evangelicals to be a Romanist plot.[14] Disestablishment was opposed by many Presbyterians because, although the state recognised as they saw it the wrong church, it was still a Protestant one, and to disestablish was to bow to the whim of Rome (Wallis and Bruce, 1986: 235; J.J. Shaw (1988), however, claimed that Presbyterians supported disestablishment but opposed Home Rule). A sense of shared Protestantism caused several leading Presbyterians to attack disestablishment as a Romanist plot (for example, see Hempton and Hill, 1992: 64–5) and to advocate reform of the Anglican Prayer Book because it was too Catholic (Akenson, 1971: 303–4). Membership of the Orange Order by Presbyterians rose dramatically after disestablishment (D. Bowen, 1983: 197). Fears abounded, therefore, that a weak government in Britain, by which Cooke understood to be a Whig government, would give concessions to Catholics and abandon Protestants. Such conciliation endangered the Protestant community. The *Dublin Evening Mail* responded to disestablishment by claiming that concessions to Cullen meant concessions to Rome, for he served the papacy, not Irish Catholics.

This sense that Protestants were under threat was reinforced by other developments. The growth of Irish nationalism amongst Catholics, particularly the emergence of the 'physical force' tradition with the Irish Republican Brotherhood, caused considerable anxiety amongst Protestants. Two uprisings had occurred around this period, in 1848 and 1867, the latter being notably larger,[15] which intensified Protestant insecurity. Further, Orangeism was growing in influence within the Protestant cross-class alliance, fed by support from landlords and the Protestant workforce in industrialised Ulster, and it came into conflict with an industrialising and urbanising Catholic population of landless labourers moving to Ulster's towns, especially Belfast. It was amongst these Catholic labourers that the 'devotional revolution' occurred after the famine, since the middle classes had long been devout, making Catholicism more significant to the poor as an ethnic identity but simultaneously intensifying it as a social marker for the Protestant working class. But it was not just the Catholic working class who encroached on Protestant territory and jobs, for the Catholic middle class had become securely established by the mid-nineteenth century, in farming, in official positions within the state bureaucracy, in servicing their own community in schools, hospitals and church organisations, and in the professions (see Miller, 1975; Corish, 1985; Ruane and Todd, 1996: 37–9). They were confident in their Catholicism and articulate in its defence; the *Ulster Examiner* was founded by Bishop Dorrian in 1865 to 'promote the legitimate aspirations' of the Catholic people (which in effect meant the middle classes because many of the poor still could not read). 'Of your politics', Bishop Dorrian wrote in an open letter in the first edition, 'I need not speak. They will be Catholic.' There was also at this time Catholic newspapers like the *Belfast Morning News,* founded in 1855, and later the *Northern Star,* founded in 1868. The consolidation of the Catholic middle class destabilised the established patterns of social closure which favoured Protestants, and the Protestant middle class thus fully engaged in the alliance with Orangeism to defend the prosperity and cultural status which Union had given them by the mid-nineteenth century. Few middle-class Protestants in the North rose above sectarian notions that Ulster was in a zero-sum conflict between two competing groups, defined by religion. So successful was this ideological construction of Protestant–Catholic relations, that even the Catholic Church was reproducing it in Cullen's ultramontanist and anti-Protestant form of Catholicism. These factors bore fruit by mid-century and Belfast was ripe for an outburst of unusually violent anti-Catholicism.

Relations between Protestants and Catholics were sometimes good in the rural areas and mostly quiescent. The urban areas were different. Belfast had been transformed by the Industrial Revolution occurring in the Lagan Valley, by its strategic position as a port, and by shipbuilding. Its population grew rapidly in the nineteenth century, including Catholics. By 1861, the Catholic population of the town had increased ten-fold from 1812, and comprised a third of its total population. The expansion had been alarmingly quick, for the Catholic population had doubled since 1834, the year of Cooke's famous speech declaring Protestant unity. Local

Protestants faced a massive influx of poor Catholics from the countryside, putting strain on the resources and infrastructure of the town, bringing overcrowding and the threat of disease, and raising all sorts of other fears. Belfast's workforce was at this time overwhelmingly Protestant and known, as Goldring argues (1991: 60), for its sectarianism. Orange lodges were organised in the workplace and workers used a deeply entrenched anti-Catholicism to defend their jobs. The Protestant Working Men's Association was established on a platform of anti-Catholicism to protect Protestant access to jobs; it nominated a leading Orangeman, convicted of riotous behaviour and violence towards Catholics in 1867, for Parliament when he had been disowned by the Conservative Party; he was duly elected Member for South Belfast (for a study of sectarianism in the Protestant working class in Belfast, see Patterson, 1980). The influx of poor Catholics appeared to Protestant workers like these as an invasion. In the linen industry, for example, skilled Protestant men were surrounded by poorly paid and unskilled Catholics, mostly women. Unskilled Protestants, however, faced the fiercest competition for jobs with the newcomers, and they were even more sectarian than their skilled co-religionists. Court records show that ringleaders in riots were younger and less skilled Protestants (Goldring, 1991: 61).

Anti-Catholic violence, however, was more than a defence of jobs. It was, fundamentally, a defence of the way of life and identity of neighbourhoods, streets and homes. With such enormous and rapid population growth, Catholics invaded territory long seen as belonging to Protestants. It is for this reason that the sporadic outbreaks of anti-Catholic violence in Belfast did not correspond to economic crises which risked Protestant jobs. Belfast's streets had become sectarian, an extension of sectarian divisions of labour within the workplace, and anti-Catholic violence was about defending the Protestantism of neighbourhoods. This is why house-wrecking by Orange mobs was so common, and why Orange marches were so important, for they helped to define the territory which Protestants claimed as their own. By 1830, there were already thirty-two Orange lodges in Belfast (Hempton and Hill, 1992: 127), and the number had grown by the mid-century when parades were used to mark out ethnic and religious territory against the Catholic newcomers. Foster notes that membership of the Order had declined in the rural areas but had trebled in Belfast, following Northern Ireland's patterns of industrialisation and urbanisation (Foster, 1988: 390). Marches thus became larger and more frequent in Belfast. As Hempton and Hill argue, where you could walk, you could control (1992: 127), and underpinning episodic outbreaks of anti-Catholic violence in Belfast was the battle for power, resources and space, from the allocation of housing to graveyards, or from the protection of jobs to whole neighbourhoods.

At the level of ideas, anti-Catholicism spread amongst the Protestant working class as evangelical societies worked in Belfast's poorer districts. Indeed, Hempton and Hill claim that evangelical religion took a foothold in the Protestant working class only because it kept sectarian divisions alive (Hempton and Hill, 1992: 123). William Murphy, for example, noted for his claim that the Virgin Mary was a Protestant, said during one lecture that 'every Popish priest was a murderer, a cannibal, a liar, and a pickpocket' (see Montgomery, 1993). The Rev. Hanlon, during his famous walks among the poor of Belfast, blamed Catholics for their poverty because their faith taught them no moral virtue. But two protégés of Cooke, the Rev. Drew and the Rev. Hanna, were notorious for their anti-Catholicism. Drew was a radical in politics, who criticised the landlords for their control of parliamentary representation, but was conservative in theology and vehemently anti-Catholic. As Grand Chaplain to the Orange Order and a minister in the Church of Ireland situated between the Catholic Pound district and Protestant Shankill, he conceded nothing as sensitive or delicate and used fanatical and inflammatory speech. Catholicism was a 'blood stained' religion, Catholics had 'strained on the rack the limbs of delicate Protestant women', and priests had 'dabbled in the gore of their helpless victims'. The Pope's prisons were paved with 'the calcined bones of men and cemented with human gore and human hair'. The emotive rhetoric at open-air preaching like this, played on long-established Protestant fears of massacre by Catholics. It was also claimed that Catholicism was bent on annihilating Protestantism, so Protestants were warned of the risk to their heritage, and given supposed biblical proof thereof. Drew wrote Orange songs and pamphlets, and in his *Twenty Reasons for Being an Orangeman* he said that one learns that by the 'doctrines, history and daily practices of the Church of Rome, that the lives of Protestants are endangered'. In a speech on 12 July 1867, he stated that the 'lives and property of the Protestants of Ireland are prey to the despoiling priests'.

The Rev. Hanna, or 'Roaring' Hanna as he was known, was Presbyterian and equal in his reputation for anti-Catholicism. The Catholic Church was the Scarlet Woman, the Whore, and the Pope was the antiChrist. He warned Protestants that their 'blood-bought and cherished rights' were at risk from Catholics. Protestants were urged to resist, 'not to be bullied or cajoled out of their rights'. Protestant crowds were easily whipped up into frenzy by the fears created by preaching such as this, and violence often ensued. After violent riots in 1857, the Belfast presbytery appealed to Hanna to desist 'as a matter of Christian expediency from open air preaching till excited passions cool'. The government report into the 1857 riots singled out as causes, inflammatory open-air preaching and the provocative marching of Orangemen. Both had contributed to 'violence, outrage, religious animosities, hatred between classes, and bloodshed and loss of life'. When asked by the members of the inquiry whether he would consider it his duty to preach knowing riots would ensue, Hanna replied 'I would, sir ... our most valuable rights have been obtained by conflict; and if we cannot maintain them without that, we must submit to the necessity' (quoted in Miller, 1978a: 86).

Protestants were thus encouraged by some clergymen to believe that violence and harassment were theologically sanctioned. 'We will fight', said the dying Henry Cooke in 1868, 'as men alone can fight who have the Bible in the one hand and the sword in the other ... and this will be our dying cry, echoed and re-echoed, "No Popery", "No Surrender"' (quoted in Kee, 1995: 138). Anti-Catholicism at the level of behaviour therefore often showed itself in violence. Religious riots began in Belfast in 1813, but were rare before 1830 (Hempton and Hill, 1992: 108). What clashes did occur in the North were associated with the linen area in Down and Antrim, incidents surrounding Orange marches, and occasional inexplicable outrages such as the massacre of Struel Wells in 1802. But by the 1850s, intercommunal violence was urban. Indeed, for a period after the famine, and prior to the conflicts associated with Home Rule, Bardon describes rural Ulster as 'remarkably tranquil' (Bardon, 1992: 307), but anti-Catholic violence had shifted to the towns. The 1857 riot in Belfast, for example, was the worst violence witnessed for two centuries. After a sermon from Drew, which was like a call to arms in the fears it created of imminent danger to Protestantism, Orangemen emerged from his church near to the Catholic Pound district and attacked Catholics. A small section of the police supported the Orangemen when Catholics defended themselves. Ten days of rioting followed. Catholics defended themselves with force, but they were numerically inferior and less well-armed. Catholics were killed in the cathedral; Orangemen in ditches, well-armed, fired without intermission, killing several Catholics including a young mill girl. Houses were burned and neighbourhoods wrecked; some buildings were demolished in the Pound to provide cover for the shooting. Even the police could not contain the Orange mobs until reinforced. Home-wrecking and shooting, uncommon before 1852, became typical forms of anti-Catholic behaviour during 1857 and after. Riots broke out again in 1864, 1867, 1872, 1886 and 1898, with smaller incidents in 1880 and 1884, and house-wrecking and gunfire featured every time. Gunmen opened up on Catholics sitting in the Guildhall in Derry in 1883 while they were listening to a lecture on franchise reform, and subsequent rioting lasted a week.

Catholics in Belfast were attacked by Orange mobs with guns in 1864, to an extent that the Protestant *Belfast Newsletter* expressed concern. A group of new rural migrants to Belfast, employed as navvies to dig out a dock in one of the shipyards and unused to the ways of sectarian Belfast and not inured to it, retaliated by downing tools and marching on a nearby Protestant area where they attacked the premises of a local school, although no one was injured. Shipyard workers, solidly Protestant, working class and Orange, on hearing news of the attack and that the navvies were Catholic, downed tools, marched to the city centre and ransacked gunsmiths' and hardware shops for weapons. Six hundred shipwrights attacked the navvies, commemorated ever since in an Orange song, 'The Battle of the Navvies', which eulogises 'noble' Orangemen and dehumanises the Catholic victims as it records them scrambling through the mud and being shot in the back (the song is reproduced in Devlin, 1981: 20). The men attacked a Catholic church with such concentrated fire that bullets 'pierced the air'. Several weeks of rioting followed, with gunfire the norm, leaving eleven dead and three hundred injured, a third of which suffered gunshot wounds. The death of a Protestant, after injuring himself at the shipyard in a riot, was turned into a massive display of Orange strength. Most mourners were armed. A Presbyterian minister gave evidence that on the evening of the funeral, 'the mobs in my neighbourhood hunted poor Roman Catholic neighbours out of their houses ... I could have wept' (quoted in Bardon, 1992: 351).[16] And all of this occurred while Northern Irish Protestants were experiencing a wave of the religious renewal, known famously as the 1859 Revival. But Christian tolerance and love did not break out for it was a renewal of evangelistic and conservative Protestantism, which was inherently anti-Catholic. If anything, the 1859 Revival was taken by Protestants as confirmation of God's approval of their campaign against the Whore and the antiChrist (this is certainly the theme of Ian Paisley's book on the Revival – see Paisley, 1958).

The Issue of Home Rule

The promise of, or threat of, Home Rule activated Irish politics for half a century from 1870 and gave full opportunity to vent anti-Catholicism, since, as the *Belfast Newsletter* first opined in February 1874, 'Home rule is simple Rome rule'. Protestantism was put at the service of the Union and defence of the Union became a test of a person's Protestantism. The first serious threat from Britain to Union was perceived with disestablishment of the Church of Ireland in 1869. Great public meetings were held by members of the 'one Protestant family', as Henry Cooke described it, to protest against the move, and speakers declared that they suspected the hand of Rome pulling Gladstone's strings. To endanger the Established Church was to endanger Protestantism; the breach of state recognition of Protestantism was a breach of the Act of Union. Indeed, it threatened the Empire and predicated civil war, according to some spokespeople. By the time Home Rule became government policy a few years later, the rhetoric became more foreboding. The Irish Methodist *Christian Advocate* stated that 'home rule for Ireland means war against Christ ... its inspiration is religious antipathy, its methods plunder, its objects Protestant annihilation' (quoted in Hempton and Hill, 1992: 175). Again it was affirmed that God was for Empire, Protestantism and Union; and the fact that English Methodists, and others, supported Gladstone's proposals merely confirmed for the newspaper that 'English Protestants had gone soft on Romanism'; 'the duty of opposing Rome has altogether disappeared from quarters where it used to be paramount'. It was not just Irish Methodists who claimed such. Too many people, the Rev. Ellis said when speaking to Orangemen in Portadown in 1885, had sacrificed their duty to God as a result of 'Popish compromise'. The leaders of all non-conformist denominations in Ireland spoke in similar terms, and 96 per cent of all non-conformist ministers in Ireland signed an address denouncing a separate Irish Parliament or any legislation which imperilled the Union. As Hempton and Hill note (ibid.: 180), this opposition to Home Rule amongst non-conformist denominations had the effect of Ulsterising the resistance by concentrating on the one geographical area where non-conformism was strong; the census of 1881 showed that three-quarters of all Irish Protestants lived in Ulster – more, if one excluded its border regions like Donegal, Cavan and Monaghan – and that the non-conformists were concentrated in Antrim and Down.

Anti-Catholicism was high on their list of objections to Home Rule. Loughlin (1986: 295–6) has shown that amongst the thirty Ulster Unionist speeches made against Home Rule in 1886, the major complaint was that an ascendant Roman Catholicism would persecute Protestants. Other anti-Catholic objections included claims that Catholics had no respect for law and order, and that they would deliver Ulster into social and economic chaos. Many historians dismiss the focus on anti-Catholicism by observing that a large number of these speeches were given by ministers of religion, but the fact that ministers were invited to speak on Home Rule at political gatherings illustrates how politicised theology had become and how central anti-Catholicism was to the campaign against Home Rule. Nor was it just ministers of religion who drew on anti-Catholic ideas in articulating opposition to Home Rule. Wesley de Cobain MP, a strong supporter of Orangeism, in one speech started to describe the Pope 'as an ecclesiastical dignitary presiding over a system of sensualism, superstition and sin'. Home Rule was widely presented as Rome Rule; this became a prominent motif of the political campaign against Gladstone. It is not difficult to see why once the Protestant anti-Home Rule mind-set is entered.

The history of Protestant–Catholic relations in Ireland since plantation had produced a mind-set amongst Protestants in which Home Rule had pull and push factors. The positive attractiveness of Union was argued vehemently, as well as the negative consequences of Home Rule; and anti-Catholicism featured in both. The positive benefits of Union were two-fold. Protestantism had made Ulster what it was, and any threat to Union was an attack on Protestantism and risked losing its benefits. Ulster was prosperous, industrious and protected from economic and social vagaries because it was Protestant (recent historical research has shown the positive contribution made to economic growth in the nineteenth century by the Catholic Church: see Kennedy, 1996: 103–16). An editorial in the *Presbyterian Churchman* in 1886 reminded readers that Ulster was once the least favoured of Ireland's provinces, but had now become the leading one because of 'Presbyterian industry and energy'. Indeed, allowed to continue and flourish untrammelled by Home Rule, Presbyterian effort would 'transform the people into the greatest Protestant Empire that has yet existed in the world'. With florid rhetoric, speakers would draw attention to Belfast's humble origins as a mere village, but the majestic sights it now rose to – its streets, parks, public buildings, industries, mills and shipyards – were a product of the 'genius of Protestantism'. Who else but a chosen people specially favoured and blessed by God, could have transformed the barren wasteland into such a place of promise? The scriptural allegory was obvious. Ulster Protestants were modern Israelites, encouraged to see themselves as the 'holy remnant', 'the faithful few' whose loyalty to God had been rewarded by worldly success in Ulster. Hence the Rev. Ellis contrasted those who had been disloyal to God and sacrificed their duty on the altar of 'Popish compromise', with the sons of Ulster, 'loyal sons of Judah amid the faithless men'. A breach of Union risked God's wrath and the ending of His blessing on Ulster. Practical men also realised that Union linked Ulster with the Empire and thus located its economy within a larger market that was critical to continued prosperity. Ulster's export-driven form of industrialisation was particularly dependent on imperial markets, and this was seen to be threatened by Home Rule. The big industrialists all supported Union for this reason (Foster, 1988: 388). But even here, an anti-Catholic spin was put on the need for Empire trade, because Catholics were supposedly slothful, backward and lazy; exports to the Empire needed the Protestant qualities of hard work, self-improvement, sobriety and industriousness (see Goldring, 1991: 111).

The negative case against Home Rule was also replete with anti-Catholicism. Home Rule meant a society governed by the Catholic Church, under the rule of the Vatican, and dominated by Catholics whose race and creed made them unsuitable for naught but servanthood and labouring, and then only under the strictest of supervision. Lord Salisbury, leader of the Conservative Party, which in 1886 had developed an Ulster Unionist group under the leadership of Edward Saunderson as the forerunner of the Ulster Unionist Party, said that authority within democratic society demanded people of the Teutonic race. The Celtic Irish were like the Hottentots in being incapable of governing themselves. The evidence of this was provided, supposedly, by contrasting the qualities of Victorian England with the poverty and turbulence of Ireland. 'The widespread belief that Irish poverty and turbulence originate in the baleful influences of creed and race', remarked Mabel Sharman-Crawford in 1887, 'is very generally held as unquestionable truth in north-east Ulster' (quoted in Bardon, 1992: 407). Protestants were obviously racially and culturally superior; Home Rule meant accepting rule by people who might make 'excellent soldiers and servants when under strict discipline' but who were incapable of government. Catholic parts of Ireland were denigrated and held up as a lesson for what Home Rule would mean for Ulster. Such was the colonial mentality through which Home Rule was perceived.

The debate over Home Rule thus reinforced the ideological construction of Ulster as a society in a zero-sum conflict between two competing groups which had incompatible sets of interest. As Miller stresses (1978a: 90), the case for Union and against Home Rule argued for the maintenance of Protestant ascendancy, and thus the notion that politics was basically about the dominance of one side over the other. Home Rule would bring domination by Catholics. As the Rev. Hanna explained in a sermon reproduced in the *Belfast Newsletter* of 14 June 1886: 'we stand for right and truth against the forces of error and tyranny. Our safety for every interest that is dear to us lies in the union. We shall enter into no political partnership with the apostles of sedition, we shall defend ourselves against domination.'[17] Protestants were led to believe that Home Rule would put them under the heel of people who hated them and would do everything in their power to humiliate and dispossess them, if not complete annihilation. According to Miller (1978a: 90), Catholics found it hard to grasp why Northern Protestants could not regard Home Rule as a gain for all Irish people; after all, Parnell reassured Protestants that Ireland 'wanted all creeds and classes', but in the Protestant mind-set Home Rule was a zero-sum game, and it involved loss not gain.

This explains the passion with which Protestants fought Home Rule. Belfast experienced another wave of anti-Catholic violence in 1886, at the height of the furore over the first Home Rule Bill, described as Belfast's worst riots. A battle broke out in a shipyard after a Catholic worker remarked that the days of Protestant dominance were over, and to demonstrate the error of the claim a thousand Protestant workers set upon Catholic navvies. Harland did not on this occasion threaten to sack Protestant workers for victimising Catholics, and workers ran amok in places of work and on the streets. Instead, William Pirrie, chairman of Harland and Wolfe, threatened to withdraw the great shipbuilding works from Belfast to the Clyde should Home Rule come to pass. Under such a state, he said, 'there would be no fair play for loyalists in the North of Ireland' (quoted in Bardon, 1992: 404). With support like this, Protestants besieged the police and magistrates who tried to protect Catholics. Bardon notes that all Catholics were driven from the shipyards, although seventy-seven did eventually return, and upwards of fifty people were killed (ibid.: 382).

The first Home Rule Bill was defeated in 1886, and news of it encouraged Protestants in their anti-Catholic violence during the summer, a victory which the Rev. Hanna said was God-given. The fight against Home Rule saw an alliance cemented between the British Conservative Party, which supported Union, and the various constituencies in Ulster which challenged Home Rule, such as the Protestant churches, the newly formed Ulster Unionists and, of course, the Orange Order. Support for the Conservative Party rather than the Liberal Party grew dramatically in Ireland, and its power base reflected the location of Protestant interests, such as urban areas and Ulster (Foster, 1988: 389). Belfast Protestants, whether industrialists or labourers, were Tory. Tory leaders from London met with burly Orangemen from the shipyards and were united in opposition to Home Rule. It was thus 'the labourers and artisans, officered by the landlords', who held Ulster for the Queen, 'not the farmers', Lord Salisbury was told in 1885.[18] Lord Randolph Churchill, on visiting Belfast to campaign against Home Rule, said much the same when commenting that it was best beaten by playing, in his oft-quoted phrase, 'the Orange card'. That is, Home Rule could be defeated by forging an alliance between the traditional anti-Catholicism and sectarianism of the Protestant working class and the imperial and land interests of Ulster's industrialists and landowners. Moderate Conservatives realised the benefit of drawing on Orange anti-Catholicism, amongst other things. The English Captain Seymour, after a public meeting in Belfast, was told by his uncle to see 'in future more business about "William III" and "No Surrender" [are] put in' (quoted in Walker, 1989: 75). Advisers told their candidates in elections to play on Orange fears; advisers to one candidate told him to portray his opponent as having Catholic support, for 'the less the Orangemen will like it' (see ibid.: 88). Orangemen thus played a considerable part in local Conservative associations – tenants and landlords, industrialists and workers alike (ibid.: 101) – and the Tories drew on familiar Orange and anti-Catholic themes. The traditional sectarian notions of Orangemen and the Protestant working class assumed even greater importance in parliamentary politics once the franchise was enlarged in 1885 to include labourers and artisans. Hence the Liberal's *Northern Whig* attacked the Conservative Party in its issue of 27 August 1872 for trading on 'the worst sectarian passions of the populace and ostentatious encouragement of the cry "No Popery"'. With evangelical Protestantism as the sacred canopy, and thus anti-Catholicism as one of its enduring themes, Protestants were actively mobilised as a united force to oppose Home Rule by appeal to notions like 'No Popery'.

The alliance between land and industry within Protestantism against Home Rule is worth emphasising. Parnell's Land League, articulating the demand for tenant rights and land reform, politicised rural Catholics, but was, in theory at least, equally attractive to Protestant tenants. The Land League did not represent the 'physical force' tradition of Irish nationalism; it was not responsible for the Phoenix Park murders in 1882, and fomenting agrarian violence was done by secret societies like the Irish Republican Brotherhood (see Foster, 1988: 406). In fact, the murders, as they always do, put the constitutional nationalists in a difficult position and set back the political gains Parnell was winning (Kee, 1995: 131). Some landowners responded to the campaign for land reform by evicting tenants, alienating even further the Catholic rural poor; more tenants were evicted between 1879 and 1883 than in the previous thirty years (Foster, 1988: 408), ably assisted by the Royal Irish Constabulary, forever after giving them a negative image amongst Catholics (see Brewer, 1990). Another response was to use Orange lodges to mobilise against the Land League, despite its obvious benefits to Protestant tenants, and to stymie the developing co-operation between Protestant and Catholic tenants. There was less tenant dissatisfaction in Ulster because of the advantages of the property right known as the Ulster Custom, which gave security of tenure and allowed for compensation when improvements were made (see Vaughan, 1984), but Orange lodges were mobilised by landowners into organisations like the Property Defence Association and various local vigilante groups, in which Orangemen drilled and organised patrols. They were successfully mobilised in this way by anti-Catholic and sectarian notions which presented Parnell as about to 'invade Protestant Ulster', by the claim that Catholic tenants were using reform to buy farms to the disadvantage of Protestants (see Walker, 1989: 20), and by stressing the connection between land reform and Home Rule.

The mobilisation of traditional Orange fears of 'Popery' also caused Parnell's support amongst Protestant tenants to dwindle. Protestant tenants in the rural hinterlands of Ulster were initially predisposed to the Land League, and some Presbyterian ministers appeared on platforms in support of land reform. In fact two Orange lodges in Fermanagh were banished from the county lodge in 1880 because members had been seen with Catholics at a Land League meeting (ibid.: 21). While it is an exaggeration to claim, as A.M. Sullivan did in his 1877 booklet *New Ireland*, that sectarian animosities were decreasing in Ulster, there was some co-operation in rural areas over land reform, and at one point Catholic and Protestant tenants voted en masse for a liberal candidate in a 1881 election against a leading Conservative and Orangeman, to the disgust of one of the latter's supporters who described it as the 'death blow to Protestantism'. But Parnell's shift in focus towards Home Rule saw this Protestant support decline as Orangeism mobilised Protestant tenants on the basis of anti-Catholic notions of what Home Rule would entail. The editor of the Fermanagh-based *Impartial Reporter* expressed the point. 'Are you prepared', he told his readers, 'to allow Parnell, the leader of the enemies of our united empire, the champion of the principle Ireland for the Irish, meaning Ireland for the Romanists, are you prepared to accept that Protestants are aliens in their land?' (quoted in Bardon, 1992: 372). Thus, by 1882, Sir Thomas Bateson was writing to Lord Salisbury about Protestant tenants in the following terms:

> I have just come back from the north of Ireland. There has been a considerable change in the feelings of the better class of liberal Presbyterians ... The same applies to the democratic Presbyterian farmers ... There seems to be a growing feeling that the policy of the national party is to stamp out the English garrison and make Ireland a purely Roman Catholic country. There is throughout Ulster a growing distrust of the Roman Catholics on the part of the Protestant farmers. I speak of the Protestant districts of Ulster only.   (quoted in Walker, 1989: 22)

Hence, by the 1886 General Assembly, the Presbyterian Church in Ireland was condemning Home Rule and regretting its association with land reform. A policy of Home Rule would threaten Presbyterians, for it 'would empty their mills, clear their rivers and shipyards, would stop their looms, would make the voice of the spindles silent, and would cause a complete destruction of the industry that has made the province so prosperous' (quoted in Holmes, 1982: 546): the 'sacred canopy' protected the Union and Protestant churches blessed the cross-class alliance which upheld it. Ulster landowners and industrialists, along with their tenants and workers, thus found unanimity with the Protestant churches in Union, for the alliance stabilised patterns of land ownership and industrial wealth in Protestant hands. The 'Orange card' which united them was in essence an anti-Catholic one because of the fear of Protestant losses following Home Rule.

The period of the first and second Home Rule Bills, the last quartile of the nineteenth century, is frequently presented as the point when political polarisation emerged in Ulster (for example see Walker, 1989), but polarisation was not fully complete, for some Protestants were Home Rulers and, in its early stages, Home Rule was distrusted by Catholic bishops. The radical Presbyterian tradition, whose heyday was represented by the United Irishmen, although overridden by Cooke's Old Light conservative evangelicalism, was not completely extinguished. There was a base in opposition to landlordism, which meant that some Presbyterians continued to support land reform, and no little support amongst some for Home Rule. The Rev. Armour, from Ballymoney, declared in 1893, at the time of the second Home Rule Bill, that Home Rule was a Presbyterian principle, and he derided his colleagues for their 'senseless fear of Romanism' (quoted in Bardon, 1992: 440). Presbyterian candidates sometimes stood as Home Rulers for the Liberal Party in general elections, some in Belfast, although most Protestant support for Home Rule was from the South. The Irish Protestant Home Rule Association represented two social bases: the liberal Protestants who remained in the North, loyal to Gladstone's liberalism and offended by the bigotry of most Northern Protestants; and Southern Protestants, scattered as small businessmen and professionals in rural Ireland, dependent on the goodwill and patronage of Catholic neighbours (Loughlin, 1985; Hempton and Hill, 1992: 185). However, the space for the liberal tradition to operate in Ulster diminished further as society polarised and the attitudes of congregations and elders, colleagues and superiors, constrained Protestant Home Rulers. These Home Rule Protestants need to be distinguished from the much larger group of what is called 'constructive unionists', who were conciliatory towards Catholics but only in the hope of being 'able by kindness to kill home rule', to use the famous phrase of Gerald Balfour.

The policy established with Cullen of preferring Catholic politics, that is political activity which the bishops could control and which served the Catholic Church first and the Irish people only secondarily, meant there was some initial suspicion of Home Rule within the Catholic Church. Secular forms of Irish nationalism, particularly if they risked violence, were opposed by the Catholic hierarchy. Parnell's commitment to Home Rule was seen by some bishops as reeking of Orangeism, and reminiscent of radical Presbyterianism in its call for an Irish Parliament, while others feared that it would leave them prey to further domination by Protestantism (Rafferty, 1994: 165). When Parnell's adultery became public knowledge, the Catholic Church condemned his morality. A priest said, 'Parnellism is simple love of adultery and all who profess Parnellism profess to love and admire adultery. Their cause is not patriotism, it is adultery' (quoted in Kee, 1995: 141). The truth was that the bishops felt unable to control Parnell's movement and unable to stop those of their priests who supported Irish nationalism. A third of the League's conventions were composed of Catholic clergy (Foster, 1988: 417) and priests played an important role in selecting parliamentary candidates for the 1885 election (Hempton, 1996: 86). Yet the official position was initially against Parnell; only briefly did the Church support the National League once Parnell aligned himself with some of the Catholic concerns of the bishops, such as criticism of the secular Queen's Colleges for their supposed 'Godlessness'. His adultery led to renewed opposition. Some priests reproduced this line in their sermons; one from Meath told his flock that 'you cannot remain Parnellite and remain Catholic' (quoted in Foster, 1988: 424). Cullen's policy of opposition to secular nationalism remained alive after his death, and only by becoming identifiably Catholic in issues and concerns (rather than in support) could the Church offer support to the Home Rule movement.

With the ultramontanist victory won, the new Cardinal, Michael Logue, the first Northern bishop to be made a cardinal, sought to establish good relations with the British, a position supported by the Vatican. It was the Vatican which urged Catholic bishops to present an address of loyalty to Queen Victoria on the occasion of her golden jubilee. And when she visited Ireland in 1900, Logue went out of his way to pay respects (Rafferty, 1994: 169), although one bishop found it necessary to leave the country to avoid her. Apparently Logue confided to Lord Denbigh, during dinner with the Queen, that in politics he was, if anything, a conservative and he wished Catholics could 'shake off these English radicals' (see ibid.: 170). Moreover, Bishop Dorrian, overseeing Belfast, took every opportunity to display Catholic loyalty to the institutions of the state by his presence at public and ceremonial occasions. He was also, initially, against Home Rule on much the same terms as Ulster Protestants, in that it would lead to decay in trade and agriculture – a remark he made, inauspiciously, on St Patrick's Day when toasting the Queen. The Catholic hierarchy, however, did come eventually to support Home Rule, but always preferred the identifiably Catholic organisations rather than secular ones, such as the Belfast Catholic Association. The bishops were strong in using the pulpit to urge the laity to support the Church's preferred organisations against their secular rivals. The fact that the advice was ignored by many Catholics shows the limits of the Church's ideological control. Some clergy ignored them too, and secular nationalist organisations like the United Irish League attracted support from Catholic laity and clergy. This reflected the fact that, at the beginning of the twentieth century, political developments overtook the Catholic Church's ability to control them.

The Path to Partition

The policy of the Conservative government after the fall of Gladstone was to be as 'relentless as Cromwell in enforcing obedience to the law', remarked Arthur Balfour in 1887, but in reform 'as thorough as Parnell': an unfortunate couplet as far as many Irish Catholics were concerned. By 1895, his brother Gerald, now Irish Secretary, remarked that the government, led by his uncle, Lord Salisbury, would be glad if they were 'able by kindness to kill home rule'. In a study of this 'constructive unionism', Gailey (1987) shows that Irish nationalism was immune to British kindness since the policy proved tardy in its generosity and short on acts of kindness. As an alternative to Home Rule it failed miserably to stem the pressure for independence. Indeed, by conceding a case for devolution of powers to Ireland, the Conservatives undermined the Ulster Unionists by reducing Union to a form of quasi-Home Rule (ibid.: 2). Gailey argues that instead of ending the demand for Home Rule, the Tories had unintentionally killed both Unionism and kindness itself (ibid.: 319), for they had weakened Ulster Unionists, strengthened the case for Home Rule, and created a climate for polarisation in which compromise and concessions no longer solved the 'Irish problem'. They had, in short, started down the path that led eventually to partition. Thus, astute Conservatives later wondered how it was that they had ever let the Union slip so far. Waltar Long asked 'why were these things done in the name of the unionist cause? Why, when the unionist flag was flying, were principles adopted which were not consonant with unionist policy?' (quoted in ibid.: 2).

When the Liberal Party assumed power after the 1906 election, they made the first tentative step toward Home Rule by creating an Irish Council, partly elected, with control over local government, education, public works, and agriculture. They described it as a 'little, modest, shy, humble effort' to give administrative power to Irish people; so modest that the Irish nationalists rejected it, but effort enough to outrage the Unionists. It was introduced at a time when Unionists were sensitive. The cross-class alliance within Protestantism was giving the appearance of crumbling under forces of modernisation, evinced most spectacularly in 1907 in the non-sectarian dock strike in Belfast, and the ultramontanist Catholic Church appeared rampant in its anti-Protestantism with the papal decree *Ne Temere* in the same year. The Church decreed that mixed marriages required a special dispensation, should be officiated by a priest, and that children of such marriages should be brought up Catholic. Protestants in the South of Ireland were the most affected but those in the North made the most vociferous complaint, since it confirmed their worst fears about an ascendant Catholicism. The furore was heightened when, supposedly, a priest in Belfast persuaded a husband of a mixed marriage to abandon his wife and take his children when she refused to 'remarry' according to Catholic rite.[19] He later described her as a meddling sectarian shrew who cursed the Pope all day and sang hymns. The children were seen as having been kidnapped by the priest, the Catholic Church as having undermined British law, and all had their suspicions confirmed that Catholicism would domineer and annihilate Protestantism under Home Rule. If it was a gift to Orange propagandists, as suggested by Joe Devlin, nationalist MP for West Belfast, it also raised the level of hysteria amongst Northern Protestants about rampant Catholicism.

Above this, however, Unionism felt challenged by the cracks appearing in the cross-class alliance within Protestantism. Under the forces of modernisation, Belfast's huge Protestant working class, mobilised effectively in the past by conservative evangelicalism and Orangeism, were developing class interests that matched those of their Catholic co-workers. Modern ideas like socialism and trade unionism developed strongest in Belfast, where there had been a branch of the Independent Labour Party in Belfast since 1892, and the labour voice had long been a feature of local politics (Foster, 1988: 439). Labour issues were on the whole linked to a Protestant populism and hence to the Union rather than socialism, especially in labour leaders like William Walker, but the first decade of the twentieth century saw alternative allegiances appear. The Independent Orange Order was established in 1903, stressing the original class interests of the Orange Order and the need to protect the interests of Protestant workers against Protestant industrialists. This threatened the unity of the cross-class alliance by suggesting that the Protestant working class had separate interests from the landowners and industrialists. The Ulster Unionists felt threatened by the Independent Orange Order and began to work more closely with the Orange Order to bolster its position. Some members from the Independent Orange Order stood as candidates against Conservatives and Ulster Unionists, attacking the large industrialists for their record on labour relations, and critical of Conservative Party links with big business (Patterson, 1980: xii). Intra-Protestant conflicts began to emerge.

It was one step further to the argument that Catholic and Protestant workers had shared class interests, and some people began to make appeals across the sectarian divide. Notable amongst these was the labour leader James Larkin, of the National Union of Dock Labourers and the Independent Labour Party, and the politician Lindsay Crawford, Grand Master of the Independent Orange Order. Crawford in particular had a background of anti-Catholicism, even complaining once of the Romanist tendencies of Anglicanism, and he had mobilised support in working-class districts by the motif 'Home Rule is Rome Rule'. But he became sympathetic to the new labour movement in Belfast, in which non-sectarian socialist ideas were taking root, and a convert to Home Rule. One of Larkin's Protestant supporters expressed the view: 'What [has] Orangeism or Protestantism got to do with men fighting for their just rights, when the issue lies not in religion but in bread and butter?' (quoted in Foster, 1988: 441). Not all class consciousness amongst Protestant workers manifested itself in non-sectarian form, for people like Tom Sloan, leader of the Belfast Protestant Association, articulated the interests of the Protestant working class against industrialists and big business while remaining firmly wedded to Protestantism and Unionism. Sloan, for example, when standing against a Conservative candidate, described himself as a representative of 'Protestant democracy' and criticised 'Romanism' extensively (Patterson, 1980: 45); he won. However, some labour leaders took a leap forward by realising the common interests of the working classes across the sectarian divide. Under this realisation, the old moulds of confessional loyalty seemed as if they could break, and the alliance which held Protestantism together smash along with them. Thus, Canon Hannay of the Church of Ireland began concocting a scheme for a radical alliance between Sinn Fein and the Independent Orange Order, and Arthur Griffith of Sinn Fein met Crawford under the auspices of Hannay, who was ecstatic that some Orangemen were declaring Unionism to be a discredited creed and calling for unity between Protestant and Roman Catholic (see Gailey, 1987: 307–8).

The 1907 dock strike was the measure of how far the moulds really had broken. In May 1907, employers locked out dockers who went on strike for better pay and conditions and drafted in blacklegs. A riot ensued in which the dockers attacked the strike breakers and the police who were trying to protect them; a police mutiny eventually occurred after a policeman refused to sit alongside blackleg drivers. Employers took to laying off thousands of men because of copy-cat strikes. Belfast was paralysed as strikes broke out in various industries. The Independent Orange Order supported the strikers. So did some Protestant clergy. One minister, drawing on a long heritage of Presbyterian radicalism, described the men as fighting against an 'aristocratic and selfish monied class'. Another described the battle as one between 'classes and the masses, and the masses will ultimately win'. Larkin and Crawford took the opportunity to bring together Protestant and Catholic strikers. Crawford urged men on, based around the strength of organised labour and 'the unity of all Irishmen'. Posters were distributed amongst the strikers and their families, appealing to common class interests. One handbill read: 'not as Catholics or

Protestants, as Nationalists or Unionists, but as Belfast men and workers, stand together and don't be misled by the employers' game of dividing Catholic and Protestant' (quoted in Bardon, 1992: 430).

But while the strikers stood shoulder to shoulder regardless of religion, their non-sectarianism did not resonate widely. Labourism was restricted to Belfast, and even there sectarian patterns were too long established and embedded. The whole of Ireland was alarmed at the police mutiny and many people in the North were disturbed by what they considered open lawlessness. The Catholic Church warned against the strike, seeing socialism as a dangerously modern idea, and nationalists like Devlin used the strike to mobilise on a sectarian policy of anti-Britishness rather than anti-employer. Devlin, through his newspaper the *Northern Star*, was openly anti-Protestant. Unionist labour leaders also became involved, pushing a narrowly sectarian line aimed at Protestant workers only. Protestant newspapers played equally on anti-Catholicism. The *Belfast Evening Telegraph* drew attention to the fact that some strike leaders were Catholic and posed the question to readers: 'are the Orangemen of Belfast going to allow themselves to be led by a Fenian?' Moreover, Home Rule was becoming a spectre again with the introduction of the Bill to establish an Irish Council, and there was a concerted campaign to associate labour radicalism with Irish nationalism. Edward Carson, the doyen defender of Unionism, a few years later expressed the link as follows: 'these men who come forward posing as the friends of labour care no more about labour than does the man in the moon. Before we know where we are we will find ourselves in the same bondage and slavery as the rest of Ireland' (quoted in Devlin, 1981: 50). Traditional Orangemen thus withdrew from a class consciousness that required unity with Catholics. The Independent Orange Order also held back as a result; Crawford was thrown out in 1908 for advocating Home Rule. The Independent Labour Party was wiped out in council elections the following year, and Larkin was marginalised within the dockers' union, leaving in 1908 to form the Irish Transport and General Workers' Union. He eventually went to Dublin (Foster, 1988: 441–2). Non-sectarian forms of organisation proved short-lived; the mould was solid. Thus, looking back in 1912, Ramsey MacDonald described well the prospects of labour organisation in Belfast: 'in Belfast you get labour conditions the like of which you get in no other town. It is maintained by an exceedingly simple device. Whenever there is an attempt to root out sweating in Belfast, the Orange big drum is beaten' (quoted in Farrell, 1976: 17).

It was beaten all the louder when a narrow English majority for the Liberal Party in 1910 strengthened again the hand of the Irish nationalists in Parliament, placing Home Rule on the British political agenda for the third time; and by now the House of Lords had lost its power of veto. Northern Protestant resistance to Home Rule was stronger than ever before. Sir Edward Carson, before assuming charge of the Ulster Unionists, wanted reassurance that 'the people there really mean to resist. I am not for a game of mere bluff.' He got whatever assurances he wanted, since Unionists had been planning to buy arms for a year before Carson offered his leadership. He invoked the 'help of God', as he put it to a meeting of 50,000 Orangemen and Unionists, in order to ensure the resistance came with moral justification. Gone was the faith placed in parliamentary action to stall Irish independence; Orange lodges, Unionist associations and vigilante groups started mobilisation to help Carson protect Protestants in the whole of Ireland from Home Rule. Only later would it emerge that partition was an option to protect Ulster Protestants alone.

The liberal strain within Protestantism was marginalised to those few with a fondness for romanticised Gaelic culture and language –it is sometimes forgotten that the revival of Gaelic culture at the end of the nineteenth century received active support from some Protestants – and the small band of Protestant Home Rulers. The size of their support is reflected in the vote within the General Assembly of the Presbyterian Church in 1912 on Home Rule, with 43 in favour and 922 against. The Rev. Armour, Presbyterian minister for Ballymoney, attacked Carson as the greatest enemy of Protestantism and criticised the way he inflamed men of violence. Armour's public meetings, however, were not well-attended.

When eventually published in April 1912, the Home Rule Bill was a modest measure of devolution, but gave the promise of further independence. It also gave Ireland control over its judiciary, and nationalists in the Irish Parliamentary Party welcomed it; Sinn Fein rejected it, as did Cardinal Logue, on similar grounds, in that the powers were hedged with various restrictions. Unionists, however, were outraged. In response, the threat of force was made frequently. The Leader of the Opposition in Britain, Bonar Law, of Ulster Presbyterian stock, declared that 'I can imagine no length of resistance to which Ulster can go in which I should not be prepared to support them'. Catholics took the opportunity to engage in senseless anti-Protestant violence, as members of the Ancient Order of Hibernians attacked a Sunday School outing, injuring several children, although there was a similar incident involving Catholic children from the Sisters of the Sacred Heart Convent in Lisburn. The next day, Protestant workers rounded on Catholics in the shipyards. Shots were also exchanged between rival gangs of football supporters, leaving sixty injured. But the formation of the Ulster Volunteer Force (UVF) threatened to project the violence on to a different plane. Civil war was threatened, Protestant newspapers openly warned of violence, and the Volunteers claimed they had the arms and the will to use them.

But the battle was as much spiritual as military, and Bible and rifle were the Protestants' weapons. Unionists understood the 'Irish question' at bottom to be 'a war against Protestantism', as a Presbyterian minister put in on Ulster Day, during a large religious service intended to seek divine assistance. He went on, 'it is an attempt to establish a Roman Catholic ascendancy in Ireland', which was also the major complaint made at the 1912 General Assembly of the Presbyterian Church. Preaching on the theme of stewardship, he showed it to be a scriptural injunction to keep that which God has entrusted to you. Everyone there had Ulster in mind: it was God's gift to Protestants and it was their divine obligation to keep it thus. To reinforce the notion that Ulster Protestants had a contract with God, Carson resurrected the idea of the covenant. Used by Irish Protestants in the past, the purpose of covenants was to pledge support for each other in public banding and to portray particular state–society arrangements as ordained by God. The 1912 Ulster Covenant had some significant differences, however.

Covenants have their origins in the Old Testament. God's promise to the Israelites took the form of a covenant, but they entered Ireland through the Ulster Scots Presbyterians, who borrowed the idea from the Scottish Kirk. Covenantal theology was thus Presbyterian rather than Protestant. In his account of the covenantal culture of the Ulster Scots, Akenson (1992: 149) argues that the widespread support for the 1912 Ulster Covenant amongst Anglicans, Methodists and others from the Reformed tradition illustrated the extent to which the Presbyterians held sway. In fact, the cultural hegemony was supplied by conservative evangelicalism rather than Presbyterian theology, a more embracing and general theological position. The covenantal theology associated with Presbyterianism was entirely absent from the contents of the Ulster Covenant, which was a political declaration with secular tones rather than a theological statement of God's agency in their affairs. It was not, as Akenson claims (ibid.: 186), redolent with Scottish covenanting antecedents; it drew on God for succour, but theology was scant.

> Being convinced in our consciences that Home Rule would be disastrous to the material well-being of Ulster, as well as of the whole of Ireland, subversive of our civil and religious freedom, destructive of our citizenship and perilous to the unity of the Empire, we, whose names are underwritten, men of Ulster, loyal subjects of His Gracious Majesty King George V, humbly relying on the God whom our fathers in days of stress and trial confidently trusted, do hereby pledge ourselves in solemn covenant throughout this our time of threatened calamity to stand by one another in defending for ourselves and our children our cherished position of equal citizenship in the United Kingdom and in using all means which may be found necessary to defeat the present conspiracy to set up a Home Rule parliament in Ireland. And in the event of such a parliament being forced upon us, we further solemnly and mutually pledge ourselves to refuse to recognise its authority. In sure confidence that God will defend the right we hereto subscribe our name. God save the King.

Even the ancient Scottish covenants were political, but the absence of covenantal theology in the Ulster Covenant shows the shift in focus towards secular political concerns by 1912. The Presbyterian Church's own convention declaration was more typical of ancient Scottish covenants in the focus given to The Almighty and the trust in Him which they invoked rather than faith in any secular support: 'Our Scottish forefathers cast their burden on the Lord Omnipotent, who gave them signal victory. Facing, as we do, dangers similar to theirs, we shall follow in their footsteps and emulate their faith. In the profound belief that God reigns, we commit our cause in all confidence to Him.'

Most of the Protestant community, however, absorbed the historical message Carson wished to convey. Theirs was an ancient struggle, the courage and will of people long dead called the living representatives of that lineage to defend their heritage with vigour. Virtually the entire adult male Protestant population in Ulster signed the covenant on Ulster Day, with a separate one for women. The Ulster Covenant was denounced as a silly masquerade, an impressive farce, and anarchic hectoring by Catholics, but Carson was successful with the historical symbolism. Again the motif rang: God was for Ulster, Union and Empire. As the *National Review* said: 'Sunday after Sunday, in every whitewashed, unadorned church, these modern covenanters stood face to face before Him to whom Empire belongs' (quoted in Goldring, 1991: 118). With the Bible in one hand, signatories of the Ulster Covenant were recruited en masse into the UVF, to be given a rifle for the other – at first perhaps a wooden replica, but after the gun-running incident in 1914 most likely a real one. The government feared that Ulster would be seized by show of force and that the Ulster Unionist Council would set itself as a provisional government (Bardon, 1992: 441). But the First World War intervened, and instead of dying to defend Ulster against Home Rule, members of the UVF died on Flanders field.

It is often forgotten that as many Catholics enlisted and died in the war as Protestants. The Catholic Church urged Catholics to forget 'petty animosities' and enlist (on the position of the Catholic Church on the war, see Rafferty, 1994: 191ff.). That it should describe Home Rule and Irish nationalist interests as 'petty animosities' reflects the stance the Catholic Church took on the issue. The whole thrust of the Pope at this time was toward moral and political conservatism. Pius X was anti-modernist, and a series of decrees preached against secular and modern trends, such as the growth of socialism and trade unionism, the development of cinema, and pornography (including immoral literature, suggestive songs and smutty postcards). The Pope was against modern forms of political protest and violence, and against popular forms of secular life-style such as drinking. This affected the Catholic Church in Ireland, and gave the impression of anti-Protestantism and anti-Englishness. The modern evils were subsumed by the Irish Church's *Catholic Bulletin* under the idea of Anglicisation, which was described in pejorative terms which made reference to 'slime' and 'sewerage', with allusions to the Devil and his 'hoof and horns'. Only Catholicism could maintain moral virtue and resist the forces of secularisation. Further, the Catholic Church insisted in proclaiming itself, Cullen-like, as the one true universal church, with Protestants as 'separated brethren' who needed to be brought back to the bosom of the Holy Church. It followed that Protestants were considered prizes for conversion and that Anglican orders and mixed marriages were considered invalid. All of these unfortunate ideas were expressed during the debate about the third Home Rule Bill. 'Ireland sober, Ireland free', was a couplet frequently seen in Ulster; Home Rule was presented as an opportunity for a conversion crusade in the North, and the *Catholic Bulletin* claimed in an issue in 1913 that Britain was a pagan society, where 'hoof and horn' and 'black devils' abound. An earlier issue in March 1912 said that Home Rule gave an opportunity for a radical programme of conversion of 'separated brethren'; 'the time has now arrived for action. The day of Ireland's missionary heroism is at hand.' The Catholic Church thus fed the fears of Protestants. Its position on Home Rule, however, was equivocal.

Cardinal Logue considered Britain's Home Rule policy modest, and some of his bishops, like MacHugh from Derry, wanted an aggressive parliamentary campaign in favour of Home Rule, but Logue had an intense dislike of secular nationalism, especially Sinn Fein, and the physical force tradition. The Irish Republican Brotherhood were condemned, as were the Irish Volunteers, set up in 1913 as a response to the UVF. The Church actively campaigned to get protest marches by the Volunteers in favour of Home Rule stopped after being asked to do so sometimes by the British; sometimes by Redmond, leader of the Irish National Party in Parliament. The Volunteers were denounced from Catholic altars throughout Ulster. Any priest who supported secular nationalist organisations was condemned. The bishops warned their clergy not to meddle in politics but to 'live up to their high calling' of pastoral ministry. Yet forms of nationalist expression and politics which the bishops could control, and which were Catholic in character, were supported, and the equivocation expressed by Cardinal Logue mostly reflected fears about provoking a Protestant backlash. Logue wrote in 1912 that as far as the interests of the Church were concerned, it might be best to continue to live under an Imperial rather than Home Rule Parliament because of the anti-Catholic hostility Home Rule was provoking. What the Catholic Church wanted was Home Rule, but by peaceful means and without stoking anti-Catholic hostility. With this an impossibility, it thought it best to take a low profile. It denounced the Easter Rising for example. Although it may be true that one of Pearse's first acts after taking the GPO was to summon a priest to hear confession, and that the last act of the surrendered men was to say the rosary (Liechty, 1993: 42), bishops condemned the uprising. Logue described it as 'foolish and perverse' and had the idea of having a church-door collection for those who suffered as a result of the rebellion. He only supported a reprieve of Casement's death sentence, he said, from 'motives of mercy and charity and not for any sympathy whatever with the unfortunate cause' (quoted in Rafferty, 1994: 195). And just after the end of the war, when Sinn Fein stood for election in Logue's own constituency, he made sure he did everything he could to ensure their defeat.

The Catholic Church was decidedly against any suggestion that Ulster be treated separately from Ireland as a whole, on the grounds that 'it will leave us more than ever under the heel of the Orangemen. Worst of all, it will leave them free to tamper with our education' (Cardinal Logue quoted in ibid.: 190; on the Catholic Church and the foundation of Northern Ireland, see Harris, 1993). Yet partition was an option as early as 1913, when it was proposed that Ulster counties could opt out of Home Rule for up to six years. Carson described this as a death sentence with a stay of execution, and demanded the complete exclusion of Ulster. He got his way, and Ulster remained with the United Kingdom. The Rev. Armour, a lone voice from radical Presbyterianism, described partition as a form of Home Rule which the Devil himself could never have imagined, and Southern Protestants felt abandoned by the

Northerners' haste to ditch them. But the *Belfast Telegraph* put it bluntly: 'if a ship were sinking and there were only enough life boats for two thirds of the passengers, should they all drown rather than leave anyone behind?' (quoted in Farrell, 1976: 24). The General Assembly of the Presbyterian Church equally welcomed partition. The 1921 Assembly made reference to events during the bloody conflict leading to partition that, in their atrocity, 'find no parallel since the massacre of 1641', as if, somehow, only Protestants were killed in the war of independence. But it thought that partition would enable two communities 'which are different in many respects, to carry out its own ideals with the least possible friction'. It made reference to covenantal theology in what it clearly saw as an offer of magnanimity to those Catholics who remained in Northern Ireland: 'one of the fundamental principles of the reformed faith is the right of conscience, the right of very man to think for himself according to the light which God has given him. True to that principle our Presbyterian people wish to live at peace with their Roman Catholic fellow countryman in the new order of things.' Sadly, there was faint hope of that as anti-Catholicism continued in Ulster's own version of the ascendancy.

3   Northern Ireland: 1921–1998

Introduction

Northern Ireland was not the invention of a cartographer who quickly scrambled together an inchoate border in a situation of rapid and violent decolonisation; it had roots, it had cultural and political coherence, and an economic base (cf. the claim of Bowyer Bell (1996: 223) that Ulster had no history or heritage). Protestants did not have to artificially construct a sense of nationhood, for they had long defined their identity around two antinomies or opposites; the one religious, the other national. Northern Ireland defined itself by its Protestantism against Catholicism and by its Britishness against Irishness; Protestantism and Britishness were its core values and they had been established as symbols of Ulster centuries before. This also meant, however, that anti-Catholicism and anti-Irishness continued as central defining tenets of the new state.

However, partition of the island of Ireland solved nothing for Protestants. It may have kept from them a Catholic Ireland, but the old problems were transported with them into the new territory. The same dimensions of differentiation occurred, and around them the same conflicts. The same zero-sum framework was applied to Protestant–Catholic relations in Northern Ireland, by the perpetuation of traditional anti-Catholicism and anti-Irishness, in order to achieve the same ends – protecting the security of Protestants, which simultaneously meant the domination of Catholics. Supporters of partition were aware of this, for they argued at the time that a smaller area with as large a Protestant majority as possible was preferable to the whole of the ancient province of Ulster, with its unsafe Protestant majority (Farrell, 1976: 24). So Unionist leaders deliberately decided, if reluctantly, to jettison Protestants in Cavan, Monaghan and Donegal in order to protect their dominance in the six counties and Ulster's religious, economic and national-identity interests (Ruane and Todd, 1996: 50). The historian A.T.Q. Stewart explains that the rationale was the 'simple determination of Protestants in north-east Ulster not to become a minority in a Catholic Ireland' (Stewart, 1977: 162); ensuring they had majority status in the new territory was the main point. The Unionist *Belfast Telegraph* reassured readers, should they feel guilty, that it was better for two-thirds of passengers to save themselves than for all to drown. Had the newspaper made an elision back to the *Titanic*, it would have been prophetic for the development of the new state.

The Catholics who remained in the North felt as abandoned as Protestants in the South. It is forgotten by Unionists in Northern Ireland, who bemoaned the position of Protestants in the South at having to confront, as they portrayed it, a social structure which excluded them and a cultural value system to which they felt outsiders,[1] that this was precisely how Catholics felt in the North at the time of partition.

87

They lacked a separate cultural identity as Northern Catholics, they had no secure national identity, no long local roots in Ulster, nor any political coherence, and they were defined as outsiders by the state's core values of Protestantism and Britishness. They were offered citizenship in the new state but on terms which made their Catholicism and Irishness problematic, and their position in the social structure made them second-class citizens. Accordingly, they mostly withheld legitimacy from the state, adding yet more tensions to Protestant–Catholic relations in Northern Ireland. This made the stakes even higher in the long-standing zero-sum conflict, for the losses and gains for either side now included the very existence of the state. The history of Catholic progress in Northern Ireland, however, shows their transition from a fragmented and subjugated community to a position of growing self-confidence, cultural self-awareness and cohesiveness, and political assertiveness. This may or may not have occurred more rapidly without terrorism, but the sustained period of civil unrest since 1968, known colloquially as 'the troubles', has polarised Protestant–Catholic relations and reinforced the zero-sum framework within which group interests are constructed by both communities in Northern Ireland. The violence has made traditional hatreds worse.

Developments in Northern Ireland have also confirmed Protestants in their mind-set. Political domination by Protestants proved to be weak and insecure; the economic base of Ulster similarly so. The re-emergence of terrorism confirmed many Protestants in their opposition to a united Ireland and fed their negative attitudes toward Catholics. Terrorism, in this sense, enabled anti-Catholicism to be disguised by elevating it into an issue of law and order. Violence has also disguised anti-Catholicism by allowing Protestants to claim that they are objects of a process of anti-Protestant ethnic cleansing. The tendency has been reinforced for Protestants to be insular and incestuous, to see themselves as beleaguered and threatened, perpetually insecure and undermined, unable to rely on anyone but themselves. The only security comes from the old shibboleths, 'No Popery', 'No Surrender', 'not an inch', even if such 'hard shell defensive posturing', as Akenson (1992: 184) calls it, excludes them from Catholic neighbours, people in the Irish Republic, from Britain and the international community. Insecurity has been reinforced by British–Irish relations as well. From the beginning of Northern Ireland, the Unionists let it be known that Britain should let them get on with running the province, and Britain seemed content to let them away with it until the wide-scale unrest provoked in 1968 by the demand for Catholic civil rights. Direct rule in 1972 transformed the relationship with Britain, and increased Protestant suspicions of Britain's innate untrustworthiness and duplicity in Irish matters, especially since the British government has begun to allow the Irish Republic more influence in Ulster's affairs – the very circumstance partition was supposed to avoid and which Protestants have struggled to resist since the seventeenth century. If Britain seems prepared so easily, as Unionists see it, to sacrifice this historical struggle for expediency in British–Irish relations, the burden of the history is a greater weight on Unionists who cannot, or will not, transcend the past. They cannot transcend history because these past struggles to defend their Protestantism and Britishness have helped shape who they are, and who they are not: they are not Catholic, they are not Irish.

Anti-Catholicism is therefore not just a feature of Protestant historical traditions, it determines the views many have of the options for the future. That the future goes backwards – back to the plantation society, back to the old anti-Catholic ideas, back to sixteenth-century definitions of group interests – does not seem to bother many Protestants in Northern Ireland. Many find security in their history, comfort in the old shibboleths, and reassurance in past victories. Many ordinary Protestants also lack the foresight and the courage to move on because they receive no encouragement to do so from Unionist politicians and Orange organisations, which fail to offer new options for the future. In fact, the tragedy of Northern Ireland is that most people, irrespective of political and religious hue, only want more of the same.

Protestant Insecurity and the New State

Insecurity was built into the very foundations of the Northern Irish state. Although Protestants saw Northern Ireland as a sacred entity, watched over by God, the template was Old Testament Israel, which was continually embattled from external threats and internal disaffection. Northern Ireland's first prime minister is reputed to have said, after a meeting in London to discuss the terms of partition, that a verse in Scripture shows Ulster 'to be born to trouble as the sparks fly upward' (see Bardon, 1992: 495). Leaving aside the licence necessary to see Scripture as in any way referring to Northern Ireland, it does indicate the tenor of prophetic theology amongst Protestants, who were not triumphalist with partition but mindful of the struggle ahead implied for them in the Old Testament.

The insecurity came from several sources. The first was external threat, either from the Boundary Commission which was left to finally determine Northern Ireland's territorial borders, or the new government in the South, whom they feared still had designs on Ulster. The first was rapidly dispensed with in 1924–5 by ignoring the Commission's recommendations, but the second was a persistent fear, even if never real. The Southern government gave some early financial assistance to Northern Catholics to undermine partition, and it later claimed jurisdiction over Northern Ireland in its constitution, but its support for Northern Catholics was mostly symbolic. It initially hoped that the Irish Free State would set a model which would encourage Protestants to voluntarily cede themselves to a united Ireland, but this misunderstood Unionists and, as Southern politicians themselves realised, the civil war in the Free State over the terms of the Anglo-Irish treaty made faint hope of it. As Kevin O'Higgins said, when making reference to Ulster Protestants during a speech in the Dail: 'we had an opportunity of building up a worthy state that would attract and, in time absorb and assimilate those elements. We preferred to burn our houses, blow up our bridges, rob our own banks ... We preferred to practise upon ourselves worse indignities than Cromwell and now we wonder why Orangemen are not hopping like so many fleas across the border in their anxiety to come within our fold' (quoted in Kee, 1995: 204–5). The Free State remained an object of fear and loathing, but the only occasion when the South seriously reopened the issue of partition was during the Second World War, when de Valera made it a condition for Irish assistance during the war. At one time it looked as if the British would accept, but it was de Valera who withdrew the suggestion on realising the opposition of the Cabinet in Northern Ireland (Bardon, 1992: 558).

The major source of threat to the new state was internal. It came, however, in various guises. Protestants feared the Catholic Church in Northern Ireland, which opposed partition, although it eventually accommodated itself to it. In the early years of the state, Cardinal Logue was often stopped and searched by the police, and on one occasion had a rifle poked into his ribs. The homes of other leading bishops were also raided (Rafferty, 1994: 216–17). This did not endear the Catholic Church to partition, and the Catholic Church underwent a process of radicalisation in the North. Cardinal MacRory even once denied that Protestantism was Christian, and the Catholic hierarchy steadfastly refused to excommunicate IRA members,[2] although the Bishop of Waterford came near to it when he said that it was a mortal sin to be a member of the IRA; other bishops described the IRA as not serving the interests of Ireland and of making the situation of Catholics in the North worse. The Church persistently attacked the use of violence by Republicans. Political violence was described once as the gravest of sins against the laws of God, pastoral letters were issued against radical groups, which were described as being banned by the Church, and moderate Church-controlled nationalist organisations were supported. On occasions the bishops even took to persuading nationalists in the Ulster Parliament to take their seats. But the Catholic Church remained opposed to partition, despite the accommodation to it. Partition was described in 1938 by Bishop Mageean as having been introduced for the sole purpose of keeping alive 'those religious animosities that have so long disgraced the north-east corner of Ireland in the eyes of the civilised world' (quoted in Rafferty, 1994: 239).

It only needed the Catholic Church in Northern Ireland to show even tacit support for the Irish Free State and the Unionist press would attack their duplicity. The beatification of Oliver Plunkett, for example, in 1920, at which 'archbishops, bishops and priests' supposedly sang rebel songs, was presented by the *Belfast Newsletter* as intended to give encouragement to rebellion. After all, Plunkett was himself 'an Irish rebel hanged for treason'. Indeed, the Catholic Church was frequently blamed for outbreaks of Catholic violence against the state: sometimes for not controlling the mobs; sometimes because it was thought to be behind it. Thus, the *Belfast Newsletter* said once that 'the bigotry of the Church and its constant efforts, open and secret, to increase its powers, [has] brought a large part of Ireland to lawlessness'. In 1929, when the Vatican appointed a papal nuncio in Dublin, and the Dublin government a minister at the Vatican, the fear of Rome, the papacy and rampant Catholicism was given full vent. The claim in 1931 by Cardinal MacRory that Protestants were not even Christian was met with equal insult. It was claimed that Catholicism was a tyranny that menaced mankind, a delusion, and a corruption of true faith. MacRory's anti-Protestantism, however, was not representative of the Catholic hierarchy, and some bishops came out in public support of the view that Protestants are part of the Church of Christ. Protestants none the less perceived that the Catholic Church showed them little generosity (for example see Dunlop, 1995: 113).[3]

The education issue shows the extent of Protestant fears of Catholicism in the first years of the new state. Lord Londonderry was a noted liberal, and as Minister in charge of Education in 1923 he introduced integrated education at primary school level and abolished religious instruction in an attempt to introduce non-denominationalism. To encourage the Catholic Church to end its separate system, which it had earlier refused to do, and to participate in the new structure, the grants they received were to be abolished. Protestant Church leaders and Orangemen criticised the legislation and the United Education Committee of the Protestant Churches was formed to pressure the government to change it. The Catholic Church disliked it too because it diluted the Catholic ethos of schooling; some Catholic teachers refused grants and salaries under the new structures for political reasons.[4] Protestants wanted religious instruction reinstated and, disliking the idea of Catholic teachers being able to work in state-funded schools, they demanded the power to appoint only Protestants, and to have Protestant clergy on appointment boards. 'Protestant teachers for Protestant schools' was the theme at protest rallies. People were told that the Act threw 'the door open for a Roman Catholic to become a teacher in a Protestant school', and when the Orange Order complained and a general election loomed, the Act was amended in 1925. Lord Londonderry resigned. With the departure of the liberal Londonderry, the education system was subsequently reformed again in a more sectarian direction. The 1930 Education Act was described by the Prime Minister as making the state-funded schools 'safe for Protestant children', for it established a completely separated system, with the Catholic Church agreeing to partly fund its own schools. Pupils in the state system were to receive Bible instruction in the manner of the 'fundamental principles of Protestantism', as the Catholic Bishop Mageean put, by which he meant that 'sacred scripture could be interpreted by private judgement' rather than Church tradition, Protestant clergy assisted in appointments, and the religion of candidates was allowed to be taken into account. A subsequent attempt to abolish Bible instruction was also defeated on the strength of opposition from Orangemen and Protestant clergy.

Protestants also felt that there were internal threats posed to their political dominance. Protestant citadels were sometimes breached by the ballot box. The first loss of power by Unionists in the Londonderry Corporation in the 1920s, with Derry city appointing its first Catholic mayor, provoked wide-scale rioting. The pro-Catholic *Derry Journal* set Protestant fears raging when it announced that the '"No Surrender" citadel had been conquered after centuries of oppression', quoting the new mayor as saying that 'Ireland's right to determine her own destiny will come about whether Protestants in Ulster liked it or not'. Having ensured a Protestant majority by manipulating the border, Protestants were fearful of being undermined by population changes within Northern Ireland. The fear of being outbred by Catholics made their dominance always seem fragile. The Prime Minister of Northern Ireland once said that one had to 'watch' the Catholic population because 'they breed like bloody rabbits'. 'Infiltration' by Southern Catholics was also recognised as a danger, and letters to Protestant newspapers like the *Belfast Newsletter* in the 1920s expressed fears that Southern Catholics were infiltrating Ulster, taking the jobs of loyal men, and changing the population dynamics of neighbourhoods. William Hungerford, of the Ulster Unionist Labour Association, later denounced the invasion of rural districts by Catholic 'farm boys' from the South, who could become voters after only a few days working in the constituency. 'They have no stake whatever, not owning a blade of grass. Their power in the ballot box, however, is great.' Fears of being outbred made the Prime Minister later express the thought that Ulster could be voted into the Free State, and it influenced the Grand Master of the Orange Order to urge Protestant employers to employ only Protestants because 'whenever a Roman Catholic is brought into employment it means one Protestant vote less'. The spectre was not just being voted into the Free State, but the voting in of Catholicism. Major McCormick told Orangemen: 'thousands of Roman Catholics have been added to the population. In many places Protestant majorities are now minorities and at that rate of increase twenty years would see the Church of Rome in power' (quoted in Devlin, 1981: 139).

Seasonal economic migrants from the South were also suspected of contributing to violence, for, above all internal threats, Protestants were made insecure by the constant fear that violence would be used to undermine the state. Catholics were 'the enemy within', irrespective of whether they came from the North or South; Catholics were seen as posing a security problem. The violence surrounding the war of independence, which gave birth to the new state, continued after the Treaty. The IRA announced in the spring of 1922 that it intended to continue the struggle, and, in its own words, consign 'to the flames the manufactories and businesses of the powers' behind the new state. Massive damage was caused in Northern Ireland in a series of forty-one major fires. A number of atrocities were carried out by the IRA in the early 1920s against Protestants who had given information to the police about IRA activity, which made them 'legitimate targets' as far as Republicans were concerned but which were seen by Protestants as examples of anti-Protestant sectarianism. The IRA thereby played into the hands of insecure and frightened Protestants and fed their anti-Catholic ideas about the umbilical connection between Catholicism and violent insurrection.

Enacting the Ascendancy

Anti-Catholicism in the new state of Northern Ireland existed in its pure form, operating at the levels of ideas, behaviour and the social structure, as it came to shape the society whose state Protestants now controlled. The new Prime Minister of Northern Ireland, Sir James Craig, later Lord Craigavon, was later to describe Northern Ireland as having a Protestant government for a Protestant people, in much the same way as the Irish government boasted of its Catholic character, although the size of the respective minority communities was entirely different in the two countries and there was no systematic campaign of violence and harassment against the minority community in the Irish Free State. The remark describes, however, the extent of the Protestant ascendancy in Northern Ireland.

The ascendancy in the North was effected immediately by means of the Protestantisation of the administration and personnel of the state. The civil service, police, judiciary, public services and government positions were dominated by Protestants. The civil service first operated a quota by which Catholics employed in Dublin Castle could transfer North, but this could not be filled and the proportion of Catholics even declined in the 1920s. The Ulster Protestant Voters' Defence Association sent a deputation to Craig in 1924 complaining that Catholics were receiving preferential treatment in public appointments, but such fears were outlandish fantasies, and the Catholics who did find public appointments were sometimes persecuted and harassed. The Protestantisation of the police was critical to the ascendancy. The Royal Ulster Constabulary (RUC) had a quota of one-third of its membership from Catholic members of the Royal Irish Constabulary, but it never met the quota (see Brewer et al., 1988: 48). The membership came overwhelmingly from Protestants in the old force, and the Ulster Special Constabulary, which had a reputation for anti-Catholic violence. The RUC thus absorbed remnants of the old UVF and the Specials, which made the occupational culture very Protestant and Unionist, and the new police force quickly established its own Orange lodge. Recollections by Catholic policemen who transferred to the RUC, show their awareness of prejudice against them within the new force, and the sharp contrast it made with the Royal Irish Constabulary (see Brewer, 1990). The administration of justice was also subject to Protestantisation, both in personnel and in its anti-Catholic application. According to the remark of B.J. Vorster, even South Africans envied the powers Unionists gave themselves in the Northern Ireland Special Powers Act to protect the state (on the provisions of the Act, see Farrell, 1976: 93–4),[5] and they had police forces which were similar in their ruthless pursuit of the minority community (on the South African Police, see Brewer, 1994).

The ascendancy was also enacted by means of the Protestantisation of political power. The country's borders were drawn in order to provide an inbuilt Protestant majority, and the electoral process was managed to the same effect. Proportional representation was abolished, against the terms of the Treaty, and electoral boundaries ensured that the old divisions between Unionism and nationalism continued in unequal portion. The Ulster Unionists dominated the Northern Ireland Parliament and within a few elections the bulk of seats became uncontested, such was the moribund state of politics under Unionist Party domination. Foster describes this as statis: a permanently weighted and largely uncontested Unionist majority was regularly returned, enforcing a stultifying continuity (Foster, 1988: 555). This process involved ghettoisation for Catholics, keeping them within geographical confines where overall Unionist political dominance was not threatened, ensuring that housing and population relocation became seen by many Protestants as constitutional issues. Catholic politics by constitutional nationalists was trapped in these ghettos, and elected representatives only erratically took their seats in Stormont. After 1922, campaigns by the IRA, which symbolically tried to break out from the ghetto, were few, short-lived and mostly rural-based (see Smith, 1995). Local elections were more keenly fought, but gerrymandering of ward boundaries occurred in some councils to ensure perpetual Unionist majorities. Derry city, for example, had its ward boundaries redrawn several times to contain the growing Catholic population, and by 1930, 9,961 nationalist voters returned 8 councillors while 7,444 Unionists returned 12 (Foster, 1988: 557).

Because of the Protestantisation of political power, the political myths and symbols of Northern Ireland which served the ascendancy were Protestant. Electoral politics within the Protestant community were always rendered into one issue – the defence of the Union (for an example of newspaper headlines from the *Belfast Newsletter* for five successive general elections which show this, see Akenson, 1992: 194). Electoral mobilisation, time after time, was effected by the sole clarion-call of Union. Unionists electors were mobilised, in other words, in terms of two categories which bore directly on the constitution – their Protestantism and their Britishness. Irrespective of whether or not the Union was under threat, it was presented to Protestants as if it was, and their mobilisation was by means of anti-Catholic notions like 'No Popery, 'No Surrender', and 'not an inch', making reference to the pantheon of Protestant history, the sacrifices of Protestant forefathers, the glory of past struggles, and the reassuring providence of a God that was supposedly Protestant and Unionist. In short, the political symbols and myths of the nation were anti-Catholic. Thus, the hegemony of the Ulster Unionists based around these myths and symbols could only be challenged by parties which claimed to better represent them. Liberal Unionists were left with little political space. When the Progressive Unionist Party was formed in the 1930s around the liberal economic and political ideas of a local millionaire, it challenged what it saw as the traditional sectarianism of the government and its anti-Catholic tone. The Prime Minister described them as wreckers and fought the 1938 election on the usual issue of the Union, uttering the familiar shibboleths of 'No Surrender', 'No Popery', and 'not an inch'. The new Constitution had come into operation in the Free State in 1937, later called the Irish Republic, which laid claim to Northern Ireland, feeding the fantasy that the Union was under threat, and not a single member of the Progressive Unionists was elected. The 12 candidates mustered less than 4,000 votes each, and the party quickly disappeared from the political scene.

Anti-Catholic Violence in the 1920s and 1930s

The violent events which led up to partition in 1921 left a legacy of insecurity amongst Protestants and a determination from 1922 to protect the state. Catholic alienation was unimportant, and this was demonstrated very quickly. During the First World War, Catholics had moved into industries formerly dominated by Protestants, and while there were attempts to dislodge them in riots in 1920, with the expulsion of over 2,000 Catholics from the shipyards, the orgy of violence worsened in 1922 once Protestants took control of the state. In the 1920 riots, Craig told the Protestant workers who were ousting Catholic competitors that he agreed with the actions 'you boys have taken in the past'; another 6,000 Catholics were driven from work by the end of 1920. Protestant workers thus felt morally sanctioned to violence during 1922. It was alleged by some members of the Protestant clergy that the workers expelled in 1922 were Sinn Fein supporters, but the Catholic bishops noted in a statement that Belfast was notorious for 'savage riots and murder of Catholics in the name of religion' long before Sinn Fein was heard of. Moreover, victims of the expulsion reported that Protestant workers were tearing at their shirts to see if men were wearing Catholic emblems around their neck, 'and then woe betide the man who was'.

At the level of behaviour, anti-Catholicism was expressed in violence and intimidation which was appalling in its brutality. Members of whole families were murdered while sitting peacefully at home simply because they were Catholic. It became an offence, the *Manchester Guardian* realised, simply to be born Catholic. They were 'the enemy within', supposedly all involved in insurrection; so in killing a Catholic one had, without doubt, killed a terrorist. What made the anti-Catholic violence worse was that it was occasionally done by policemen, there supposedly to protect impartially law and order. Attacks on the security forces by the IRA were often met with bloody reprisals on innocent Catholics by the RUC. In one police raid, searching for Sinn Fein members, the police killed five innocent members of one family sleeping in their beds, including a seventy-year-old man and his seven-year-old grandson lying asleep beside each other. One man in the family was bludgeoned with the sledgehammer the police used to force their way through the front door. In another raid, B Specials (a sectarian police force abolished by the British government in 1969) took a Catholic publican, his five sons, and a barman, lined them against a wall and shot five of them dead (Farrell, 1976: 51). Craig later introduced legislation which indemnified all officers of the Crown against legal action resulting from activities in the defence of Northern Ireland, another tactic which the South Africans later copied. Indiscriminate violence was equalled by Protestant mobs, co-ordinated under the paramilitary Ulster Protestant Association, formed in 1920. In 1923 even the police described the Association as dominated by 'the Protestant hooligan element [whose] whole aim and object was simply the extermination of Catholics by any and every means' (quoted in ibid.: 63). A bomb was thrown into a group of Catholic children playing outside their home; six were killed, resulting in a similar outrage against Protestant children. A group of Catholics watching the fire brigade race to a hoax call were injured when someone threw a bomb into the crowd. A bomb was thrown at people leaving mass; an elderly women died. A mob poured petrol over the housekeeper of a Catholic doctor in the staunchly

Protestant Donegall Pass area and set fire to her. Bombs were thrown on to crowded trams in Catholic areas. More people died in Belfast during three months of violence in 1922 than in the whole two years preceding the formation of the state (ibid.: 50). Virtually all the 232 victims were Catholic, and 11,000 were made jobless and 23,000 homeless as Protestants protected their access to socio-economic resources. Over 500 Catholic-owned shops and businesses were burned, looted or wrecked. Property worth £3 million was destroyed.

The violence leading up to partition was as much against Protestants as Catholics; 157 Protestants died in the two years up to July 1922, and 37 members of the security forces, compared to 257 Catholics. But the orgy of violence in 1922 once Protestants controlled the state saw Catholics alone as victims (at least, this was the case after the first month, for in May, the number of deaths across the two communities was very similar, see Buckland, 1981: 46); it was illegal for Catholics to possess weapons, while Protestant mobs engaged in massacre. The paradox was not lost on the English press. The *Manchester Guardian* commented in March 1922: 'whilst envenomed politicians in the Ulster parliament are voting themselves powers to use torture and capital punishment against citizens whom they forbid to defend themselves, whilst they scarcely attempt to protect them from massacre, some of their own partisans in Belfast carry wholesale murder to refinements of barbarity'. Anti-Catholic passions aroused by politicians during the campaign for partition reaped a whirlwind in 1922. The English *Daily Herald* observed what it called 'the blood harvest of Carsonism', as gangs who resisted Home Rule on grounds that it would lead to persecution, persecuted and denied liberty to Catholics. Liberal Protestants were appalled. Southern Protestants had earlier disassociated themselves from such activities and through the Irish Protestant Convention called for attacks on Catholics to stop. Leading Protestant churchmen had earlier condemned the violence and a joint statement specifically stated that nothing could justify the extent of violence against Catholics. Liberal Unionists in the Northern Ireland government also criticised the violence, with Lord Londonderry describing the acts in 1922 as rep-rehensible. The MP for Queen's University criticised men who were deliberately plotting 'the murder of unoffending Roman Catholics', and called on the Northern Ireland government to stop them. A group of Protestant and Catholic businessmen pleaded with Craig to try to end the attacks. So did the Catholic Church, which had earlier set up the Catholic Protection Committee to collect money for the families of victims and for Catholics forced out of homes and jobs. At one of these meetings, Bishop MacRory noted that the Protestants who talked 'glibly of civil and religious liberty', 'appear by their actions not to have even the most elementary idea of what either means' (quoted in Rafferty, 1994: 213). The Northern Ireland government responded by interning Protestants, two of whom were police reservists in the B Specials, both later re-engaged by the police – but the internment worked and the anti-Catholic violence stopped, temporarily.

Violence erupted again during the 1930s, when the economic depression intensified competition for employment and placed strain on outdoor relief programmes. The weakness of the Northern Ireland economy became apparent in the 1930s, with its reliance on traditional industries which went into decline during the decade. Economic decline, halted only by the Second World War, put strain on Northern Ireland's social structure, which was already unstable because of sectarian divisions. The outdoor relief riots of 1932, however, were remarkable for the absence of sectarian division. The grants paid to the unemployed, both Catholic and Protestant, were deemed inadequate. The Presbyterian Church in Ireland had declared the grants incapable of meeting the barest necessities of life, and Farrell (1978) and Devlin (1981) show that the relief paid in Belfast was lower than in any other British city. A non-sectarian Unemployed Workers' Committee organised a public campaign in protest. The outdoor relief workers went on strike in protest at the grant paid, the government banned all marches, and the police responded to the dense crowds of strikers with violence, Protestant and Catholic alike, although it was noticeable that they only used guns when faced with strikers in the Catholic Falls Road area. Some Protestant strikers responded by firing on the police. Police fired upon looters in Belfast city centre. Sporadic outbreaks continued until October, when the government relented by increasing the rates. Other forms of economic protest, however, took sectarian form. The Ulster Unionist Labour Association, solidly Protestant and Unionist, passed motions during the depression saying repeatedly that it 'was the duty of our government to find employment for our people'. Complaints were made that there were too many Catholic gravediggers in Protestant cemeteries, too many Catholic nurses in hospitals, and so on. Not surprisingly therefore, sectarian riots broke out in the 1930s to defend Protestant jobs. The cross-class alliance within Unionism persisted as employers and industrialists were urged to prefer Protestant labour. A well-known Loyalist, with former links with the UDA, recalls today that he knew men who were paid 50 shillings a week – 'a king's ransom' he described it as – in order to shoot at Catholics during the poor law relief riots to provoke sectarian unrest; money he claimed was paid by people in the Unionist Party at the time.

The Ulster Protestant League was formed in 1931 in the context of rising unemployment and it set its object to 'safeguard the employment of Protestants'. Amidst other activity to defend Protestantism, such as mobilising opposition to Belfast City Corporation when it had planned to allow the Catholic Church the use of the Ulster Hall for missionary work, and campaigns to hound defrocked priests, it supported the employment of Protestants. It had been influential in organising attacks on Catholics returning from Dublin in 1932 after attending an international gathering of Catholics, and the Orange Order that summer defended the attacks because Orange anger had been inflamed by the 'unchanging bigotry of Rome' and the 'arrogant, intolerant and unChristian pretensions' of Catholics. Campaigns were undertaken to ensure that Protestants employed only other Protestants. The Grand Master of the Orange Order made the call explicit: 'When will the Protestant employers of Northern Ireland recognise their duty to their Protestant brothers and sisters and employ them to the exclusion of Roman Catholics? I suggest the slogan should be: Protestants employ Protestants' (quoted in Farrell, 1976: 137). Sir Basil Brooke, at a speech in Newtownbutler in 1933, told his audience, as reported by the *Fermanagh Times*:

> There were a great number of Protestants and Orangemen who employed Roman Catholics. He felt he could speak freely on this subject as he had not a Roman Catholic about his place ... He would point out that the Roman Catholics were endeavouring to get in everywhere and were out with all their force and might to destroy the power and constitution of Ulster. There was a definite plot to overpower the vote of Unionists in the north. He would appeal to Loyalists, therefore, to employ Protestant lads and lassies.

Protestant clergymen from County Cavan complained that Protestants from the South felt repelled by his remarks (Bardon, 1992: 538), but Brooke repeated his views later in the year, saying that he was concerned that Catholics were becoming so numerous that they could vote Ulster into the Free State. When Prime Minister, Brooke was famous, as his successor complained, for never having crossed the border, never visiting a Catholic school, and never attending a civic reception in a Catholic town (O'Neill, 1972: 47). Criticism of Brooke from more tolerant Protestants led Lord Craigavon to himself affirm: 'I have always said, I am an Orangeman first and a politician afterwards. I boast we are a Protestant parliament and a Protestant state.' He had earlier said, 'ours is a Protestant government and I am an Orangeman'. Other government ministers repeated the sentiments. The Minister for Labour reassured Protestants that labour in Stormont was overwhelmingly Protestant. After scurrilous rumours to the contrary, he told the Northern Irish Parliament that only one porter out of 31 in Stormont was Catholic, and he only employed temporarily. During 1935, the Orange Order began an official boycott of Catholic pubs, supplementing the boycott of Catholic shops and businesses that had been in operation for a long time. The Ulster Protestant League urged Protestants to support the boycott in order to ensure Protestants alone benefited from Protestant consumer power. The boycott policy of Catholics was, it announced, 'neither to talk with, nor walk with, neither to buy nor sell, borrow nor lend, take nor give, or to have any dealings at all with them, nor for employers to employ them, nor employees to work with them' (quoted in Farrell, 1976: 140). Bishop Mageean noted that the boycott of Catholic business and trade was advocated and supported 'even by men holding high executive office' in the state.

During one employment rally in 1934 members of the Ulster Protestant League had told the audience to 'get training in firing' and made such outrageous remarks that two leaders – one of whom was Rev. Samuel Hanna, a Presbyterian minister – were later convicted of incitement to disorder after a mob returning from the meeting attacked Catholic homes (ibid.: 137). Shots were fired into Catholic areas, and the first sectarian killing occurred since 1922. Other outbreaks of violence took place. A kerbstone was thrown through the window of one Catholic home, killing a disabled child inside. Violence in 1935 was more widespread, since it was infused by Loyalist and Orange celebrations of the silver jubilee of King George V. Shots were fired into Catholic streets, a fifteen-year-old girl was shot on her way from mass, Catholics were beaten up on their way home from work (one so badly that he died), homes were wrecked, and one Catholic publican killed by gunfire. The province's attorney general and chief law officer remarked during the trial of the men accused of the publican's killing that the victim was 'a Roman Catholic and therefore liable to assassination'. Catholics were also expelled from the shipyards and from the linen mills. Calls for peace went unheeded. After the Church of Ireland Bishop of Down asked Orangemen to forget the old feuds, the old triumphs and humiliations, the Orange Grand Master retorted, 'are we to forget that the aim of these people is to establish an all-Ireland Roman Catholic state, in which Protestantism will be crushed out of existence ... are we to forget the heroic achievements of our forefathers?' (quoted in Bardon, 1992: 540). Some of the worst nights of disorder since 1922 followed after this invocation of the past, leading the city coroner to urge leaders of public opinion to remember that 'bigotry is the curse of goodwill and peace' and that 'the poor people who commit these riots are easily led and influenced'. 'It is not good Protestantism', he said, 'to preach a gospel of hate and enmity towards those who differ from us in religion and politics' (quoted in Devlin, 1981: 144). The funeral of one of the Protestant victims of the riots, however, saw widespread anti-Catholic violence after further inflammatory preaching.

The Ideological Construction of Difference

Protestants were a majority, but not a confident one. A sense that their ascendancy was fragile and persistently under threat led to a paranoia about Catholics, showing itself in outrageous anti-Catholic violence, unrestrained rhetoric and blatant discrimination, which gave only the illusion of strength. In this respect it was still important to maintain the dimensions of difference between Protestant and Catholic, ensuring that religion coincided with patterns of differentiation in education, housing, the economy and politics. With no compunction, for example, advertisements for jobs in the *Belfast Telegraph* stated religious preference, and most requested Protestants. In 1926, for example, it was common to see advertisements like the following: 'wanted, strong country girl for housework, must be able to milk; Protestant preferred'; 'respectable Protestant little girl wanted to mind young baby': it is not apocryphal that someone once advertised Protestant puppies for sale. The debate in the academic literature over how much discrimination there was against Catholics at the level of social structure (see, for example, Hewitt, 1981; O'Hearn, 1983; Whyte, 1983) suggests there is disagreement only on the extent, not its fact. Equally important, however, is the ideological construction of difference, the process by which Catholics were presented as second-class citizens irrespective of the discrimination they experienced in the allocation of resources. Victorian 'scientific racism' was rarely drawn on by this time to present Catholics as racially different, although ideas like this survived in some people (see Brewer, 1992: 356). The ideological construction of difference drew primarily on traditional anti-Catholicism, reproducing themes long established since the sixteenth century, but which were refashioned to reflect the new circumstances in Ulster.

At the level of ideas, Catholics were constructed as different by means of traditional anti-Catholic stereotypes which imputed to them familiar negative behavioural traits. They were dirty, for example. Government ministers reproduced this old but widespread notion when one said that an Orange hall needed to be fumigated after American Catholic servicemen had used it for mass (the Spirit of Drumcree group of Orangemen had the Ulster Hall fumigated in 1997 after its use by Sinn Fein), and another minister said that Catholic slum-dwellers had 'sub-human' habits. Similarly old fashioned but popular notions included the belief that Catholics were lazy, slothful and feckless. The Belfast Board of Guardians, for example, responsible for determining outdoor relief for the unemployed in the city, record in their minutes that it was their obligation 'faced with such sloth, fecklessness and iniquity', 'to discourage idleness and create a spirit of independence'. They were fearful of large Catholic families being a burden on the ratepayers, who were disproportionately Protestant under regulations designed to protect local election majorities. The Catholic poor were all too willing to beg instead of work but showed 'no poverty under the blankets', as a Chair of the Board once said. Some Protestant clergy criticised poor Catholics who were a 'wastrel class' and asked the Board to cut grants 'to parasites' (see Bardon, 1992: 525). Goldring (1991: 48) argues that the Board were Calvinists who believed that poverty was a judgement from God and that after partition the Board saw themselves as in the front line of a war to maintain a Protestant majority. They were thus intent on preventing Catholics from getting relief. Protestants were unemployed because they confronted unfortunate circumstances, Catholics because they wasted money on gambling and drink, and made no effort to find work (ibid.). Objections to other 'habits' led some government ministers to try to restrict British welfare dispensations, with one proposing to abolish family allowance payments for the fourth and any subsequent children. The General Assembly of the Presbyterian Church supported the views of Professor Corkey, a Presbyterian theology teacher and a former Minister of Education in the Northern Ireland government, who said that parents of large families ought to be fined for having so many children (see Rafferty, 1994: 247).

Catholics were also presented as disloyal, an idea that is as ancient as anti-Catholicism itself (on this idea, see Clayton, 1996: 124; McEvoy and White, forthcoming). The chairperson of the Commission on Education, set up in 1922 to determine the education system for the new state, set out his principles: 'there are two peoples in Ireland, one industrious, law abiding and God fearing, the other slothful, murderous and disloyal' (quoted in Kennedy, 1988: 97). The 1923 Promissory Oaths Act required all civil servants and teachers in Northern Ireland to swear an oath of allegiance to the British Crown and to the government of Northern Ireland. Notions of Catholic disloyalty resonated well with Ulster's uncertain ascendancy: Catholics were disloyal to the British Crown and to the Northern Irish state, and could not be trusted. Catholics employed in public and government service, for example, were always suspect. The Catholic–Police Liaison Committee, set up under the Anglo-Irish Treaty to try to establish rapport between Catholics and the new RUC, was undermined immediately when the Catholics on the committee were considered security risks and two were arrested by the new police force. The safety of government offices appeared paramount. After the public came to know of the fact in 1926, two Southern Catholics employed in the ministry of labour after transferring from Dublin Castle, were forced to leave by the minister, John Andrews. A Catholic gardener, with testimonials from Royalty, was still hounded out when it became known he was employed on the Stormont estate. Hunting out Catholics became press sport. The Home Affairs minister, Dawson Bates, at perhaps the most sensitive department in terms of national security, had a young typist sacked when it was revealed in the press that she was Catholic. He declared afterwards that he did not want even his most junior employee to be a Papist. Bardon notes that Bates openly regarded Catholics as enemies to be kept in check – and this a man in charge of the police and judiciary – and that he showed blatant disregard for impartial procedures (Bardon, 1992: 498). Sir Basil Brooke, then Minister of Agriculture, told the Londonderry Unionist Association in 1934 that he 'recommended those people who are loyalists not to employ Roman Catholics, ninety-nine percent of whom are disloyal. I want you to remember one point in regard to the employment of people who are disloyal, you are disenfranchising yourselves.' He said that Catholics were 'out to destroy Ulster with all their might and power'. He reassured them that the Prime Minister was behind him in such views, for Lord Craigavon had earlier said that 'the appointments made by the government are made, as far as we can possibly manage it, of loyal men and women'. It was not just politicians who argued thus. The Rev. Tolland, a senior chaplain in the Orange Order, said in 1936 that: 'Popery is the key to the problem of peace in Ireland. Popery in the past has been the curse of Ireland and there will never be peace while Popery reigns.' The Second World War, therefore, caused some people to suspect disloyalty amongst Catholics. Rumours circulated in working-class Protestant districts that Catholics were guiding in German bombers by torchlight.

It was in this sort of context that after the war, the only Belfast Victoria Cross won in the Second World War was not commemorated because the person concerned was Catholic and he found himself snubbed by the city council and ex-servicemen organisations (see Fleming, forthcoming). Allegations of disloyalty continued after the war, which shows that the idea had become part of an anti-Catholic popular culture not tied to specific instances of conflict which might provoke the claim. Thus, speaking in 1957, when community tensions had eased considerably from the first years of partition, a government minister told his audience of Orangemen in Portadown that 'all the minority are traitors and have always been traitors to the government of Northern Ireland'. As late as 1959, well before the Catholic civil rights campaign and civil unrest, the Prime Minister, now Lord Brookeborough, said that Catholics should not be allowed to join the Ulster Unionist Party or stand as candidates because they were disloyal. It would be difficult, he said, for Catholics 'to discard the political conceptions' acquired from Catholicism, 'whose aims are openly declared to be an all-Ireland republic'. The Grand Master of the Orange Order also remarked that the 'vast difference in our religious outlook' meant that Catholics could not unconditionally support Northern Ireland, although some ministers and members of the Young Unionists felt that the time was opportune for Unionists to shed their anti-Catholicism. Brookeborough, however, was locked in the past, and he regarded all Catholics as likely traitors. Some of the partition generation survived into the 1960s, similarly moribund by old controversies and fears, and content merely to repeat the old shibboleths. Robert Babington, for example, urged in 1961 that employment registers should be kept of loyalists by the Ulster Unionist Party, which employers should consult to give them first choice in jobs, but a new generation was also emerging in Ulster Unionism which would try to move Protestants into the future. Their prospects would test the extent to which Protestants could transcend anti-Catholicism under the modernisation occurring in the 1960s.

The Rise and Fall of O'Neillism

Captain Terence O'Neill was a liberal Unionist, representative of the enlightened Protestant tradition, progressive in religion and politics, and someone who wanted to transcend the old style in both. He assumed the post of Prime Minister in 1963 at a time when other progressive Unionists were calling for modernisation in religion and politics. Leading Protestant churchmen, for example, were opening up to dialogue with Catholicism and conscious of the past errors they had made in their relationship with Catholics. The 1965 General Assembly of the Presbyterian Church, for example, passed a resolution which urged upon 'our people humbly and frankly to acknowledge, and to ask forgiveness for, any attitudes and actions towards our Roman Catholic fellow countrymen which have been unworthy of our calling as followers of Jesus Christ'. Presbyterians were told to structure relations with Catholics 'always in the spirit of charity rather than suspicion and intolerance, and in accordance with scripture' (quoted in Dunlop, 1995: 55). The Church's committee on national and international problems produced a report the same year which recognised the extent of discrimination against Catholics in the North in the workplace, housing allocation and in electoral boundaries, and condemned it. The Church also gave its support to involvement by leading Presbyterians in ecumenical initiatives. By the mid-1960s, there were some joint ventures between all the main churches in Northern Ireland, and meetings had occurred. It was reciprocated by the Catholic Church, which, following Vatican II, was more open to Protestantism. Cardinal Conway made speeches which were gracious; he had earlier paid Protestants in Ireland a glowing tribute when appointed as Archbishop of Armagh. Catholic bishops began meeting with government ministers and other Unionists. They met with Belfast's lord mayor for the first time since partition in 1962; in Enniskillen the bishop met the town's Unionist mayor to restore 'friendliness and co-operation' with Protestant neighbours, and the Catholic hierarchy in Ireland supported the wider move to ecumenism following the second Vatican Council, which had highlighted the good qualities in the other Christian churches. Conway spoke of the need for unity amongst all Christians and for people in Northern Ireland to change their attitude toward each other, and an annual ecumenical conference was inaugurated in 1966. Conway was later to say that during the 1960s, the bishops gave every mark of recognition and acceptance of the Northern Ireland state, and that they met as much with government ministers in Ulster as the Irish Republic (see Rafferty, 1994: 260).

Corners of the Unionist Party were advocating similar change in politics. Younger Unionists demanded change. In 1962 Bob Cooper, then involved with the Young Unionist Council, was critical of the 'ageing tired men' who dominated Ulster politics, who were embedded in the past, 'men who cannot look forward with hope and who are forced to look back with nostalgia'. Lord Brookeborough resigned the following year and O'Neill, as his successor, reflected a new approach, bemoaning the lost opportunities and wasted time of Brookeborough's premiership. It was a tragedy, O'Neill later wrote, that Brookeborough did not try to persuade his 'devoted followers to accept some reforms' (quoted in Bardon, 1992: 621). He once referred to 'small minded men' who had removed rights from Catholics 'during the first years of Northern Ireland's existence', and who did nothing to make Catholics 'feel wanted or even appreciated'. Reform was O'Neill's watchword: on taking office he said that his task was 'literally to transform Ulster' by bold and imaginative measures. He wished to transform Ulster economically, and introduced economic planning; and politically, by building 'bridges between the two traditions in our community'. Reconciliation was declared policy and Catholics were now part of the one community, not alien outsiders to it. The old rhetoric and shibboleths were jettisoned in favour of an inclusive style, which opened up the promise of better Protestant–Catholic relations.

The climate, as far as the government could permit it, changed immediately and dramatically. Union Jacks on public buildings in Ulster were flown at half mast on the death of Pope John XXIII, and while Rafferty dismisses this as mere procedure since it was an instruction from the Queen (Rafferty, 1994: 257), O'Neill spoke generously about the Pope, announcing on his death that he had 'won widespread acclaim for his qualities of kindness and humanity'; the Governor of Northern Ireland represented the government at his funeral. The General Assembly of the Presbyterian Church in Ireland stood in silence for a minute in his honour. More significantly, contacts were established with the South. Young Unionists visited Dublin to meet Fine Gael, some Unionist politicians regularly went hunting with Southern politicians, and O'Neill followed with meetings in Dublin and Belfast between himself and Sean Lemass, the Irish Prime Minister and a former internee and participant in the Easter Rising. Unthinkable before for an Ulster Prime Minister, O'Neill said the meeting had been held because the North and South shared the same rivers, the same mountains and some of the same problems. Lemass's successor, Jack Lynch, also made a visit to Stormont. Rubicon after rubicon was crossed: O'Neill won a measure of Catholic support for the Unionist Party, saw the nationalists in the Stormont Parliament won over to recognising the Parliament, urged the ending of segregated education, met with Catholic bishops, attended Catholic schools and hospitals, and successfully shifted government rhetoric to include Catholics in citizenship and into partnership for the future. In 1966, the year in which the Labour government in Britain commended O'Neill for his modernisation, he said: 'let us be united in working together – in a Christian spirit – to create better opportunities for our children, whether they come from the Falls Road [Catholic West Belfast] or Finaghy [Protestant South Belfast]' (quoted in Bardon, 1992: 633).

The practical reforms did not, unfortunately, match the change in government rhetoric, but even the change in discourse went too far for some Protestants who wanted to hear the old anti-Catholic and Orange shibboleths, and to keep the traditional power and ascendancy they reflected. Ecumenism was abused by some Protestants and Orangemen. The Protestant churches were accused of going papist, of following a 'Romeward trend'. The government received equal wrath. O'Neill was accused of being a traitor, of 'committing spiritual fornication and adultery with the anti-Christ', and the RUC discovered that the UVF were plotting to assassinate him. Leading members of the UVF have admitted with hindsight that the resurrection of the organisation in the 1960s was in order to oppose O'Neill rather than the IRA: 'his overthrow was to take the shape of violent incidents in Belfast and Northern Ireland to hype up communal and political tension' (see Gusty Spence, in Garland, 1997: 7). O'Neill was vilified unmercifully by the Rev. Ian Paisley, whose anti-Catholicism led him to form his own political party in opposition to liberal O'Neillism and his own church in opposition to the liberal Protestantism, since both 'supped with the antiChrist'. Liberals in politics and religion were allies of Rome, Lundys [sell-outs], and traitors. O'Neill wrote later in his autobiography that his 'self-styled loyalist' critics were 'Protestant extremists, yearning for the days of the Protestant ascendancy' who threatened to light 'the fuse which blew us up' (O'Neill, 1972: 80). He had right-wing critics in his Cabinet in mind, as well as the street politicians-cum-preachers like Paisley, Foster and Porter. The old sectarian and anti-Catholic forces within Protestantism and Unionism ruled the day, leaving O'Neill to lament on his resignation in 1969: 'I have tried to break the chains of ancient hatreds. I have been unable to realise [what] I had sought to achieve ... but one day these things will and must be achieved' (O'Neill, 1969: 200). This proved to be wishful thinking because the anti-Catholic forces within Protestantism were rampant.

The fall of O'Neill shows the resilience of sectarian forms of politics in Unionism and the survival of anti-Catholic ideas in Protestantism. Both traditions were too strong to be jettisoned and the 1960s was not an opportune decade for change. The Protestant working class felt threatened in the 1960s, for it was experiencing economic insecurity arising from deindustrialisation and the decline of the traditional industries, the rise of less sectarianised forms of employment linked to multinational companies, and rising unemployment. The Catholic community was advancing economically, educationally, culturally and politically. They were unsatisfied by the pace of change, articulate and tenacious in the defence of Catholic civil rights, and their protests were about to provoke a level of violence which destablised the state. If the Protestant working class remained sectarian because of this, the Protestant middle classes were unsettled by it; the old shibboleths gave security and identity to both in a changing and insecure world. And when terrorism emerged in 1969–70, polarisation developed along with it. The extremes consumed the middle ground once violence fed ancient prejudices and fears; the extremists feasted voraciously on the violence, projecting to a high profile the fanaticisms and fears of men who otherwise might have remained on the lunatic fringe. As it was, Northern Ireland remained locked in ancient hatreds, giving a powerful voice to those people who represented the past. Paisley's rise to influence acts as a template for the failure of Northern Ireland in the 1960s to transcend anti-Catholicism.

Paisleyism

The Rev. Ian Paisley, founder of Free Presbyterianism, is often portrayed as the Henry Cooke of his century: florid in rhetoric, evangelical, covenantal and rabidly, shamelessly anti-Catholic in theology; and conservative, pro-Union and relentlessly Loyalist in politics; a Christian minister who believes it an obligation to be involved in politics, and one who sees no contradiction between his Christianity and fomenting anti-Catholic hatreds and enmities. The comparison should not be over-extended, however, for Cooke was an 'insider' to mainstream conservative Protestantism, while Paisley is very much an 'outsider'. The success of Paisley has been to use traditional anti-Catholicism as a power base which resonated in the political polarisation that occurred after terrorist violence, enabling him to broaden his appeal to an extent that the conservative and traditional forces he represents shape the agenda within Unionism – but he does so from the outside.

It is popular to portray Paisley as an aberration, a throwback to earlier times (see Moloney and Pollack, 1986; Ruane and Todd, 1996), but he represents the dominant tradition in Northern Irish Protestantism, which is evangelical conservativism expressing itself theologically in anti-Catholicism and politically in militant Unionism (studies which recognise this include Taylor, 1983; Bruce, 1986; Wallis et al., 1986; MacIver, 1987; Cooke, 1996). This tradition was challenged in the 1960s by the constructive Unionism of O'Neill, itself more like a throwback to the beginning of the century. Paisley was on the fringe while pragmatists dominated Unionism, but this only occurred briefly with the premiership of O'Neill. Paisley and O'Neill represented two directions for Northern Protestants; the one forward to new arrangements and new relationships; the other backward to the old long-standing traditions and shibboleths. They fought for the soul of Unionism, and they were implacable enemies. Through his organisation Ulster Protestant Action (UPA), Paisley abused and heckled liberals in theology and politics, and worked hard to advance the claims of 'Protestant and loyal workers in preference to their Catholic fellow workers', as the UPA put it. He attacked O'Neill unceasingly for his overtures to Catholics. Paisley's newspaper, the *Protestant Telegraph* (founded in 1966), once described O'Neillism as a policy of betraying Ulster by appeasing rebels and showing weakness to Romanism. In fact, this was amongst the least invective of the slanders: O'Neill was a Lundy, a Judas, a dupe; selling out birthright, land, hopes and the future.

Paisley also attacked the ecumenical trend in Protestantism during the 1960s. Ulster's Church leaders were selling their Protestant heritage 'lock stock and barrel ... This is not the time for a velvet tongue. It is a day of war and war to the death. The enemy we fear is the enemy within ... If they want to go to Rome, then let them go, but they are not taking Ulster with them' (quoted in Taylor, 1983: 15). They were the Iscariots of Ulster for expressing condolences on the death of Pope John XXIII, that 'Romish man of sin [who] is now in Hell'. Paisley's analysis of Protestant denominations, with the exception of his own Free Presbyterians, was they were becoming de-Protestantised (see Cooke, 1996: 69) because of their ecumenism, which is something 'blackened with the blackness of Popery', something hating, fighting, defaming, and rejecting Christ on the wickedness of Baal, something representing the machinations of the Devil (see Cooke, 1996: 70). Ecumenical activity was condemned because it involved association with Catholicism: 'there's no agreement between Protestantism and Popery, no agreement between the Gospel of Jesus Christ and the trash of the Anti-Christ, [you] can't make them agree' (quoted in ibid.: 76). Accordingly, Protestants who were ecumenical were apostate, they had abandoned their faith; they had joined Catholics as the new 'enemy within'.

Paisley, however, was not the sole representative of the conservative evangelical, anti-Catholic and militantly Unionist tradition, and there were people like Norman Porter, with his National Union of Protestants, who competed to represent the heart and soul of traditional Protestantism. William McGrath organised the Christian Fellowship and Irish Emancipation Crusade, warning of the onslaught threatening Ulster Protestantism – variously identified as communism, Catholicism and later, ironically, the UVF itself (on conflicts within the UVF and the dispute with McGrath, see Garland, 1997). McGrath feared a 'national crisis of faith', and urged resolute action: 'this crisis will eventually break into armed conflict between those who fight the "battles of the Lord against the mighty" and those who know nothing of "the glorious liberty of the children of God". Blood has ever been the price of liberty. Oliver Cromwell once said, "choose ye out Godly men to be captains and Godly men will follow them". We must do the same' (quoted in ibid.: 7). O'Neill also had his right wing in the Ulster Unionist Party, with people like Craig. But Paisley successfully associated himself in the public mind with militant Unionism by rallies, protests, stunts and florid language, and later subsumed all competitors. Instances in 1966 illustrate the early attempts he made to commandeer the high place in militant Loyalism. He shamelessly played on the mythology of Carson by dragging his son over to review the Ulster Protestant Volunteers (soon to become the new UVF) when a new bridge in Belfast was not named after the Ulster hero. He marched members of his congregation through Catholic areas on the way to the General Assembly of the Presbyterian Church in protest at their alleged Catholic tendencies, provoking a riot amongst Catholic residents, shouting 'Popehead', 'Lundy', and 'Romanists' at members of the assembly as they emerged on the street. Paisley decided to go to prison during the year rather than pay a fine for breaching public order, whipping up frenzied feelings by claiming, on the Sunday before imprisonment, that it might be his last religious service since the government had declared war on Protestantism, making it clear that he was prepared for martyrdom like other Protestant martyrs. If his life 'has to go', he announced, 'it will go in that cause'. It was a sacrifice he was willing to make (quoted in Taylor, 1983: 18). There was serious rioting outside the prison on the day Paisley went inside and a group of supporters marched into Belfast city centre rampaging and burning Catholic-owned shops (Farrell, 1976: 235). It was not just Free Presbyterians who were whipped up by Paisley's rhetoric. When the UVF that year started killing Catholics again – although they also killed an elderly Protestant woman into whose house they threw a petrol bomb by mistake – one of the convicted men told the police that he 'felt terribly sorry I ever heard of that man Paisley or decided to follow him'. Paisley denied knowing the man (although Farrell (ibid.: 236) shows the connections between Paisley and the early UVF; see also Cooke, 1996: 183–4), but the man's point was that Paisley had created in him frenzy and hate as a result of Paisley's attempt to dominate militant Loyalism. Garland looks at the links between Paisley and McGrath, who later transformed his Fellowship into the terrorist group called Tara (1997). However, Paisley was also assisted in his rise to prominence by civil rights marches and IRA activity,[6] which he exploited as posing a threat to Protestantism and Unionism. He convinced many people of the threat and O'Neill resigned in 1969. O'Neill complained of 'self-appointed and self-styled loyalists who see moderation as treason and decency as weakness'; the tradition of conservative evangelicalism, anti-Catholic and militantly Unionist, represented this time by Paisleyism, had commandeered the high place again.

The appeal of Paisleyism is three-fold (see Bruce, 1986, 1994). The class interests of working-class Protestants in the cross-class alliance are protected to ensure that 'big Unionists' and the 'fur coated brigade' within Unionism, as Paisley puts it, do not sell out working-class Protestants. Paisley's first political organisation was the UPA, which was established at a time of rising unemployment for the Protestant working class, and his latest expression, the Democratic Unionist Party (DUP), has an urban base in the Protestant working class (but also amongst conservative evangelicals in the rural areas, which is more middle class – see Bruce, 1986). But economic interests are not overt because Paisleyism's primary appeal plays on political and ethnic-national interests based around the antinomies of Britishness (against Irishness) and Protestantism (against Catholicism). The former predisposes it to militant Unionism, the latter to militant anti-Catholicism, which together comprise the motifs of Paisleyism.

Free Presbyterianism is the most extreme expression of anti-Catholicism in Northern Ireland (ibid.: 224).[7] For Paisleyites Catholicism is not only totally evil, it is very effective and powerful. A theological case is made against the Catholic Church, supposedly grounded in Scripture itself, and also a political argument in terms of its malevolence. Theologically, Catholicism is unscriptural, baptised paganism and unChristian. 'Make no mistake', Paisley once wrote in *The Revivalist*, his church magazine, 'Romanism is as far removed from Christianity as Hell is from Heaven. Anyone who denies that, is either ignorant of the Bible, or of Rome, or of both.' The problems lie in its claims to universality, the infallibility of the Pope, the place of tradition compared to the Bible, the role of the priest, the use of icons and rituals, and the adoration of the Saints and the Virgin Mary, none of which Paisley sees as scriptural. Thus during one of his sermons, Paisley said: 'if the Church of Rome is right, Protestantism is wrong. If the Church of Rome is a Christian church, that Bible is not true. The Roman Catholic Church is not a Christian church. It has insulted the doctrine of divine redemption. It has rejected the Lord of the Book. It has elevated Mary. It has rejected the finished work of the Lord Jesus Christ. A false system. It's the system of anti-Christianity' (quoted in Taylor, 1983: 99–100). The Catholic Church is believed to be the Whore and the Harlot described in Scripture, and the Papacy the antiChrist. Relevant Scripture passages in the Book of Revelation and Old Testament prophecies are taken to be covert references to Catholicism. Even the hymns purposely written for Free Presbyterians reproduce anti-Catholicism, with lines referring to Catholicism as the 'mystery of wickedness', and 'the harlot in the bride's attire' (for example, see hymn number 757 reprinted in Cooke, 1996: 42–3). As Bruce argues (1986: 224), this certainty that anti-Catholicism is scriptural fills the gap left by the absence of evidence for the malevolent conspiracies which the Catholic Church is alleged to instigate. The conservative Protestant *knows* that Rome is the Mystery Babylon, the Whore and Deceiver because they believe the Bible says so. If there is no evidence to show its malevolence it is because Rome is subtle and has lulled the rest of the world into complacency. Thus, the conspiracies are real, even though they appear fanciful.

It is therefore confidently believed that the Catholic Church is, for example, behind the European Union (see ibid.: 227). It is a Papal conspiracy, supposedly foreseen in Daniel and Revelation, by which Catholicism can succeed in its ambition for world domination. The Beast with ten heads in Revelation is claimed to symbolise the flag of the European Union. The Ulster Defence Association's *Ulster* in February 1979 suggested that the entire structure had been designed to imperil and subvert Protestant, Loyalist Ulster. Of Paisley's own position in the European Parliament he says: 'I'm going to get all I can for Ulster, every grant we can possibly get our hands on. Then when we have milked the cow dry, we are going to shoot the cow' (quoted in Taylor, 1983: 32). He has also defended his position there as ensuring that Britain, which, he claims, is the last Protestant country in the European Union, is represented by a conservative Protestant. Fascism, communism and other evils have been alleged to be the products of Catholicism; most things Free Presbyterians dislike can be lodged at the door of the Catholic Church. The Catholic Church was responsible for the Falklands War, which *The Revivalist* said in May 1982 was a curse on the Church of England because it has gone 'a-whoring after Rome'. It was behind the break-up of the marriage between the Prince and Princess of Wales, since Mrs Parker-Bowles's former husband is supposedly a devout Catholic (see Cooke, 1996: 78). Catholics have infiltrated the media – the BBC in Northern Ireland and the *Belfast Telegraph* are described as Catholic-dominated. The IRA even inform the media before they let off a bomb to ensure their Catholic cohorts are there first (see Taylor, 1983: 114). Local political events are all rendered into the malevolent influence of the Catholic Church. The IRA, civil unrest, civil rights, even disputes over parades are all plots by the Catholic Church to advance its claims to universality; Drumcree was a problem caused by the Pope's emissary who went to Portadown only to stir up conflict, for wherever there is a Jesuit 'there is trouble' (see Cooke, 1996: 208). The policies of the Northern Ireland Office have at times been explained away by reflecting the interests of the Catholics who are said to run it: it wants to take Ulster back down the Romeward road.

Conspiracy theory offers Paisleyites their explanation for 'the troubles': civil unrest is a plot by the Catholic Church to annihilate Protestantism, the IRA merely the dupes of the Pope and his bishops. The Catholic Church, it is argued, has been the instigator of persecution and revolution throughout the world, and violence in Northern Ireland is but one manifestation. The IRA are thus tools in the hands of bishops. At the beginning of 'the troubles' the IRA was described as the murder gang of the Roman Catholic Church, 'the armed wing of the Roman Catholic Church whose real aim was to annihilate Protestantism'. Bishops are described as Sinn Feiners, and murders by the IRA are portrayed as at the behest of the Catholic Church which 'still claims the right to kill Protestants'. No amount of public condemnation of terrorism by the Catholic Church alters the perception that Irish Republicanism and Irish Catholicism are indissoluble. Interviews Taylor has undertaken with Free Presbyterians show they believe Paisley's conspiracies implicitly. IRA members have been socialised into Catholicism, it is claimed, and the Church offers moral, spiritual and material support to terrorists (see Taylor, 1983: 111). Projecting the blame for civil unrest on to Catholicism in this way also ensures that they have no need to compromise in order to establish peace, since it would be compromise with the Devil. The old shibboleths, 'No Surrender', 'No Compromise', 'No Popery', 'not an inch', thus suit the time very well.

The second motif of Paisleyism is militant Unionism: Paisley puts Protestantism at the service of the Union, as this tradition has always done. A united Ireland is criticised because it would be Catholic, in the grip of priests, and devoid of civil and political liberties. Warning the Prime Minister of the Irish Republic during a speech in Omagh in 1981, Paisley described him as 'this guardian of murderers, this godfather of intended destruction, this green aggressor and conspirator', and went on to say: 'you will never get your thieving murderous hands on the Protestants of Northern Ireland because every drop of Ulster blood will be willing to be shed before we entered into your priest-ridden banana republic'. Dogs may return to their vomit, washed sows to the mire, Paisley wrote vividly in 1982 in *No Pope Here*, 'but we shall not be guiled ... By God's grace we will never return to Popery.' The defence of the Union is a defence of Protestantism because the Catholic Church would extirpate Protestants in a united Ireland. An article in the *Protestant Telegraph* described the 'jackboot system' of Rome which rules in Southern Ireland and warned Northern Protestants that any reform or compromise, any appeasement of Catholic neighbours in Ulster, was folly because 'Rome carries out an unrelenting war for the achievement of her aims. She is a past master in hypocrisy, duplicity, deceit and falsehood ... her actionists [are] preparing for the greatest onslaught ever to be launched against the forces of the Crown' (quoted in Cooke, 1996: 163).

Protestantism serves the Union in another way by defining part of the symbolic meaning of 'Britishness' which the Union is intended to preserve. The Union is valorised in part because it is a union of Protestants within Protestant Britain, representing the civil and political liberties associated with Britishness. Protestantism and Britishness are the same Janus face: thus, an attack on one is an attack on the other. Republicans who challenge the legitimacy of the British state in Northern Ireland are, in this view, really attacking Protestants. This is seen most clearly in the fabricated 'Sinn Fein oath', first appearing in the *Protestant Telegraph* in May 1966, which represents the conflict as one against Protestantism.

> These Protestant robbers and brutes, these unbelievers of our faith, will be driven like the swine they are into the sea ... until we of the Catholic faith and avowed supporters of all Sinn Fein actions and principles clear these heretics from our land ... We must work towards the destruction of Protestants and the advancement of the priesthood and the Catholic faith until the Pope is complete ruler of the world (quoted in Cooke, 1996: 149; for another fabricated Sinn Fein oath along the same lines, see the Ulster Defence Association journal *Ulster*, 15 June 1985).

The oath reveals the mind-set of the perpetrators of the fabrication: the real problem in Northern Ireland is Catholicism. 'The Roman Catholic Church lies at the heart of the problem in Northern Ireland', Paisley once said, because 'she has indoctrinated her people against everything that is Protestant' (quoted in Cooke, 1996: 60).[8] Protestantism does not just service the Union, therefore, it defines the outsider or stranger who threatens it.

Paisleyism is characterised by the belief that Protestantism and Britishness are under constant threat. The campaign for civil rights for Catholics, Republican terrorism, direct rule, the Hunger Strikes, the Anglo-Irish Agreement, the Downing Street Declaration, the ceasefires, and the post-ceasefire talks have all in their time been used to mobilise Protestants on the basis of the perpetual anxiety about the undermining of their Britishness and Protestantism (with respect to the Anglo-Irish Agreement, see Aughey, 1989). Unionists have historically always seen the Union as under threat, but these events were not, as in Brookeborough's time, fanciful fears, but real indices of how Britain's relationship with Ulster Protestants since 1969 has, in Unionist eyes, been compromised by Anglo-Irish relations, undermining their position within the United Kingdom. And as the attacks have purportedly increased in severity, so has the vociferousness of the defence mounted by Paisley. Hence the attractiveness in the academic literature of the idea of Protestant insecurity as an explanation of Paisley's support (for examples of such explanations, see Nelson, 1984; Bruce, 1986, 1994; Wallis et al., 1986; Akenson, 1992). In a situation where Protestants see (or think) their world is collapsing around them, every plank which supported their social structure being dismantled, and where their identity as British Protestants is undermined, Paisleyism offers security by aggressively defending their identity, values and way of life, and by repeating, time and time again, the familiar and comforting shibboleths from the past. Paisleyism offers continuity with tradition; and it is a history which shows that tenacity and perseverance always led to victory. Hence the perpetual cataloguing of past battles and victory cries – 'Remember 1690', 'No Surrender', 'No Popery', and 'not an inch'. It is, in short, a tradition of glorious victory that resolves the ontological anxiety of Protestants who see the Janus connection between their Britishness and Protestantism being prised apart by Irishness and Catholicism.

The past is thus a powerful resource in Paisley's political armoury (on this point, see especially MacIver, 1987). This goes beyond offering particular interpretations of history, which are on many occasions factually inaccurate, but reflects, more deeply, his conscious and deliberate attempt to associate Paisleyism with historical tradition. His Free Presbyterian sect, as Taylor (1983: 3) calls it, comprises no more than 20,000 people, but Paisley has broad appeal outside his own church (and political party) because he has successfully identified Paisleyism with the conservative evangelical tradition, dating from Henry Cooke, and the even more ancient tradition of covenanting theology, which runs back to the sixteenth century. This reflects in two ways. First, he portrays himself as the latest in a proud lineage of Protestant martyrs and preachers, beginning with Luther and including Calvin, Knox, Wesley, Cooke, Spurgeon and Whitefield. Knox is a particular favourite – both spent time in prison, both were persecuted for their proclamation of biblical truth, both felt a conditional loyalty to the state because of what they saw as an overriding loyalty to God, and both were anti-Catholic (on the similarities between Paisley and Knox, see MacIver, 1987: 374–6). Paisley frequently alludes back to Knox. In a special issue of *The Revivalist* on Knox in 1972, Paisley wrote: 'oh for men in our land today, fearless men, God anointed men, Spirit-filled men, fire baptised men, to cry out as Knox cried out against Popery and against the curse that has blighted twentieth-century Protestantism, this curse of ecumenism'. As Denis Cooke (1996: 45ff.) has shown, however, the pantheon which Paisley frequently invokes as part of the same tradition of anti-Catholicism, often differed from him in its openness to Catholics and in considering the Catholic Church as part of the Christian tradition (for Cooke on Wesley, see 1996: 49–51; on Calvin, see p. 48; on Spurgeon, see pp. 96–7; on Luther, see p. 47), something Paisley ignores by means of selective quotation.

Second, and perhaps more significant, historical tradition is used as a representation of the present. The future goes backwards in Paisleyism because the present is also understood in terms of the past. The same conflicts, battles and enemies exist now as then: they are historical universals, the unchanging unfolding of the age-old clash between biblical truth and error. An article in the *Protestant Telegraph* on 15 June 1974 expressed this succinctly: 'the Ulster situation is Protestantism versus popery. The war in Ulster is a war of survival between the opposing forces of truth and error, and the principles of the Reformation are as relevant today as they were in the sixteenth century.' In contrast to those who would forget the past, Paisley resoundly asserts its relevance for today. Wallis et al. (1986: 19–20) quote from one of Paisley's sermons in the 1960s:

> There are voices raised in our province which advocate forgetfulness. They tell us that the sooner we forget the great epochs of history, the sooner that we forget about Derry, Aughrim, Enniskillen and the Boyne, the better for us as people. There are leaders in church and state who are apostles of this doctrine of for-getfulness. Where Rome is there is no liberty. If Rome had her way in Ulster there would be no liberty. Are we going back to darkness, back to Romanism, back to the tyranny and superstition of the Dark Ages? As Protestants we must remember the past. What happened when Rome ruled supreme? Was there peace? Was there light?

Nothing is new. Ulster is enabled rather than imprisoned by its past because the old historical universals persist. Thus, Paisley offers backward-looking politics, because the age-old challenge to Union continues; and he offers backward-looking theology, because the sixteenth-century disputes grounded in the Reformation still have not seen the victory over the Whore of Babylon and the antiChrist. Thus, to him there is no shame in looking backwards because the present is a reproduction of the past.

There is a view of the relationship between theology and politics contained in this approach to history which is drawn from sixteenth-century covenantal theology. For Paisley as for the covenanters like Knox, politics must be shaped by theology. The conditional loyalty implied in covenants which commentators emphasise as a feature of Paisleyism (Miller, 1978a; Akenson, 1992: 287), adheres only because theological commitments are primary to political ones. Paisley has said that he will remain British only so long as the Queen remains Protestant, because the exercise of political liberty is subordinate to his conception of theology (Taylor, 1983: 8). Covenantal theology best summarises this position. The greater loyalty is to God, who is seen as having underwritten a set of social and political arrangements which it is one's Christian duty to uphold while God's contract or covenant remains. Defence of the Union and vilification of Catholicism are part of the covenantal obligations. Ulster is God's gift to Protestants in Northern Ireland,[9] so defence of the Union is part of his commitment to God, and since Catholicism is unscriptural and unChristian, in attacking it he is demonstrating higher loyalty to God. This makes him feel immune to criticism and attack; he is certain that in defending the Union and in attacking Catholicism he is fighting the Lord's battle.

Biblical examples are drawn on frequently to dismiss criticism, for when attacked Paisley takes comfort in the self-appellation that he is a persecuted prophet. Over time he has drawn parallels between himself and the stoning of King David, the condemnation of Jesus, and the rejection of Jeremiah, Ezekiel and Elijah. The favourite role models are the Old Testament denunciation prophets – Jeremiah, Ezekiel and Elijah – who were warrior prophets warning of imminent danger to the faithful remnant from the mortal enemies which were within and around them. These prophets used strong language, were constantly vilified by the Godless enemies without and the faithless 'enemies within' and, except for a 'holy remnant', they were mostly ignored; yet they remained true to the message God had given them to preach. Paisley once wrote to Cardinal O'Fiaich, who complained about his intemperate language: 'as Elias [Elijah] stood on Carmel and cried out against the priests of Baal, so would I. I count no words too severe. If my every speech would be a thunderbolt, and every word a lightening flash, it would not be too strong to protest against the accursed system' (quoted in Cooke, 1996: 53–4). As for criticism, it merely reflects the great commission God had given him to defend the Union and preach against the antiChrist.

> Show me a man of whom is said every evil and wicked slander. Show me a man who becomes the recipient of wave after wave of condemnation, who is condemned out of hand, who is accused of the most outrageous of crimes, and I will show you a man whom God has commissioned, whom God has called, whom God has sent to be a prophet to his generation   (quoted in Taylor, 1983: 34).

With such a view of himself, every defeat can be reinterpreted to prove that he and his followers are right, every set-back explained away, and every means of resistance permissible. 'We refuse to allow a foreign priesthood to be forced upon us', wrote the *Protestant Telegraph* on 7 March 1970, 'like the covenanters of old, we shall resist this, even to prison and to death, and God shall defend the right'.

This raises the issue of Paisley's involvement in violence. His covenantal theology permits resistance against secular forces and circumstances which breach the covenant with God. History is full of role models of Protestant Reformers who resisted in order to reinstate the civil and political circumstances that God was believed to have ordained – Knox, Cromwell, Cameron – and Scripture is not short of examples of people who resisted kings and rulers at God's command; Jesus being the least obvious, however. Paisley's sermons and writings draw these historical parallels, but he has been careful to avoid direct participation in, or encouragement of, acts of violent resistance. He threatens it, he has relationships with people and organisations who commit it, many leading Loyalist paramilitaries worship with him at his church, he has organised large rallies and protests after which acts of violence have been committed by others, he was involved with the protests surrounding the Ulster Workers Strike and the Anglo-Irish Agreement which were often bloody and disorderly, but Paisley himself has been arrested only for unlawful assembly and imprisoned for failing to keep the peace by not promising to desist from leading more demonstrations. Much as critics might regret it, acts of violent resistance cannot be attributed to him, nor is there evidence of his direct encouragement of it.

However, Paisley is culpable by contributing to a culture of violence. This culture of violence is assisted in two ways: by the oblique remarks Paisley makes about violence, and by the manner in which he uses violent imagery. In his remarks about violence he implies in vague terms that violent resistance is sanctioned, and it is regularly threatened by means of florid language and provocative acts which hint at possible violence. Paisley's 'Third Force' in 1981 is a good example. At the time of meetings between the British and Irish Prime Ministers, Paisley organised, on a hill-top near Ballymena, a military-style parade of men wearing combat jackets and brandishing gun licences in a gesture to emulate Carson's UVF threats in 1912. He even organised a similar 'Carson trail' around Ulster with an equivalent to the 1912 Ulster Covenant which was more or less identical in content. His language was florid and frenzied. He accused his opponents in the Official Unionist Party of trying to assassinate him, he said that the Southern government had a 'noose specially prepared for the Protestants of Ulster' and that their hands were dripping with blood, and he described Irish Catholics in abhorrent terms. 'Our ancestors cut a civilisation out of the bogs and meadows while Mr Haughey's ancestors were wearing pig skins and living in caves. When our forefathers donned the British uniform and fought for their King and Country, Mr Haughey's fellow countrymen used their lights to guide enemy bombers to their targets in Northern Ireland' (quoted in Moloney and Pollack, 1986: 382). At the time of the Anglo-Irish Agreement in the mid-1980s civil disobedience towards the RUC was threatened and given some vague sort of sanction because the police had, according to Paisley, 'reaped what they sowed'. In October 1997, in yet another Carson trail around Northern Ireland trying to drum up mass support against the peace talks, but on this occasion with Robert McCartney in tow, Paisley said that Ulster was about to be slaughtered by a fascist-loving government that conducts love-ins with the IRA. For participating in negotiations about peace, the Unionist Party was accused of the same treason that led to the abandonment of Protestants in Southern Ireland in 1921, and he made warnings of resistance which would set the winds of fire alight in Ulster. The paradox of the man is that when he has brought the mobs on to the streets or hill-tops, worked them to a frenzy, threatened of violent consequences and vaguely sanctioned action in some form or other, he criticises them when they go too far. He has at times condemned Loyalists who carry out acts of terrorism, while he contributes himself to the very culture which causes it.

This culture of violence is not only reproduced in his elisions to violence but in the manner in which Paisley speaks. The main offence that critics can levy against Paisley is the use of violent metaphors and images in his rhetoric, which the mindless or militant can take as exhortations to violence, although Paisley's covenantal theology legitimises his manner of speaking. Even Presbyterians outside the covenanting tradition, let alone more liberal Christians, argue that, in the words of the government and church committee of the Presbyterian Church, 'those who initiate actions in volatile situations cannot evade total responsibility for the consequences of what they begin'. But according to Paisley, God defends the right and he is simply using the vocabulary of the Incarnate Son of God, who hated evil. But it is impossible to contemplate Jesus saying the following. 'Blood has ever been the price of liberty. Historically the blood of Ulster's youth has run till Boyne rivers flow blood red ... Today the battle is not yet won and sacrifices will have to be made ... Now is the time for Ulster to prepare for the final conflict ... Ulster arise and acknowledge your God. No surrender. No compromise' (*Protestant Telegraph*, quoted in Cooke, 1996: 159). This violent discourse is reproduced in the language of his supporters. Taylor quotes a young Free Presbyterian woman: 'I would just as soon as line my four children up against the wall and shoot them dead before I'd see them into the Church of Rome' (Taylor, 1983: 94). An elderly woman from his church used the same discourse: 'we will fight if we have to. We are sick of the prevailing evil in our midst. We have a cause to live for and we are prepared to die' (ibid.: 27).

Civil Unrest and 'The Troubles'

The outbreak of civil unrest in 1968, which has continued more or less non-stop since then, had roots much further back than partition. It reaches back to plantation when inequality between Catholics and Protestants was made government policy; inequality effortlessly reproduced itself in the eighteenth and nineteenth centuries once it became embedded in the social structure and affected politics, the economy, education, housing and employment. It worsened in the twentieth century with partition only because discrimination was enhanced by Protestant control of the state. The 'physical force' tradition of Irish Republicanism fed off these circumstances and had a measure of cultural (rather than political) legitimacy. Yet, strangely, by the 1960s, the majority of Northern Catholics would have been content with civil rights within Northern Ireland rather than the ending of partition. The demand for Catholic civil rights, however, contributed in part to the resumption of the hegemony of the anti-Catholic conservative evangelical tradition, represented by Paisleyism, over the constructive Unionism of O'Neill, ensuring that demands for civil rights were given an anti-Catholic spin. Amidst television coverage of police batoning unarmed civil rights marchers, unreconstructed Unionists like Craig abused civil rights supporters as Republicans, Paisleyites harassed them on marches with shouts of the big man's name and 'one Taig [derogatory term for Catholic], no vote', and the police went wild rampaging the Bogside in Derry because Catholics had the effrontery to march through a Protestant area, which local Protestants saw as an 'invasion' (Bardon, 1992: 661). A spate of bombings were attributed to the IRA but have been shown to be the responsibility of Loyalists in order to undermine O'Neill (Farell, 1976: 256; Bardon, 1992: 664). Mrs Paisley, speaking on behalf of her husband while he was in prison, announced that the bombs were the whirlwind reaped by O'Neill for his concessions to Catholics, despite the fact that the Catholic Church withdrew enthusiasm for Catholic civil rights once it saw the violence that the demand provoked (Rafferty, 1994: 261).

The Presbyterian Church in Ireland was, however, still in its ecumenical phase at the outbreak of 'the troubles'. The Annual Report of the General Assembly in 1969 expressed grave concern at the violent response which the demand for Catholic civil rights had caused. Religious loyalties, it argued, should not be used to foster social enmity, and it was critical of politicians who used religion for party interests. Reflecting the liberal trend, the report argued that religious loyalties should instead inspire 'concern for human need, for truth and justice and reconciliation'. 'We declare ourselves ready', the report ran, 'to meet with our Roman Catholic fellow-countrymen to explore in Christian charity our mutual needs and grievances. We call upon all citizens, and all who lead public opinion, to exercise the greatest restraint in speech and action, and to make new endeavour to understand those with whom they may be in political disagreement' (Presbyterian Church in Ireland, 1969: 4). It explained the violence as the harvest of past mistrust, suspicion and non-co-operation, and it described those who attacked the civil rights marches as dishonouring the cause they profess to defend: 'a grievous betrayal of the Protestant and Presbyterian principles of civil and religious liberty and respect for conscience. Avowed enemies of Christianity could not have done more damage to the faith than the things that [they] have said and done in the name of religion' (ibid.: 6). It acknowledged the 'blood brotherhood of enmity' in the Protestant heritage in Ulster, which it compared unfavourably with the way Catholics in the South had dealt 'fairly and even generously with the members of the Protestant minority'. A ministry of reconciliation was needed, discrimination should be abolished, and the churches should not seek to impose their own convictions and principles on others. Finally, it recorded that the differences between Catholicism and Protestantism were but those between brethren belonging together to the one Church of Jesus Christ.

The polarisation that occurred with 'the troubles' saw the Presbyterian Church in Ireland undergo a conversion toward conservative evangelicalism, with a drift away from ecumenism in the direction of anti-Catholicism. The Presbyterians pulled out of the ecumenical World Council of Churches in 1980, although six ministers, including John Dunlop, Ken Newell and John Morrow, had argued since 1978 against withdrawal (the Church also withdrew from the British Council of Churches in 1989); Paisley referred to the six ministers opposing isolation from ecumenism as agents of Satan. By 1986, the Presbyterian Church in Ireland was describing a concession to Catholics like the Anglo-Irish Agreement as unjust and the cause of a breakdown in the government's relationship with Protestants (ibid., 1986a: 2–3). After expressing the same wish as in 1969 for all to seek to love their neighbour and to do all that is in their power to effect reconciliation, it argued, contrary to 1969, that religious loyalties sometimes have to become politicised. The Anglo-Irish Agreement was a matter of such national importance and so unjust that 'to remain silent is to deny the prophetic nature of the church'. It gave the Irish government a say in Northern Irish affairs which would consolidate fear and apprehension, and was a 'denial of fundamental democratic rights' for Protestants. This was tame compared to what Free Presbyterians like Paisley said, but it reflects the hardening of attitudes amongst liberal churchmen arising from the changes in Protestant–Catholic relations because of terrorism and developments in Anglo-Irish relations. Involvement by the Irish Republic in Ulster's affairs raised constitutional issues and threatened the Union, while terrorism allowed an elision between anti-Catholicism and law and order issues, and it gave substance to the fear that a process of anti-Protestant ethnic cleansing was taking place.

This was inevitable given the conceptual framework through which Protestants have the world packaged and presented for them by conservative evangelicals, militant Loyalists, and Unionists. The change in Anglo-Irish relations and events during a quarter-century and more of civil unrest and terrorism were seen in terms of the images of the past. As Ruane and Todd explain it (1996: 95), Protestants were, in their world view, being pushed out of their traditional areas, even out of Ulster itself, they were under siege, beleaguered, embattled, subject to genocidal attack and ethnic cleansing (for a study of one Loyalist community where these views were widespread, see McAuley, 1994: 129–36; see also interviews in Bruce, 1994). The claim by conservative Protestants that this represents crude anti-Protestantism resonates in this climate. As Clifford Smyth expressed it in 1996, 'horror is being inflicted on war weary Ulster Protestants': 'nearly thirty years of terrorism from the mainly Roman Catholic Provisional IRA [is] aimed at forcing Ulster's Protestants into a united Ireland, where their religion, culture, language, history, traditions and sense of place – in fact everything that makes them a distinct people – will be suppressed and extinguished' (C. Smyth, 1996: 3). Letters in the columns of the *Belfast Telegraph* in recent years give voice to the same mind-set: 'the success of sectarian intimidation and the ethnic cleansing policies of successive Dublin governments [are] to extend to Northern Ireland'; 'the Ulster people will never accept being united with those whose hands are red with the blood of our kinsmen'; 'Protestants are being culturally cleansed'; 'the campaign to suppress Protestantism increases'; 'the IRA are all devout Catholics'; 'the Pope is the anti-Christ, he believes in a united Ireland'; 'oh people of Ulster, you are God's Israel, chosen seed, God gave your forefathers this land to be a light in darkest Ireland'; 'most of the world's terrorism is committed in Roman Catholic countries'; 'our liberty, dearly bought, is being thrown away'; 'let [us] obtain an apology from the Roman Catholic Church for its involvement in the horrific massacre throughout Ulster in 1641 when at least 30,000 settlers were brutally murdered in a single day by Irish nationalists'.

Terrorism by the IRA is thus also interpreted through the lens of the past: it represents simply the latest attempt by the Catholic Church to extirpate Protestants, a continuation of a strategy begun with the 1641 massacre. Lulls in their violence or even ceasefires are illusory and not to be trusted because IRA actions are but one strategy in a universal and ongoing battle by the Catholic Church against Protestantism. Terrorism has, however, given anti-Catholicism a new twist by disguising it as an issue of law and order. It is possible to claim that it is now Catholics who are confrontational and sectarian, with Protestants as innocent, unsuspecting and bemused victims. This is a view propounded by Clifford Smyth, for example, who wrote in a letter to Cardinal

Daly in 1996: 'the challenge facing the bishops of the Roman Catholic Church is to lead the Roman Catholic people out of a spirit of confrontation and aggression against their neighbours on this island, and into a spirit of acceptance' (reproduced in C. Smyth, 1996: 58). It is also now possible to claim that Catholics and the Catholic Church lack respect for law and order; indeed, that they advocate terrorism. A defence of law and order thus involves a justifiable attack on Catholicism.

There are three claims involved in this elision between anti-Catholicism and law and order. First is that the IRA is a Catholic organisation in ethos, membership, ambition and control. It is said to be run from the Vatican, works to the behest of the bishops, and intends to realise an all-Ireland Catholic state. Second, the violence and terrorism is yet more confirmation of the lawlessness, disloyalty and untrustworthiness of Catholic people because of their faith, either because Catholicism lacks moral discipline or their church uses lawlessness to fulfil its ambitions for universality. The final claim is that the Catholic Church has done little or nothing to condemn or stop the terrorism. The first two claims bear no credence, but the third is worth addressing because it is not so immediately crackpot. Its very plausibility, however, illustrates the level of deception involved in the elision between anti-Catholicism and law and order concerns.

There are two clauses to the claim: the Catholic Church has neither stopped nor condemned terrorism. An anti-Catholic caricature lies behind these beliefs, in that it is assumed that Catholics do precisely what the bishops tell them. However, the Catholic Church is not in reality the all-powerful and omnipotent organisation it is believed to be and it has been unable to stop terrorism or stem support for radical Republicanism, like Sinn Fein, despite trying. Sinn Fein's agenda for a secularised and socialist Ireland is as unattractive to the Catholic Church as Ulster Protestants, but the Catholic Church lost control of politics in the Catholic community from the 1950s onwards. The Catholic hierarchy have given their utmost support to constitutional nationalists but voters began to turn to Sinn Fein in increasing numbers from the 1956 by-election in mid-Ulster onwards. Although it was widely believed at the outbreak of civil unrest in 1968 that the Catholic Church could control nationalist politics – and the British Army sought the assistance of priests in having barricades in 'no go' areas lifted (Rafferty, 1994: 262–3) – people do not do what priests tell them. The failure of the Catholic Church to control nationalist politics is nowhere better demonstrated than during the Hunger Strikes in 1981 when even the intervention of the Pope did not prevent ten men dying, nor prevent a massive flow of electoral support to Sinn Fein afterwards. Even the constitutional nationalists, like the Social and Democratic Labour Party, have distanced themselves from the Catholic Church, and Sinn Fein is heavily critical of the Catholic Church.

The main criticism of Catholicism in terms of law and order issues is the supposed failure of the Church to condemn terrorism rather than its failure to stop it. Historically, however, the Catholic Church has always distanced itself from the 'physical force' tradition and has never encouraged violence, save for odd remarks in the seventeenth century during plantation (although even then, it was not behind the 1641 massacre). Consistently since the eighteenth century it has broadly supported Irish nationalism but never Republican organisations and never violence. Partition did not alter this. The IRA was resoundly condemned during the war of independence and the 1922 campaign. In October 1931, the bishops repeated their pastoral warning against Republican groups, mentioning the IRA and Saor Eire specifically. It was a theme Cardinal MacRory frequently returned to throughout the decade (see Rafferty, 1994: 231). Political violence was described by one bishop as the 'very gravest of sins against the law of God'; the army council of the IRA wrote to MacRory complaining of such pronouncements. The IRA's 1950s campaign, coinciding with an electoral breakthrough of Sinn Fein, alarmed the Catholic Church. Bishops D'Alton and Farren said that the violence only achieved bitterness, and a statement read at all masses in January 1956 solemnly denounced violence: indeed, the Catholic Church outlined in this statement a position on the use of force that was similar to Northern Protestants. Their covenantal theology legitimated resistance when against the evil men who were disowning the social and political arrangements supposedly ordained by God, while the Catholic Church argued that 'sacred Scripture gives the right to bear the sword and to use it against evil doers to the supreme authority, and to it alone' (quoted in ibid.: 251). It also declared in January 1956 that, 'it is a mortal sin for a Catholic to become or remain a member of an organisation which arrogates to itself the right to bear arms; it is sinful for a Catholic to co-operate with, express approval of, or otherwise assist any such organisation' (quoted in Cooke, 1996: 62–3). Lord Brookeborough welcomed the statement but added churlishly (and inaccurately) that he regretted it had not been made before. It came a few months before Paisley used vivid and violent imagery in *The Revivalist*: 'action speaks louder than words, and it is action – aggressive, militant, uncompromising action – which alone can save us. Oh for the sword of Gideon to slay the apostates and rid the land of tyrants': and this in response to education reform proposals which he felt sold 'Ulster Protestants down the river'.

The denunciations of violence by Catholic bishops have increased with the prolonged and violent IRA campaign since 1968, to a point where the bishops declared, in 1975, that 'our vocabulary of moral condemnation has been virtually exhausted'; no more stronger words were available to say 'unequivocally that it is utterly immoral' (quoted in Rafferty, 1994: 272). But the early years of 'the troubles' were problematic for the Northern hierarchy. Their flock had become politicised, widening the gulf between the Catholic Church and Catholic communities in the North, and the deterioration in law and order affected the partisanship of some priests. On an occasion early in 'the troubles', when one bishop preached against the IRA and told Catholics to stop supporting them, his house was surrounded by an angry crowd. The bishops refused to denounce internment and the Catholic Church on many occasions risked Republican anger. But in as much as the bishops lacked the power over ordinary Catholics that is ascribed to them, they also occasionally failed to influence the clergy, and in the early period of 'the troubles' there were demands from some priests for stronger statements in favour of Irish nationalism and weaker ones condemning violence. The Ulster Branch of the Association of Irish Priests, for example, wanted the hierarchy to condemn internment as immoral and a violation of basic human rights, although Paisley also criticised it when it meant the internment of Protestants (Cooke, 1996: 171). The official position of the bishops remained, but the actions of the priests have imprinted on the memory of critics of the Catholic Church. Actions by a few pro-IRA priests feature prominently in anti-Catholicism, but this loses sight of the small proportion they comprise and that it mostly occurred at the beginning, when violence by Loyalist paramilitaries and the British Army made it appear that the Catholic community was under siege. Two monks, for example, tried to assist escaping internees (see Rafferty, 1994: 267), and were fined £600. There was a general politicisation of the lower clergy in the first years of the civil unrest, and forty announced in April 1971 that they intended to boycott the 1971 census. Four months later the first priest was shot dead by the British Army while giving the last rites to another of their victims; a Church of Ireland bishop was condemned by the vestry of his diocese for attending the funeral since it was 'incompatible with the teaching of the church' to attend a Catholic mass. In December the Association of Irish Priests issued a statement supporting a united Ireland, and the following month a group of sixty priests disputed the view of the bishops that armed resistance could never be justified. Coogan's study of the IRA records that one priest went to the army council asking them to assassinate Paisley (Coogan, 1995: xiii). Rafferty reports that some lower clergy were disgruntled at the moderate stance taken by their bishops (Rafferty, 1994: 268), although greater numbers denounced violence and called upon Catholics, for example, to support the security forces. An interview with veteran Republican Jimmy Drumm, the most interned man in the British Isles, who has been interned in every decade from the 1930s to the 1970s, revealed that in his estimate, the IRA received most opposition from the Catholic Church. Priests refused them the sacraments, bishops influenced priests to be hostile, and he claimed that no priest was ever a member of the IRA.

The lower clergy began to be depoliticised with direct rule in 1972, which the Catholic Church welcomed, and the escalation in the barbarism during the early 1970s, with the arrival of no-warning civilian attacks by both sets of paramilitaries. The scenes of devastation on days like 'Black Friday', when the IRA let off twenty-two no-warning bombs on civilian targets, appalled priests, and there were ecumenical services held on the sites, although Paisley abused them in the *Protestant Telegraph* as 'ecumenical stunts' and reminded readers that 'Rome is behind the troubles – that is an indisputable fact'. But the violence ended any romantic notions priests had about the IRA. Later in 1972, for example, groups of clergy in Belfast and Derry called on the IRA to stop the violence, and bishops took to visiting internees and prisoners in the hope of persuading them to use their experience to encourage colleagues on the outside to desist (Rafferty, 1994: 271), although writing in the *Protestant Telegraph* Paisley asserted that this merely confirmed that the 'Provisional IRA is in reality the armed wing of the Roman Catholic Church. Its real aim is to annihilate Protestantism'. The Catholic Church signed up to a joint declaration by all the main churches in 1976 which stated that Christians had a *prima facie* moral obligation to support the authorities in Ireland, North and South, against paramilitary forces; Free Presbyterians did not attend the meetings to draw up the declaration. Some priests refused burial services to dead terrorists, others agreed only if there were no Republican emblems. 'Paramilitary funerals' have thus been rare, and in 1975 Edward Daly, Bishop of Derry, warned the IRA that there would be a total ban on funerals unless Republican paraphernalia was removed from the coffin before being brought into church (ibid.: 272). However, the Catholic Church was sending out conflicting messages by the end of the decade. On the one hand Tomas O'Fiaich, as the new Cardinal, called in 1979 for British withdrawal, while during his visit to Ireland the same year, the new Pope issued a passioned plea for peace:

[violence] is unacceptable as a solution to problems. Violence is a lie [It] destroys what it claims to defend: the dignity, the life, the freedom of human beings. Peace cannot be established by violence, peace can never flourish in a climate of terror. Nobody may ever call murder by another name than murder. I appeal to you in language of passionate pleading. On my knees I beg you to turn away from the paths of violence and return to the ways of peace. Violence only delays the days of justice.

This was said despite the claim of the Orange Order that the Pope acquiesced in the rape of Ulster and in the murder of its citizens, and some Northern Presbyterians refused to meet him because of 'theological differences'. The Reformed Presbyterian Church in Ireland reminded people that Catholicism 'is the negation of the gospel of Christ'. Paisley also criticised the visit and took another opportunity to proclaim the Pope as the antiChrist, 'the man of sin in the Church'. On this occasion he added, inaccurately, that the papacy had been behind the 1916 Easter Rising.

Cardinal O'Fiaich's stance was a minority position, however. Cahal Daly, later himself to replace O'Fiaich as leader of Irish Catholicism, took a strong line against the IRA. At the time at which the Cardinal was urging British withdrawal, meeting with Sinn Fein, and comparing the conditions in Long Kesh to that of the homeless in Calcutta, Daly took his lead from the Pope and told the IRA and Sinn Fein that the Catholic Church would not support the right to political status for terrorist prisoners. The IRA's was an 'immoral and anti-national campaign which respected no one's rights' (see Rafferty, 1994: 278). Both Daly and O'Fiaich, however, urged the hunger strikers, protesting at the removal of political status, to relent; so did the Pope, and all were ignored. The death of the first hunger striker was not marked by a public mass for him in his diocese. It was a Catholic priest who eventually negotiated an end to the protest (see Beresford, 1987), and Daly later issued the following pastoral letter: 'no end, however good, can ever justify means which are evil ... when the means are evil, the ends they achieve will be evil also. This is nothing to do with politics. This is a question of morality' (reproduced in Daly, 1983: 14–15). In short, violence is sinful. This became hegemonic when Cahal Daly assumed the position of Cardinal on O'Fiaich's death in 1990. In 1991 he wrote categorically of Republican paramilitary organisations: 'no faithful Catholic can claim that there is moral justification for the violence of these organisations' (Daly, 1991: 52–3). He said this at a time when Paisley was writing about what he called 'the Roman Catholic Irish Republican Army'. But perhaps the final remark to quell the idea that the Catholic Church has not condemned IRA terrorism could be left to Edward Daly, Bishop of Derry, speaking in 1986, when some Protestant clergymen and preachers, amongst others, were threatening, advocating and, in some cases, participating in violence in protest against the Anglo-Irish Agreement. Daly wrote in the *Irish Voice* that men of violence and their supporters lived totally contrary to the teachings of Jesus, and he warned them in words which were also relevant to the Protestant churchmen who were associating with acts of violence at the time:

> If you wish to choose the devil rather than Christ, be honest with yourselves and declare yourselves to be no longer Christians because your lives and your actions are utterly inconsistent. If you cannot accept Christ's words and teachings or utterly reject him, then leave Him, leave Christ.

Anti-Catholicism in the Late 1990s

Direct rule has limited the extent to which anti-Catholicism permeates Northern Ireland's social structure because Protestants no longer control the local state, but it continues at the levels of ideas and behaviour. It also exists outside the ideas and behaviour of the prominent leaders of Northern Irish Protestantism and Unionism, and can be found in the comments and conduct of ordinary people who do not feature in historical narratives. Here I will demonstrate some of the more mundane reproductions of anti-Catholic ideas and behaviour in the last decade of the second millennium, nearly five centuries after the Reformation.

Anti-Catholicism has political and theological expressions in the comments of ordinary people today, but is primarily oriented to local political concerns. However, the formulaic phrases grounded in theology are reproduced in interviews. A middle-aged male Free Presbyterian said of the doctrine of the Roman Catholic Church, 'it is a false church based on a lot of tradition ... the Church of Rome will head for the judgement of God, as it says in Revelation 17'. An interviewee with the same background said much the same: 'I don't believe in the Church of Rome, their doctrines and what they teach, yet I do believe there are Christians in it, but they should come out of it ... I believe the Roman Catholic Church is the Whore of Babylon, a system which is contrary to the word of God.' A trainee minister in the Presbyterian Church expressed only a slightly more liberal view: 'I see the Roman Church as a Christian church in error. I believe there are people who are saved or born again within that Church, but the church itself isn't in standing with the Christian community as such, and would need reform.' Another Presbyterian ministry student said that 'evangelical Catholics need to withdraw from that Church'.

Ecumenism is anathema to these sorts of respondents. A Free Presbyterian said: 'I could not sacrifice biblical doctrine because of unity. A man would have to believe in the doctrines I love in order to truly have fellowship.' Another said, 'I honestly have no time for the ecumenical movement ... To me there can be no reconciliation between what Rome teaches and the Scriptures. I don't believe light can have any fellowship with darkness.' Ecumenism was to blame, according to one Free Presbyterian, for all the ills of Northern Ireland: 'the ecumenical movement is set for a one-world Church. There'd be no leader but the Pope. That's why the country's in the state it's in. People are confused, all these ecumenical services where it doesn't matter what you believe, anything goes.' A trainee minister for the Presbyterian Church was in favour of ecumenism so long as it was restricted to Protestant churches: 'I have no problem with ecumenism within Protestant denominations, but I would see areas where the Protestant churches should not be working with the Catholic Church ... In the Protestant churches the word of God would be central to our worship, I'm not sure that's central to the Roman Catholic tradition.' However, a middle-aged Baptist woman said of such attitudes: 'I'd love to see one Church, we could all be Christians together. I think ecumenism is frowned upon because they don't know exactly what is involved in it. I'd love to see all denominations worshipping together, I would include the Catholic Church.'

The letters pages of local newspapers often give vent to theological disputes, especially at critical junctures in wider Protestant–Catholic relations. Following a high-profile ecumenical event in 1995, readers were reminded by one letter-writer that, 'the Roman Catholic system is not only imperfect it is unreformable. Its very foundation is built on erroneous revelation ... Catholicism is not Christian.' Another correspondent argued, following the same event, 'Bible-believing Christians should not be sitting down in fellowship with Roman Catholics'. Any shift away from biblical truth amongst conservative evangelicals pours forth people pointing out the error. The attendance at an ecumenical event of a particular Presbyterian minister who had strong connections with the Orange Order, provoked much advice about the risk to his salvation. By his attendance he had been sinful, and contravened the Orange Order oath: 'he should strenuously oppose the fatal errors and doctrines of the Church of Rome and scrupulously avoid countenancing any act or ceremony of popish worship'. The furore provoked by the Irish Republic's President, Mary McAleese, receiving Communion, as a Catholic, in a Protestant church in December 1997, led to a spate of letters. It put some conservative evangelical correspondents in a difficult position. The criticism of President McAleese by the Catholic hierarchy, for trying, as Monsignor Denis Faul put it, to impossibly serve two churches, two brides and two loyalties at the same time, only confirmed them in their suspicion that the Catholic Church is imperialist and unreformed in believing itself the one true church, even though only 12 per cent of ordinary Catholics supported the hierarchy's criticism in a public opinion poll, while also confirming for them that ecumenism is a 'Romeward trend' from which nothing good can come.

Mostly, however, articulations of anti-Catholicism by ordinary people link it to various political conspiracies and events. In interviews conducted during 1997, many respondents felt Catholicism to be a political phenomenon not a religion. As one Free Presbyterian said: 'the Roman Catholic Church is a political organisation. The Vatican is a political state.' Another member of the same denomination said: 'the Church of Rome is involved in politics ... I think Rome has a big say in the back room.' An elderly Presbyterian businessman described Catholicism as fascist, which he compared to the 'tremendous amount of free thought' in Presbyterianism, commenting, without seeing any irony, 'we tolerate people with diverse views'. While Catholicism was inclined to fascism, for another interviewee Protestantism inclined to Unionism: 'Unionism is based around the historic fact of Great Britain's system of government being based around Christianity. The Irish Republic is anti-English, anti-Protestant, which is why I believe Unionism is right.' This is why one Free Presbyterian said charmingly, 'I would have no problem with a united Ireland if it was under British rule ... [but] I believe it would be a Roman Catholic dominated thing, the British way of life would be what I would favour.' However, other respondents did not feel that Unionism was anointed by God, 'I don't think it's a case of "For God and Ulster".' Interviews undertaken by Duncan Morrow amongst Protestants in the Portadown area following the stand-off at Drumcree in 1996, which saw widespread disorder before the Orange Order was permitted to walk the Garvaghy Road, show the fears ordinary Protestants have of Catholicism's alleged political activity (Morrow, 1997). 'It's a land thing', one said, 'the Protestants here are afraid of being taken over. They see the border creeping down and there's no place to run' (ibid.: 14). 'I just feel the Protestants are losing their foothold. I feel that the government is always trying to woo Sinn Fein' (ibid.); 'there's a suspicion here. They don't trust the Roman Catholics. They've all lost relations. They tend to equate Roman Catholicism with republicanism' (ibid.: 19); 'there's a real fear of Roman Catholicism and its imperialist methods. They're seen as wanting to dominate' (ibid.: 31). Thus it was that 'King Rat', a Loyalist in Portadown who was connected with the Loyalist Volunteer Force before his assassination, allegedly killed a Queen's graduate, Michael McGoldrick, in response to Drumcree because he was the nearest available Catholic.

Such is the commode-like quality of anti-Catholicism, that all issues can be interpreted as evidence of the political malevolence of the Catholic Church. Writing in the letters column of the *Belfast Telegraph* on 31 July 1996, one correspondent from Portadown said that the Drumcree stand-off between the RUC and the Orange Order proved that Roman Catholicism is the 'supreme embodiment of fascism ... The Roman Church seeks to regain its spiritual and social ascendancy in Europe.' Although it was the Orange Order who did battle with the police, and Loyalists who rampaged throughout Northern Ireland when the Orange Order was initially refused permission to march, Drumcree supposedly saw Catholicism at its worst, secretly, surreptitiously working in the background to defeat Protestantism and Unionism. Thus, one of Morrow's interviewees said that the 1996 stand-off was necessary because it was a zero-sum conflict between 'them or us': 'in Drumcree, if we lost we'd lose everything. We've given and given and given and we've nothing in return. The whole problem was the Roman Catholic Church; their church backs them' (Morrow, 1997: 46). In 1997, when the Orange Order was allowed to march down Garvaghy Road for the third year in succession and this time Catholics went on the rampage, the Catholic Church was blamed again for orchestrating the disorder. 'Fascism, the child of Romanism is not dead', said a speaker to the Independent Orange Order in Ballycastle on 12 July 1997. The IRA was described as 'the Beast of Roman fascism', and the speaker went on to say that eight out of ten Protestants in the South had been eliminated – 'shades of Hitler' – and Protestants in the North could expect the same from residents groups who challenged the right of Orangemen to march.

The high level of fancy involved in this historical fiction shows how the issue of Orange marches in the late 1990s touches something more important than space and territory, for it is being interpreted by Protestants in terms of the age-old elision between space, territory and identity. A denial of the right to march by residents' groups is seen as a denial of Protestant identity and heritage; the defence of the right to march is a defence both of Union and Protestantism. The right to march is thus understood in terms of the same two antinomies that have governed Protestant identity since plantation, for marching is an expression of Britishness (against Irishness) and Protestantism (against Catholicism). Hence, anti-Catholicism is an inevitable by-product of the marching issue. The defence of the right to march is given an anti-Catholic spin, and attacks on residents groups which deny this right feature abusive anti-Catholicism.

This is illustrated well by demonstrations like those at Harryville, in Ballymena, where a Catholic church had been surrounded by Loyalists and Orangemen and women for nearly two years, with worshippers harassed, intimidated and abused at the church, in protest at the denial of the right to march. The protest is presented as a response to the actions of the residents in Dunloy, assisted by the RUC, who successfully challenged the right of Orangemen to march through the Catholic village, a few miles from Ballymena. But the fact that the protest focuses on a Catholic church in nearby Ballymena, the heart of the fundamentalist 'Bible belt' in Ulster, reveals the anti-Catholicism wrapped up in it. During a sermon in Ballymena, a visiting pastor, Alan Campbell, argued that what is really going on in Harryville is the ancient battle between the true Church, Protestantism, and the Whore, the Beast, and the Baal worshippers within Catholicism.[10] He told listeners that this had to be a battle to the finish, and one which the Harryville worshippers had to lose to avoid Protestantism suffering a major defeat and Romanism and ecumenism a triumph. In Campbell's mind-set the marching issue represents an 'orchestrated campaign by Romanism to face Protestantism down', an example of 'bigoted Romanist sectarianism'. The defence of space and territory in Dunloy thus becomes translated as an issue of identity fought out in Harryville. The protesters supposedly were representatives of the true Church, with an illustrious heritage of ancestors burned alive because they would not worship the wafer God; they were Protestant, loyalist, Unionist and British. The

Catholic church subject to the protest was referred to continually as a 'Romish mass house', and worshippers abused by being called 'Ballymena Papists', 'Romanists', 'Baal worshippers', 'Republicans', and 'worshippers of a wafer God'. The police who protected the worshippers from the baying crowds were 'guardians of the wafer God', and Protestants who joined the worshippers in a show of support were ecumenists 'kissing and hugging papists', who had 'allied themselves to God's enemies', 'playing footsie with the Beast, Scarlet Woman, Mother of Harlots and Baal worshippers'.

The absorption of space and territory into identity is reflected in other incidents in the late 1990s where Protestants have defended a locality against what is seen as encroaching Irishness and Catholicism, the antinomies against which Protestants define their identity. Thus, in June 1997, residents in a working-class Protestant area drew on such themes to understand the social changes affecting their area as a result of the operation of the housing market. The area is near to Queen's University and two hospitals and has become a popular location for students and young professionals. House prices have risen, properties have been converted to flats, outsiders are moving in, and local families feel squeezed. However, these processes were presented to residents in terms of the identity concerns of Britishness and Protestantism. Posters were displayed in the area saying that Loyalist people have 'tolerated long enough the nationalist scum that have flooded into the area due to the unscrupulous behaviour of greedy landlords'. The detrimental effects this had on the Loyalist community were understood as increasing the risk to them from Republican terrorists. 'Do you know who lives next door to you', the poster asked, and it went on to warn that it is 'unwise to have a nationalist as a neighbour and even worse to befriend them'. 'As from 12 noon on the 1 July 1997,' the poster read, 'the Loyalist people will no longer be able to guarantee the safety of any nationalist who chooses to remain within the area, nor can they guarantee the safety of any property where nationalists are dwelling.' It was perceived by others as a Catholic witch-hunt.

Because identity is treated as equivalent to space and territory, the boycott issue has also become an expression of anti-Catholicism (and anti-Irishness). The boycott strategy was employed in Northern Ireland in the twentieth century first by Protestants who sought to advantage Protestant unemployed during the 1930s, although it goes back to the nineteenth century when Catholics used it first in the dispute over evictions.[11] However, it was used effectively in some local areas after the 1996 Drumcree stand-off, when some Catholics boycotted the businesses of Orangemen who had been allowed by force to march in Catholics areas. To someone like Clifford Smyth, however, boycotts represented an attack on Protestant space and territory by denying Protestants their livelihood, forcing them from areas where they had long been, which was an attack on their identity. In his pamphlet on the boycott in 1996, Smyth claims that the strategy is prophesied in Scripture as a feature of the 'beast system' and the antiChrist, understood to be Catholicism and the Pope, which are using the strategy to suppress and extinguish Protestantism in Ulster (C. Smyth, 1996: 3). It is, he says, 'silent ethnic cleansing' by pushing Protestants from

areas formerly their own, and represents the latest example of the Roman Catholic community's persecution of Protestants: it is 'terrorism without the sound of exploding bombs', and represents an attack on the Britishness and Protestantism of Ulster. Amongst the claims made in advancing the argument are that the IRA is Catholic (ibid.: 3) and supported by the Catholic hierarchy and priests (ibid: 27), that Catholicism is the antiChrist (ibid.: 2, 30), that it is linked to international conspiracies like the rise of Nazism (ibid.: 12–13), that it predisposes believers to violence (ibid.: 25), that it dupes and intoxicates the unsuspecting (ibid.: 30), and that Catholics are always whining and complaining, never being satisfied (ibid.: 62). An attack was made also on Irishness, with the Republic supposedly ignoring the 'sufferings of those who refuse to embrace' an Irish identity (ibid.: 17), there was a process of Hibernicisation of culture in Ulster (ibid.: 26), and that it was only with plantation that a Christian culture was introduced in Ireland (ibid.: 34). He ended his analysis by predicting civil war in Ulster (ibid.: 36) unless people embraced Protestant, Christ-centred religion.

One of the saddest manifestations of the elision between space, territory and identity was the murder of Bernadette Martin in July 1997. She was a young Catholic who had a Protestant boyfriend, at whose house in an overwhelmingly Protestant village she occasionally slept. Bernadette was invading space and territory, and thus this harmless teenager, whose father said at her funeral that she did not even know who the Provisional IRA were, was killed in the dead of night, with four bullets pumped into the back of her head, simply because she threatened the Protestantness of the village. Five days later an IRA ceasefire was announced, although her murderers were Loyalists supposedly already under a ceasefire. The IRA ceasefire was ridiculed by the leading churchmen and politicians of the conservative evangelical and militantly Unionist tradition on grounds that it imperilled the Union and threatened Protestantism. A Baptist woman could have spoken to the churchmen who said thus, when in one of our interviews in 1997 she remarked: 'if political parties want to call themselves "Christian", they need to take their Bibles a bit more seriously and love one another instead of always looking to the past'.

Part II

Sociological Features of Contemporary Anti-Catholicism

Part I has attempted to show that anti-Catholicism in Northern Ireland is a sociological process for the production of different rights, opportunities and material rewards between people in a society where religious labels are used to define group boundaries. However, to fully understand and locate a sociological process, more is necessary than simply explaining its origins and use in terms of the 'social item' it produces, for it is also important to describe its character and form as they help to produce this social item. It is thus important to outline the types of contemporary anti-Catholicism and identify the ways in which they produce social stratification and social closure. An analysis of contemporary articulations of anti-Catholicism demonstrates that it has distinct modes. Not all function as resources in this manner but the main types, called the covenantal and secular modes, produce social stratification and social closure within a distinct cultural milieu. Anti-Catholicism does not operate as a resource to produce these social items in every society, for it is demarcated by a cultural context in which theology can stand for and represent other sorts of differences and conflicts between people.

It might be doubted that there are distinct types of anti-Catholicism, since from the beginning of the nineteenth century, conservative evangelicalism has provided the sacred canopy around Protestants when their identity seemed to be under threat from local Catholics, the British, or Anglo-Irish relations generally, and this casts anti-Catholicism in a single form. The canopy first appeared in the 1830s at the time of Catholic emancipation and other events, and it showed itself forcefully whenever people's Britishness and Protestantism seemed under threat from their antinomies (Irishness and Catholicism respectively), such as during debates about Home Rule and partition, the O'Neill period, and throughout 'the troubles'. Conservative evangelicalism offers a secure identity in its very strong invocation of the two defining tenets of that identity, Britishness and Protestantism, which is attractive when either seems threatened. This accounts in the modern period for the appeal of Paisleyism (see Bruce, 1986, 1994; Wallis et al. 1986; Akenson, 1992) and explains why his Free Presbyterian Church, established in 1951, languished until O'Neillism emerged in the mid-1960s (Bruce, 1994: 19).

However, this is not to argue that conservative evangelicalism is the preferred form of religious expression for Protestants, nor that all Protestants are religious. It means only that conservative evangelicalism successfully articulates an identity, and people can buy into the identity it constructs – Britishness and Protestantism – during a crisis or threat even if they are not themselves conservative evangelicals or religious (a similar point is made by Bruce, 1994: 25). Wright (1973) has shown that secular Protestants, who are not churchgoers themselves, none the less still impart the conservative evangelical tradition to their children by insisting on attendance at Sunday Schools and membership of youth brigades, and would themselves have attended the same and imbibed the symbols, myths and paraphernalia of evangelicalism. They may now be uncertain or marginal believers but Wright argued that they see 'belief as a "good thing", something to be valued', even if for others (1993: 245–6). Wallis et al. likewise argue (1986: 5) that secular Protestants in Northern Ireland are attached to the symbols of religion despite their own low level of church participation because they are so exposed to conservative evangelicalism. In part this is also because there are no alternative lines of division other than religion in Northern Ireland around which to construct identity, as Bruce later argued (1994: 28), so closely do religion, politics, nationhood and locality coincide; the simple zero-sum is a binary game. There are 'Bible Protestants', the religious fundamentalists like the Free Presbyterians and the small gospel-hall-goers, who would be conservative evangelicals, but it is the identity conservative evangelicalism constructs that *most* people find appealing rather than conservative evangelicalism itself (a similar point is made by Bell, 1990: 64). This explains why Paisley, for example, attracts support well beyond the numbers in his church and amongst people whose ethics, beliefs and behaviour are not religious, let alone evangelical (see Wallis et al., 1986: 25; for comments made by Protestant youth which illustrate this, see Bell, 1990: 164).

Notwithstanding this powerful argument, however, conservative evangelicalism is not the sole rallying cry for Ulster Protestants. Because it is an identity that most people are buying into rather than conservative evangelicalism itself, there are alternative sources from which people can purchase this pro-British, pro-Union identity, such as secular forms of militant Loyalism and secular Unionism. In what is now a very popular duality, Todd (1987) contrasted Ulster Loyalist and Ulster British identities, the former seeing themselves as Ulster Protestants first and British second; the latter, vice versa (for another attempt to classify types of Unionist identity see Porter, 1996; on developments within what he calls 'new Unionism', see O'Dowd, 1998). Porter (1996: xi) has argued that the former identity, which he calls 'cultural unionism', exaggerates Protestantism as an identity marker. However, Ulster Loyalists are divided between what Bruce (1994: 2) calls the evangelicals and the gunmen; that is, the conservative evangelicals and the secular Loyalists, for whom Protestantism is an ethnic and social identity rather than a theological commitment. The Ulster British identity on the other hand valorises Britishness and, if not secular, is liberal in its Protestantism, and mostly puts a hermetic seal between religion and politics. Porter (1996: xi) described it as 'liberal unionism' and said that it stripped Unionism of its Protestantism, aspiring to a liberal politics in common with the rest of the United Kingdom, in which religion is kept out of public life. In secular forms of Unionism and Loyalism, the defence of the Union is inviolate but their articulation of the other trait historically important to Protestants, their Protestantism, is underplayed or is nominal, ensuring that they have difficulty in appealing to 'Bible Protestants', leaving them with a constituency for whom Protestantism is less central to their identity. Bruce (1994) argues that it is for this reason that conservative evangelicalism is the most attractive and popular articulation of identity because it puts value on both Protestantism and Britishness, and resonates with the high levels of religiosity in Northern Ireland. But not all Protestants are religious, nor do all see the two tenets as indissoluble or value them equally, and competing sources of identity construction challenge the dominance of conservative evangelicalism.

Empirical data on identity amongst Protestants focuses on national identity, a narrower issue, but some findings are revealing. Reviewing the survey evidence on Protestant national identity since 1968, Trew (1996: 142) shows that the proportion of Protestants describing themselves as 'British' rose from 39 to 71 per cent between 1968 and 1994, with a similar reduction in those describing themselves as 'Irish' or 'Ulster', the latter falling from 32 to 11 per cent. This reflects the polarisation that occurred during 'the troubles' and the security many Protestants found in Britishness as an identity. Analysing 1994 data from the Northern Ireland Social Attitude Survey on national identity, Breen shows that four-fifths of Protestants defined their national identity as either 'British' or 'Ulster', only 3 per cent said 'Irish' (Breen, 1996: 37). Of the 'British' or 'Ulster' identifiers, 94 per cent supported Union. He concludes that irrespective of any differences between 'British' or 'Ulster' identities, in their constitutional preferences they are the same (ibid.: 45). Thus, if Protestantism is not necessarily a strong source of identity among secular Unionists and Loyalists, Britishness and the Union is. Union is important to other Protestants, however, precisely because it is indissoluble from Protestantism, while to others it is less important than Protestantism, some of whom would wish to remain British only in so far as Britain remained Protestant. This is relevant to anti-Catholicism because it is a mistake to see it as monolithic in character, associated only with the tradition of conservative evangelicalism. Protestants can construct their identity from other sources, religious or secular, and anti-Catholicism remains an important part of that identity, although it takes on a different form than in conservative evangelicalism. In short, anti-Catholicism is still integral to secular forms of Protestant identity.

Anti-Catholicism is a general cultural motif in Northern Ireland, with strong historical roots and many contemporary cultural representations, from Orange marches, doctrinal statements of faith by churches, to graffiti on gable walls. It is something which can be internalised without forethought, and reproduced unthinkingly in language – 'Taigs', 'Fenians', 'Papists', 'fuck the Pope' – because it is represented in so much cultural iconography, such as paintings, murals, poems, songs, writings, and painted kerbstones. It is reproduced on Orange Order banners, in church hymnals, and by means of tattoos – 'Remember 1690', 'No Surrender', 'UVF' can be seen on some bare-chested torsos. It is part of the sectarian culture of the place – it seeps into the very pores of the province – and like many cultural symbols it can be imbibed unreflexively, without thought or systematic formulation, and reproduced unthinkingly in language with no malicious or discriminatory intent. Where anti-Catholicism is unsystematic at the level of ideas and not reflected in behaviour it can be described as 'passive anti-Catholicism': the kind that some Protestants have transmitted to them as part of their social learning but which remains as a cultural backdrop, rarely articulated or enacted. 'Active anti-Catholicism' is something different and represents a fully formulated structure of ideas, language and behaviour. It is this kind that anti-Catholicism that is addressed in the typology.

Three types of active anti-Catholicism are distinguishable, called the covenantal, secular and Pharisaic modes. They are empirical rather than ideal types. That is, they exist as real types used by real people, although they are not pure types in that an individual's anti-Catholicism is rarely composed of just one. However, they do have a 'primary constituency' to which the type mainly appeals. They are systems of real belief and action, and they have an identifiable structure and form, as represented in Figure 3.

Each mode has a common structure, with its own set of foundational ideas on which it is premised, using a characteristic form of rhetoric by which to express anti-Catholicism; each emphasises different things in the articulation of anti-Catholicism, appeals to a different primary constituency and has different implications for relationships with Catholics. A summary of the three modes is reproduced in Figure 4.

It was argued in the Introduction that anti-Catholicism has political and theological dimensions, which were presented in diagrammatic form in Figure 1 (p. 4). The modes stress the political and theological dimensions of anti-Catholicism in different proportion, as shown in Figure 5. This diagram neatly captures the paradox of anti-

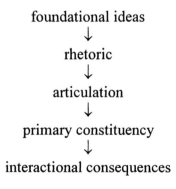

foundational ideas
↓
rhetoric
↓
articulation
↓
primary constituency
↓
interactional consequences

Figure 3   The structure of the three modes of anti-Catholicism

Catholicism in Northern Ireland, in that it can be grounded in an interpretation of Scripture (covenantal and Pharisaic modes), which may (covenantal mode) or may not (Pharisaic mode) have political expression, and also be relatively devoid of theology and highly political (secular mode), emphasising an approach to the Union much like one of the more theological modes (the covenantal). This highlights the point that although they are empirical rather than ideal types, they do not exist in pure form in people's language and behaviour because there is overlap in the concerns of each mode and people articulate this cross-over in their own version of anti-Catholicism. There is cross-over, for example, between the anti-Catholicism of, say, Paisley and militant Loyalists: Paisley incorporates both convenantal and secular modes, while militant Loyalists usually draw on the secular mode and

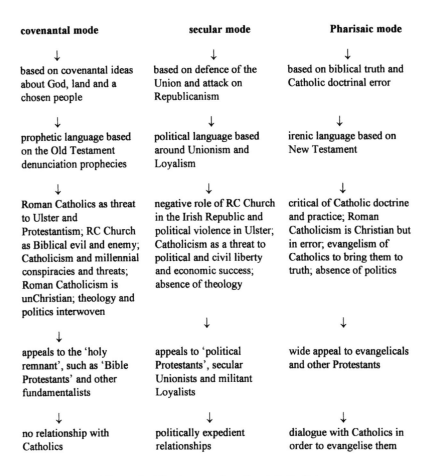

covenantal mode	secular mode	Pharisaic mode
↓	↓	↓
based on covenantal ideas about God, land and a chosen people	based on defence of the Union and attack on Republicanism	based on biblical truth and Catholic doctrinal error
↓	↓	↓
prophetic language based on the Old Testament denunciation prophecies	political language based around Unionism and Loyalism	irenic language based on New Testament
↓	↓	↓
Roman Catholics as threat to Ulster and Protestantism; RC Church as Biblical evil and enemy; Catholicism and millennial conspiracies and threats; Roman Catholicism is unChristian; theology and politics interwoven	negative role of RC Church in the Irish Republic and political violence in Ulster; Catholicism as a threat to political and civil liberty and economic success; absence of theology	critical of Catholic doctrine and practice; Roman Catholicism is Christian but in error; evangelism of Catholics to bring them to truth; absence of politics
↓	↓	↓
appeals to the 'holy remnant', such as 'Bible Protestants' and other fundamentalists	appeals to 'political Protestants', secular Unionists and militant Loyalists	wide appeal to evangelicals and other Protestants
↓	↓	↓
no relationship with Catholics	politically expedient relationships	dialogue with Catholics in order to evangelise them

Figure 4   The three modes of anti-Catholicism

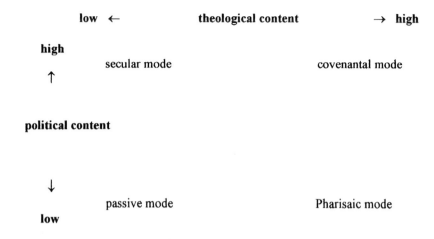

Figure 5   Plotting the modes of anti-Catholicism along the two axes

borrow very rarely from Paisley's theological ideas. Other points follow from the schema in Figure 5. The different primary constituencies to which each mainly appeals points to the fragmentation within Protestantism between the political and theological, the secular and religious modes of expression and sources of identity, which challenges the notion that conservative evangelicalism is the sole or primary source of identity. Second, the implications each type has for establishing relationships with Catholics illustrates the difficulties ahead for peace and compromise during the second ceasefire unless there is a decommissioning of Protestant mind-sets as well as of Republican arms. Part II identifies the modes of anti-Catholicism and addresses some of the sociological features which underlie them and by means of which the modes help to produce social stratification and social closure. These features include examination of the common-sense reasoning processes which support anti-Catholicism, the 'cognitive map' on which it is based, and the sociological dynamics of the language used to express it.

4 The Modes of Contemporary Anti-Catholicism

Introduction

This chapter will address the three modes of active anti-Catholicism, since they constitute the forms and nature of contemporary anti-Catholicism in Northern Ireland. However, each mode can itself be sociologically unpacked, and this chapter identifies the character of each mode, focusing on four themes which define their nature: their foundational ideas, the form of rhetoric deployed, the content of the articulation, and their primary constituency. The chapter also addresses the implications of each mode for Protestant–Catholic relations, and identifies the main challenges that can be made to its foundational ideas. The covenantal mode is considered first, followed by the secular and Pharisaic modes. The latter has no implications at the social structural level and is not used as a resource in social stratification and social closure, but it none the less constitutes an important type of active anti-Catholicism.

The Foundational Ideas of the Covenantal Mode

The defining ideas of the covenantal mode of anti-Catholicism are found in the biblical notion of covenant, and its reformulation by Ulster Scots to describe a political contract between ruler and ruled. In Scripture, God makes a binding contract with His 'chosen people' to give them land so long as they show unstinting loyalty to Him. Both parties are obligated by the terms of the covenant, including God, who promises undreamt of blessings for those who love Him, but the loss of land and prosperity for those who renege. Israelites kept their covenantal terms by following the Judaic Law established by Moses as God's Commandments; God kept His covenantal terms by continuing to bless His people by tying them to the land of Israel. As reformulated by Scottish Presbyterians and Ulster Scots in the sixteenth century, covenants are as much political contracts as theological ones, for they underwrite a set of social and political arrangements which are seen as God-given and which are said to reflect loyalty to Him. These notions shape the foundational ideas of the covenantal mode of anti-Catholicism.

The following beliefs define the foundational ideas of the covenantal mode: Protestants in Ulster are modern Israelites, a (but not *the*) chosen people; Ulster is God's gift of land and prosperity to Protestants; Scripture is replete with allegories and prophecies relevant to Ulster; Ulster's social and political arrangements are God-given; reform of these arrangements is a breach of loyalty to God; since covenants are theological and political contracts, there can be no separation of politics and religion; covenants are unchanging, unless ordained to do so by God, so that historical continuity with the past is essential; covenantal terms are difficult to maintain against the threat posed by faithless outsiders and the backsliding 'enemy within', but a 'holy remnant' remains loyal to the covenant and has strong and defiant watchmen or shepherds to protect them.

The notion that Ulster Protestants are modern-day Israelites, the 'loyal sons of Judah', as the Rev. Thomas Ellis put it in 1885, expresses itself in direct analogies with biblical Jews, as well as in references to Ulster Protestants as a chosen people. The *Protestant Telegraph* thus wrote in its Christmas edition in 1968: 'the Almighty does not make mistakes. Our presence in Ulster is no accident ... We have a historic and divine commission ... we are a special people, not of ourselves but of our divine mission.' Free Presbyterians, for example, are frequently told by Paisley that 'God has chosen Ulster' (Taylor, 1983: 12). It follows, therefore, that Ulster is a modern Israel, God's gift of land to His people as their source of prosperity. In biblical times Israel had to be fought for and protected from the faithless Hittites and Canaanites, who were evil, in order to be given to the chosen, the elect, to whom God had promised it. Despite the opposition of incumbent natives, Israel was given to the Jews because it was His blessing to a special people. The same applies to Ulster (those who recognise that some Protestants appropriate this to themselves include Holmes, 1985: 9; Bruce, 1986: 10; Akenson, 1992: 119). Ulster is for Protestants: fewer people believe this than they did in the eighteenth century, but some still do. As one said, when describing what the phrase 'for God and Ulster' meant for him: 'Ulster is worth living and dying for. Such patriotism could not survive without the strength of God's love' (collected by the Evangelical Contribution on Northern Ireland in Thomson, 1996: 43). Thus, Pastor McConaghie, in defining the same phrase, remarked: 'as a Bible-believing Protestant, I am for Ulster. I am for her continued enjoyment of her God-given blessings, which are protected in the United Kingdom, but which are at best only tolerated where Rome's influence is felt. I gladly take to myself the label, "for God and Ulster"' (ibid.: 85). It follows further that these ideas legitimise the dominance of the chosen elect. The Irish natives were the heathen, the evil Canaanites, those whom God has not called to salvation (on the application of this idea to Ulster Protestants see Wallis and Bruce, 1986: 273). If Ulster prospered materially and economically, it was because it was Protestant, and, as Bruce argues, if Protestants prospered 'it was because it pleased God to let them prosper; if Catholics were poor, it was because they had not been saved' (Bruce, 1994: 27). Scripture is therefore said to be replete with allegories and prophecies relevant to Ulster, which confirm both its sacred position and Protestants' divine blessing. Some Protestants thus believe that Scripture contains direct advice on how Ulster should act, has many parallels to experience in Northern Ireland, and numerous analogies applicable to a myriad of situations (on this point see Akenson, 1992: 118). As one example, a daily prayer for deliverance was printed in the church page of the *Belfast Telegraph* during the furore over the Anglo-Irish Agreement in 1985, invoking a verse from Isaiah 14, that no weapon could prosper against those to whom

God had promised the blessing of land. The prayer continued: 'O people of Ulster, you are God's Israel, chosen seed, God gave your forefathers this land, these promises are yours' (other examples are this kind are found in MacIver, 1987: 362).

However, the Old Testament covenant is not the only frame of reference, for the political contract embodied in sixteenth-century Scots Ulster covenants is also a template. In this view, God upheld a contract between ruler and ruled, so long as the ruler kept to a set of social and political arrangements which reflected God's divine will. Loyalty to the ruler was guaranteed, as a reflection of loyalty to God, so long as these social and political arrangements remained (hence the notion of *conditional* political loyalty; see Miller, 1978a). Civil and political liberty, parliamentary democracy and the Protestant religion are indivisible in such covenants. Reform which threatens any one, threatens them all, and would be a sacred betrayal of the covenant. Governments therefore needed to be moral, but primarily had to uphold the socio-political arrangements which God blessed. As taken up by the Scots Ulster covenanting tradition, God ordained the British Constitution. As Bill Malcolmson said, when describing what the phrase 'for God and Ulster' meant to him, God 'has given nations the moral law, he has instituted governments to promote righteousness ... we desire our British government to follow this course set by God, and to do so in Ulster ... by the very instincts of our nature we love our native soil' (Thomson, 1996: 83). It also follows from this covenanting tradition that covenants have an inherent political dimension. Politics is indivisible from religion, so that political involvement is a theological necessity. For this reason, some Protestant clergy have unashamedly used their clerical position for partisan Protestant causes, since it followed naturally from the view that God involved Himself in government. Political battles, such as those against Irish nationalism, are equally religious battles. 'My politics are not divisible from my faith', Alan Wright, a Salvation Army member and committed Loyalist once said, 'it's Protestantism versus Rome' (quoted in Bruce, 1994: 25). When politics departs from God's ordinance, His blessings fade. As one interviewee said, 'I mean, law and order has broken down, in the home, in the schools, it's broken down everywhere because man has tried to go his own way and forgotten about the teachings of God. You can only go God's way. If you go God's way, everything will be OK.'

Because these divinely ordained social and political arrangements were drawn up long ago and have not changed, because God is eternal, the past is the prism through which the present is viewed: the 'martyrs' blood still cries to God', as Paisley once vividly expressed it. Continuity with tradition is the important standard by which to judge present practice, and specific social and political arrangements have to be viewed in terms of their conformity with this tradition. The past sets the standard by establishing the social and political arrangements which God ordained and which need to be maintained, and it identifies the problems that arise when any departure from them occurs. The 'fingerprints of the eternal God', Paisley once said, can be traced in history, and they rewrite history. The same loyalty is required to God's will (which never changes, since God is eternal), and the same threats exist to God's moral government and to God-given social and political arrangements. History repeats itself. But it does so in terms of both events and choices. Events recur as threats to God's ordinances but they also recur as opportunities to choose loyalty to God by keeping faith with the covenantal terms. As Paisley once said: 'the same terrorism, the same tyrannies, the same superstition, the same episcopacy, the same prelacy, the same popery are rife in our land today' (quoted in MacIver, 1987: 367). Thus, history also always presents the same choice between truth and error. In the words of the *Protestant Telegraph* there is an eternal conflict between truth and evil and as events arise Ulster, Protestants have to choose to be 'defenders of Truth in this province and in this island'. Thus, the Pope's appearance at the European Parliament in 1988 represented for Paisley the recurrence of an age-old threat and an opportunity for the same choice between truth and evil. As he wrote on the occasion in *The Revivalist*: 'this is the battle of the ages which we are engaged in. This is no Sunday School picnic, this is a battle for truth against the lie, the battle of heaven against hell, the battle of Christ against the anti-Christ.'

The covenantal terms are thus difficult to maintain in the face of such recurring threats without determined and watchful shepherds to protect the 'holy remnant' who have kept faith. In the Old Testament a prophet whom the Bible tells us spoke the same unpalatable words as Jeremiah, fled in fear of opposition to Egypt and died, while Jeremiah kept faith with his unpopular message – even to the point of being thrown into a pit – and he remained alive. Shepherds are necessary because the faithless outsiders are joined by the 'enemy within' to attack the commitment and loyalty of the 'holy remnant', who become the last bastion of faith, the last to uphold the covenant. Thus, the *Protestant Telegraph* wrote once that this remnant are the 'last defenders of Truth', 'the last bastion of evangelical Protestantism in Western Europe', and they 'must not let drop the torch of Truth'. Enemies outside the covenanted community, like Catholicism and secularism, and enemies within, such as apostate Protestants and ecumenism, pose equal threats and can weaken the holy remnant's resistance. Hence the constant need for warrior prophets, discerning watchmen, to act as protectors. 'Our leaders in church and state today', Paisley once said in a thanksgiving service in 1964 to commemorate a UVF gun-running incident in 1914, 'have either lost the great vision of our Protestant heritage or else are practising deliberate treachery.'

The Form of Rhetoric of the Covenantal Mode

Commentators have noted that Ulster Scots are people of the Old Testament rather than the New (MacIver, 1987: 361, 363; Akenson, 1992: 117), for just as the Old Testament furnishes many of the foundational ideas of the covenantal mode, it also supplies its characteristic style of rhetoric, which replicates the Old Testament denunciation prophecies. This prophetic rhetoric, as it can be called, is marked by vivid imagery, strong and florid language, and intemperate tone. It is marked also by focus on damning denunciations of the faithless, alarming warnings of danger unless people return to covenantal obligations, but the comforting reassurance of marvellous blessing if they do. The rhetoric is shrill, vivid and rich. Fee and Stuart (1982: 160) refer to these denunciations as 'woe oracles', used by prophets to warn of imminent doom. They contain three elements, an announcement of distress, an explanation of the reason for the distress, and a prediction of distress unless change is made, and all spoken in vivid rhetoric. But the denunciation prophets like Jeremiah, Elijah and Ezekiel also employed 'salvation oracles', through which they promised future blessing if there was radical reform, which meant a return to the past in the form of a restoration and repair of the covenant. As Akenson put it (1992: 135), evil is all around, inside and outside the covenanted community, and denunciations (and promises) are necessary if the holy remnant is to remain faithful, addressing backsliders and outsiders alike. Prophetic messages can thus be unpopular and the language strong enough to provoke opposition, but this is usually taken as a sign of their authenticity (ibid.: 134). Therefore, during a sermon on 1 August 1993, Paisley remarked:

> I will not compromise Christ's truth. I will not allow His person or His passion to be vilified by the enemies of the gospel and not make the most vehement of protests. I must, I will, stand up for Jesus. That's what I've got to do. No words of mine can be too strong to condemn those who blaspheme my Lord. They are the brood of Judas. They are the offspring of Iscariot. They are the generation of that viper Satan.

Compare this with the words of Isaiah, perhaps the most favourite of Old Testament prophets: the darkness around people will turn to the brightness of noon, he writes, 'if you do away with the yoke of oppression, with the pointing finger and malicious talk' (Isaiah 58:9).

Alarming warnings and florid language also sometimes had to be made to Israel's kings, the powerful and mighty, at great risk to the prophet – many denunciation prophets risked their life for God's calling: they were persecuted prophets. Likewise in Ulster. The characteristic form of florid rhetoric used in the covenantal mode, even when addressed to the powerful and mighty, is represented well by one of Paisley's letters to Queen Elizabeth II in 1970, after she met a Catholic cardinal.

> We would remind your Majesty, humbly, of the terms of your Coronation Oath and, in the name of Almighty God, warn you of the disasters that must come to our nation through any entanglement or alliance with the Roman anti-Christ. Idolatry means the curse of the Almighty, and that curse must, of necessity, fall upon all those who identify themselves with that system of idolatry depicted in the Holy Scripture as 'Mystery Babylon the Great, Mother of Harlots and the abominations of the earth.'   (taken from *The Revivalist,* February 1970)

The Articulation of Anti-Catholicism in the Covenantal Mode

Anti-Catholicism in the covenantal mode reflects the foundational ideas of this type, so that the themes articulated in this mode blend theology and politics. Dealing with theological claims first, Irish Catholics are Ulster Protestants' Canaanites and Hittites, the evil outsiders to the covenanted community, from whom land was taken at the behest of God and who pose a constant threat to their continued possession of God's favour. Dispossession of the land, however, is not the cause of conflict in Ulster. A prominent theme in the articulation of the covenantal type of anti-Catholicism is that Ulster is one site of the recurring conflict between good and evil, truth and error, which are age-old battles. While this is a universal conflict – 'you are fighting the same battle in this country as we are in our country', Paisley once told American fundamentalists, 'it's the same devil, the same spirit of the anti-Christ, the same apostasy' – Ulster is somehow special. It is special because some Protestants see Ulster as having a divine mission; 'little Protestant Ulster', as Paisley sometimes describes her, has a special mission because the 'light of Protestantism' burns so brightly there. A minister in the Reformed Presbyterian Church in Ireland said in 1996: 'I am thankful to be British, part of a nation unusually favoured and used by God. I believe that the Roman Catholic system has been responsible for keeping much of this island in spiritual darkness' (Thomson, 1996: 47).

Ulster is special also because the forces of evil and darkness are thought to be so powerfully focused on her, as represented by the scale of the threat posed by the IRA, which is the Roman Catholic Church incarnate. James Allister, one of Paisley's leading supporters in the Democratic Unionist Party (DUP), once expressed this allusion well: 'The somewhat unique aspect of Irish Roman Catholicism is its inseparable affiliation to militant Irish Republicanism. This affiliation means that Irish Republicanism [has] a fevour imbued by abject loyalty to the teachings of the Church ... Goaded on by a crusading religious mission, militant Irish Republicanism [is] a holy war against Protestantism' (quoted in Taylor, 1983: 112). Therefore, one of the most important themes in the articulation of anti-Catholicism in the convenantal mode is that Catholicism represents theological evil and is doing its damnedest to annihilate Protestants in Ulster because they represent theological truth. A local councillor for the DUP is reported in the *Irish Times* to have said at its 1991 annual conference, using typical prophetic rhetoric: 'Rome's aim is to destroy Protestantism, our children and our children's children, our way of life and our Bible. Popery in Rome, with the aid of Romish priests, ensured the demise of the B Specials, of which I was a member. The UDR [Ulster Defence Regiment, abolished in security reforms] attempted to defend Ulster from Romanism, but it too has fallen.' Thus, the evil hand of Catholicism is behind any and every social and political evil and ill (see Bruce, 1994: 22), such is its powerful malevolence. It is behind the IRA, as James Allister alluded, and another overarching theme within the covenantal mode is that the Catholic Church supports and promotes terrorism. The Rev. Martyn Smyth thus said recently that the IRA is Roman Catholic and its members 'act in the cause of religion rather than politics' (Thomson, 1996: 105).

Not only are Catholics theologically unsaved and outside the elect, they are not blessed by God, being in receipt of no favour or promise from God because Catholicism as a system is unChristian. This is another prominent theme in the articulation of anti-Catholicism in this mode. Using the florid rhetoric of this type, the covenantal mode suggests that Catholicism is 'baptised paganism', worshipping wafers, idols, and pre-Christian deities. In one of comics published by Chick Publications (*Why is Mary Crying?*) the Virgin Mary is said to represent the witch Semiramis, who became Queen of Babylon, and who, with her husband, Nimrod, was used by the Devil to form a satanic cult whose power is still felt. According to *Why is Mary Crying?*, it was this cult which developed the idea of the confessional and celibacy for the priesthood, and motivates much of the doctrine and practice of Catholicism. In another of their comics, *Are Roman Catholics Christian?*, widely on sale in Northern Ireland, Chick Publications argues that Catholics are being deceived; the confessional is used only 'to find out what is going on, and to control and blackmail', Catholic forms of devotion replicate Baal worship, and that Satan devised the Catholic mass. One of Monica Farrell's pamphlets, *Why am I a Protestant Daddy?*, has a father instructing his daughter on the evils of Catholicism in which the young girl comes to realise that Catholicism brings 'paganism inside the Christian Church' (Monica Farrell, 1986: 9). Thus, a common theme in the covenantal mode is that Catholicism represents the Babylonian system referred to in Scripture, the Harlot, the Whore, the Beast and the abomination described in the Book of Revelation. In a comic called *The Beast*, Chick Publications draws a picture of a young Catholic family with the mark of the Beast on their foreheads (666), as described in the Book of Revelation, being blessed by the Pope. The Pope is referred to as Satan's masterpiece, using a bank of computers in the Vatican to control 'every person on the globe', as part of the plan to unite people under the false religion headed by 'the beast'. The world then would become one gigantic witches' coven, with Satanism saturating the world in the guise of Catholicism. The Pope is therefore the antiChrist predicted in Scripture, that 'man of sin who claims to be God'. Thus, according to one pamphlet produced by the Pilgrim Tract Society, *The Pope's Blessing*, anyone receiving a blessing from the antiChrist has awful things happen to them, although it sometimes takes a lifetime before they die. These views are not restricted to crackpot comics, and they permeate beyond Free Presbyterianism. Thus, an Elim pastor recently wrote (in restrained language, however), 'I am against Roman Catholicism, which I consider an idolatrous and blasphemous religion – the largest false religion. Roman Catholicism I believe to be openly hostile to God and His will' (Thomson, 1996: 84–5).

Given this evil, challenges to Catholicism are one's Christian duty, and another anti-Catholic theme in the covenantal mode is the contrast made between the enervation of Catholics and the eulogy for Protestant opponents. It is the Protestant's sacred duty to oppose Catholicism, giving legitimacy and status to its opponents, which contrasts with the way individual Catholics are stripped of moral value, marked as they are with '666' on their foreheads, the sign of the antiChrist. To those people who criticise their tendency to remain locked in the past, covenantal type Protestants declare it their sacred duty to valorise history in order to demonstrate the continued threat posed by sixteenth-century battles. The allegation that they are bigoted as a result of hanging on to the past in this way, is naught compared to serving Christ. Thus, Monica Farrell writes:

> everything our forefathers resisted and died to procure, is being given away to Rome and anyone who tries to raise a voice against it is called a 'bigot' or 'extremist' ... Protestants, whose forefathers resisted the domination of Rome, and who secured Ulster in union with Britain, can now see it being handed over to the very people who stabbed Britain in the back, while they are being lectured by Westminster politicians 'to forget their past history'. These men utterly refuse to take into account Vatican policy ... They don't want to know it [but] Britain will yet suffer at the hands of Rome.   (Monica Farrell, 1986: 23–4)

The political contract implied by covenants furnishes further themes for the articulation of anti-Catholicism in the covenantal mode. Catholics are either outside this contract or engage in actions which abrogate it. The civil and political liberties associated with Protestantism are God-given, which makes them right and just. There can thus be no entertainment of the view that these social and political arrangements are unjust to Catholics; claims of injustice are either denied in the covenantal view or seen as irrelevant because Catholics are outside the political contract. Reflecting the former view, it is a popular theme in the covenantal mode to argue that Catholics are ungrateful whingers, and exploit the benefits of the state while withholding legitimacy from it. Clifford Smyth (1996: 62) expressed this theme when he wrote that Catholicism inherently causes its adherents to have a sense of grievance. And the whinging is unjustifiable. According to 'Realist', writing in the letters column in the *Belfast Telegraph* on 22 April 1972, 'there is nothing in Ulster now – nor has there ever been – that a Protestant gets that a Roman Catholic doesn't get'. As an illustration of the claim that Catholics exploit just and fair systems, Taylor quotes from one of his interviewees in the Free Presbyterian Church: 'we have been good neighbours and held out an open hand of friendship. But they [Catholics] have infiltrated this place [Ulster] to get all the benefits and they still want a United Ireland. They have no intention of recognising either the Queen or the courts of law. We are really fighting for our livelihood because if we give up here they will take over everything' (Taylor, 1983:105). Another said, using more characteristic florid rhetoric, 'we wouldn't give anything to the Taigs that they are getting now. We wouldn't give them social security, there wouldn't be as many Taigs who would want big families. A lot of Taigs are living on the state [and we] would cut a lot of that out. They would work or want' (ibid.: 106).

That Catholics are outside the contract is evidenced, in the covenantal mode, by the social and political arrangements that obtain in Catholic-ruled countries, which contrast so negatively with those in Protestant countries, and an important theme in the covenantal type of anti-Catholicism is a denigration of the Irish Republic. It is devoid of civil and political liberty, and its social and political arrangements have not been blessed by God, as shown in the supposed tyranny and poverty in the South. Ian Major, a missionary pastor, thus said of the contrast between Ulster and the Irish

Republic: 'using the motto "for God and Ulster" my forefathers united to keep their nation free from religious and political tyranny. Today, I stand in their place with those same noble desires, knowing that history, in the sectarian record of the Irish state, has vindicated their assessment' (Thomson, 1996: 80). There is slavery in the South because Catholicism dominates and God has not contracted the relationship between ruler and ruled, so there are no civil and political liberties as under the Williamite British Constitution. Referring to the Ulster Protestant defence of Union, the Deputy Grand Chaplain of the Grand Orange Lodge recently claimed: 'this was the safeguard against "Rome rule". The choice was between freedom or slavery, and they chose to embrace the freedom of British democracy rather than the slavery of a state dominated by the Roman Catholic Church' (ibid.: 71). That it is a society that lacks value for civil and political liberty is further shown by the Southern government's orchestration, in league with the Catholic Church, of the terrorist campaign against 'little Protestant Ulster'. God's failure to bless the Irish Republic with economic prosperity is also claimed to show that Catholics are outside the contract. In the absence of God's blessing, Catholics live in poverty while the Catholic Church in Ireland is wealthy, which only confirms Catholicism's exclusion from the contract. One Free Presbyterian remarked of his experience of holidaying in the Irish Republic (the irony appeared to have gone unnoticed): 'the poverty was unbelievable. The people were very poor but in nearly every village there was a brand new chapel glistening in the sunlight' (Taylor, 1983: 107).

According to Paisley, God curses a nation that does not repudiate Popery. Anti-Catholicism thus must become national policy (MacIver, 1987: 372), which explains why perhaps the most important theme in the covenantal mode's articulation of anti-Catholicism is the danger of the unification of Ulster and the Irish Republic. Union with the United Kingdom is an obsessive theme, for without Union Protestants would be aligned to a nation dominated by Popery and would thus lose their covenant with God and sacrifice all the blessings it brings in politics, economics, culture and theology. 'Rome', said Pastor McConaghie, is 'the sworn enemy of civil and political liberties', existing 'primarily for the accruement of political power' (Thomson, 1996: 85), and all dangers mustered in the prophecies of the Old Testament denunciation prophets would befall should Ulster ally itself to Catholic Eire. Prophesying the future, Old Testament woe oracles saw Israel's integrity potentially impugned by the faithlessness of its people, and so Union is threatened by the faithless, unChristian – even anti-Christian – dogma of Catholicism. Writing in the *New Protestant Telegraph* in May 1995, Paisley projected into the future to warn readers: 'Ulster is to be sold out by a leading British Roman Catholic to a senior Republican Roman Catholic. There is a major conspiracy to destroy the Protestant inheritance of this island and to deny Protestants their rights.' During one of his sermons outlining such dangers, Paisley used the prophetic rhetoric of the Old Testament in saying: 'the land of my fathers, God's heritage is at stake. And you Christians, if you do not pray and dedicate yourselves to God, the blood of the whole land will be upon you and you will be judged by it' (printed in *The Revivalist*, June/July 1973). In this mode of anti-

Catholicism, however, Union is not just threatened by the weaknesses of the 'holy remnant', but by weak leadership that seeks to undermine Protestantism. Paisley's abuse towards Prime Minister Thatcher arising from the Anglo-Irish Agreement, summarises well what the covenantal mode thinks of Union and how anti-Catholicism is articulated around it.

> The Protestantism of Ulster is an embarrassment to her. The old way of thinking that the Bible is true ... that there is a separation demanded between God's people and those that live for the devil and sin, she does not like. So she takes Ulster and puts Ulster into a marriage bond with the Republic in order to destroy the identity of the Ulster Protestant people. She is saying to us 'where is the Lord thy God? You defiant little people, you do as I say. Where is the Lord thy God?' I have news for the prime minister. God is in heaven ... The day of glory for Margaret Thatcher is over. The day when she was hailed in the robes of glory has passed. The robing of this woman is going to be the robes of shame, for God will take her in hand ... We hand this women over to the devil that she might learn not to blaspheme.   (*The Revivalist*, January 1986)

The Primary Constituency of the Covenantal Mode

The covenantal mode of anti-Catholicism is restricted on the whole to the 'holy remnant' left in secular society, who see themselves loyal and faithful to God's mission for Ulster, which is to be a light in an otherwise dark island. They sometimes describe themselves as 'Bible Protestants'. The covenantal mode appeals to conservative evangelicals and other religious fundamentalists, spread across many denominations but dominating only perhaps in the Free Presbyterian Church and the gospel hall tradition. They are people who see themselves as a holy people, surrounded by the evil and profane, representing the only true and faithful believers left in an otherwise corrupted nation. They are the descendants of the Reformers and martyrs in the militancy of their defence of the Protestant faith and its social and political arrangements. Theirs is thus a proud pantheon of Protestant self-sacrifice, denial and righteousness. Loyalty to God and to their forefathers thus has the same animus, and leads to the same conclusion: Britishness at the expense of anti-Irishness, and Protestantism at the expense of anti-Catholicism. That they are now beleaguered and embattled as a result is of no matter in face of the necessity to remain true to God and Ulster. Gregory Campbell, a DUP councillor in Derry, described this 'holy remnant' as: 'A beleaguered, embattled people, having been so vilified that they must seek a refuge which will not betray them'; a refuge he says they find in the evangelical witness in Northern Ireland that understands and accepts the essential nature of the dispute between Protestantism and Roman Catholicism (Thomson, 1996: 36–7). Conservative evangelicalism in otherwords, with its strident but peculiar form of anti-Catholicism, gives meaning and identity only to a small group which perceives itself in a battle with the Catholic Church. Clearly, therefore, conservative evangelicalism is not any longer the sacred canopy which binds all Protestants together (a point emphasised also by Akenson, 1992).

The Implications of the Covenantal Mode for Relations with Catholics

Most advocates of the covenantal mode draw a distinction between individual Catholics and Catholicism, stating that their opposition is to the Catholic Church, not people. One of our interviewees put the distinction as follows: 'The Roman Catholic Church is contrary to the word of God, that doesn't mean to say I hate all Catholics.' A trainee minister said the same: 'it's not against the individual that I disagree, it's against the church'. Paisley makes the same contrast. It permits people to have relationships with individual Catholics while denigrating the church to which they belong. But these relationships must be entirely outside the context of religion (which is why Paisley, for example, can, and does, work tirelessly for his Catholic constituents in the European or Westminster parliaments). Even going to a Catholic church is impossible for many covenantal mode anti-Catholics; other forms of relationship in a church setting are entirely unacceptable. The Rev. Martin Smyth's attendance at a united prayer breakfast, in which some Catholic clergy were also involved, resulted in outraged complaint from some people. Letters in the correspondence columns of the *Belfast Telegraph* said the following: 'he should strenuously oppose the fatal errors and doctrines of the Church of Rome and scrupulously avoid countenancing by his presence or otherwise, any act or ceremony of popish worship'; 'the Roman Catholic system is not only imperfect is it unreformable. Its very foundation is built on erroneous revelation. Catholicism is not Christian.' Dialogue with Catholics about religion is also beyond the pale – ecumenism is going too far for anti-Catholics of the covenantal type. A correspondent in the *Evangelical Times* in December 1991 pointed out the reasons why dialogue with Catholics about religion is impossible: 'one cannot be a Roman Catholic and an evangelical at the same time. They are mutually exclusive doctrinal systems, opposed on every essential and fundamental matter.'

The distinction, however, is difficult to maintain because of Catholicism's commode-like quality: because Catholicism inveighs its way into everything, many non-religious relationships are not permitted because Catholicism is somehow involved in the background. Politically expedient relations with individual Catholics, for example, are ruled out because covenantal type anti-Catholics cannot separate the individual from the system. This particularly affects local politics, which is said to be controlled from Rome. Thus, for example, meetings with the IRA or Sinn Fein could not even be contemplated, nor relationships with Dublin politicians. This puts the DUP, for example, in a difficult position because politically expedient relationships are constrained by the theological stance of Paisley. There are several instances where DUP politicians have been censured for meeting individual Catholics, presumably on grounds that Catholicism so penetrates and inveigles politics that some individual Catholic politicians are indistinguishable from the system. Thus, a DUP mayor in Larne was forced out of the party for visiting Dublin (Taylor, 1983: 181), and a Belfast councillor left the party because he was censured for attending a diamond jubilee service for the RUC at which a Catholic priest read a lesson (Wallis et al., 1986: 25).

The distinction is difficult to maintain for another reason. Because the covenantal mode openly denigrates the faith of the individual Catholic, they meet so few Catholics that there is little opportunity for secular forms of relationship, except for purely economic exchange, which allows them to make this distinction without having to practise it. But whether or not this distinction is practised – and many would claim they do – the covenantal mode does not permit relationships with individual Catholics over the very issues which keep them apart, politics and religion. This maintains the old zero-sum frameworks and ancient stereotypes, and keeps most relationships to functional ones of economic exchange. Even here, however, individual Catholics rather than the system of Catholicism can be mistreated. Two of Morrow's respondents from rural Armagh speak volumes about this distinction: 'just near here there was a farm come up that was going for good money. There was a danger that an RC would buy it, so the Orange Order bought it, I know of a couple with a small business in the village who might want to retire, but their children aren't interested in it and the most likely buyers are RCs'; 'one of our builders employs Roman Catholics though he'd prefer to work with Protestants. He said to me "I'll get you a window cleaner and he'll be a Protestant". He wouldn't want Catholics around the church' (Morrow, 1997: 20).

Challenging the Covenantal Mode

In challenging the different modes of anti-Catholicism it is pointless to criticise them for what they are not – that they are not open, inclusive, good-neighbourly, or whatever. It is more important to criticise them on their own terms. This involves challenging the foundational ideas on which each is based, so that, hopefully, adherents at least pose themselves certain questions which strike literally at the foundation of the system of beliefs and practises which characterise the mode. Several challenges can be mounted to the covenantal mode in its own terms.

The first is the relative stress laid on the Old Testament compared to the New. 'Bible Protestants' and covenanters are Old Testament people. Many of the stipulations in the Old Testament by which the Israelites kept their covenantal obligations to God are impossible to keep for modern Christians because they no longer apply. Worship at the Temple, for example, is impossible because the Temple no longer exists, and the sacrifice of animals as described in the Law would be illegal. Biblical scholars argue that the Old Testament as a whole, rather than the Judaic Law stipulated in the Books of Exodus through to Deuteronomy, represents the Laws that Jesus came to complete and fulfil (see Fee and Stuart, 1982: 135ff.). Yet Jesus says that that He did not come to abolish the Law and that not a single letter will disappear from it 'until everything is accomplished' (Matthew 5:18). Two biblical scholars, Fee and Stuart, contend that what Jesus meant by this was that while the old Law remained, and was impossible to amend, it no longer applied to those who accepted the new kingdom by following Jesus (Fee and Stuart, 1982: 138). Modern-day Christians should therefore respond to the Old Testament as follows (ibid.: 136–43). First, they should see it as a statement of the covenantal terms which God required to demonstrate the Israelites' loyalty to Him. Second, that it was thus the Israelites' testament not ours; that is, it represents the old covenant which followers of Jesus are not obligated to follow unless its stipulations and laws are specifically renewed and repeated in the New Testament. Fee and Stuart argue that modern Christians should assume that none of the stipulations in the Old Testament apply unless Jesus says they are binding (ibid.: 137). Third, New Testament scholarship shows that most of the stipulations in the Old Testament have not been renewed, such as those referring to Israel's civil and ritual laws. However, fourth, some aspects of the Old Testament were renewed, notably the ethical aspects of the Law which serve to support the two basic laws of the New Testament as Jesus Himself defined them (Matthew 22:40) – love the Lord your God with all your heart, soul and mind, and love your neighbour as yourself. These repeat ethical laws from the Old Testament (see Leviticus 19:18 and Deuteronomy 6:5) and their applicability to the new covenant is indicated by Jesus's restatement of them. The same applies to the Ten Commandments which are recited in various ways in the New Testament. In the absence of such reinstatement, therefore, the old laws do not apply. As Fee and Stuart remark, 'only that which is explicitly renewed from the Old Testament can be considered part of the New Testament "law of Christ"' (Fee and Stuart, 1982: 139). This does not deny that all of the Old Testament is the *word* of God, but it shows that it is not necessarily still God's *command* to us. Covenanters, however, believe the latter.

This relates to a second challenge to the covenantal mode, which is the relevancy of Old Testament denunciation prophecies in the modern world. Biblical scholarship indicates that prophets in the Old Testament did seek to foretell the future but it was the immediate future of Israel, Judah and the surrounding nations, not the prediction of events far distant from their own day. Moreover, prophesy in the Old Testament was not so much the foretelling of the future but a direction about the present. Most prophets told oracles which spoke the word of God to contemporaries, and most feature what God said *could* happen rather than what was to happen. Thus, Fee and Stuart (1982: 151–5) argue that the function of Old Testament prophets included the enforcement of the old covenant, rather than the new one arising with Jesus. To support these claims, it is worth noting that the sixteen prophetical books of the Old Testament relate to the period 760–460 BC when there was enormous upheaval in the region, a massive degree of religious unfaithfulness, and great shifts in populations and national boundaries, which had potential to weaken conformity to Judaic Law. This reinforces Fee and Stuart's point that prophecies are intended primarily to enforce the old covenant and are aimed exclusively at Israelites in a specific historical context (ibid.: 157).

Moreover, prophets relayed God's instructions and words, not their own, to the people to whom the message was directly and unambiguously aimed. The prophecies were not the word of God as the prophet interpreted it or saw it, but the direct command of God as God wished the prophet to present it; prophecies were given on God's command and authority, not the prophet's own. Jeremiah, for example, warned of 'false prophets' who 'speak a vision of their own heart, not from the mouth of the Lord' (Jeremiah 23:16), and some denunciation prophecies were aimed at false shepherds who spoke lies. Therefore, prophecies which require acts of imagination or interpretation in order to apply them to a people, time or events not indicated in God's actual command at the time are not appropriate to today. Bickle (1995: 229) uses the following tests to see if an Old Testament prophecy is relevant to the new covenant arising with Jesus. Does it bring honour to the person of Jesus? Does it produce a greater hatred of sin and a greater love of righteousness? Does it produce a greater regard for Scripture? Does it lead people to truth? Does it produce a greater love for God and our neighbour? Anti-Catholics of the covenantal mode would wholeheartedly contend that their favourite prophecies do that (although critics would not) because Catholicism is against Christ; it is the Beast and the Whore of the Book of Revelation. This claim is part of a New Testament prophecy (the Book of Revelation), which is significant to the argument because it is thus part of God's word for today.

The authenticity of the traditional interpretation of the Book of Revelation, however, mounts a serious challenge to the covenantal mode. According to Fee and Stuart (1982: 205ff.) and Hunter (1972: 189–97), the symbolism of the Book of Revelation must be interpreted in the context of the first century rather than the twentieth or twenty-first. Moreover, the Book contains three different literary genres: apocalypse, prophecy and epistle. The apocalyptic passages look forward to when God will bring a violent and radical end to history, the final triumph of truth over evil. Apocalyptic writing, however, is not prophecy because it is not a direct word of God. The writer of the Book (either the apostle John or John the Seer – see Hunter, 1972: 190), is told to write what he has seen (Revelation 1:19), whereas the prophets were told to speak what God had told them. The apocalyptic passages are human *interpretations* therefore, not God's spoken word. Further, these human interpretations are couched as fantasy. The images of the apocalyptic passages, like the Beast with seven heads and the women clothed in the sun, are forms of fantasy, dreams and visions, which contrast markedly with the allegories used by Jesus which were intended to be unambiguous, for while Jesus often uses symbolism in His parables, the images are all real and concrete to make them immediate (Fee and Stuart, 1982: 207). John's apocalyptic passages on the other hand offer an interpretation or vision of a far-off triumph of Christ. The prophetic passages, however, were, according to Fee and Stuart (ibid.: 208), aimed directly at the first-century Church, providing a word from God for the Christians' immediate situation, which was one of persecution and oppression. To prophesy in the Bible does not mean to foretell the future, but to speak God's word to the people at the time at which He gave them, and the prophetic passages of Revelation are God's word to some churches at the end of the first century. This is reinforced by the epistle passages, which are letters of encouragement and instruction to meet the specific needs of churches experiencing persecution during the first century.

It follows from these arguments that much of the Book of Revelation is not intended for transport to the third millennium, and its meaning was intended to be understood by those to whom it was directed, first-century Christians, rather than Christians twenty centuries later. As Hunter writes (1972: 195): 'John's book must be read in the light of the times when it was written, his allusions looked for in the persons, events and even rumours of the last decade of the first century AD.' Those to whom it was directed would be expected to be able to interpret the symbolism – this was God's point: messages from God which cannot be understood are pointless. Fee and Stuart (1982: 209–10) argue that the exegetical task required in interpreting the symbolism would have been easy for those to whom the revelations were directed because the interpretation was either intrinsic to the text or available from the historical context at the time. John himself assists in the interpretation by identifying some of the symbolism in the text itself. Thus, for example, the Harlot is the 'great city', which in the first century would have meant the city of Rome; the seven heads are the seven hills on which the woman sits, meaning the seven hills around the city of Rome; the seven stars and the golden lampstands refers to the seven Christian churches experiencing persecution (see Fee and Stuart, 1982: 210); and Babylon refers to the Roman Empire (Hunter, 1972: 193). The Beast, with 666 marked on its head, which was drunk with the blood of God's people, would have been understood at the time as referring to Emperor Nero (who had committed suicide and was rumoured to return from the underworld to continue his persecution of Christians – see ibid.: 195) – since the Greeks and Hebrews used the letters of their alphabet also as numerals, so the Greek *Neron Kaiser*, transliterated into the Hebrew script, produces 666 (ibid.: 194). The 'worshippers of the beast and its image' (Revelation 14:9–11) were thus those followers of Nero who had been instructed to accord divine honour to all emperors, and to worship their statues, under the 'emperor cult' which made them into gods. The 'Beast' who rises up to challenge Christ was thus a Roman emperor, who was persecuting the Christian churches at that time and demanding allegiance to pagan religion (also see Fee and Stuart, 1982: 215). The historical context of the Book suggests that many of the other images would have been seen at the time as referring to the Roman Empire, but were written in allegory to protect John from the Romans who were then occupying the whole area. The 'city of earth' which persecutes God's people thus becomes the city of Rome. What was described in the Book as doomed was the Roman Empire and its emperors, who were the antiChrist, so the 'fall' is in fact a description of the end of a political and colonial system rather than a religious one. Biblical scholarship thus shows the tremendous leaps of human imagination to see the images referring to Catholicism and the Pope. It was not until the seventeenth century, in the context of religious conflicts over the Reformation, that two Protestant scholars 'unlocked' the mysteries of the Book of Revelation by identifying the Catholic Church and the Papacy with the images threatening the victorious Christ (see Clouse, 1980), and it has been ritually reproduced this way in the evangelical tradition ever since. The same applies to the notion of the antiChrist as referring to the Pope, which Barkley (1967) shows only began with the Reformation, when writers became preoccupied with a fear of the Catholic Church and a wish to denigrate it.[1] It is, in short, human imagination not divine revelation to claim that the Catholic Church and the Papacy are demonised in Scripture (see Bruce, 1986: 221–2 for the beliefs of Free Presbyterians on this point).

The final challenge that can be made to the covenantal mode relates to the tradition of identifying Ulster as God's promise to Protestants. An Old Testament scholar recently argued that the scriptural tales of Israel's divine deliverance by means of God's assistance in battle, of which there are many, do not necessarily imply God's complete approval (Johnston, 1997: 8–9). God's verdict on a people, even His 'chosen people' of Israel, is never final, and terrible judgement can befall a once divinely-delivered nation. On the basis of his analysis of the scriptural texts which describe Israel's changing fortunes, Johnston remarks, 'the God who promised His people land, city, temple, monarchy and independence, and delivered them in times of crisis, still judged their lack of faith' (ibid.: 9). From these Old Testament lessons Johnston draws the conclusion that Ulster's 'deliverance' from Popery in William's victory in 1690, does not necessarily mean that God approved of her cause or her heroes, nor that He necessarily continues to approve, even if He once did, or that any approval excuses contemporary injustice and sectarianism or any breach of Jesus's commands to love each other. Israel's persistent sinfulness, after all, did not protect her in the long run despite God's original approval of His chosen people. Moreover, God's will for the nation of Israel was not fixed, such that history was a poor measure of what God willed at any specific juncture; in Isaiah's time God's will for the nation was to stand alone from a neighbouring powerful nation (Egypt), in Jeremiah's it was to submit to another nation (Babylon). Magee also makes the interesting point (in Thomson, 1996: 78) that even though the Hebrew people were full of national pride and had originally been given the promised land, Jesus made no reference to love of nation. Nor did Jesus restrict His promises and blessings to any one land, territory, nation or people. The new covenant with God described in the New Testament gospels, by means of which God's blessings are gifted to anyone who believes in His son, is entirely devoid of linking the covenant to land. Even the Old Testament glimpses of Jesus and the new covenant make this clear. In one of Jeremiah's salvation oracles, in which God outlines future prosperity for His people, He outlines the nature of the new covenant: 'The Lord says "the time is coming when I will make a new covenant. It will not be like the old covenant I made with their ancestors. The new covenant will be this: I will put my law within them and write it on their hearts"' (Jeremiah 31:31–3). Land and nation are irrelevant to the new covenant. Billy Mitchell, one-time terrorist with the UVF and now a committed Christian, warns that some people can be guilty of building a god in their own image by seeing God as gifting Ulster to Protestants (Thomson, 1996: 86), for the idea that God is associated with one political and territorial entity and its inhabitants is not taken from the Gospels. The kingdom of God that Jesus offered was not a kingdom in any geographical sense, unlike the kingdom offered to Abraham and his descendants, but rather the rule of God in people's hearts and minds. This is why the Old Testament mark of the covenant, circumcision of the penis (physical circumcision), is replaced in the new covenant by circumcision of the heart (spiritual circumcision),[2] as the New Testament makes clear, and why Jesus says that the kingdom of God is within one. The key to this kingdom, therefore, is not turned by nationality or ownership of land or title but, as George Crory, a Belfast Baptist pastor, said, 'by repentance and faith in the Son of God' (ibid.: 41).

Other Modes of Anti-Catholicism

The covenantal mode is the type most people recognise as anti-Catholicism. The grounds of objection to Catholicism are manifestly theological and much reference is made to religion, so that it appears to be the thing its nomenclature describes, a form of opposition to Catholic doctrine. Its dominance as a mode in people's thinking is reinforced by the prominence in Northern Ireland of Paisleyism which represents this type to the world. Yet the grounds of objection within the covenantal mode are not solely theological, for politics is inseparable from theology in covenantal thinking, and covenantal type anti-Catholicism in Northern Ireland links strong theological objections to Catholic doctrine with vociferous defence of the political, economic and cultural Union with Britain. Secular concerns thus form part of anti-Catholicism, even in its obvious form. It is not contradictory therefore to describe another mode as secular, since its focus is almost exclusively on the political, cultural and economic dimensions of Union, which Catholicism supposedly threatens. This ensures an overlap with the political concerns of the covenantal mode. However, there is an absence of theology and little reference to doctrine in the secular mode, with the focus being on the actions of Catholics and the Catholic Church in Ireland (and sometimes more broadly) as they affect the Union. The Pharisaic mode, however, completely neglects politics to focus entirely on Catholic doctrine, ensuring overlap with the theological approach of the covenantal mode, although its theological focus is different, owing more to the New Testament than the Old and being devoid of covenantal notions. Though the covenantal mode is in most people's eyes the prototype of anti-Catholicism, it is therefore necessary to distinguish other modes which contrast markedly with it in terms of foundational ideas, rhetoric, articulation, the constituencies to which they appeal, and their implications for relationships with Catholics (as summarised in Figure 4, p. 133). The secular mode will be addressed first.

The Foundational Ideas of the Secular Mode

The ideas that form the foundation of the secular mode are support for, and vigorous defence of, the Union with Britain; the claim that the Irish Republic is a degenerate and backward state; that Union is under threat, especially from the Irish Republic and a duplicitous Britain; that the major problems to Union are political and that theology is either irrelevant or secondary to political circumstances. There is, accordingly, a sharp division between religion and politics, with the struggle being seen as a political rather than religious one.

Defence of the Union is the *idée fixe* of the secular mode, which it shares with the covenantal mode, but Protestantism in the secular mode is a social marker rather than an expression of religious commitment, and although it is a religious marker that is used as the self-appellation, what it stands for is thoroughly political and secular. Protestantism represents and stands for the Union; it is a constitutional rather than a theological commitment. This has long been recognised by British and Irish politicians who sought to use Protestantism as a mobilising resource. O'Connell, the forerunner of Irish nationalism, once described Northern Protestants as 'political Protestants' only, wedded to a constitutional rather than a theological position. Some Unionist politicians felt much the same. Speaking in 1874, for example, William Johnston, standing as a Conservative parliamentary candidate, said the following to his Belfast electors: 'you will stand up for conservative members because they are Protestants. I would not ask you to support conservative candidates if they ceased for a moment to conserve Protestantism and conservatism. And the conservative that would not stand for Protestantism is not a conservator of the British constitution' (quoted in Walker, 1989: 110). One of the leading figures in the Progressive Unionist Party (PUP) said in an interview in September 1997 that the conflict in Northern Ireland is a political one not a religious one, and that when he hears some people talk about the 'Protestant people of Ulster' he feels alienated by its parochialism, since he is a citizen of the United Kingdom of 56 million, and by its use of religion as an identity marker. Likewise, Gary McMichael, from the Ulster Democratic Party (UDP), said in interview that religion divides people, being part of the problem not the solution, in that theology acts like a set of blinkers, giving people baggage which prevents them from being able to transcend tribal politics. In this manner, Protestantism stands for a position on the British Constitution and is, for all intents and purposes, secularised because, above all, it represents a political affiliation. Protestantism stands for civil and political liberties, established by the Glorious Revolution, and a political identity, deriving from the constitutional link with Britain. Thus, Captain Corry, standing in the 1874 general election in County Tyrone, said: 'as a conservative I shall always seek to maintain the integrity of this great empire; and as a Protestant, I shall use my utmost endeavours to uphold our glorious constitution, granting at the same time to every man the fullest civil and religious liberty' (quoted in ibid.: 92). David Ervine, of the PUP, said in an interview that Unionism is not a political philosophy, it lacked a social and economic programme, and that it was just a form of political identity. If the Protestant religion is a commitment at all in the secular mode, it is a weak one – they are not 'Bible Protestants' – and secular Protestants do not subscribe to the ethical values of the Protestant faith, such as Sabbatarianism, temperance, regular church attendance, and religious observance.

A distinction is thus made in the secular mode between religion and politics, and if religion is not kept out of politics, it is made subservient to it. This is an important foundational idea of the secular mode: the name of the game is politics not theology. In one of the best attempts in the 1980s to move Loyalism into politics and away from theology, John McMichael and Ray Smallwoods, from the Ulster Defence Association, published *Common Sense* (UDA, 1987), in which they set out proposals for an agreed political solution in Northern Ireland. It forms the basis of the UDP's present political platform. In the document, the terms 'Catholic' and 'Protestant' were put in quotation marks to signify that religion is not seen as the social marker (on political developments in the UVF in the 1980s, see Garland, 1997). The new Loyalist parties, like the PUP and UDP, have socialist or social democratic bases, not theological roots. They recognise the class interests of their section of Loyalism. Working-class Loyalists were never part of the Protestant ascendancy; David Ervine said they might have 'belonged' in the way that the Catholic working class did not, but Stormont 'was a one-party elitist state' which benefited the 'fur-coat brigade' in Unionism. Gusty Spence also challenges the idea that the Protestant working class were ever ascendant (in Garland, 1997: 13; see also respondents in Nelson, 1984). Ervine said that he and his colleagues in the UVF had been used as cannon-fodder by these sorts of Unionists in the past. Sammy Wilson, a working-class politician representing secular Loyalism, once defended his membership of Paisley's DUP by arguing that the DUP was not a conservative organisation dominated by the clergy, but a vehicle for the political aspirations of working-class Protestants who otherwise would not have been in politics because 'they did not have the right accent, did not live in the right area, had gone to the wrong school and did not have hyphenated names' (Wilson, 1984). His motivating concerns were to address politically the problems of poor housing, low pay, social deprivation, social security, and education. Religion was a backcloth to this because Irish Presbyterianism, Wilson argued, was a radical force (claiming that it was behind the American and French Revolutions) and faith is therefore 'bound to manifest itself in radical social concern and action'. But the primary focus for Wilson was political rather than theological, being to challenge politically 'the structures of society which work against the disadvantaged'. Of course, Union with Britain is the other backcloth to these concerns, for it is the only guarantee of civil and political liberty, and another of the foundational ideas of the secular mode is that the Irish Republic is politically, economically and culturally backward. Republicanism, whether represented by the IRA or the Irish Republic, is bankrupt.

If Union with Britain is one *idée fixe*, the degeneracy of Catholic, nationalist Ireland is another. J. Bowyer Bell, who recently wrote a sympathetic account of what he called the Protestant case (Bowyer Bell, 1996), said that the twenty-six counties were both threatening and a failure (ibid.: 182). Of its failure he wrote: 'in truth, the Republic is much as Protestants suspect rather than as its citizens assume' (ibid.: 99);

the Republic is a failed entity. The national dream, because of the malign influence of Catholic, Gaelic society, has led to disaster ... led to tragedy, a futile, authoritarian society without grace or enterprise. This is not some fervid Orange speech but reality: look at the record, read the statistics, see the evidence beyond the travel posters and government claims ... Free Ireland is an unhappy state filled with unhappy people.   (ibid.: 175)

His remarks border on old-fashioned racism:

Beyond the insidious doctrines and prevalence of the Roman church, the society of the Gael is a secondary but real disaster, less threat than failure, a failure due to the very nature of the Irish-Irish. And that central Irish nature, a compound of invader ethics, island habits and an imaginary golden age, was at worst a wild and barbarous core that saw indolence as grace and violence as recreation.
                                                                  (ibid.: 234)

The twin obsessions in the secular mode – Union with Britain and the degeneracy of the Irish Republic – feed off each other because the Irish Republic is seen as posing a threat to Union, such that the link with Britain is perceived always as fragile, although such fragility lies also in British untrustworthiness and duplicity. As a member of the West Belfast UDA once said: 'for four hundred years we have known nothing but uprising, murder, destruction and repression. We ourselves have repeatedly come to the support of the British Crown only to be betrayed ... Second class Englishmen, half-caste Irishmen' (quoted in Farrell, 1976: 314). This is a recurring idea in the secular mode; the backs of Protestants are continually against the wall, backing southwards to the Republic or across the Irish Sea to Britain. 'We are fighting for our very survival', the Ulster Freedom Fighters said in 1973, 'our backs are against the wall. We have more in common with the state of Israel ... like the Jewish people, each time an act of aggression is committed against our people, we shall retaliate in a way that only the animals of the IRA can understand' (quoted in ibid.: 314). This remark is useful as it epitomises the political focus of the secular mode. Like the covenantal mode, an analogy is made with Israel, but it is not with biblical Israel. In this view Protestants are not like the Old Testament Jews, with covenanted land and under a special blessing from God, but like modern-day Jews facing problems from enemies who challenge the political legitimacy of the state.

The Form of Rhetoric of the Secular Mode

The language of the secular mode is political rather than theological; it is about the state, social and political problems, Republicanism, terrorism and threats, not covenants, biblical prophecy, God, and divine blessings or denunciations. Reference is made to Protestantism, but it is primarily used as a political identity marker and political affiliation. Little stress is laid on the theological dispute with Catholicism; the complaint is more with the political and constitutional position that Catholicism represents. Ritualised phrases against the Catholic Church are occasionally issued, but they are few and the intent is political, the context secular: the struggle is clearly identified by the rhetoric as a political one. The following poem taken from *Loyalist News* on 25 November 1972 presents a good example of the use of this political rhetoric.

> Dare to be a Protestant, Dare to stand alone,
> Dare to fight with purpose true against the Church of Rome.
> Dare to stand beside those men preparing for the fray,
> Dare to fight the priest, his witchcraft, his tool, the IRA.
> Dare to arm united, for Ulster take your stand.
> Dare to join the UVF, a rifle in your hand.
> Dare to join our struggle and hit the rebels hard.
> Dare to stand as UDA or Protestant Vanguard.
> Dare to lay your life at risk, to win a victory grand.
> Dare to test your loyalty to Ulster's Red Hand.

With such rhetoric, the label 'Protestant' stands as a marker for political aspirations (see Bell, 1990: 64, for a similar point). Protestants are thus dared to take on Republicanism, not Catholicism; to defend the Union, not the Reformation. It is Republicanism not Romanism which seeks to destroy Ulster, and no rigorous attempt is made to represent the two as synonymous. Compare the above poem with the comments of a local councillor from the DUP, whose rhetoric was more covenantal and prophetic. He was quoted in the *Irish Times* in 1991 as saying: 'Rome's aim is to destroy Protestantism, our children, our children's children, our way of life and our Bible.' In the latter view, it is 'Popery in Rome, with the aid of Romish priests' which ensures the demise of Ulster; in the former it is political circumstances which are usually the culprit (terrorism, Irish or British governments, Republicanism). Hence, David Ervine, for example, said that 'Rome rule' is too simple a description of Southern Irish politics and that ideas of papal conspiracies were nonsense; indeed, covenantal theology like Paisley's was described as 'a load of crap'. In his interview, Gary McMichael described Paisley's theology in similar terms, describing Paisley personally as a fanatic who was blinkered by his theology.

The Articulation of Anti-Catholicism in the Secular Mode

The question thus arises of whether the secular mode is a type of anti-Catholicism at all. It is, because Catholics are criticised for their politics, if not their religion, and negative consequences follow at the levels of ideas and behaviour for Catholics because of what Catholicism is said to stand for politically. In this mode, the articulation is about what Catholicism represents politically rather than using this alleged political malevolence as an opportunity to criticise the nature and designs of the Catholic Church. The political rhetoric combines with a secular focus to shift the balance of emphasis toward the stance, affiliations, conduct and consequences of the Republican politics of Catholics as they affect Union. But Catholicism is presented as standing for these things, and the Catholic identity of Republicans is woven into the articulation, so that the attack on Republicanism is simultaneously also a criticism of what Catholics support politically. Thus, the articulation of anti-Catholicism in the secular mode points to such things as the threat of Republicanism to the Union (coupled with the untrustworthiness of British governments), the threats of a united Ireland, the degeneracy of Irish nationalism and the Irish Republic, and the authoritarianism and lack of political and civil liberties in the South, all of which are represented as Catholic and are said the highlight the dangers of Catholic politics. Sometimes, even, the secular focus is reinforced by avoidance of the use of the term 'Catholic' when criticising a political affiliation, but it is made perfectly clear, none the less, to whom it is referred. A good example is the following statement by Myrtle Boal, a member of the Conservative Party in Northern Ireland, and a Baptist:

> today we have the privilege of democracy, a privilege worth defending. While no country is fairer to its citizens than the United Kingdom, sadly, in this part of the Kingdom, some have benefited from the largesse of our country. Because of the country's sense of fair play, our government has bent over backwards to listen to and accommodate this lawless, ungrateful minority, compromising the loyal, law-abiding majority, who continue to suffer in silence.
>
> (quoted in Thomson, 1996: 33)

Others are less circumspect in attributing as Catholic political affiliations, conduct and behaviour they disagree with and oppose (and if not 'Catholic' they use interchangeable terms like 'Taig' and 'Fenian'). Thus, according to the UDA's *Combat*, Loyalist prisoners are 'banged-up inside' because the lawyers, magistrates and judges who framed evidence were Fenian. If not pulled by strings from the Vatican, the IRA is at least Catholic. Two of Bruce's respondents recounted how this affected their view of ordinary Catholics. 'The ordinary Catholic does not mind benefiting from the work of the gunman. When the gunman kills a farmer, who buys the farm? When the gunman kills a shop keeper, who buys the shop? The ordinary Catholic tolerates the IRA and votes for the IRA and takes the benefit from the IRA because they want our country'; 'ordinary Catholics have had long enough to stop the IRA. Everyone says they are not supporting the IRA but then who is?' (Bruce, 1994: 43). It is one step further to claiming that the Catholic Church supports, even controls, the IRA, and occasionally, secular Loyalists quote from Paisley's covenantal-type claims to this effect. Thus *Ulster* once carried a report that priests served in the IRA, quoting Paisley extensively, and *Combat* at the time of the Pope's visit to Ireland referred to the 'Papal anti-Christ' and made occasional reference to things like the 'spirit of the covenanters which still inspires the faithful few in defence of our Protestant heritage'. Early in the current round of 'troubles', there was a closer relationship between the Loyalist paramilitaries and Paisley; for example, together they organised the Ulster Workers' Strikes in the 1970s. This left the secular Loyalists open to the influence of covenantal theology and rhetoric. A good example is the Ulster Vanguard Oath, which, as a pamphlet, was pushed through the homes of Catholics in the 1974 Ulster Workers' Strike. It weaves together political complaint against Republicanism (Fenianism) with theological notions and rhetoric.

> I swear by Almighty God, by all heaven and earth, by the Holy Bible of the true Protestant faith, by our glorious Queen Elizabeth II and by our noble and victorious leader William Craig, supreme ruler of the Loyalist people of Ulster, to fight until we wade triumphantly through the rebel blood of every Fenian tyrant and murderer in our glorious Ulster. That these Fenian robbers and villains, these unbelievers of our glorious faith, will be driven like the swine they are unto the sea by the bullet, fire or sword, until Ulster is of the true Protestant [faith] and the Vanguard movement is indeed victorious and that all Fenian rabble is driven from our land ... We must shed the blood of all Fenian rabble and we must penetrate by whatever means, all Roman Catholic business and employment, that will cause ill feeling among their own kind. Above all, we must keep our deeds secret, using any methods of deception to gain our ends towards the downfall of the Roman Catholic heretics. I also swear that for every one of the British soldiers murdered by cowardly Fenians we shall exterminate one Fenian man, woman or child or a Fenian priest. This I swear to do before Almighty God. God save our glorious leader William, our Queen Elizabeth and the Rev. Martin Smyth. Above all keep Ulster Protestant.

However, most of the overlap with the covenantal mode today results from drawing on its political rather than theological analysis, and there are more criticisms of Paisley than eulogies. For example, members and supporters of the Loyalist para-militaries dislike Paisley's tone and manner, what Bruce (1994: 33) refers to as his 'bluster'. Some refer to him as the 'Grand Old Duke of York', who, through militant talk, led them up the hill, only to withdraw when the firing started as they turned his rhetoric into action, after which he disowned them. Gary McMichael, for example, described Paisley as a hypocrite, for he disowned the paramilitaries on occasions and drew on them at other times. Other working-class Loyalists use different military analogies, describing themselves as Paisley's cannon-fodder, people who do the dying or the prison term, while Paisley shouts the bluster from his safe home in a middle-class suburb. The animosity between Paisley and Gary McMichael is known to be intense, going back to the difficult relationship between Paisley and Gary's father, John McMichael, who criticised Paisley for offering nothing politically at the time of the Anglo-Irish Agreement except 'Ulster says no' (which *Common Sense* (UDA, 1987) was a response to). It is for much the same reason that conservative evangelicals criticise the secular Loyalists, despite common ground in their political analyses, because of their moral turpitude. In an interview David Ervine said that Paisley 'hated his [Ervine's] guts'; Clifford Smyth, connected with Inheritance Ministries, described the Loyalist paramilitaries as an amalgam of thieves who were mere tools of British intelligence and incapable of saving Protestant Ulster (C. Smyth, 1996: 35). Pastor Kenny McClinton, a former member of the UVF who once advocated beheading Catholics and impaling their heads on railings in Loyalist areas but who underwent a religious conversion to conservative evangelicalism in prison, said in interview that his former colleagues from the UVF, who had themselves undergone a political conversion, were a group of thugs, criminals and drug pushers. The acronym UDP stands, he said, for the 'Ulster Drug Party', and the new Loyalists lack any moral integrity; Ervine was described as a drunk. From his interviews with respondents from both camps, Bruce describes the views of conservative evangelicals towards secular militant Loyalists as unfriendly. They see vigilante violence as unacceptable and perpetrators as unsaved and lacking proper moral virtues (Bruce, 1994: 34). Secular Loyalists, meanwhile, do not find Paisley's religion agreeable; it's crap according to Ervine. Bell (1990: 164) recorded the following conversation between members of a Loyalist flute band in Derry:

> A: If we had Ian Paisley as prime minister we would have no drinkin' or anything
> B: There would be fuck all ... I don't agree with their religion, the DUP, their politics, aye, but not their religion, not this business about Sunday
> A: No swimmin' pools, no leisure centres, nothin' like that.

Even some of those band members who supported Paisley's Sabbatarianism did so for political reasons rather than religion: 'It's the day the Fenians go out to enjoy themselves, that's what Paisley's against, the Fenian Sunday ... yer got to stop the Fenian day' (Bell, 1990: 165). What religious commitment there was amongst the lads was nominal. 'I went [to church] this time last year ... I just did my communion and that was me. It's boring just listening to yer man shoutin' his head off. Jesus, it's wild boring. Yer canne sneeze or nothin' (ibid.: 163).

One of the important features of the secular mode's articulation of anti-Catholicism is criticism of the Irish Republic. Again, reference is sometimes made to the dominance of the Catholic Church in the South, and its identity as a Catholic country is continually stressed, similar to the covenantal mode, but the balance of the criticism is towards the socio-economic and political features of the Irish Republic which make it a failed entity that no one in their right mind would want to be united with. 'Fuck it', said one of Bruce's respondents in the UDA, 'we will not lose, we cannot lose. My grandfather joined the UVF to prevent a united Ireland and I joined the UDA for the same reason' (Bruce, 1994: 109). The Irish Republic is authoritarian, jackboot politics operate, and tyranny rules. By the same logic, opposition to the Orange Order by Republicans is said to show the same disrespect for civil and political liberties, and the evidence of 'Free Ireland' simply confirms it. This is not just code for the dominance of the Catholic Church in the Irish Republic, it is also a statement about Southern politicians and governments. Thus *Combat* argued at the time of the Pope's visit in 1979 that he should be allowed to visit Belfast in order to be able to compare everything with the Republic; he would then not listen to his cardinals again. Covenanters would not countenance a visit, but the secular mode was unconcerned about theological propriety and more interested in undermining the case for a united Ireland amongst Northern Catholics. *Combat* believed it had done this, for it wrote in 1979 that 'Northern Catholics are allied to Northern Protestants in wanting nothing to do with a failed Southern entity'.

Ulster once wrote that 'Eire is the most repressive state within Europe', and proceeded to document, not the conduct of the Catholic Church, although it had done so, but the activities of the Republic's security police and government figures. It was a country in which politicians 'still ignore the social and political injustices in their very midst, and the human right to a decent job and a fair wage shall remain only a forlorn hope for the many thousands who stand in the dole queues. As the harsh winds of winter descend on Dublin, cold and ragged children will continue to beg from passers-by.' That the article was written from Dublin by the paper's Dublin correspondent shows, however, their willingness to associate with Catholic Ireland in order to denigrate the Republic; and the denigration is as much cultural and economic as political. The cultural values of the Irish Republic toward divorce and contraception, for example, rooted in Catholic doctrine, match the unattractiveness of its social and economic policies. In his account of the 'Protestant case' against a united Ireland, J. Bowyer Bell said that 'the statistics of prosperity, the failures of policy and the futility of most national endeavours, from the welfare system to all sorts of economic and social gauges, indicate that all is not well. Behind the doors are ruined building sites, the green fields are badly tended, the people not so lovely close up' (Bowyer Bell, 1996: 193). 'Protestants know in their heart of hearts' the costs that a united Ireland would impose, 'inferiority and oppression by the lesser breed', and he went on to state: 'actually no-one has disproved this case' (ibid.: 93). He described it as priest-ridden, and its high culture contaminated by economic failure and Catholicism, with 'the finest artists driven abroad, if not by poverty then by the Pope' (ibid.: 179): 'a futile society without grace or enterprise, a tragedy for the Catholics already and a tragedy proposed for the Ulster Protestants' (ibid.: 175).

The Primary Constituency of the Secular Mode

Sir Fred Catherwood, a well-known Christian businessman born in Northern Ireland and President of the Evangelical Alliance, tells a story of how Protestant women from West Belfast were once besieging a government minister in a local hotel. A spokesman for the minister said to the women that he was 'not much of a Christian, but I know that Christians are meant to love their neighbours and you want to shoot them'. The women replied quickly, 'we're not Christians, we're Protestants' (recounted in Thomson, 1996: 38) – thus, some Protestants define themselves in terms of political and constitutional issues rather than a theological position, and the identity suggested by the appellation 'Protestant' is not a religious one. While there may well be a respect for 'Bible Protestants' amongst some secular Protestants because conservative evangelicalism is such a part of everyday life, it is also because of the political stance adopted by many Bible-believing Protestants. One of Bell's respondents from a flute band told him that 'Free Presbyterians are the most Protestant of the lot. I'm not a Free Presbyterian myself but I'd say they are the most loyal bunch' (Bell, 1990: 164). The secular mode of anti-Catholicism appeals to people like this. Its constituency is amongst the secular, and even anti-religious, or the liberal Protestants whose religious commitment is kept private and separate from politics; people who are militantly Loyalist and pro-Union, but who wish to keep covenantal theology and the Protestant religion out of Unionism; people whose contempt for Catholics arises because of the political position which Catholicism is said to stand for, and for the kind of society that Catholics offer as the alternative to Union with Britain; people who, because their anti-Catholicism has no religious trappings, can think of themselves as not being anti-Catholic at all but, instead, see themselves as political opponents of Republicanism, although the allusion between politics and Catholicism ensures that theirs is a secular form of anti-Catholicism.

The Implications of the Secular Mode for Relations with Catholics

Politically expedient relations are permissible – not only permissible, said David Ervine, but necessary. McMichael shares this view, for it is only pragmatic to recognise the need for relationships with Catholics. What objections there are to some forms of relationship arise from political circumstance and ideology rather than theology. The absence of theological commitment ensures that there are no problems in the secular mode to meeting Catholics as Catholics. Relations are also permissible outside the context of politics. Being secular or liberal in religion, attendance at a Catholic mass is even possible under some circumstances (mixed marriage ceremony, funeral etc.), and other mixed relations are permissible. Mixed marriage itself is more feasible under the secular mode because opposition is to a political position rather than religion, and sometimes the crude equation of the two can be overcome by personal knowledge and contact. That is why Bell (1990) found that even amongst his militant Loyalist respondents in Derry, some youngsters were in mixed relations, especially the girls,[3] something unimaginable for the young people of either sex in congregations in the Free Presbyterian Church or in the gospel halls dotted around Northern Ireland. Most members of Loyalist paramilitaries – whom Bruce (1994) calls the 'gunmen' – and their followers are secular anti-Catholics.

The Loyalist Volunteer Force (LVF), however, formed in Portadown in 1996 by Billy Wright, has appropriated covenantal theology as a result of Wright's conversion to conservative evangelicalism while in prison. Before his murder in 1997, Wright came under the influence of the Rev. William McCrea of the Free Presbyterian Church and Pastor Kenny McClinton. The old Tara paramilitary group in the 1970s was also covenantal in its theology because of the influence of William McGrath, and had difficult relations with the UVF as a result (Garland, 1997: 10). McClinton revealed in interview that one of the three conditions necessary to join the LVF's wing in the Maze Prison is regular church attendance. But the LVF is opposed by the other Loyalist paramilitary organisations and their political representatives, in large part because Wright's covenantal thinking permitted no political contact with Catholics. Wright opposed both the Irish cultural dimension recognised by the main Loyalist paramilitaries and their readiness to talk with Sinn Fein. In an interview with the *Sunday Life* on 2 November 1997, Wright explained that he objected to the move toward politics evident in the UVF since the 1970s (on which, see Garland, 1997), and to the atheism of the new Loyalists, although he said they were no longer Loyalists because of their readiness to develop politically expedient relations with Irish nationalists. 'You can't leave faith out of the equation', he said. The LVF broke away from the UVF in 1996 over the issue of political contact with Catholics, and there is the prospect of a bloody feud breaking out between them, although after Wright's assassination, some of the murders of Catholics in retaliation were admitted by the UFF, the mainstream paramilitary group linked to the UDA and to McMichael's UDP, which suggests a rapprochement. This does not appear to extend to the UVF. Pastor McClinton, who has spoken up for the LVF in the past (he denies that he is their spokesperson), was shot at in August 1997 and intimidated out of Belfast, and Belfast UVF men have assaulted some of Wright's supporters in Portadown. David Ervine's view of his former colleague's conversion was cynical – 'Wright always finds God in a crisis' – and Ervine objected to the LVF's naked sectarianism during the 1994–6 ceasefire, when it purposely shot innocent Catholics in order to try to draw in the IRA to protect the Catholic people. In interview, he said that the PUP's conflict with the LVF was part of the international process of urban versus rural splits, and was explained further by mid-Ulster's reputation as the heartland of sectarianism and tribalism, which the LVF sought to reinforce rather than challenge.[4] McClinton's view, on the other hand, is that 'tribal Protestantism', as he described it in interview, is ingrained in people in Ulster like a 'sort of conditioning', and that the secular Loyalists will face a cap in their support because they fail to represent Protestantism. Gary McMichael believes, however, that people's political and theological loyalties are not the same as they once were in Northern Ireland, so that the grain has changed: 'people are not the same as they were in 1920, society is not the same as it was in 1920, things have changed, and Unionists need to change with it'.

Challenging the Secular Mode

Various questions can be posed about the foundational ideas of the secular mode of anti-Catholicism. The first concerns the claim that Catholicism stands for a particular political position opposing Union, which misrepresents the Catholicness of Republicanism. On the one hand, Catholic constitutional preferences are mixed, for Breen (1996: 40–6) has shown from a 1994 survey that a quarter of Catholics want the Union preserved. Even a third of those respondents who described themselves as having an Irish identity preferred retention of the Union. While almost all Sinn Fein supporters favoured a united Ireland, a ratio of one to three SDLP supporters favoured the Union. On the other hand, it is erroneous to suggest that Republicanism is Catholic in ethos, motivation and ambition, as pointed out in Chapter 3. Republicanism is opposed by the hierarchy of the Catholic Church and it is thoroughly secular in its goals and aspirations. A similar exaggeration arises with the identification of Protestantism with certain civil and political liberties, largely based on a misrepresentation of the Irish Republic. This presents the greatest challenge to the foundational ideas of the secular mode for their view of the South is highly questionable; they see it, much like Ulster itself, through the prism of the past.

The covenantal view of the Irish Republic is simple – it is under 'Rome rule'. The secular mode, however, sees the country in more complex terms, although it is equally negative. To liberal Unionists it is a foreign country; whatever relations there are with the Irish Republic of an economic, business or political kind it is none the less still contact with a foreign country. The Loyalist view is more hostile and extreme. Pastor McClinton described the Republic as foreign soil, led by a foreign government: 'two countries, two states, two peoples; the Ulster-Scots are the indigenous population pushed North [and into Scotland] by the invading Gaels from Europe'. As Ruane and Todd (1996: 257) put it, Loyalist ideology presents the South as a Third World country, its economy bankrupt, its politics typical of banana republics. It is dominated by the Catholic Church and is unfriendly to Protestants, its culture is parochial and backward, and its people untrustworthy and devious. 'Rome rule' is thus only one of its problems. There was credence to some of these views once, but not all, and that was long ago. As David Ervine admitted in interview, 'Rome rule' is too simple a description of Irish politics and some allowance should be made for the changes that have taken place politically, pointing to the fact that a government fell recently because of the activities of a paedophile priest, something he considered unthinkable years ago.

At the time of partition, Cardinal Logue saw the Free State as a Catholic country, and reminded those drawing up the Constitution that the political blue-print 'must be submitted to the Bishops and a committee of theologians aided by a lawyer should be appointed to examine it and see that it is in accordance with Catholic principles' (quoted in Rafferty, 1994: 220). Fianna Fail's Ireland was, according to Foster (1988: 547), a nation set apart by Catholicism and Irish nationalism. Dennis Kennedy (1988) has demonstrated that Protestant attitudes in the North were seriously affected by the nationalist violence directed against Southern Protestants in the period 1920–2 but also by the adoption of an explicitly Catholic Constitution in 1937. Yet the portrayal of this as a form of fascism exaggerates the point. The Catholic Church has never been the established state church in the way that the Church of Ireland was until the mid-nineteenth century, and the Constitution merely recognised 'the special position' of the Catholic Church as the religion of 'the great majority of its citizens'; the Article was removed from the Constitution in 1972. Moreover, Protestants have never been systematically discriminated against. It has never been state policy and the advertisements carried in Unionist newspapers in the North explicitly stating that no Catholics need apply were not paralleled by anti-Protestant discrimination. There has been no physical extermination, nor enforced abandonment of the Protestant faith. In the view of Kurt Bowen, Protestants in the Republic have been a privileged minority (K. Bowen, 1983). The numbers of Southern Protestants have fallen considerably since partition, but this is the result of voluntary acts, such as migration North, lower birth rate, and mixed marriages. The birth rate for Protestants for two successive decades was half that of Catholics (Whyte, 1990: 153), and the rate of intermarriage grew rapidly from the 1950s. By the 1980s four out of every ten Protestants married Catholics (Ruane and Todd, 1996: 248). However, research has also shown that 40 per cent of the children from mixed marriages were baptised Protestant (Inter-Church Council, 1993: 79). Protestants faced a value system which did not reflect their religion, in that the society prohibited divorce and abortion, made it difficult to obtain contraceptives and permitted censorship of literature, although conservative evangelicals would approve of many of these if they had not been at the behest of the Catholic Church. But there is no evidence to support Loyalist claims that the minds and attitudes of faithful Catholics have been turned against Protestants by the Catholic Church. Southern Protestants never were a downtrodden and disadvantaged minority. Economically they were privileged and secure, and research shows them to be over-represented in the upper reaches of the class structure (summarised by Whyte, 1990: 152). There is evidence of considerable cultural assimilation rather than isolation or ostracism, as Protestant schools, clubs, colleges, newspapers and businesses have opened up to Catholics and become more mixed. Community relations are good, which is quite the opposite to the North, where communal divisions are enshrined in separate and exclusive associations.

Moreover, the political influence of the Catholic Church has not been uniform, and little account is taken of the separation of Church and state in modern Ireland. Whyte summarises his own research on Church–state relations by arguing that the influence of the Catholic Church declined from the 1950s onwards, most notably after the public outcry following the abandonment of the mother-and-child welfare scheme in 1951, which the Catholic hierarchy objected to on grounds that it was counter to Church teaching. In the earlier period the state enacted laws enshrining Catholic values in divorce, contraception, and censorship, but these were later modified or repealed. The Catholic ethos of the state has been diluted in part because of changes in attitude within the Catholic Church and in part because of the secularisation of the state. With respect to the former, the Second Vatican Council led to considerable reform of the Catholic Church, and by 1983 Cardinal Cahal Daly said that 'the Catholic Church totally rejects the concept of a confessional state. We do not seek a Catholic state for a Catholic people. We believe that the alliance of church and state is harmful ... We in no way seek to have the moral teaching of the Catholic Church become the criterion of constitutional change or have the principles of Catholic faith enshrined in civil law' (quoted in Dunlop, 1995: 53). The state became more secular as well, reflecting the opening up of its economy, the introduction of multinational companies, and entry into the European Union. Traditional Catholicism, Ruane and Todd write (1996: 246), is now a residual identity, and there is increasingly vocal anti-clerical and anti-Church sentiments; mass attendance is falling; numbers entering the priesthood and closed orders are declining; and the public devotion of Catholicism has been replaced by a more private and family-centred devotion, much as in secular societies like Britain. This contrasts markedly with the North, where politics and public displays are more religious.

Other comparisons work to the favour of the South. The crime rate is lower and crime is less violent (see Brewer et al., 1997), and the Southern economy is now stronger as a result of industrial expansion and growth in the Irish Republic and deindustrialisation in the North, both occurring in the 1960s, to the point that the Republic has been compared with the 'Tiger economies' of the East; the Republic's economy is referred to as the 'Celtic tiger' (see O'Connell, 1996). The comparison of the Irish Republic with Third World economies was described recently as fatuous (Kennedy, 1996: 178), and reviewing economic, social and health indicators, Kennedy argued that the South was one of the richest countries in the world, with the living standards of its inhabitants within the top 20 per cent in the world (ibid.: 180). The image of poverty and impoverishment was not true historically either. One of the most important measures of poverty is the infant mortality rate, and Kennedy shows how Ireland's rate was lower in 1900 than countries such as England and Wales, Denmark, Belgium, Austria, Hungary, Spain, Portugal and France, constituting leading nations in Protestant and Catholic traditions. By mid-century, Ireland was still lower than them all, save Denmark and England and Wales (ibid.: 183). Reviewing the evidence of poverty in the European Union, Ramprakash (1994) showed that the Republic has less poverty than the United Kingdom, and less than many other member countries in the European Union, although recent research has shown that the number of children living in poverty is higher in the Republic than the United Kingdom, reflecting larger family size amongst the poorest families (see Oppenheim and Harkin, 1996: 160; this data does not disaggregate Northern Ireland figures – on poverty levels in Northern Ireland see Mallett, 1997; in the Republic see National Anti-Poverty Strategy, 1997).

The Foundational Ideas of the Pharisaic Mode

The Pharisees were commended by Jesus for their knowledge of Judaic Law and their observance to it, and thus for their devotion to God. They were pious and devout, but also self-righteous in the conviction of their own salvation. Pharisees believed they knew the way to Heaven, which they saw as strict observance of Judaic Law, and they were exceedingly conscientious in sticking to the letter of the law. They believed they possessed knowledge of the Truth, which was available to all since it was contained in the Law of Moses, but that they alone practised it. The Pharisees were thus, in their own eyes, specially blessed by God as the only sect who followed His commands. This self-righteousness merged with a sense of superiority to set the Pharisees apart from ordinary believers. This apartheid was important to the Pharisees, for although God's Truth was available to all and Pharisees felt obliged to remind believers of the way to possess it, Pharisees prided themselves that ordinary Jews found observance of the Law too difficult, allowing them to see themselves as superior. This sense of pride was important and whenever it was threatened their separateness was reinforced by stricter and stricter reinterpretations of Judaic Law, which defined the boundaries of God's eternal truth narrower and narrower. Hence the major complaint that Jesus made against the Pharisees was that they had built more and more human-made regulations on top of God's commands, which both loaded people down with unnecessary human-imposed burdens and distorted God's Truth.

Jesus rejected the idea that strict observance of Judaic Law represented Truth and ensured salvation, and He redefined the righteous life as one which followed the spirit rather than the letter of God's Law. The spirit of this Law was significantly simplified when Jesus said that it could be summarised as the injunctions to love God completely and fully, and to love one's neighbour as oneself. In simplifying it, Jesus simultaneously made the boundaries of Truth exceedingly broad (although not necessarily any easier to practise), eliminating the exclusivity and superiority surrounding the Pharisees. The gates to Heaven are narrow, as Jesus says, for God's Law is difficult to practise, but everyone has the opportunity to enter, and the criteria for access are sufficiently wide to include everyone who believes in Jesus and can love both in the way Jesus says we should and the people whom we are supposed to. Jesus saw these criteria as more inclusive than observance of Judaic Law, and although the Pharisees were recognised by Jesus as very religious in their devotion to God, and very legalistic in observing injunctions, they were criticised by Him for placing too much emphasis on doctrine and not enough on love, and practising the outward form of religion but having a heart that was not open to Him. Jesus spoke to the Pharisees in such terms: 'You diligently study the Scriptures because you think that by them you will possess eternal life. These are the very Scriptures that testify about me, yet you refuse to come to me in order to have life ... I know you. I know that you do not have the love of God in your hearts' (John 5:39–42).

The third mode of active anti-Catholicism is called Pharisaic because its foundational ideas are reminiscent of the Pharisees. There is a sharp distinction made in the Pharisaic mode between biblical Truth and Error, from which arises a self-confidence that they possess knowledge of it and a recognition that they have a responsibility to share this knowledge with those who lack it by means of conversion attempts. Within the Pharisaic mode, people are pious, devout and very religious, but there is also a sense of superiority and exclusivity arising from the notion that they alone possess and practise biblical Truth. There is the same self-righteousness as the Pharisees but what distinguishes them is the definition of what constitutes such truth, which is no longer Judaic Law and its observance but Reformed theology. A major foundational idea of the Pharisaic mode is thus the stress on Reformed theology. It is now the right doctrine rather than the right interpretation of legal instructions that defines God's Truth and ensures salvation. However, maintaining the distinction between Truth and Error remains as important now as at the time of the Pharisees. Thus, Ankerberg and Weldon (1994: 111) write: 'what is salvation? What is the knowledge of the truth? If a knowledge of the truth and of salvation mean something different to Catholics and Evangelicals, how is it "loving" to ignore the fact? Unity and love among true Christians is always important, but so is doctrinal truth and the inevitable division it brings for those who openly reject such truth ... Love is a commitment to God that does not compromise truth.'

The 'right doctrine' they refer to is presented as Reformed theology, particularly as this understands the issue of personal salvation. Faith, and faith alone, is the way to salvation in Reformed theology. This is faith in Jesus, not trust in good works or any other intercessor than Jesus, such that salvation comes from the grace of God as His choice rather than anyone's own efforts; salvation is gifted not earned. Nor is salvation obtained by belief in Church tradition or teachings. The Bible is the word of God and it alone is the standard by which to judge His commands. Moreover once salvation is gifted – by the individual being 'born again' or renewed as a result of the Holy Spirit acting in their life – it cannot be lost. Once sins are forgiven by God as a result of accepting Jesus as one's personal saviour, they are forgiven for all time; and only Jesus can forgive sins. This is biblical truth – the right doctrine – as the Pharisaic mode presents it. As Ankerberg and Weldon write (ibid.: 244–5),

> Catholicism teaches that a Christian may lose their salvation. This is not biblical teaching. Jesus Himself taught that faith does bring the right to salvation. The Bible clearly teaches that by faith alone people can know that they are eternally saved because, at the moment of saving faith, they possess eternal life ... They can know this by truly trusting in Christ for forgiveness of sins and making Him their personal Lord and Saviour.

The Pharisaic mode shares this foundational idea with the covenantal mode, but there are significant differences in the way they make use of Reformed theology. In the Pharisaic mode Reformed theology is not understood through the notion of covenant, it is focused on the New Testament rather than the Old, since Jesus changes the means of salvation away from observance of Judaic Law towards belief in Himself, and it is devoid of the political dimension wrapped up with covenants. The Pharisaic mode is thoroughly apolitical, stressing the theological dimensions of Protestantism rather than the political ones attached to it in Northern Ireland. Thus, in one of our interviews, an elderly Presbyterian commented: 'the Church can't go any further than the Ten Commandments. If it starts to devise political structures, it's not really competent to do so ... Once the Church begins to talk politics, it gets itself into a mess.' This is not to say that such people have no political beliefs, but a hermetic seal is placed between them and their religion. Moreover, there is a tolerance of other Christians and other faiths even though this is combined with the certainty that their own beliefs are right. The above respondent continued: 'Presbyterianism does allow for a tremendous amount of free thought. We tolerate people with diverse views very easily as long as they still maintain the central belief.' As David McCarthy, General Secretary of the Evangelical Alliance in Northern Ireland, said: 'if Christians who are Evangelicals are to be consistent with their beliefs they will not be able to accept a tolerance which implies pluralism, but they will fiercely defend and uphold that tolerance which promotes the equal value and dignity of each person irrespective of their beliefs' (McCarthy, 1997: 14).

Being convinced, as they are, that they know and possess biblical Truth, advocates of the Pharisaic mode feel obliged to share such knowledge with those whose beliefs they see to be in error. That it is possible and necessary to convert people to the right doctrine is an important foundational idea of the Pharisaic mode. Attention is therefore focused on the theological problems of Catholicism rather than any political activity allegedly associated with it which might prevent the possibility of conversion. The covenantal mode thinks of Catholics as a collectivity under the control of the Pope and enslaved to the system of Catholicism, and has little contact with individual Catholics to make it possible to convert them, even if they thought that this was possible (and many conservative evangelicals believe that God has nothing to do with Catholics because they are non-Christian and thus He would not extend His grace to them). However, the Pharisaic mode, while also recognising the necessity for Catholics to convert to the Truth, tolerates individual Catholics to the point that there are relationships which can form the basis of conversion attempts. The leads to a further foundational idea, which is that Catholicism is Christian but in error. As Christians in error, God could extend His grace to individual Catholics to bring them back into Truth, hence the necessity for conversion attempts. As one of our respondents said of becoming a Christian, 'it's a purely personal decision ... the Holy Spirit may talk to anyone. The Spirit is supreme. I can't make the distinction about who is and isn't a Christian.'

The Form of Rhetoric of the Pharisaic Mode

The characteristic rhetoric of the Pharisaic mode is irenic, tending to be inclusive and conciliatory. Catholics are not condemned, belittled or demonised. Their doctrine is wrong, but even in declaring this point, Catholicism as a set of beliefs is not denounced in the terms or rhetoric of the covenantal mode. The irenic rhetoric of the Pharisaic mode is gentler, and less grating and harsh. In its softness it seeks to promote openness amongst Catholics to the idea of conversion rather than alienating them by denunciations, and vivid and lurid prophetic rhetoric. Having abandoned almost all covenantal theology, including the Westminster Confession and other covenantal statements, the irenic rhetoric of the Pharisaic mode does not convey that the Pope is the antiChrist and that the Catholic Church is the Whore of Babylon. As Bruce (1986: 221) says, such rhetoric would be embarrassing to liberal Protestants. A good example of irenic rhetoric is contained in the opening passages of a book intended to persuade Catholics that their doctrine is in error and that they should conform to the biblical Truth found in Reformed theology:

If Roman Catholicism and Evangelical faith are both biblical, then fine; we can both worship together in each other's churches without fear of violating our conscience or scriptural standards. But if the Bible reveals that either Protestantism or Catholicism is wrong, then one or the other should conform itself to biblical standards. Of course, even the most liberal Evangelical would agree that there are significant aspects of Protestantism as a whole that are unbiblical and oppose the teachings of Christ. And even the most traditional Catholic would agree that there are powerful elements within modern Catholicism that do the same.

(Ankerberg and Weldon, 1994: ix)

The tone is soft, conveying the idea of openness and conciliation, even that there are things wrong in every set of beliefs, while at the same time conveying that Catholicism is contrary to biblical standards.

The tolerance towards Catholics which is part of the foundational ideas of the Pharisaic mode conditions this irenic rhetoric. The rhetoric cannot be denunciatory with the idea that Catholics are fellow Christians, brothers and sisters in Christ, who have strayed and need to be brought back into Truth. Such tolerance also expresses itself in the idea that Catholicism contains many evangelicals within it who 'truly believe in Jesus Christ as their Lord and Saviour and trust in Him alone for their salvation' (ibid.: 100). Of such Catholics Ankerberg and Weldon (ibid.: 100) say, 'we warmly accept these as brothers and sisters in Christ'. These are people with whom there can be 'spiritual fellowship', which is typical irenic rhetoric. However, evangelical Catholics need to leave the Catholic Church because the Church is in error. No compromise is made with this idea despite the open and welcoming irenic rhetoric. This was conveyed in the remarks of one of our respondents, a ministry student training for the Presbyterian Church, who utilised typical irenic rhetoric:

I would define Christianity within any denomination as someone who has recognised their need for Christ and Christ alone for the forgiveness of sins and peace with God, from whatever denomination that person comes from. Christianity is focusing on Christ and acknowledgement of Him alone for salvation. I believe we find that in the Roman Catholic Church as well. There would be areas of fundamental disagreement with Catholicism but those on the periphery I would be flexible about, but I couldn't the flexible about the fact that Christianity is about faith in Jesus Christ alone for salvation.

There are thus areas which Catholics and evangelicals can agree about, but the Truth is the Truth, and no matter how irenic the rhetoric, Catholics are told firmly they are in error if they do not believe in faith alone as the means to salvation. Thus the stress in the Pharisaic mode is on the differences in theology rather than the areas of doctrinal concord. 'To say that Evangelicals and Catholics are brothers and sisters in Christ', write Ankerberg and Weldon (1994: 109), 'assumes beforehand that Catholics have experienced true, regenerating faith. But this is impossible for any Catholic who is seeking to attain salvation by both faith and works as taught by [the] church. To assume that the average Roman Catholic is just as saved as the average Evangelical is a terrible mistake. Catholics need to be evangelised.'

The Articulation of Anti-Catholicism in the Pharisaic Mode

J. Bowyer Bell wrote, when formulating the 'Protestant case' that, 'a great many of those Protestants in British Ulster who seek moderation and understanding, who support fellowship and ecumenical gestures, still find the Roman church distasteful and authoritarian and much that is Irish-Irish unattractive and often inferior, and so says the record and observation' (Bowyer Bell, 1996: 264). In the Pharisaic mode, toleration of others and irenic rhetoric still involves negative stereotypes of Catholics and the Catholic Church, an arrogant self-righteousness that one's own doctrine is not just the better but the only way to Truth, and the view that Catholicism is morally and theologically wrong. There is still fear of Catholicism, even if this fear is not linked to local or international political conspiracies, and a lack of acceptance of Catholic doctrine and practise. Anti-Catholicism in the Pharisaic mode does not articulate political concerns but addresses theological issues, like the claims that the Catholic Church is in error, that traditional Catholics lack piety, devotion and the prospect and promise of salvation, and that Catholic doctrine is unreformed and unreformable in its essential beliefs.

Most mainstream Protestant denominations have now overturned the anti-Catholic doctrinal statements that were first formulated in the sixteenth and seventeenth centuries at a time of struggle between the Reformation and Counter-Reformation. The Presbyterian Church in Ireland, for example, decreed in 1861 that the Catholic Church was a Christian church, replacing the views of the Westminster Confession, but it argued instead that the Catholic Church was 'in much error'. This is the view of a trainee minister in the church who told us in interview: 'I see the Roman Church as a Christian church in error. I believe there are people who are saved or born again within that Church – individuals – but the Church isn't in standing within the Christian community as such, and would need to reform right back to the basic doctrines, Mariology, the mass, the basics of the Church.' The validity of Catholic doctrine is not recognised; it is morally and theologically wrong. It is not that the Catholic Church's politics are anti-Union or anti-Northern Irish Protestant – its doctrine is just plain wrong. A Protestant, active in the peace movement, ecumenism and cross-community relationships could still thus confess: 'if my daughter got engaged to a Free Presbyterian I'd be sorry because I would expect to get a bigoted son-in-law; but if she chose a Catholic, no matter how tolerant he was, I'd be more disturbed. I'd feel she was allying herself with something that's morally wrong' (quoted in Inter-Church Council, 1993: 15). The failure of traditional Catholics to be 'saved' and 'born again' ensures both that they lack the piety and devotion associated with a moralistic private life, and that they lack eternal salvation. Stereotypes of traditional Catholics (as opposed to evangelical ones) in the Pharisaic mode recycle old-fashioned anti-Catholicism, even if expressed politely – they are going to Hell, are immoral, untrustworthy and objects of fear, and belong to a church that prevents them or makes them incapable of receiving the Truth.

The Pharisaic mode makes allowance for the changes in doctrine and practise that have followed the Second Vatican Council, unlike the covenantal mode. Pastor McClinton, for example, said that Vatican II was just a veneer, a coating, and that it had made no real change, but Pharisaic-type anti-Catholics recognise the change. Yet the Pharisaic mode still criticises the Catholic Church because Catholicism has been left in a state of confusion and disarray, as official doctrinal statements are contradicted and diversity is permitted. Catholicism is evolving as tenets like papal authority give way to people's authority, but this results only in confusion and divergence. This is a no-win situation: the Catholic Church is criticised for moving away from established doctrine, but also for not changing the fundamentals of its doctrines. It has changed too much and not enough. Ankerberg and Weldon, for example, complain that there is a 'degree of confusion and divergence in Roman Catholicism as a whole' (Ankerberg and Weldon, 1994: 19), and they cite with support the views of theologians who complain that an examination of Catholic doctrine is now difficult because it is no longer uniform (ibid.: 18, 19). But they also criticise Vatican II for its failure to address the central issue of personal salvation: 'No one can deny that substantial changes have occurred in the Roman Catholic Church since Vatican II ... Nevertheless, one of the most serious issues is its unwillingness to accept biblical authority' (ibid.: xi–xii). Catholicism thus becomes 'hedged with unbiblical trimmings' which 'revise, neutralise or nullify' Truth (ibid.: xii). Even with the absence of vitriol, venom and denunciation, this represents anti-Catholicism because Catholicism is not recognised as a valid expression of Christian duty, nor a reassurance of salvation. In short, all Catholics should leave, even the evangelical ones. As one of our interviewees said, 'we need to draw a line and not compromise. I think from Scripture [that] evangelical Catholics would need to withdraw from that church.'

The Primary Constituency of the Pharisaic Mode

If the covenantal mode has a primary constituency in the 'holy remnant' of religious fundamentalists, the Pharisaic mode appeals to those Protestants who are religious but disavow politics or denunciation. The tolerance and openness of the Pharisaic mode and its inclusive irenic rhetoric, combined with the self-righteousness that Protestantism is right, ensures that it appeals to the pious and devout Protestants of the liberal kind. Its avoidance of politics also gives it appeal to those Protestants who have either withdrawn from worldly contamination, as Bruce (1994: 35) puts it, to focus on God, such as the exclusive Brethren who eschew all political involvement, or those who draw a sharp distinction between religion and politics and wish to keep the two separate. This does not involve a political withdrawal, just a religious faith free of politics. Such a thing is possible in Northern Ireland.

Researcher: Could you tell me a little bit more about how your Unionism interacts with your Christianity?

Respondent: For God and Ulster? I would see them as two distinct things. I believe in God first, and politics and everything else, comes after that. My politics happen to the Unionist, but I don't think it's a case of 'For God and Ulster'.

Researcher: So is Unionism anointed by God?

Respondent: Not for me.

Politics in such an approach is viewed in rationalistic and pragmatic terms, with political conflict in Northern Ireland being resolved by compromise, tolerance and conciliation. But since as a religion Catholicism is uncompromisingly wrong, a hermetic seal needs to be put between politics and religion as the best way of handling this. This divorce from politics adds to the appeal of the Pharisaic mode of anti-Catholicism.

The Implications of the Pharisaic Mode for Relations with Catholics

Because the Catholic Church is recognised in the Pharisaic mode as a Church of Christ yet is in much error, there is an acceptance of some Catholic doctrines. As a Christian church, Catholicism has areas of common ground. There is also a recognition that the Universal Church of Christ should have no denominational boundaries. With such views, people in the Pharisaic mode would see themselves as able to engage in many Church-based relations with Catholics. There is also contact with Catholics in order to convert them. The Pharisaic mode lends itself to ecumenism and other inter-church activities, but this is always under the recognition that Catholicism is wrong in several doctrinal beliefs and practices. In the covenantal mode, ecumenism is abhorrent. Paisley has said this many times, and Pastor McClinton described it as the greatest blight on the province of Ulster. Protestant churchmen who were ecumenical had 'sold their birthright to get into bed with Rome'. Within the Pharisaic mode, however, ecumenism is endorsed but only up to a point, and for some it may not extend to joint worship. In an interesting piece of survey research on the 'Protestant mosaic' in theological preferences, Boal et al. found that of those Protestant churchgoers they defined as liberal, most would have contact with the Catholic Church on religious and social matters, while those defined as 'conservative liberals' would be more hesitant about religious association but have little resistance to social contact. Those they defined as fundamentalists avoided the Catholic Church on all matters (Boal et al., 1991: 78). Only around a third of all churchgoing Protestants were prepared to worship with Catholics. Ecumenism for some conservative-liberal Protestants, therefore, falls well short of joint worship, yet there is still contact of a kind and a general tolerance of Catholics. Two of our respondents expressed this well.

I would see Christianity not necessarily in a list of do's and don't's or creeds but it's focusing upon Christ and acknowledging Him alone for salvation. We find that in the Protestant Church and I believe we find that in the Roman Catholic Church as well ... I have no problem with ecumenism but I would see areas where the Protestant churches should not be working with the Catholic Church. If you're talking about heading down the road of joint worship I would have difficulty with that.

I'd love to see one church without denominations, we could all be Christians together. I think ecumenism is frowned on because they don't know exactly what's involved in it. I'd love to see all the denominations worshipping together. I would include Catholics with the exception of the Mass because of what they believe about transubstantiation. The Pope being infallible, that's the only other major one.

The relatively open-minded nature of this mode of anti-Catholicism therefore permits several forms of relationship in a religious context, although the line gets drawn somewhere before full ecumenism. The ecumenism of the Pharisaic mode therefore needs to be distinguished from those ecumenical Protestants who are devoid of any anti-Catholicism.

Since theological concerns are the only impetus to the Pharisaic mode, relationships with Catholics in non-religious settings are not problematic, some of which may, however, be used as attempts for the conversion of Catholics to Reformed theology. The absence of political impulse ensures that politically expedient relations with Catholics are possible. In this mode, moreover, the Republic of Ireland presents no special fears or objections, culturally or politically, and adherents of this mode of anti-Catholicism are the most open to visiting Southern Ireland and to developing cross-border relations. It is people with the Pharisaic mode of anti-Catholicism who are likely to be those Protestants whom Ruane and Todd (1996: 258) describe as having an 'orientation [which] sees the South as another jurisdiction and as culturally different, but not "foreign" in the normal meaning. Their own criticisms of the South are nuanced, problems are seen in context, misunderstandings are open to correction, and "positive" changes in the South are acknowledged.'

Challenging the Pharisaic Mode

Since the focus of the Pharisaic mode is entirely theological, challenges to the foundational ideas of the mode must also address the theological misunderstandings surrounding anti-Catholicism. This is done in greater detail in Chapter 5; suffice here to say that there are two specific theological challenges to the Pharisaic mode: the value placed on doctrine above love, and the association of the doctrine of justification by faith with biblical Truth. In the Apostle Paul's discourse on love in 1 Corinthians 13:1–13, he tells us that 'if I have no love, I am nothing'. Knowledge without love is pointless Paul says, for 'what I know now is only partial'. Human-made doctrines offer only partial truths; Scripture must be the source of doctrine, and in Paul's formulation of Scripture, he balances the relative merits of various spiritual gifts. He mentions the importance of good preaching, a faith powerful enough 'to move mountains', and the possession of knowledge deep enough to 'understand all secrets'. Yet above all these, he says, is love. It is greater than faith and hope; good doctrine does not even get a mention when he lists the three enduring qualities: faith, hope and love; the greatest of which, Paul writes, is love (1 Corinthians 13:13). Elsewhere in Scripture we are told that love builds one up while knowledge puffs one up, and there are several warnings against the conceit of thinking that human wisdom is divine. Therefore, people within the Pharisaic mode need to ask themselves whether their capacity to love those who have different doctrine is placed below the stress on possession of the right knowledge; Scripture says it should be reverse.

This leads to perhaps the major challenge for the Pharisaic mode, which is whether or not justification by faith is the Truth. Justification by faith is a clear injunction of Paul's letters in the New Testament, but the Book of James, for example, places as much stress on good works. But leaving aside disputes between the apostles, the critical measure for the Pharisaic mode is provided by Jesus' own actions and words. He, after all, is the One recognised as the object of faith and veneration, not Paul or James. Jesus has a very broad understanding of personal salvation. He says often that He is given only those whom the Father gives to Him, supporting the view that salvation is God's gift, but Jesus never mentions justification by faith as the means to personal salvation, nor does He restrict salvation to the possession of a corpus of knowledge. He asks everyone – anyone – simply to come and believe in Him as the Son of God. Faith *is* the critical measure, but what is important is the object of this faith. For Jesus it is faith *in Jesus* that is the means to personal salvation, not faith in the doctrine of justification by faith. The latter is a narrower doctrinal statement developed by the Protestant reformers at the time of the Reformation to distinguish themselves from what they saw as the teaching and practice of the Catholic Church, and is more exclusive than Jesus' own standard. The doctrine of justification by faith is a human-made measure of personal salvation, and as such is the very thing that Jesus warned against. What was necessary to Jesus to ensure salvation was faith in Him. 'Whoever comes to me I will never drive away', Jesus is quoted as saying in John's gospel (John 6:37). No mention is made about the doctrine that is needed in order to come to Him. Implications for doctrinal beliefs follow on from faith in Jesus – one cannot hold sets of beliefs which contradict His teachings – but the doctrine of justification by faith is not one of Jesus' teachings. Moreover, implications for good works also follow on from faith in Jesus, as the necessary working out of His teachings. Those who believe in Him are enjoined to walk like Him, as the first of John's letters make clear (1 John 2:6), which has consequences for what ordinary Christians do and say, although these works are clearly presented by Jesus as not ensuring entrance to the gateway to salvation, they are more the consequence of already having passed through it as a result of believing in Him.

In addition to its very narrow interpretation of personal salvation, the Pharisaic mode also has a distorted interpretation of what Catholic teachings are on personal salvation since the Second Vatican Council. The Catholic Church no longer teaches salvation by works, and places belief in Jesus at the centre. These points, which seriously challenge the foundational ideas of the Pharisaic mode, will be addressed further in Chapter 5.

5   Common-sense Reasoning
and Theological
Misunderstandings

Introduction

The intention in this chapter is to address some further sociological features of anti-Catholicism by identifying the common-sense reasoning processes involved with it. This complements the more macro-level analysis of the operation of anti-Catholicism in Northern Ireland's social structure in Part I by focusing on micro-level issues relating to identity, language and common-sense knowledge. While the focus is on the theological misunderstandings surrounding Catholicism and the distorted common-sense notions about what Catholics are supposed to believe, there is a sociological base to the distorted theological ideas on which anti-Catholicism is founded. Two issues are addressed in particular to demonstrate this claim. The common-sense ideas and reasoning processes which support the 'cognitive map' of anti-Catholicism help to create, amongst other things, distorted theological understandings; and the socio-linguistic features of the language used in theological debate, have more to do with representing different identities than differences in doctrine.

Common Sense and Anti-Catholicism

'Common sense' is a frequently used term in the vocabulary of sociologists, and although there is no agreed theoretical understanding of the term (see Brewer, 1984), it is understood widely to refer to a body of beliefs, maxims, ideas and types held by ordinary people in the street, constituting lay notions of social reality, rather than scientific ones. The normal contrast is between common-sense knowledge and science, with lay notions being seen as opposed to scientific ones, although common-sense notions can incorporate science by including lay interpretations of scientific ideas. This is exemplified, for example, by the lay understandings of the medical evidence about drinking and driving which distorts the scientific evidence about the negative effects of alcohol on driving ability. Anti-Catholicism involves common-sense knowledge about theology rather than science, for lying behind these distorted theological ideas about Catholicism is a body of common-sense knowledge which sustains and supports it, including common-sense ideas about theology and the place of Catholic doctrine and practice in relation to it. This common-sense knowledge also includes a host of other maxims lying outside of theology, such as common-sense notions about Catholic politics and the Catholic Church's alleged support for terrorism, ideas about Britain, the Irish Republic and Ulster, as well as judgements about Catholic attitudes, behaviour and life-style, amongst many other things.

It is recognised in sociology that common-sense maxims, types, ideas and beliefs are often vague and contradictory, but are extremely immutable and resistant to change, since common-sense knowledge is the primary realm of relevance through which people understand and interpret the world. Common-sense is believed by lay people to make sense, in that it supplies the categories, types, and interpretative processes necessary to understand the world. This suggests that 'common sense' is much more than a stock of ideas, for it is fundamentally a process of reasoning. It involves a reasoning process in which this stock of common-sense knowledge is routinely drawn on by lay people to construct their interpretations and understandings of their everyday world. If the stock of common-sense knowledge on which people draw in their reasoning process is shared within a group, in that the ideas, notions and maxims adhere to a group or collection of people, the common-sense knowledge will be socially transmitted amongst them, ensuring that they reason in similar ways and thus construct similar understandings of the social world. The phrase 'cognitive map' is a useful description of this process. A person's 'cognitive map' includes their stock of common-sense ideas, which may be shared collectively with others, as well as their practical reasoning processes which utilise this common-sense knowledge to map or understand the world.

Anti-Catholicism highlights this process well. The modes of anti-Catholicism form discrete common-sense understandings of the social world, based on different, though related, common-sense maxims, ideas and notions. These common-sense ideas adhere to collections of people, who thus come to construct similar understandings, as exemplified within each mode of anti-Catholicism. The modes thus represent different, though related, stocks of common-sense knowledge, which are socially disseminated and transmitted and therefore readily available as a resource. Anti-Catholicism also involves a practical reasoning process in which anti-Catholics draw on their stock of socially available common-sense knowledge to understand the world, rather than formal theological knowledge which contradicts it. I begin by outlining what might be called 'the cognitive map of anti-Catholicism' by describing the common-sense reasoning process which supports the stocks of common-sense knowledge about Catholicism.

The Cognitive Map of Anti-Catholicism

Four features characterise the common-sense reasoning process that supports and sustains anti-Catholicism, which, in a remarkable piece of alliteration, can be called distortion, deletion, distance and denial. Distortion occurs when evidence is turned around, manipulated or even invented in order to fit a generalisation about Catholicism; deletion involves the removal of evidence from deliberation and consciousness when it contradicts or complicates the generalisation; denial occurs when evidence against the generalisation is falsified by denying events or circumstances occurred; and distance occurs when evidence against the generalisation is avoided, ignored and overlooked. The employment of these cognitive processes ensures a very self-contained and closed cognitive map, and they mutually reinforce each other in their antipathy to Catholicism.

Distortion is by far the most obvious element of the practical reasoning which supports anti-Catholicism. It involves distorted views of Irish history as a whole, as well as of specific events and circumstances. As Hempton (1996: 108) describes it, the 'Ulster-Protestant world view' offered appeals to history which 'not only fore-shortened the past', but manipulated history to suggest they were 'part of a tradition protected by divine providence'. He enthusiastically endorses Roy Porter's view that 'those who appeal to bygone ages are often those who know least about them; the present can invent the past according to its own preferences' (quoted in ibid.: 177). The 1641 massacre, for example, has been distorted to support contemporary conflicts. It is widely understood in Protestant mythology as the first sectarian killing in Irish history, suggesting that sectarianism begins only when Catholics kill Protestants. Some Protestants reason that they are thus the victims rather than the perpetrators of sectarianism. The Rev. Ivan Foster, from the Free Presbyterian Church, wrote in the letters column of the *Belfast Telegraph* on 12 July 1997 that there had been a sectarian war waged against the Protestant people for centuries, invoking the 1641 massacre, and warned readers that the time had now finally arrived for them to resort to the same tactics used against them, at long-last fighting sectarianism with sectarianism. The claim that sectarianism begins with the massacre overlooks and ignores the fact that Catholics had been killed for decades prior to 1641 (that is, the claim also involves distance), and it distorts the scale of the Protestant deaths in the massacre. The practice of what historians call 'presentism' – the process of interpreting the past through the perspective of the conflicts and concerns of the present – distorts the 1641 massacre in other ways. Paisley has referred to the massacre as the first attempt at Catholic interference in Ulster, deleting obvious evidence that Ulster in its present form did not exist then and that Catholics were, anyway, the original inhabitants of the old province of Ulster (indeed, of Ireland).[1] An elder in the Free Presbyterian Church told Taylor that 'it all started in 1641 when the Catholics massacred Protestants and stacked up thirty bodies at the front door of the church' (Taylor, 1983: 95). Another of his respondents is quoted as saying that the River Bann 'was full of the bodies of Protestants and the Catholics walked over their bodies to get to the other side' (ibid.: 104). Other people also distort the scale of atrocities. One correspondent to the *Belfast Telegraph* alleged that 30,000 Protestants were killed; *Ulster* claimed it was over 150,000 whereas impartial historical evidence shows it to be between 3,000 and 10,000 at most (see Chapter 1). Further distortion results in the claim that the Catholic Church orchestrated the killings and that it was done by Irish nationalists, both of which claims involve projecting backwards into history someone's current foes. This is most clearly evident in the claim of *Ulster*, a Loyalist magazine, that 'the present struggle in Ulster commenced with the massacre of 154,000 Protestants in 1641', and that it was an attempt by 'Romanism, joining hands with that other religion of hate, Communism', to 'clear every Protestant off the soil of Ireland'.

It is not just the scale of atrocities in specific conflicts that can be distorted, for the placing of blame and responsibility is also distorted by common-sense practical reasoning. For example, to some Protestants, the only deaths that occurred during the Reformation were of Protestants, and the only church responsible was the Catholic Church. Only Catholic monarchs left a legacy of misdeeds; Cromwell, instead, was described by one member of the Free Presbyterian Church as the greatest Englishman. Paisley has also eulogised Cromwell, saying on one occasion that he 'thanked God' that he decapitated people, suggesting that he wished Cromwell could 'swing his sword today' (quoted in Taylor, 1983: 97). This finds a parallel today in the idea that only the IRA is responsible for deaths in 'the troubles'.

One more example can suffice of historical distortion arising from presentist concerns. The Orange Order's Brian Kennaway, convenor of its Education Committee, recently wrote about the origins of the Order, claiming that it was a response to 'defenderism', which was described as a group of 'Roman Catholic Revolutionaries', and part of the 'ethnic cleansing programme to remove Protestant witness from Ireland' (Kennaway, 1997: 8). The claim conveniently deletes mention of the violence of the Peep O'Day Boys and their own attempt to protect access by Protestants to the linen industry, to which defenderism was a reaction. The Peep O'Day Boys were so called because they were given much to terrorising Catholics at dawn, harassing them from their homes and papering their doors with notices to remove themselves to Hell or Connaught, a reference back to Cromwell's depredations (see Kee, 1995: 137).

Distortion does not just occur as a result of presentism, where current conflicts and concerns are projected on to the past, for the present itself can be distorted. For example, characterisations of the contemporary Irish Republic are made through the operation of practical reasoning rather than appropriate statistical evidence, and show similar distortion. Common-sense notions that the Republic is an economic banana republic are not supported by the evidence, nor is the notion that the Republic is worse than the North in terms of social measures like crime and poverty. Generalisations like this are made about a whole number of Catholic countries, whose contemporary circumstances are believed to be negatively affected by the limitations of their religion. Taylor quotes one of his respondents in the Free Presbyterian Church as saying that the 'mental health of a country' can be ascertained from its religion, and he went on to say: 'if you notice, in Roman Catholic countries there is always poverty and in Latin America particularly, you find witchcraft mixed with religion. The priest could not get rid of it so they accommodated themselves' (Taylor, 1983: 107). Many distortions exist around the modern period of terrorism in Northern Ireland. One is that Northern Ireland was at peace before the outbreak of civil unrest in the late 1960s and it was only the propensity of Catholics to complain about citizenship rights which disturbed the peaceful equilibrium (see Bowyer Bell, 1996: 343). Another more popular common-sense notion is that the Catholic Church endorses, even encourages, the violence. This claim illustrates that distortion often occurs in conjunction with deletion, which involves ignoring counter-evidence. In the common-sense reasoning process within anti-Catholicism, the claim that the Catholic Church endorses or encourages terrorism is mutually reinforced by removing from consciousness and deliberation the counter-evidence that, in fact, the Catholic Church has been amongst the fiercest critics of the IRA, as veteran Republicans like Jimmy Drumm comment. The distortion that the 1916 Easter Rising was blessed by the Pope, often quoted by Paisleyites, deletes from consciousness the fact that William of Orange, the symbolic figurehead of Protestant Ulster, was blessed by the Pope before the Battle of the Boyne and was actually supported by the Catholic Church at the time against King James II. Conversely, Rafferty (1994: 194) shows that the 1916 Rising was not supported by the Catholic Church (see also Chapter 3).

Deletion and distance are similar cognitive processes. The former involves the conscious removal of well-known counter-evidence from historical and narrative accounts of events, the latter the overlooking and avoidance of counter-evidence. Thinking in terms of stereotypes and categories involves distance, for it requires avoidance of evidence drawn from personal knowledge in preference for bold generalisations drawn from typifications. Within anti-Catholicism, individual Catholics are thus treated as types and countervailing evidence drawn from personal contact with particular Catholics is overlooked. Bowyer Bell, in putting the 'Protestant case', describes what he calls the Protestant stereotypes of 'the other' and demonstrates how easy it is to reason by them rather than on the basis of personal experience (Bowyer Bell, 1996: 145): 'the others, the Fenians, are not British, not proper Christians, imprudent, wastrels, profligate, not redeemed, beyond redemption. Better to imagine the slothful, drunken Catholic, surrounded by squalling children, living on the dole, slipping off to mass on the way to the pub, there to sing rebel songs, to contribute to Sinn Fein. It is far better than meeting the harried, desperate husband, unemployed, willing and desperate, determined that his lot will get out of Unity Flats [an estate of tower blocks in a hardline area] and into a decent school, and not at all concerned with the authority of Rome or the agenda of Sinn Fein. Better to imagine the Irish rebel, cold, merciless, cruel, a nationalist monster.' Taylor's analysis of Paisleyism recognises the effects which follow from people thinking only in terms of stereotypes of Catholics, for he notes that this reasoning process supports a range of common sense notions which are anti-Catholic: 'the view of Free Presbyterians that Catholics are "second class citizens" produced by a church which holds them under its spiritual domination, is derived more from an inherited set of historical prejudices and values than from direct personal experience of Catholics' (Taylor, 1983: 116). This is a good example of what results when distance affects common-sense reasoning.

Distance is also close to denial, in that the latter cognitive process involves falsification in order to deny counter-evidence. The application of stereotypes involves denial in that it falsifies evidence which shows that ordinary Catholics do not fit the typification. Denial, however, is also a broader cognitive process. A good instance of denial in relation to anti-Catholicism concern claims from its members that the Orange Order, for example, is tolerant toward Catholics and hostile to Protestants who 'persecute, injure or unbraid any man on account of his religion' (Kennaway, 1997: 9). Catholic parishioners of Harryville church in Ballymena, who have now had members of the Orange Order harass and abuse them outside church for nearly two years, could reasonably query this statement, but it forms part of a larger exercise in practical reasoning in which anti-Catholics deny they are bigoted or prejudiced toward individual Catholics, or that they are to blame for any of Northern Ireland's ills. It is only denial which allows anti-Catholics to believe common-sensically that the bitterness and enmity comes from one side alone. Thus, a member of the Free Presbyterian Church told Taylor (1983: 103) that 'the Free Presbyterians are much more tolerant of the Catholics because they are concerned with their souls'. Another of his respondents said that Protestants have extended the hand of friendship only to be scorned by Catholics. 'Let me put it this way', she said, 'we let them have their worship and we mixed with them and for all our love, they became our enemies' (ibid.: 108). Denial like this of the extent of Protestant hostility and enmity towards Catholics in the past, is an important part of the common-sense reasoning process of anti-Catholics, and involves considerable distortion of the historical record, as well as much deletion of counter-evidence. The common-sense idea that anti-Catholics really love individual Catholics is a gross distortion, and it is not just a feature of the common-sense reasoning of anti-Catholics today. The Rev. Henry Cooke, the arch-conservative evangelical and rabid anti-Catholic of the nineteenth century, argued against O'Connell's demands for Catholic emancipation on the grounds that it destabilised Protestant–Catholic relations which had hitherto been good, primarily as a result of the 'brotherly kindness' associated with Protestantism:

> hitherto the Protestants and Papists of Ulster had lived together in peace. Those feelings of brotherly kindness which Protestantism inculcates, had produced a salutary effect upon all parties. The vast body of Roman Catholics showed no jealousy at Protestant success. The spirit of fanaticism which generally charac-terises their faith had well-nigh disappeared. Under the influence of O'Connell, a system of agitation was inaugurated which changed the whole tone of society in Ulster.   (quoted in Porter, 1871: 393)

Distortion, deletion, distance and denial clearly appear together in the common-sense reasoning process within anti-Catholicism, and many common-sense notions can only be sustained because distortion, deletion, distance and denial mutually reinforce each other in sustaining antipathy toward Catholicism and Catholics. Their mutual reinforcement of antipathy results in a cognitive map which is very closed and self-contained, and one that is immutable and resistant to change. The closed and self-contained character of the cognitive map of anti-Catholicism is reinforced by various religious and secular artefacts and behaviours which sustain and support anti-Catholicism. These range from the Bible version they read, the King James version being the preferred version for anti-Catholics;[2] the church to which they belong and the ministers to whom they listen; the hymns which they sing; the other Christian groups and organisations with which they have fellowship; the secular newspapers they buy; the political parties and politicians they support; the marching organisations to which they belong; the area where they live; the places where they shop, send their children to school and spend their leisure; and their places of work, entertainment and pleasure. All these can reinforce the closed cognitive map of anti-Catholicism because they are the mechanisms by which the stocks of anti-Catholic ideas and notions are socially transmitted and disseminated to the group, or because they involve sectarianised forms of social interaction which prevent or restrict contact with Catholics, ensuring that common-sense stereotypes, ideas, maxims and beliefs are not undercut by personal experience. These artefacts and behaviours ensure that people's anti-Catholic notions are immune to empirical test in day-to-day life and, instead, are reinforced continually by the social dissemination and transmission of anti-Catholic common-sense knowledge. Wright once argued that 'Protestant ideology' structured the experiences of ordinary Protestants rather than the other way round (Wright, 1973: 246; a view supported by Taylor, 1983: 116), in that their knowledge of Catholics is based on what they have been told about them rather than as a result of first-hand experience, a tendency reinforced by residential segregation in most working-class districts of Northern Ireland. This is particularly applicable to anti-Catholicism. The cognitive map of anti-Catholicism structures how anti-Catholics perceive, understand and 'know' the Catholic Church and its members, ensuring that relations with them, if there are any, are affected by a stock of anti-Catholic common-sense notions, such that this common-sense knowledge about Catholicism is reproduced in a self-fulfilling way. This reinforces the anti-Catholic's belief that this common sense actually makes sense, ensuring that it continues to be used as the primary realm of relevance for understanding Catholicism and individual Catholics. In short, the cognitive map remains closed, self-contained and impenetrable.

Common Sense, Language and Identity

The facility of language is perhaps the single most defining characteristic which distinguishes human beings from other species. But it is not so much the ability to speak that is important but what language does sociologically; language does a great deal more than speech. People's experiences and ideas are subjective and personal, but their expression through the medium of language translates them into linguistic categories which suggest that these experiences and ideas are common and shared. People's biographical stock of common-sense knowledge is partly structured as a body of collective and shared ideas because the language which expresses it simultaneously renders it into intersubjective form. Language does so because it typifies experiences and ideas, giving the impression that common-sense knowledge is indeed common. Language is therefore integral to the process of common-sense reasoning because it translates subjective notions into socially available and recognised linguistic categories which appear to make such notions intersubjective. In short, language helps to structure the process of common-sense reasoning by allowing people to see their common-sense knowledge as part of a broader social world. It is, therefore, an important mechanism for socially disseminating common-sense ideas amongst a group because it socially transmits common-sense knowledge while simultaneously reinforcing the belief that one's personal stock of common-sense notions is collective.

Language not only helps to construct the social world as an intersubjective one; it simultaneously reflects that social world. Underlying language is a social world which permeates the talk, allowing it to achieve its communicative purpose. It is prosaic in the anthropology of language to argue that culture conditions and produces language. Gumperz (1982), for example, argued that culture affected language in at least three ways. It assisted in speaking, in that it defined the appropriate ways of articulating ideas; it assisted in listening, in that culture both helps 'inferencing' (ibid.: 19), which is the way to 'hear' ambiguous words; and it assisted in understanding words used as 'codes' (on the use of language in cultural representation see S. Hall, 1997). The sociology of language shares the view that language reflects society, but extends the argument by suggesting that it helps in part to construct or constitute society: it reproduces rather than merely represents society. Language embodies social forces and processes, and can thus reflect structural differentiation according to inequalities of power, class, gender, ethnicity, race, age, or whatever. It reproduces, in other words, dimensions of difference in linguistic form, reflecting society's patterns of differentiation. In the work of 'critical linguistics', like Pecheux, Foucault and Fairclough, language is said to show the effects of ideological struggle (see Fairclough, 1994). Pecheux and Foucault, for example, argue that ideologies can become expressed in 'discursive formations' which determine what can be said and the semantic form in which it is said. These discursive formations often contain 'preconstructeds', which are ready-made and ritualised expressions used to reflect ready-made ideological presuppositions. In this way, language is said to be constitutive of society, in that it reflects the forces, processes and struggles that go to make up society.

To appreciate how language is said to be constitutive of society, it is necessary to understand that language does not just report experiences but helps to define and shape experiences. This is what is known as the Sapir and Whorf hypothesis, based on combining together the work of both linguists, and Hoijer (1967), in his analysis of the argument, points out that language is constitutive of experience because it shapes as well as reports it. It does so by directing the perceptions of speakers, by providing speakers with habitual modes of analysing experience, and by supplying the categories, types and units through which experiences are understood. The very act of speaking simultaneously becomes the act of perceiving because language supplies the linguistic categories used to interpret the reported experience. Experience

is thus constitutive of the language used to report it. This applies more generally. Society is constitutive of the language used to reproduce its structural forces, patterns and processes. The same is also true of identity. Language not only describes identity, it provides the categories and units which are used in constructing and shaping it and which give it meaning: identities are described by means of language, but they are also in part constituted by means of language. Language provides the categories, units, typifications and stereotypes by which one 'knows', commonsensically, one's own identity and those of others. For example, moral boundaries are drawn by means of language, and notions of social distance and the identities of 'the stranger' and 'the outsider' are expressed in linguistic form. However, the language used to report these in part constitutes the very identities people possess since the language used in categorising identity helps to draw the boundary markers and define the experiences and way of life which constitute the identity (see Jayyusi, 1984). Language, in other words, is constitutive of identity, constructing as well as reporting on categorisations of 'us' and 'them'.

This discussion of the sociological characteristics of language is relevant to anti-Catholicism in Northern Ireland in several ways. Language is one of the mechanisms by which the modes of anti-Catholicism are socially disseminated amongst the collectivity which constitute its primary constituency, but the rhetoric characteristic of each mode also reproduces the foundational ideas as intersubjective and shared notions belonging to a group. The intersubjective categories contained in the language used by each mode, helps to create the modes as mini social worlds exiting beyond the ideas of the individual. This sustains and reinforces anti-Catholicism because language transforms it into an intersubjective reality, allowing the individual to elevate it to something other than personal prejudice or bigotry. The claim that most anti-Catholics make that they are not bigoted is in part the result of the language used to articulate anti-Catholicism, since it suggests that the common-sense ideas and notions are part of a broader social world rather than adhering to their personal prejudices.

In functioning in this way, anti-Catholicism constitutes a 'discursive formation'; that is, a discourse which reflects in linguistic form patterns of power in society and the dominance of some group or groups in social and political struggles (anti-Britishness amongst Republicans is a similar 'discursive formation'). Anti-Catholicism in Northern Ireland is a discursive formation for describing ways of speaking about and understanding Catholic theology and its followers in a society where Catholics have less power, having been defeated in past social and political struggles. As Part I showed, it emerged as a discursive formation in Irish society with the plantation and has continued in Northern Ireland as a way of determining what can be said about Catholics, and the ways in which it can be said, because the structural conditions of differentiation it reflects as a discursive formation still hold in the North. Anti-Catholic rhetoric thus reflects the social world in Northern Ireland, including its patterns of differentiation, the operation of political power, and enduring ideological and political struggles. Thus, the language of anti-Catholicism helps to put Catholics in their place – 'Remember 1690', 'No Surrender', 'not an inch', 'Home Rule is Rome rule', 'Ulster will fight and Ulster is right', 'for God and Ulster' – constituting shibboleths which refer back to battles which Catholics lost and in which power was wrested from them; it is a language of power reflecting the past reality of power, and is hung on to tenaciously as a discursive formation, even when this power is ebbing away. Therefore, anti-Catholic discourse helps to signify society in Northern Ireland, giving it meaning because it reflects and helps to constitute its patterns of differentiation. Alternative discourses – based, for example, around social class, race or gender – are not discursive formations with any influence because they do not reflect structural conditions and lines of differentiation in Northern Ireland and thus cannot capture what needs to be said, what can be said, or how it can be said, because they speak about the wrong things.

Discursive formations contain 'preconstructeds', which are the ritualised phrases, formulaic expressions and standardised remarks which speak of what needs to be said, how it can be said, and the way it can be said but do so by a kind of linguistic short-hand. The ritualised expressions, as short-hand, can be quickly committed to memory and can be easily reproduced, yet they speak volumes: 'No Surrender', 'no Pope here', 'to Hell or Connaught', 'Taigs out', 'the antiChrist', 'the Whore of Babylon', 'fuck the Pope', 'No Popery'.[3] These formulaic phrases also assist in 'hearing' and 'inferencing' when the meaning of words is ambiguous (such as 'to Hell or Connaught'). A special kind of 'preconstructeds' are 'codes', which are short-hand indices reflecting a wealth of unstated meaning. Good examples of anti-Catholic 'codes' in Northern Ireland are 'ye must be born again', 'grace alone', 'justification by faith and faith alone', and 'by Christ crucified'. They are indexes which open up a whole social world of unstated meaning against Catholic theology and its followers. They can be seen pasted on billboards, nailed to trees and posts, written on walls, pinned to church notice boards, referred to in advertisements on the side of buses, and published in the personal columns of local newspapers. They are short, punchy, and can be written easily and read quickly, but they describe a vocabulary of unstated assumptions, meanings and typifications, and reproduce a whole social world of differentiation and stratification.

The discursive formation of anti-Catholicism not only provides for ways of talking about Catholics, these linguistic categories simultaneously supply the terms for perceiving them. Talk about Catholicism, therefore, is talk about identity in Northern Ireland as much as it is about doctrine. The anti-Catholic rhetoric of this discourse defines the moral boundaries between the groups in Northern Ireland, identifies social distance by defining Catholics as those with whom it is desirable to restrict social relationships, and locates the identity of 'the stranger' or 'the outsider' as being Catholics, nationalists, and republicans. Anti-Catholic language, therefore, contains habitual ways for both describing and perceiving 'the other'. The 'codes' like 'ye must be born again', mark the moral boundaries of those with the right theological doctrine and the right political and national identity, and the ritualised and formulaic phrases, like 'no Pope here', '1690', and 'No Surrender', mark the identity of those with the power and those without. The discourse marks the user as an insider against those who are the subject of the discourse. But the discourse does more than that, for the anti-Catholic language helps in part to constitute what it means to be Protestant as anti-Catholics construct this identity: it means to be in power, to be dominant, to feel superior, to have won in 1690, to not want 'Rome rule' or 'Popery' in Northern Ireland, to never having had to surrender, to have the right to march in Catholic areas, and to have God, supposedly, on Ulster's side. Anti-Catholic language, in short, is constitutive of a certain kind of Protestant identity.[4]

This can be illustrated further by analysis of 'Papist' (synonymous with the code 'Romanist') as a well-used and popular 'code' within the discursive formation of anti-Catholicism. 'Papist' is a 'code' that constitutes a common-sense category or typification for describing the 'extreme' or 'fanatical' Catholic, as people differently put it, who needs to be distinguished from what people call 'the ordinary decent Catholic', although a few anti-Catholics use the category 'Papist' to refer to all Catholics (for a discussion of categorisation generally, see Jayyusi, 1984; for a discussion of how members of the RUC draw distinctions between 'ordinary decent Catholics' and the rest, see Brewer, 1991: 130–5). It is a very stable category, and is not temporarily or locally occasioned, and constitutes a primary status for the person who is so classified. 'Papist' comes with 'category bound activities', which are common-sensically associated with the category. In their worst form, these category-bound activities are theological (worshipping the 'wafer God', submission to priests, worship of pagan deities, glorification of the Saints and the Virgin Mary on a level above Jesus, and so on), as well as political (disloyalty, support for or participation in terrorism), social (being lazy, slothful, licentious, dishonest, drunken, and so on), and cultural (anti-British, anti-Protestant). They define past behaviour and attitudes and predict future ones. Hence, they describe, for example, how 'Papists' have acted in past ceasefires and how they will act in the current one, and how they have been wedded to violence in the past and will remain so in the future. These category-bound activities become attached to every Catholic who is classified as belonging to the category, and they perform a number of interactional purposes, such as apportioning blame and responsibility, assisting in evaluation and judgements, and describing the moral performances of those Catholics seen as extreme enough to be classified as 'Papists'. The category presupposes others to which it is related, such as 'idolater', 'pagan', 'anti-Christian', 'scrounger' or 'terrorist', which have their own elaborated forms of category-bound activities. The category also presupposes others with which it is in asymmetry as part of a dualism or pair in the way that, for example, 'police officer' and 'criminal', or 'doctor' and 'patient' are pairs. The asymmetrical pair partner for 'Papist' is 'Bible Protestant' (which is synonymous with 'fundamentalist' and 'conservative evangelical'[5]), which has asymmetrical category-bound activities which predicate opposed moral evaluations and define contrasting patterns of past and future behaviour. The standard relational pair of 'Papist' and 'Bible Protestant' thus stand as 'codes' for two identities forged in opposition to each other, and the language used to describe them, whether stated and unstated, at the same time both reports the differences and constitutes them. It is thus constitutive of 'Bible Protestant' identity to be loyal to the Crown, to be peaceful, opposed to terrorism, to be hard working, a devout Christian and so on. This is simultaneously also the very language used to describe the moral boundaries between themselves and 'Papists'. Talk about 'Papists' is therefore also talk about identity.

Common Sense and Anti-Catholic Theology

In the discursive formation of anti-Catholicism, most people's understanding of Catholic theology and doctrine is reduced to the formulaic and ritualised expressions based on what they have been told about what Catholics are supposed to believe (likewise for 'Brits' within the discursive formation of Republicanism). These common-sense assumptions about Catholic belief and practice constitute what anti-Catholics 'know' about theology, and they hold to it with the same certainty and taken-for-grantedness as all common-sense knowledge. Theology, in other words, is for most people reduced to common-sense notions about theology, which is something different altogether from proper theological awareness. This is why the numerous areas of great similarity between Catholic and Reformed theology do not count for the anti-Catholic – and four-fifths of the doctrine between the two is the same; neither do the marked differences in theology count within the Reformed tradition. What counts to the anti-Catholic is the assumed difference between Protestant and Catholic theology as understood common-sensically; and one needs to look outside theology for an explanation of why small differences in religious belief are magnified.

The common-sense notions about what Catholics are supposed to believe theologically portray them, among many other things, as having a Bible which does not contain Chapters 17 and 18 from the Book of Revelation (see Free Presbyterian respondents in Taylor, 1983: 103), since these contain the prophecies about the antiChrist and the Whore which the Catholic Church allegedly wishes to suppress; they are said to believe that they literally eat the flesh and drink the blood of Jesus in Communion – 'when [a Catholic] takes the wafer god during holy communion [they] must believe [they are] eating the creator of the universe' (*Are Roman Catholics Christians?*, by Chick Publications); because of the 'physical presence' of Christ in the Communion elements, Catholics are thus said to believe that Christ is recrucified at every Eucharist (see Boettner, n.d.); they worship and adore the Virgin Mary to the point where she replaces Jesus as mediator between them and God – 'the Roman Catholic Church in actual fact worships Mary more than it worships either God or Christ' (Rockwood, 1984: 27); they are subjects of 'priestcraft', much associated with 'witchcraft', by which priests keep the Bible from ordinary Catholics (see Free Presbyterian respondents in Taylor, 1983: 103); ordinary Catholics do not know or read the Bible and are kept ignorant of Christ's Gospels – 'the tragic reality is that the overwhelming majority of Catholics have either never personally studied the Bible or have only done so under the strict supervision and scrutiny of their church' (*The Bible and Roman Catholicism*, by Chick Publications); they believe that it is the priest rather than God who forgives sins and who offers salvation – 'I look forward', said one of our respondents, 'to another Reformation when the power of the priest is lessened. The power of the priest is such that he is seen as the gift of eternal life among men'; they are said to believe that 'good works' rather than faith will bring salvation, that eternal life is thus capable of being earned rather than something gifted as grace from God; the Pope's word is said to be seen by Catholics as above that of God's, and that they give their first loyalty to the Vatican rather than God; that Catholics see church-defined traditions as more important to their lives rather than the word of God; and that with their rosaries, medallions, figurines and statues, Catholics worship idols and graven images.

It is worth measuring these common-sense notions of Catholic theology against official Catholic doctrine. Before doing so, however, it is important to stress the changes that have occurred in Catholic theology since Vatican II. Attitudes change slowly in divided societies where attitudes reflect identity, and many anti-Catholics have not caught up with changes in Catholic theology and teaching. However, contemporary anti-Catholicism is not characterised so much by an imperceptibility about post-Vatican II reform but a refusal to believe any real change has occurred. The Pharisaic mode is most likely to recognise change, but even here the Catholic Church is still said to be a departure from biblical Truth (Ankerberg and Weldon, 1994: xii). A well-known Christian academic, active in Conservative politics in Northern Ireland, who, on his own admission, would be a Pharisaic type, said that he would dissent from the view that there is no biblical basis to anti-Catholicism, although he accepted that some of the extreme notions contained in the Westminster Confession lacked scriptural support. Covenantal types are likely to express more vividly the sentiment that no real reform has taken place since Vatican II. *The Bible and Roman Catholicism*, published by Chick Publications in 1985, states: 'the Roman Catholic Church has traditionally suppressed, opposed and forbidden the open use of the Bible. Though external pressures have caused Rome to relax its restrictions and opposition against the Bible, the Bible is still widely withheld and its distribution and free use discouraged in many countries heavily influenced by Roman Catholicism.' After reading one of its publications on the Whore and Beast of Babylon, which disputes that any fundamental change has occurred in Catholicism's evil, a correspondent in 1996 wrote to *Battle Cry*, the magazine of Chick Publications, stating that the Roman Catholic Church were Nazis in religious garb who fitted perfectly the picture of religious hypocrites described in Matthew 23 (which, ironically, makes reference to the blind leading the blind). A Northern Irish Presbyterian minister, in a pamphlet published by the Presbyterian Fellowship, decried Vatican II as changing nothing (Montgomery, n.d.: 8). Conversely, some Irish Catholic theologians have described Vatican II as profound in the extent to which it borrowed from, and imitated, important Protestant traditions (McDonagh, 1996: 18; a view shared by a former Moderator of the Presbyterian Church in

Ireland – see Dunlop, 1995: 34); and this from theologians in a country where Catholics are more traditional than most, as Geraldine Smyth, Director of the Irish School of Ecumenics, described it in an interview. Thus the gulf between Catholic theology and common sense notions of Catholic theology since Vatican II is wide.

The issue of transubstantiation concerns the debate over whether Christ is a real bodily presence in the Communion elements of bread and wine. It long detained theologians at the time of the Reformation by defining one of the central differences between Catholicism (bodily presence) and Reformed theology (substantial but not bodily presence). The issue is important to anti-Catholics today because it is the foundation of many other differences in practice – and differences are what needs to be highlighted for anti-Catholics – and it permits lurid caricatures of Catholic beliefs, such as the claims that Catholics believe themselves to be eating the flesh of Christ and drinking His blood, and that they believe He is thus recrucified at every Eucharist. Therefore, resolution of the hoary contrast of bodily versus substantial presence, dissolves much more besides. Recent theological interpretations of the medieval doctrine of transubstantiation have addressed both the nature and scope of Christ's presence. The Rev. Richard McBrien, in his acclaimed documentation of Catholic theology (1994; also see McBrien, 1996), explains that Catholic doctrine now stresses that the presence of Christ extends beyond the Eucharistic elements into the community assembled together for worship as well as the *office* (not the person)[6] of the minister presiding (McBrien, 1994: 827). Fr. Paul Tang Ing, a leading Jesuit theologian, wrote an account of Catholic beliefs and described the nature of Christ's presence as spiritual rather than symbolic or bodily. 'He is not there in physical flesh and blood as an animal that has just been killed. He, as the resurrected Lord, is there in a spiritual way' (Ing, 1984: 66). Christ's 'real' presence is manifested in spiritual rather than physical form; and most Protestants believe Christ to be 'real' in His spiritual presence amongst them. Thus, one of the private prayers in the Catholic liturgy following communion records sentiments with which Protestants could not disagree:

> It is at mass above all that we celebrate the presence of your kingdom already in our world and look forward to its final establishment in glory. It is at mass that we become conscious of ourselves as a community who belong together in your body as the church. The mass gives us our commitment to serve one another, to give to one another.

Christ's presence is there in the body of His church, manifesting itself in service to each other, a presence marked spiritually by His kingdom on earth, since Christ, as all denominations accept, is not bodily present on earth but is inside all Christians as a spiritual presence ('the kingdom of God is within you' remarks Jesus in Luke 17:21). It follows, therefore, that the Catholic mass is not a physical repetition of Christ's sacrifice. As Fr. Ing put it: 'we come to Mass to ask for God's forgiveness and for God's strength (love) to do His will. It is making "my own" the power that Christ has gained for me through His eternal sacrifice. It not a repetition of Christ's sacrifice, which is once and for all' (Ing, 1984: 74). The mass is thus meant for Catholics to relive the *memory* of His sacrifice rather than its physical repetition: 'When Christ said "Do this in memory of me", he meant us to relive in faith the memory of His life, death and resurrection in such a way that the power of His sacrifice becomes present to us here and now' (ibid.: 75; see also McBrien, 1994: 832 who describes the Eucharist as an act of remembrance). Catholic teaching is thus that the power of Christ's sacrifice becomes manifest spiritually in Catholics at the mass as they relive the memory of His death and resurrection: He is not repeatedly sacrificed. It follows from this that Catholicism teaches that Christ died once and for all, from which it also necessarily follows that that God's forgiveness of our sin has already been given once and for all by Jesus' death. The Catholic sacrament of reconciliation (penance, performed on the instruction of the priest after confession) is thus not based on any refusal amongst Catholics to believe that God alone forgives sins – let alone a belief that the priest or the Pope has the power to forgive sins. It is a means of being healed by helping sinners to accept that they have indeed been forgiven by God. As Ing writes, 'forgiveness is not for God; it is for us. We have broken the relationship with Him', and penance is 'our human expression of sorrow and desire to mend the broken relationship' (Ing, 1984: 78–9). Moreover, confession and penance is a form of public repentance for sin, much as Jesus told His followers to do when He encouraged His disciples to 'confess your sins to one another, and pray for one another, that you may be healed' (John 5:16). The penance is done by the sinner, only in mark of sorrow, the forgiveness only by God, in mark of His desire for our healing; common-sense misunderstandings translates this into the notion that Catholics believe that priests and popes forgive sins.

The modern Catechism of the Catholic Church states this categorically: 'Since God alone can forgive sins, it is God who, in Jesus, his eternal Son made man, will save his people from their sins. The name "Jesus" signifies that the very name God is present in the person of his Son. It is the divine name that alone brings salvation. There is no other name under heaven given among men by which we must be saved' (Roman Catholic Church [hereafter RCC], 1994: 96–7). A considerable degree of distortion and denial has to take place in the process of common-sense reasoning for anti-Catholics to claim that Catholics do not place Jesus at the centre of their faith in face of statements from Catholic theologians like the following: 'Christ is the foundation of His church. Without Christ there is no church. Christ is not only the saviour of Christians, He is also the life of Christians' (Ing, 1984: 101). Neither the office of the papacy, the teachings of the Catholic Church, nor received tradition are therefore above the word of God (ibid.: 108). The Bible is thus recognised by Catholics as the inspired divine word (ibid.: 96). 'Sacred Scripture', the Catechism writes, 'is the speech of God as it is put down in writing under the breath of the Holy Spirit' (RCC, 1994: 25). The role of Church tradition is seen by the Catechism as transmitting 'in its entirety the Word of God', and its place in Catholic theology comes only as a result of it being seen to express divine commands, which is why Church tradition is called 'sacred tradition', in order to stress its intent to transmit in different form the same sacred word of God. Reformed theology claims there is no need for anything but Scripture itself to discern and transmit the word of God, and anti-Catholics common-sensically see their own denominations as bereft of doctrinal statements or Church traditions. However, as the Rev. Kinahan, a Church of Ireland minister, explains, not only do Protestant denominations have a doctrinal interpretation of Scripture, they accord Church tradition a role in interpreting God's word and tend to see their own tradition as the only right one: 'each Protestant denomination has tended to make its own tradition of biblical interpretation the infallible yardstick of doctrine' (Kinahan, 1995: 80). He went on: 'we Protestants insist on *sola scriptura* (only scripture) and damn Rome for her additions or developments. But that condemnation is hardly convincing when there are literally dozens of little churches, all claiming to be faithful to holy scripture, yet all with vastly different theologies, church orders and practices' (ibid.: 89). The Presbyterian Church of Ireland recognises this and calls its traditions of doctrine and practice 'subordinate standards', the intent of which, however, is still to 'serve as a testimony for truth and against error' (quoted in Dunlop, 1995: 98), at least as they define truth. Cooke has shown a similar process in the Free Presbyterians, where Paisley imposes a doctrinal orthodoxy in the training seminaries (Cooke, 1996: 121–4). Bruce (1985c) explains how this occurs, for it lies in the innate tendency within Protestantism to schism and differentiation because they place so much emphasis on human-made interpretations of truth (although these are always claimed to be Spirit-led interpretations). These human-made interpretations soon establish themselves as doctrine for break-away churches, loyalty to which becomes in future a test of orthodoxy. The Catholic Church is thus no different in establishing a body of Church-based doctrine, and it, like Protestant denominations, would see this tradition as only better serving God's purpose as revealed in His word and is thus subservient to Scripture (the Protestant position), or at least not superior to it (the Catholic position).

In as much as Scripture defines Jesus as the mediator between fallen humankind and God, Christ must be at the matrix of people's relationship with God. The common-sense understanding anti-Catholics have is that a crowd of others vie with Him for this, including the Virgin Mary, all the Saints, and, of course, the Pope. Their position as mediators is reinforced by the various statues and portraits of such people to which Catholics pray, which only adds to the profanity. However, the Nicene Creed, which is an important article of faith and doctrine in both Protestant and Catholic traditions, calls believers to affirm that 'we believe in the communion of saints', and recent Catholic teaching argues that devotion to the Saints follows on from one's relationship with God. This does not mean, however, that the Saints are adored above God. Fr. Ing states that devotion to the Saints draws one nearer to God and it does not 'take away from Christ His unique role as the sole mediator between God and Man' (Ing, 1984: 120). The Catholic Catechism says the same. 'Those who dwell in heaven fix the whole church more firmly in holiness', but Christ Jesus is 'the one mediator between God and men', so 'our communion to the saints joins us to Christ' (RCC, 1994: 219). The Catholic Church is clear on this, for the Constitution of the Church says 'we have but one mediator', by which is meant that Christ is the 'meeting point' between the divine and the human. The Virgin Mary or the saints do not replace Christ in this role. Ing (1984: 129) refers to their role as 'secondary mediations', and he argues that Christ Himself did not cut off humankind from these 'secondary mediators' when He defined Himself as the matrix, since He clearly identified a series of events (repentance for sin), activities (collective worship) and places (church meetings, wildernesses and quiet places) where it is possible for us to meet Him in order for Him to mediate for us. Ing sees the Saints and the Virgin Mary as simply people who perform the same role, allowing others to indirectly meet Jesus (ibid.: 129), just as evangelical Protestants believe we meet Jesus indirectly in any person who is Spirit-filled. Thus, Catholic theology teaches that Mary is venerated because people glimpse Jesus in her, representing as she did, a model of faith and discipleship. She is claimed by the Catholic Church to be the mother of God, which is not to claim, as anti-Catholics misinterpret it (see Rockwood, 1984: 28), that she herself is God. In claiming Mary as the mother of God, Catholics affirm the divinity of Jesus: Jesus is within the triune God, Mary is the mother of Jesus, Mary is the mother of one of the God-head. To deny that role to Mary is to deny that Jesus is within the triune God, but she herself is not seen as part of the same trinity. Jesus, and no other, is the matrix to humankind's relationship with God.

In as much as the crowds of others involved in this relationship are secondary to Jesus, the statues, portraits and images which capture their likeness are not adored, so they are not idols which take adoration away from Jesus. As Fr. Ing writes, these objects are merely material representations of the spiritual, and they find parallel in many behaviours and artefacts in Protestant worship: 'our statues and images are to remind us of the persons represented. We do not believe that these persons are really present in them. They are like photographs of people we love which we place on our tables. Neither do we worship them. We worship only the One true God. The bowing of the head and joining of hands and other postures when praying, these are all material mediations of something spiritual' (Ing, 1984: 132). He could have added hymn singing, church music, other forms of praise like dance and theatre, and things like prayer walks, the 'walk for Jesus' and other marches and parades which are physical and material representations of spiritual devotion to God. 'Adoration', says the Catholic Catechism, 'is due to God alone': 'religious worship is not directed to images in themselves [they] lead us on to God incarnate' (RCC, 1994: 463–4).

Semantic differences, however, make all the difference to anti-Catholics; it is not enough to worship the same God, it has to be done with the same words, and the language needs to possess the same meaning. The distinction between the veneration of an image as a spiritual representation of devotion to God, and the adoration of that image in itself, is not one which anti-Catholics are willing to make. They wish to remain in their belief that Catholics venerate the person represented by the image and that Catholics do so to such a level that it constitutes adoration, something which, rightly, should be reserved only for God. The same applies to Catholic interpretations of salvation, where semantics are used to maintain the divide in the post-Vatican II period between the understanding of 'justification by faith' in Catholic and Reformed theology.

On many occasions Jesus refers to belief in Himself, as the Son of God, as the sole means to salvation. John's gospel, for example, quotes Jesus as saying that anyone who believed in Him believed in God, the one who sent Him (John 12:44), that anyone who believed in Him would have eternal life (John 3:16), that He Himself is the bread of life (John 6:47), that anyone who believed in Him would not remain in darkness (John 12:46), that He is the gate for the sheep and that anyone who comes to Him will be saved (John 10:7–10), that Jesus is the resurrection and the life and that anyone who believes in Him will live and never die (John 11:25), and that He is the way, the truth and the life, and no one can know the Father but through Him (John 14:6). Luke quotes Jesus as saying that anyone who declares publicly that they belong to Jesus will have Jesus speak on their behalf before God (Luke 12:8). Moreover, such faith was gifted by God. 'No one can come to me', Jesus says in John 6:65, 'unless the father has enabled him.' This idea imprinted itself on the Apostles, and they stressed, for example, that to be able to confess 'Jesus is Lord' meant one was filled with the Holy Spirit (Paul in 1 Corinthians 12:3; John in 1 John 4:2),[7] and that to be able to declare that Jesus is the Son of God meant the person lived in unity with God (1 John 4:15). Paul used the phrase 'justification by faith' (especially in his letter to the Romans) to describe Jesus' view – salvation came from faith in Jesus, which was a gift of grace from God.

However, a whole doctrine has been established around Paul's terminology by Reformed theologians, which can be called 'the doctrine of justification by faith', to distinguish it from Jesus' (and Paul's) meaning. The origins of this doctrine are in the Reformation. Luther has been described as reducing Christianity to an essence, which he derived from Paul's writings on faith, bringing every other part of Christian doctrine under the judgement of this single, simple, principle (Collinson, 1990: 257). The Reformation, in other words, was Pauline in its direction: the Gospel of Christ according to Luther was the Gospel of Paul, at least as Luther understood it.[8] Luther described Paul's epistle to the Romans as 'the chief book in the New Testament and the purest gospel' (Hunter, 1972: 94); Paul's epistle to the Galatians was described by Luther in exaggerated tones – 'it is my epistle; I have betrothed myself to it; it is my wife' (quoted in ibid.: 118). What Luther took from Paul was his stress on justification by faith. The subsequent doctrine developed from that includes the following tenets: salvation comes from faith and faith alone; justification is not obtained by works or a person's own efforts; salvation is a gift of God, the result of God's saving grace; grace is received through hearing the word of God; it comes in the form of the Holy Spirit during a conversion experience when one is 'born again'; the justified are still sinners but are not seen as such by God; justification brings forth 'good works', which are not done to earn spiritual reward but from the love of God; real goodness is the result, not the prerequisite of faith. As Collinson (1990: 159) emphasises, the implications for the Catholic Church of Luther's formulation of 'the doctrine of justification by faith' are limitless. The sacraments, the priesthood, the mass and all other devotions are radically undermined because they are 'works' with a false motivation. There is no longer a rationale for monasticism or clerical celibacy, since they are 'works', and the distinction between priest and laity evaporates under the impulse of the 'priesthood of all believers' because the priests may have false motivations for their vocation. The tenets of the doctrine of justification by faith also become 'codes' within anti-Catholic language – 'ye must be born again', 'saved by grace', 'faith not works' – which index a world of social meaning distinguishing Protestants and Catholics. The codes are like theological shibboleths, dividing Reformed and Catholic interpretations of salvation. And the conflict over 'justification by faith' has been a lengthy one, constituting a bitter polemic since the Reformation: Bishop Jansen was denounced as a heretic by the Pope for advocating views on grace during the seventeenth century similar to the Reformed theologians. However, two points should be made: 'the doctrine of justification by faith' inserts faith in the language of the doctrine, rather than faith in Jesus *per se*, as the means to salvation; and Catholic teachings on salvation since Vatican II do not conform to the common-sense view.

New Testament Scripture makes it absolutely clear that people are justified by faith: Jesus' meaning is unambiguous – faith in Him gives eternal life. We are, however, justified by faith in Jesus, not by the language of the doctrine of faith (for a similar point see Monaghan, 1997: 12). Faith in Jesus can be articulated with different words than the doctrine of justification by faith and it will still bring salvation. The Rev. Kinahan (1995: 77–8) makes the point that the New Testament writers were more interested in the life-style of the first Christians than in the exact details of what they believed, and more concerned with the ethical fruits of faith than with its doctrinal dogmas. There are many instances in the Gospels of Jesus accepting people without asking them about the doctrinal view which accompanied their faith, or what they understood by faith: believing in Him was enough. The prisoner hanging on a cross beside Him was told that he would that day be in paradise with Jesus because he had believed that Jesus was about to go to His kingdom (Luke 23:42–3); Jesus' healing of beggars and the sick was never accompanied by requests to know what the sick believed before they were cured – the woman who simply touched the edge of his cloak in a large crowd, for example, was instantly healed and told by Jesus that it was her faith that had cured her (Mark 5:21–34). To elevate a particular form of wording in describing justification by faith into the sole standard of salvation is to impose human-made criteria on faith, which contradicts the original meaning of the term. After all, Paul, who first used the phrase, was equally capable of statements which criticised the reduction of salvation to doctrine: 'for it is not by hearing the law that people are put right with God, but by doing what the law commanded' (Romans 2:13); 'God will reward every person according to what he has done' (Romans 2:6); 'for all of us must appear before Christ to be judged by him. Each one will receive what he deserves, according to everything he has done, good or bad, in his bodily life' (2 Corinthians 5:10). Moreover, Paul stresses that Jesus' church is composed of different forms with a plurality of gifts and witness, describing it as a 'body with many parts' (1 Corinthians 12:12), which suggests diversity rather than a narrow orthodoxy (a point also made by Kinahan, 1995: 83). In the Book of Romans where Paul introduces the phrase 'justification by faith', he also states that Christ's followers were to accept (some translations use 'welcome') Gentiles 'for the glory of God', as Christ had accepted them, an injunction which came without any reference to the dogma necessary for them to receive this acceptance or welcome. Other parts of the New Testament recognise the importance of 'right action' as much as 'right belief'. The Book of James, for example, states that faith without proper action will not result in salvation (James 2:14 and 2:26); if faith is alone and includes no action 'then it is dead' (James 2:17), and James goes on the list Old Testament figures who were 'put right with God' (that is, justified) through their actions (James 2:25), including the prostitute Rahab, the great-great-grandmother of King David, in whose line Jesus came. James saw faith and works as inseparable, each leading to the other, and Jesus did the same, as the following passages illustrate: 'not everyone who calls me "Lord, Lord" will enter the Kingdom of heaven, but only those who do what my Father wants them to do' (Matthew 7:21); 'you will be able to enter the Kingdom of heaven only if you are faithful in doing what God requires' (Matthew 5:20). As Kinahan shows (1995: 77), in Jesus' parable of the final judgement, the righteous are measured by what they did not what they believed (Matthew 25:31–46). False prophets were to be discerned not by their doctrine but by their actions – 'you will know them by what they do' (Matthew 7:16). In short, Jesus considers faith in Him as the means to salvation, a faith which inevitably outworks in good deeds because God's law is written on the heart of anyone who believes in Him; it is not measured by conformity to the language spoken in the 'doctrine of justification by faith'.

The interpretation of Paul's writings on faith by 'the doctrine of justification by faith' is unbalanced. Theologians interpret the Apostle Paul's emphasis on faith as a critical reference to other notions of salvation current at the time, which stressed conformity to Jewish Law and thus to works (see Hunter, 1972: 103; Ing, 1984: 156; a view shared also by the Methodist minister Johnston McMaster, 1996: 39). This was a Law which Jesus came to transcend by His death. Paul's passages on faith were therefore set to contrast with the idea that works alone bring eternal life. The 'grand assumption', as Hunter puts it, of Judaic Law was that works ensure salvation (Hunter, 1972: 103), so that it was 'works by law' which Paul attacks, that is, the idea that conformity to Judaic Law earned credits in the ledger of Heaven (ibid.: 171). To apply Paul's' writings to Catholicism is thus a huge leap. Moreover, Paul's passages on faith alone need to be set in contrast with those where Paul properly balances faith and works, as did all the other Apostles. The mark of Paul's recognition of the indissolubility of faith and works is marked by his references to the role of proper conduct and 'agape' (selfless) love in salvation, in addition to faith. This is best demonstrated by his famous discourse on love in 1 Corinthians 13, where he states that faith without love leaves the person bereft and empty (13:2).[9] John said the same, when he wrote in 1 John 4:8 that 'he who does not love does not know God, for God is love'. The agape love that is referred to here is more than a romantic feeling. It is commitment to action toward the object of that love, arising from compassion, empathy and kindness. Hence Jesus says that to know and love Him is to give food to the hungry, water to the thirsty, clothing to the stranger, and to visit the sick and prisoners (Matthew 25:42–3). Love, thus, inevitably shows itself in compassion to others out of a commitment to God. That is, love leads to good works. Faith, love and works are indivisible. Paul believed this too, outlining in several passages how people ought to live a life of goodness once they have received grace and developed faith: real goodness is the result of faith, not its prerequisite, but faith and works are tied umbilically. Faith must be lived out in love, which is itself expressed in good works.

'The doctrine of justification by faith' distorts this equilibrium by undervaluing works and by claiming that Catholic theology sees 'good works' alone as the guarantor of salvation. However, any understanding of salvation must accept faith in Jesus as its standard, if not a formulaic wording or doctrine to express this faith. The issue thus becomes whether Catholic theology is Christ-centred and its teachings on salvation stress faith in Him, irrespective of the language and 'codes' used. The Catechism of the Catholic Church outlines teaching on salvation thus:

> Believing in Jesus Christ and in the One who sent Him for our salvation is necessary for obtaining that salvation. Without faith no one has ever attained jus-tification, nor will anyone obtain eternal life. Faith is an entirely free gift that God makes to man. Faith is the beginning of eternal life. Faith is a personal act – the free response of the human person to the initiative of God who reveals himself. But faith is not an isolated act. By my faith I support others in the faith. We do not believe in formulae, but in those realities they express, which faith allows us to touch   (RCC, 1994: 41–2).

The Catholic Church 'is not the author of our salvation', which comes from God alone (ibid.: 42), although in Catholic theology any faith God gifts to the Catholic expresses itself in the Catholic Church, through its teachings about faith and its guardianship of the faithful. Without this emphasis on the Catholic Church as one expression of grace, these teachings are very Protestant. And although it does not use coded phrases like 'born again', the Catechism refers to newness and rebirth once God's grace is gifted. 'Christ liberates us from sin; by his resurrection he opens for us the way to a new life. This new life is above all justification that reinstates us in God's grace, so that we too might walk in newness of life. We are [Christ's] brethren not by nature but by the gift of grace' (ibid.: 150). The Catechism tells us from whence this grace comes: 'the grace of the Holy Spirit has the power to justify us, that is, to cleanse us from our sins and to communicate to us the righteousness of God through faith in Jesus Christ' (ibid.: 432). It also comes through infant baptism, which is the point at which most evangelical Protestants would beg to differ (although Free Presbyterianism practises infant baptism), but Catholic theology also recognises the work of the Holy Spirit in rebirth and renewal through conversion. 'Through the power of the Holy Spirit we take part in Christ's passion and resurrection by being born to new life ... The first work of the grace of the Holy Spirit is conversion; moved by grace, man moves towards God' (ibid.: 432). Thus, while the Catholic Church teaches that people may be saved through its institution, it is the grace of God that does the saving, and salvation can come outside the Catholic Church through a conversion experience. Catholic understanding of salvation is thus very Christ-centred. Pope John Paul II made this clear in a letter to the Sixth World Council of Churches in 1983: '[We] confess faith in Jesus Christ, believing that there is salvation in no one else, for there is no other name under heaven given among men by which we must be saved. Jesus is the crucified saviour, the redeemer of all, the Lord of life' (quoted in Cooke, 1996: 43).[10]

Such views on salvation permit dialogue with Protestant denominations whose Reformed theology does not now appear quite so different. In 1988, a joint Baptist and Roman Catholic Report referred to a shared faith in the centrality of Christ, a belief in the revelation of God, and agreement on Christ's sole mediation between God and humankind. This built upon a similar concord with the Lutheran Church in 1983, where the parties accepted that humankind's entire hope for justification and salvation rested on Christ Jesus and that the two churches should not place trust in anything other than God's promise and saving work in Christ. Gassman (1996) outlines what articles of doctrine the two parties signed up to: human beings are unable to effect or merit their justification; sinners are justified; justification is through grace alone; justification is received by faith; Christians are justified and sinners at the same time; the justified are assured of their salvation; the justified are called to good works. In 1994, forty leading evangelicals in the US met with Catholic theologians to discuss 'evangelicals and Catholics together in the third millennium', declaring themselves brothers and sisters in Christ because they were all Christ-centred and 'accepted Christ as Lord and Saviour'.[11] Other American evangelicals determined to show that the Catholic Church had not changed its basic doctrines and could not be trusted (see, for example, Ankerberg and Weldon, 1994). Some local evangelicals in Northern Ireland responded by writing a letter to the *Belfast Telegraph* on 23 December 1995 reminding readers of a letter published in the *Evangelical Times* in December 1991: 'one cannot be a Roman Catholic and an evangelical at the same time. They are mutually exclusive doctrinal systems, opposed on every essential and fundamental level.' Through a process of common-sense reasoning, which distorts what Catholic theology actually teaches, 'the doctrine of justification by faith' remained as the single, simple measure to divide these correspondents from Catholic believers.[12]

One other significant change in Catholic theology since Vatican II, which common-sense notions amongst anti-Catholics have also not caught up with, is the Catholic Church's stance on ecumenism and its position toward Protestantism (for a recent statement on this see Vatican, 1993). Cardinal Luciani, who was to become Pope John Paul I, once remarked during the discussions at Vatican II, that with respect to relations with other churches 'we had been wholly wrong' (quoted in Dunlop, 1995: 33). What he came to accept was the principle of religious liberty and freedom, and to understand the reality that salvation exists outside the Catholic Church. In 1965 the Catholic Church recognised religious freedom as an intrinsic universal right (for the statement, see Inter-Church Council, 1993: 130), and accepted the salvific role of other Christian churches, which have 'significance and importance in salvation', and while the Catholic Church, naturally, saw itself as offering the fullest means of salvation, other Christian churches did not 'lack all the means of salvation' (see ibid.: 128–9). Protestants were thus no longer seen as spiritually defective: 'by the Holy Spirit's gifts and graces, his sanctifying power is also active in them [Protestants] and he has strengthened some of them even to the shedding of their blood' (ibid.: 129). The unity of Christ's church was thus sought on the basis of co-operation rather than fostering, as it once had been, the return of all Protestants back to itself as the 'one true church of Christ'. The use of terminology like 'heretic' and 'schismatic' to describe Protestants was replaced by phrases like 'separated brethren'. The commitment to good ecumenical relations with Protestants is outworked in many ways, from ecumenical dialogue, common Bible work, common liturgical texts, ecumenical co-operation in catechesis, co-operation in institutes of higher education and in seminaries and undergraduate studies, as well as in missionary work (Vatican, 1993: 78–100).

It does not outwork well in two thorny issues – mixed marriages and shared Communion. It is not that the Catholic Church prohibits inter-church marriages, but it likes the children brought up Catholic, although no formal written or oral promise is now required to this effect (ibid.: 73). The Church stresses, however, that in other aspects of their upbringing, partners should share responsibility and obligations (see Inter-Church Group on Faith and Politics, 1989: 90), and that it respects the 'conscientious duties' of the other partner's religion (ibid.: 77). The marriage ceremony can also now take place in the church of the Protestant partner, and in most cases the church of the bride. Yet these moves do not alter the common-sense perception of some Protestants that the Catholic Church is imperialist in demanding children of mixed marriages be raised Catholic, although John Dunlop points out that in some cases priests informally require only that the children be raised as Christians (Dunlop, 1995: 35). Couples of mixed marriages, however, are still not allowed to share Communion since the Catholic Church imposes requirements that participants in the Eucharist be in oneness with the Church in faith, worship and ecclesial life (Vatican, 1993: 68). However, intercommunion is permissible in extreme circumstances, which Cosgrove (1996) outlines: that the person greatly desire to receive the sacraments; that they freely request them; that they manifest a faith in what the Catholic Church professes with regard to the sacraments; and that the person be unable to have recourse to Communion in their own church for a prolonged period. An encyclical letter on Christian unity in 1995 deleted the last condition, which makes it only marginally easier for intercommunion, and it took fifteen years of agitation from ecumenical Catholics for this small change to occur. The opposition of the

Catholic hierarchy to President McAleese taking Communion in a Protestant church illustrates how far the Catholic Church needs to go to resolve this issue.

It could be argued in defence of the anti-Catholic position that traditional Catholics have themselves not caught up with official Church teaching and practice, such that many ordinary Catholics still believe what common-sense theology has as being their formal doctrine: Vatican II might have changed official Catholic theology, but Catholics themselves are still medieval in what they hold to be true. This is not a defensible argument because it means that the *system* of the Church is no longer unproblematic, with the conflict lying in the individual's interpretation of doctrine. This would place the Catholic Church in no different a position than any other denomination, whose members appropriate in differing degrees particular articles of doctrine. This is noticeable even in one of the Free Presbyterian respondents we interviewed, who looked critically on his congregation and declared than many were not Christian because of their personal beliefs. It also reverses the anti-Catholic's normal dictum, that opposition is to the institution of the church not the individual believer. To now accept that the problem lies with personal interpretations of Catholic doctrine rather than the theology itself, would require an acceptance of the system. Hence, anti-Catholics are unable to countenance that changes have occurred to formal Catholic theology, so that their common-sense theology remains immutable.

Common-sense Knowledge and the Bible

Anti-Catholicism is not just premised on common-sense misunderstandings of Catholic theology, for the common-sense reasoning on which it is based also contains peculiar notions about the Bible. Chief amongst these is the idea that there is a Protestant Bible, or at least a Protestant version, in the form of the Authorised King James version. Thus one of our respondents, a Free Presbyterian, said in interview: 'I believe the Authorised version is the Bible that was given to us. I believe it's the word of God, and the way I look at it is, the 1859 Revival came about by the Authorised version. Now today, we've all different translations, and there's verses missing from them all. Unfortunately most of those are Roman Catholic inspired translations ... Only the Authorised version – King James 1611 – can be read or quoted in [my] hall.' Another of our Free Presbyterian respondents quoted Paisley, whom he referred to as 'the Doc', to support the claim that this version must be specially blessed by God because it had been the translation involved in several evangelical revivals. Moreover, it is a version which is supposedly very accurate in its translation of God's word. A third Free Presbyterian respondent said in interview: 'the King James version is the only book. When men did translate it, they were very careful to make sure they didn't get it wrong, and everything was checked and rechecked.' De Semlyen writes (1993: 199) that 'leading scholars today' recognise that 'the King James version is the only true Protestant Bible and the only one which really lends itself to the historical interpretation of the anti-Christ'. Formal theological scholarship is also supposed to tell us that 'virtually all the other translations are regarded as having leanings toward Romanism' (ibid.). Protestant Bible societies, like the Trinitarian Bible Society and the Evangelical Protestant Society, lend authority to these common-sense renderings of theology by endorsing the claim that theological scholarship 'proves' the King James version is the accurate standard against which all others are distortions. These societies then go on to claim that the evil hand of Rome is working in the distorted translations. Thus, Hugh Farrell, for the Trinitarian Bible Society, wrote that the Revised Standard Version, for example, was part of a Romanist plot to achieve predominance, politically and educationally (H. Farrell, n.d.: 2), and left out verses or distorted them to suit its perverted theology (ibid.: 8–14).[13]

In fact, biblical scholarship shows the King James version to be the most unreliable. The only Greek text available to translators in 1611 was based on late manuscripts and had accumulated all the mistakes of a thousand years of copying. The Cambridge historian Owen Chadwick argues that the Greek manuscript known as Greek Septuagint, on which the King James version is based, itself makes reference to an earlier Hebrew manuscript, and that in modern times a hoard of earlier manuscripts have been found, including the Dead Sea Scrolls, which are more original than the Septuagint (Chadwick, 1990: 351). Fee and Stuart describe the mistakes in the King James version as numerous and often making a significant difference in the meaning of specific verses (Fee and Stuart, 1982: 34). They conclude that one should 'use almost any modern translation rather than the King James version' (ibid.) because contemporary translations use older and more original manuscripts and have eliminated the non-original matter in the Authorised version (ibid.: 42). John McManners, the Oxford theologian, describes the translators of the King James version as having shaky knowledge of Hebrew and completely ignorant of early manuscripts of the New Testament (McManners, 1990: 284). Moreover it was unpopular when it first appeared, with Archbishop Laud continuing to use the Genevan Bible. Obedience to the King James version is thus a human-made tradition, which is only common-sensically presented as a theologically valid preference. The reason why taste and tradition dictate the use of the King James version for certain Protestants is because it was conceived and presented as an avowedly anti-Catholic translation. In the Epistle Dedicatory to the Bible, in honour of King James, reproduced thereafter in every copy sold, the translators set up the conflict with Catholicism, contrasting their endeavours with those 'Popish persons at home and abroad, who will malign us because we are poor instruments to make God's holy truth to be yet more and more known unto the people, whom they desire still to keep in ignorance and darkness'. Thus, even the translators in 1611 omitted the Apocrypha, which devout Protestants thought of at the time as Papist. The preface to many a copy down the years by various writers, picks up the anti-Catholic context of the Authorised version. Dr John Eadie, for example, in the preface to the 'Working Man's Family Bible', an ornate reproduction of the King James version, writes that 'the glory of our land is its Bible ... the estimate in which we hold the Bible will always be a criterion for our superiority. Popery stands in opposition to a gospel.' The author makes reference to Papists as deluded and fanatical, and describes Catholicism as 'an unhallowed usurpation of Christ's title and prerogative'. Thus, the Authorised version is, indeed, a Protestant Bible, but not because it proves the doctrinal truth of Reformed theology, but because it is perceived, common-sensically, to be anti-Catholic; the preference for it is based on tradition not correct theology.

Matters of social taste and fashion also affect interpretations of specific pieces of Scripture. This creates instances where common-sense practical reasoning misunderstands fundamentally certain key New Testament passages. Three examples can be cited: interpretations of the antiChrist; Jesus' injunctions to love one's neighbour, the alien and outsider; and His absence of comment on the Christian's political role. It is a key foundational idea of the covenantal mode of anti-Catholicism that the Book of Revelation refers to Catholicism as the evil which threatens the Church before Christ's second coming, and that the papacy is the antiChrist and the Catholic Church is the Whore spoken of in the vision. That the Pope is the antiChrist is one of those 'codes' which is so quick and easy to reproduce in language that it often extends into other modes, to become a prominent feature of the discursive formation of anti-Catholicism generally. While the claim is thought to be based on sound theological scholarship, and believed to be true for that reason by many who reproduce it in their talk, it is only common-sensically theological, for it is based on a misunderstanding of biblical scholarship. That it is none the less still believed to be true by anti-Catholics shows the immutability of common-sense theology in the face of formal theological knowledge; that the claim continues to reproduced, shows the immutability of human-made tradition and of social tastes and fashions.

Professor John Barkley, a Northern Irish Presbyterian theologian, has analysed interpretations of the antiChrist and shown them to be tied to social context and time (1967)[14] – even the Spice Girls (an all-girl British pop group, popular especially with young girls for their promotion of 'girl power') have now been referred to as the antiChrist, like Napoleon, Hitler, Marx and the Beatles before them, amongst many others. The term itself did not appear until about AD 50–60, but the underlying theme can be traced to the Old Testament. The Book of Daniel, for example, introduce the idea of a God-opposing power, although Jewish scholars were unsure as to whom it applied, and by 63 BC were describing Emperor Pompey in this manner because of his desecration of the Temple during the conquest of Jerusalem. Another Old Testament pillar to the New Testament notion of the antiChrist was the Belial myths, which introduce the idea of a superhuman satanic being. A third pillar from the first century was the Nero myth, in which it was believed that the recently dead Emperor, killed by his own hand, would return from the dead as the antiChrist, as a Belial-like figure who was God-opposing. The Book of Revelation in which the phrase 'antiChrist' appears, drew on these antecedents and the reference is widely understood to refer to Nero (Barkley, 1967: 6; Hunter, 1972: 194). The Book of Revelation does not speak of an ecclesiastical power but a political power, and its allusions are to the Roman Empire. As stated in Chapter 4, the mark '666', for example, which is carried on the forehead of the antiChrist, is a reference to Nero; Greeks and Hebrews used letters also as numerals, and the Greek *Neron Kaiser* in Hebrew numeral transliteration is 666 (Hunter, 1972: 194). The concept of the antiChrist appears elsewhere in the New Testament and these references are unaffected by the allusions to the Roman Empire, which shape John's vision, but they also cannot be seen as referring to the Catholic Church. In the second of Paul's letters to the Thessalonians, written circa AD 50 (ibid.: 143), before Nero committed suicide and the myth of his return became established, Paul refers to a Man of Lawlessness, conceived as a God-opposing individual with satanic powers. But he was understood as a false messiah sent specifically to punish the Jews for rejecting the true Messiah (Barkley, 1967: 6).

Leaving aside the apostolic period, Barkley shows that the early church in the first six centuries used the term antiChrist frequently, and did so to refer to the political powers of the Roman Empire. Irenaeus, for example, about AD 185, spoke of the antiChrist as a crouching lion, a rebel and persecutor, and argued that '666' referred to the Roman Empire, the Greek word for which was *Lateinos*, the sum of whose digits is 666 (ibid.: 8–9). Hippolytus, a few decades later, also used the term to refer to the Roman Empire, as did numerous others in the first centuries (see ibid.: 10). Thus, the people to whom John's apocalyptic vision in Revelation was supposed to have meaning, understood it clearly to describe a political power, not a church, and to refer to the Roman Empire, not the Roman Catholic Church. The location of the antiChrist with Nero was advanced by people like Commoduanus, Lactantius and Victorinus, whose commentary on the Book of Revelation was revised by Jerome and was quoted by St Patrick.

Early medieval understandings of the term located the antiChrist as a Jewish figure, coming from the East, rather than a Christian figure like the Pope in the West. It could not have been understood as referring to the papacy because the title of Pope was not confined to the Bishop of Rome until the eleventh century. The Crusades against Islam at the time tended to locate Mohammed as the antiChrist. It was not until 1316 that a particular Pope was referred to as the antiChrist, and that because the term was used by a Catholic opponent with whom he was in conflict over the nature of monastic life (ibid.: 14). It was, however, a reference to an individual person, not the papacy as a whole. By 1378, the 'great schism' occurred in the Church, where for a time there were up to three Popes, and during this period one Pope often called another the antiChrist. It was at this time that John Wyclif referred to all Popes as representing the antiChrist, and it was this idea that critics latched on to two centuries later in their attack on the Catholic Church during the Reformation. In 1520, for example, Luther held that every Pope was an antiChrist, and so did Calvin some years later. Thus, it was only during the intellectual attack on the Catholic Church during the sixteenth century that it became widely fashionable to locate the antiChrist with the papacy. This was precisely the time that Protestant churches made their doctrinal statements of faith, like the Westminster Confession (1644) and the Irish Articles (1615), which, given the understandings at the time, slavishly reproduced the idea that the papacy was the antiChrist. The Westminster Confession, for example, refers to the 'Pope of Rome' as 'that antichrist, that man of sin, and son of perdition, that exalteth himself in the church against Christ, and all that is called

God'. Thereafter, these confessions of faith have supplied anti-Catholics with the theological justification for the claim that the Pope is the antiChrist, but these doctrinal statements were themselves products of human-made tradition and social taste, whose declarations bore no relation to what we now know to be biblical scholarship. Hence, the Presbyterian Church in Ireland no longer requires subscription to the statement that the Pope is the antiChrist, and in 1988 the General Assembly passed a resolution stating that it is not scriptural to locate the antiChrist with any Pope or the Papacy as a system. Amongst anti-Catholics, however, common-sense theology is immune to formal theological argument; common-sense understandings of Scripture dominate over biblical scholarship. That the Pope is the antiChrist is thus a myth.[15]

Common-sense theology affects the reading of those passages in Scripture where Jesus enjoins Christians to love their neighbour and to show kindness, compassion and love to aliens and outsiders. These passages pose considerable problems for anti-Catholics (as for many others), and common-sense practical reasoning is necessary to interpret them in such a way that they permit hostility and enmity, in language and deed, toward Catholics. In a sense, Jesus' injunctions to love each other summarise the essence of Christianity as Jesus Himself portrayed it. This was something Paul recognised in his discourse on love in 1 Corinthians 13 and when he also told believers in Corinth that 'knowledge puffs up but love builds up' (1 Corinthians 8:1). Thus, upon being asked, for example, to state the greatest of God's Commandments, Jesus answers, 'love the Lord your God with all your heart and with all your soul and with all your mind. This is the first and greatest commandment. And the second is like it. Love your neighbour as yourself' (Matthew 22:37–9). It is significant that in being asked for one, Jesus gives two, for they are seen as inseparable. It is not that they are two different Commandments that could be in conflict, and that one might have to abandon the second in order to keep the first, for Jesus says categorically that the second 'is like' the first. The Rev. Roy Magee makes the point that Jesus gives a second Commandment, when He was only asked for one, because He is trying to convey that our love for God is manifested in our love for other people (see Thomson, 1996: 78). Elsewhere Jesus tells us what we are to do with those who are God's enemies and our own: 'you have heard that it was said "you shall love your neighbour and hate your enemy". But I say to you, love your enemies' (Matthew 5:43–4). From Jesus' parable of the good Samaritan (Luke 10:25–37), where He repeats His description of the two great Commandments, we are told whom are neighbours are – and it is not just people of our own kind, culture, nationality and linguistic group. To be a neighbour is to show mercy (Luke 10:37), even to people who are entirely different to us. Hence Jesus says in the Beatitudes (Matthew 5:46) that we get no reward just by loving those who love us (who are like us). Rather we should love others as we would like to be loved, do unto others as we would have them do to us (Matthew 7:12), and do good to those who hate us (Matthew 5:43).

This is one of those instances where Jesus's 'new covenant' does not restate the obligations and commands of the old, but transforms them completely, changing the nature of God's word in the New compared to the Old Testament. Under the old covenant, Jews were called to be a special people, different from other nations, who should not follow the life-style and religion of others. They were called to be a 'light to the nations' (Isaiah 49: 6) by showing the blessings that follow from trust in and devotion to God, but they were not called to love those nations and peoples who were God's enemies (see Inter-Church Council, 1993: 37). On occasions God instructed His chosen people to persecute and kill enemies. For example, when Moses explains to the Jews the Ten Commandments given him by God, he summarises them in a long discourse contained in Deuteronomy. After being told to love their God with all their heart, soul and strength (Deuteronomy 6:5), God's people are told to drive out the nations, destroy them completely and show them no mercy (Deuteronomy 7:2). King Saul was rejected as king because he had spared the lives of God's enemies (1 Samuel 15:17–23), Elijah massacred the prophets of Baal (1 Kings 18), Ezra persuaded the people to divorce all their foreign wives in fear that they would lead husbands astray (Ezra 10), and there are frequent places where God is called upon to bring down vengeance against the enemies of His people. In one of the Psalms, for example, King David asks God to cut off and destroy David's enemies (Psalm 143:12). But there are also passages where God enjoins His people to show compassion to strangers and foreigners. Elijah, for example, is sent to a foreign widow and is sustained by her, in return for which she receives undreamt-of blessings (1 Kings 17), and God reminds the Jews on occasions that they were once strangers in Egypt and that they should love their neighbours as themselves: 'the stranger who sojourns with you shall be to you as the native among you and you shall love your neighbour as yourself; for you were strangers in the land in Egypt'. These passages were undoubtedly glimpses which God gave of the 'new covenant' (as He also gave glimpses of His Son) and in the New Testament this inclusivity, generosity and compassion towards neighbours, strangers and foreigners is transformed into the overriding expression of love for God. This is why Jesus deliberately returns to the expressions used in Deuteronomy to turn them on their head by refocusing the emphasis. Jesus uses the same words in the first of those two great Commandments, which He says sum up our obligations, in describing how we should love God; but the second is not now to destroy our neighbours, as it was in Moses' time, but to love our neighbour. God's love in Christ is for all – even God's enemies, for Paul writes in Romans 5:10 that 'while we were yet enemies, we were reconciled to God by the death of His Son'. This radically alters how Christians are supposed to treat neighbours, foreigners and strangers alike. 'There is no question here', Paul writes to Christians in Colosse, 'of Greek and Jew, circumcised and uncircumcised, barbarian, Scythian, slave or freeman; but Christ is all and in all' (Colossians 3:11). Peter, Jesus' rock on whom He built His church, was given a vision by God to enter the home of a Roman centurion, an official in an army which was persecuting Christians, and he understood God's message in the vision. The Book of Acts records: 'Then Peter began to speak. "I now realise how true it is that God does not show favouritism but accepts men from every nation who fear him and do what is right"' (Acts 10:34). Jesus lived this in His ministry. The opposition the disciples faced in Samaria led them to ask Jesus if they should bring down fire from Heaven to destroy the Samaritans, as Elijah had done, whereupon Jesus rebukes them and says that He has come to save lives not destroy them (Luke 9:55). His encounter with the adulterous Samaritan woman at the well (John 4:1–42) breached several boundaries which divided righteous Jewish men and sinful Samaritan women, but Jesus showed compassion and love to her, and extended to her salvation. Scripture records that the woman was filling her pitcher in the day and by herself. Normally, this was a task done communally by all the women at first light. That she was alone most likely shows she was ostracised by the other women because of her adultery. It was not acceptable for Jewish men to talk to women alone, let alone a sinful one, but Jesus broke both taboos. Samaritans as a whole were ostracised because they were not part of the circumcised, those whom God had blessed in the original covenant with Abraham, which reinforced the national, linguistic, ethnic and cultural barriers dividing them from Jews. Jesus stepped over all such boundaries, and the story of the woman at the well is a powerful message of the inclusivity and universality of Jesus's love under the 'new covenant'. John's gospel records that many Samaritans came to believe in Jesus – and thus receive salvation – through Jesus' encounter with her. As Sr. Geraldine Smyth (1996: 48) also points out, Jesus was the one who dipped bread in the same dish as Judas, knowing what He knew, and who continued to acknowledge Peter after he had denied Him three times, eventually restoring him to wholeness.

The thrust of Jesus' words and ministry is that under the 'new covenant', there are only two absolutes – love of God and love of neighbour – and that faith in Him must be lived in compassionate, kind, loving and constructive good works toward both. The common-sense reasoning process of anti-Catholics reinterprets these Scriptures in two ways. First, they hark back to the old covenant, represented by the Old Testament injunction to 'go ye apart and be ye separate', in which God was a separatist and selected an exclusive and special people to whom He restricted His blessing and to whom He gave the instruction to remain apart. This completely fails to recognise the new covenantal obligations introduced with Jesus in which there is a universality and inclusiveness, with salvation open to all who come and believe 'from East and West' (Matthew 8:11). But Paisley, for example, continues to see God as a separatist, decrying those who preach Jesus' new covenantal obligations of love as 'these lovey dovey fellows' (*The Revivalist*, February 1980: 10). 'I want to tell you', he went on, 'God declared war on the Devil in Heaven and cleaned the Devil out of Heaven. God is a separatist. Christ said "I saw Satan cast as lightening from Heaven". A clean sweep.' Separatism such as this thus requires that Catholics be enervated by common-sensically believing them to be as evil as the Devil. Hating Catholics is permissible, under the old covenant, *if* they are seen as God's enemies, but is indefensible under the new covenant *even if* they remain seen as

God's enemies. Hence, common-sense theology amongst anti-Catholics reverses the overturning which Jesus did. In doing so, comfort is found in the few New Testament passages which appear to reintroduce separation between believers and God's enemies. Paul writes in 2 Corinthians 6:14–15 that light and darkness cannot live together, so believers should not try to work with unbelievers as equals, and in his epistle to Titus Paul urges that after a third warning, believers should have nothing to do with those who cause division (Titus 3:10–11). Common-sense theology can only appropriate these to rationalise anti-Catholicism if Catholics are seen as unbelievers, which explains why there is such extreme common-sense distortion about what Catholics really believe. Hence Pastor McClinton said in interview: 'fellowship with anyone who is a Christian is an obligation, a necessity, but Roman Catholics are not Christian. The Church of Ireland are the same. Roman Catholicism uses priests as intercessors, uses the confessional to forgive sins, believes in baptismal regeneration and Mariology, [and] offers salvation always with Jesus and something or someone else when it's only Jesus.'

It is also only possible to appropriate these passages from Paul to rationalise anti-Catholicism if people allow the entire thrust of Jesus' message to be blunted by a few comments from Paul. This often happens, for a second response amongst anti-Catholics is to common-sensically reinterpret Scripture in order to put limits on Jesus' injunctions to love neighbours, strangers and outsiders. In an article in *The Revivalist* in June 1993, Paisley explains what he thinks Jesus's injunctions mean, and it is a travesty of Jesus: 'for a Christian to love is simply to desire with all the heart for everyone to love and obey Jesus Christ'. Paisley's usual response to these injunctions is to ignore them in his preaching and writing. Cooke concludes his survey of Paisley's preaching and writing by saying that Jesus's commandments have received only one slight and indirect reference (Cooke, 1996: 96). Paisley has said more often that it is correct to hate the sinner as much as the sin – to do otherwise he has said is unscriptural (see Cooke, 1996: 96), which involves further travesty of Jesus's injunctions. Other Free Presbyterians have taken a slightly different argument in claiming that the neighbour Jesus was referring to as the object of our compassion, kindness, love, mercy and good works was, in fact, merely someone like us in having our citizenship, nationality and culture by being 'a citizen of the country in which we live' (Mervyn Storey, quoted in Thomson, 1996: 112). Pastor Kenny McClinton's reasoning places Catholics outside citizenship. Citizenship, he said, brings rights and responsibilities, and the full rights of citizenship cannot be extended to those who evade responsibilities like obligations toward the state, flying its flag, and recognising the authority of the state's forces of law and order. 'Irish nationalists claim they're second class citizens', he said, 'well, they are.' The phrase 'for God and Ulster' allows many anti-Catholics to interpret 'neighbour' as Ulster Protestants only, or, at least, to treat as an outsider to this commandment anyone who does not support Ulster.

Common-sense theology amongst many anti-Catholics, especially the covenantal types, also distorts the New Testament, therefore, by making an equation between

God and country. Two consequences follow from this equation. First, a country's borders are seen as theologically inviolate.[16] Pastor McClinton, for example, said that while God's Kingdom is not of this world, He gave us responsibilities to the land, any land. While these borders are underwritten by international law, which should not be breached, the force of the Old Testament supersedes this, for God told His chosen people not to move ancient boundary stones, and he told Joshua to possess the land. He draws from this that Ulster is thus an integral part of the United Kingdom because the Bible tells us so. The second consequence of this equation is that political participation on behalf of one's country, even to extreme levels, is a theological obligation. It might be an obligation for other reasons, but it becomes so for religious ones only if common-sensically one assumes that religion and country are indivisible. They are so in Old Testament notions of the covenant, but Jesus' 'new covenant' did not link loyalty to God with valorisation of nation and land, as Chapter 4 made clear. In fact, the one judgement Jesus makes about countries was that they should not be separated into groups which are divided from each other, which seems to further undermine any interpretation of covenants which link God's blessing to a special land or group. Jesus says: 'any country which divided itself into groups which fight each other will not last very long. And any town or family that divided itself into groups which fight each other will fall apart' (Matthew 12:25). Conversely, Jesus said naught about the political role His followers should adopt and He purposely avoided setting Himself up as a political zealot, intimating that politics be kept separate from faith when He told His followers to render unto Caesar that which is Caesar's and unto God that which is God's. Some of Morrow's respondents who were Protestant ministers reported their interpretation of the New Testament position: 'I see boundaries between politics and the Church'; and 'politics and the pulpit don't go together' (Morrow, 1997: 23; see also Kinahan, 1995: 37). For this reason also, therefore, anti-Catholics have to remain wedded to the Old Testament and to blunt the edge of Jesus' 'new covenant', since the Old Testament supports national and patriotic political sentiment. Hence, Pastor McClinton argued:

> a Christian's obligations under the New Testament are not much different from under the Old Testament. Moses, David, the prophets, Judges, they were all politicians, spokespeople for the people. Christians have an obligation to participate in politics, to stand against evil and to stand up for justice and truth, which means political involvement. But it must be peaceful, be within the law, and be democratic.

Conclusion

Professor Bruce, an avowed agnostic, once perceptively wrote that if God is so all-powerful, it should not be beyond His capabilities to allow people to find Him through both 'the florid Catholic Mass and the Quaker shared silence' (Bruce, 1994: 149). Although undoubtedly true, the problem with the common-sense theology underpinning anti-Catholicism is that it believes God to be on its side. God is their God, who stands for and defends their Bible, who shows preferential treatment and special favour to their position, and who protects their version of biblical truth. Thus, areas of theological common ground with the Catholic Church are ignored, as are profound differences in worship, liturgy, praise and doctrine within Protestantism. The small differences with Catholicism make all the difference to the anti-Catholic's common-sense reasoning; it exaggerates the theological chasm with Catholicism and makes this one set of differences the sole measure of theological Truth. But even if the doctrinal differences with Catholicism were huge, this would still not justify the level of abuse, ridicule and sectarian hostility toward Catholics and the Catholic Church. The New Testament makes many severe warnings against false doctrine and prophets, but Jesus said these would be identified by their fruits – 'a good tree cannot bear bad fruit, or a poor tree good fruit. That is why I say you will recognise them by their fruits' (Matthew 7:15–20). They will not be recognised by Christians engaging in name-calling, vengeful abuse and spiteful ridicule to differentiate them. Nowhere did Jesus say that this was the way to treat those with whom we disagree; not even, any more, God's enemies. James warned against a harsh tongue (James 3:1–12) and Jesus warned: 'you can be sure that on Judgement Day everyone will have to give account of every useless word he has ever spoke. Your words will be used to judge you – to declare you either innocent or guilty' (Matthew 12:36). The obligation for a Christian was to ensure that they are righteous in Jesus' eyes rather than right in their own. It was only the powers of Satan which Jesus rounded on harshly and with force of deed and tongue.[17] And this is why, in the common-sense reasoning of many of the most extreme and rabid anti-Catholics, they have to believe Catholic theology to be so evil and satanic, for their abuse is thus justified and they are saved from condemnation in the final judgement.

Conclusion

Introduction

In an analysis of ethnic differentiation in Northern Ireland, Richard Jenkins, one of its foremost analysts, claimed that local Protestants had used ethnicity as 'a social resource' in their dominance (Jenkins, 1997: 90), and while he rightly renders ethnicity in its Northern Irish expression to be manifested by religion, he dismisses anti-Catholicism as an expression of ethnic conflict because doctrinal differences have not everywhere produced conflict on the scale of Northern Ireland (ibid.: 112). This is not the point: anti-Catholicism in some settings is, indeed, much more than doctrinal differences but a sociological account is needed to distinguish these occasions from settings where the differences remain theological. In 'situational' theories of ethnicity, ethnic boundaries are not genetic or kinship based, but locally determined and appropriated contextually whenever ethnically based mobilisation occurs. Modern cultural studies have shown the vast array of cultural resources used in constructing identity, including national and ethnic identity (Hall and du Gay, 1996; Woodward, 1997). Anti-Catholicism has been used as a resource in localised and situational circumstances, such as in Britain between the seventeenth and nineteenth centuries, where it was mobilised in different sorts of conflicts, and in Ireland. The imperative is to explain why theological and doctrinal differences took on such sociological import in Northern Ireland and why they have continued to do so when they have diminished in saliency elsewhere.

It is significant that anti-Catholicism functions this way in Northern Ireland not some other resource, such as anti-Irish racism. Old-fashioned notions of 'race', popular in the nineteenth century, have never been appropriated in social stratification and social closure in Ireland, even though anti-Irish racism was once used in this way in Britain. This is because 'race' has no resonance in Ireland, historically or today, but religion always did, and still does. Or at least, the early resonance of 'race' was always reducible to religion because Gaels were Irish Catholic and the Ulster Scots and English planters Protestant, which explains why 'race' did not sustain itself as a line of differentiation independent of religious difference much beyond the seventeenth century (on the overlap between lines of differentiation, see Ruane and Todd, 1996). 'Ethnicity' in some general sense does not act as a resource either because religious difference, as Jenkins rightly argues, is its sole component in Northern Ireland in the absence of other ethnic regional, cultural or linguistic differences: ethnicity is reducible to religion in Northern Ireland (a point stressed also in the work of Bruce, see especially Bruce, 1986, 1994).[1] Thus, religious difference has always been the only resource on which to call situationally whenever ethnic mobilisation was necessary, and the saliency of religious difference to the lives of ordinary people in Northern Ireland ensured that mobilisation was always on ethnic grounds rather than by alternative forms of mobilisation based around class – or at least, attempts to mobilise on class grounds, such as during the 1907 dockers' strike and the outdoor relief riots of the early 1930s, did not sustain themselves because of the saliency of ethnic differences as marked by religion. Such religious difference finds its ultimate expression in anti-Catholicism, although there is no inevitable reason why it should. The point, therefore, is to explain why religious difference was expressed in this extreme form for so many people in Northern Ireland, and has done so for so long. These, and many other issues, need to be addressed in any sociological account of anti-Catholicism.

The Sociology of Anti-Catholicism

A sociological account of anti-Catholicism needs to proffer a definition of the phenomenon in such a way as to identify it as a sociological process with import beyond mere doctrinal differences, in order to explain why, in some settings, it becomes situationally wrapped up in a range of other, broader processes; to describe its forms and types, and some of the sociological features underlying them; to identify the situational and localised circumstances in which anti-Catholicism becomes used as a resource in group mobilisation; to explain why its saliency as a resource continues, even thrives, in some settings when it has declined or disappeared in others; and to describe the sociological dynamics of its reception amongst an audience or primary constituency. The previous chapters have attempted to address these issues, and pulling together the arguments in summary form here is useful to stress the sociological character of anti-Catholicism.

Anti-Catholicism has its roots in a theological debate, beginning in the Reformation, about the doctrine and practice of the Roman Catholic Church. Anti-Catholicism, however, is not just a theological dispute about salvational truth, but can also be understood as a sociological process. Sociological processes are methods of doing or producing an identifiably social item, and act as resources in that they are a means to expedite goals, a source of support in time of need, and a supply of material aid or prosperity. Anti-Catholicism as a sociological process can be defined as the determination of actions, attitudes and practices by negative beliefs about Catholics or the Catholic Church as an institution, which results in these negative beliefs being invoked as an ethnic boundary marker in group identity, which can be used, in some settings, to represent social stratification and conflict. Thus, the social item produced by anti-Catholicism is social stratification and closure. But it operates for this purpose in a restricted social setting. In Northern Ireland's case, this setting is distinguished by two kinds of social relationships into which anti-Catholicism needs to be located: an endogenous one between Protestant and Catholic, and an exogenous one between Ireland and Britain generally. The colonial relationship between Britain and Ireland ensured that the social structure of Irish society was dominated by the endogenous relationship between Catholics (natives) and Protestants (settlers), which remained in Northern Ireland after partition. But the broader relationship negatively affected the internal one in other ways. Local Protestants were caught between 'natives' and the British, making them cling tenaciously to that which identified them with Britain, mostly their Protestant religious identity and beliefs, and political union (on 'settler ideology' in twentieth-century Ulster, see Clayton, 1996). But the relationship of local Protestants with Britain was always unstable, because of the changing position of Ireland as a colony in the exogenous relationship, resulting in a paradox which has dogged Irish (and then Ulster) Protestants. In terms of their relationship with Catholics, local Protestants felt a sense of superiority, ascendancy and dominance, while the Irish–British relationship gave them a sense of grievance, threat and fear, similar to colonial settings elsewhere in which religion was absent. Superiority and suspicion mixed in equal proportion amongst local Protestants, structuring the role of anti-Catholicism in group relations in Ireland. Thus, anti-Catholicism can be conceptualised as a sociological process for the production of different rights, opportunities and material rewards between people in a society where religious labels are used to define group boundaries (such as in Ireland and then Northern Ireland) or, more narrowly, where religious labels are used to define the boundaries of an out-group in a society differentiated on other lines (such as in Britain).[2] It is thus one of the tap roots of sectarianism and is similar as a sociological process to anti-Semitism, although, on the whole, anti-Semitism reflected the use of religious labels to define an out-group in societies differentiated by other processes.

The sociological definition of the process can be extended. Anti-Catholicism occurs at three levels – that of ideas, individual behaviour and the social structure. There is nothing inevitable about the progression through these levels, but in its worst manifestations, such as Northern Ireland, it occurs at all three. Anti-Catholicism (like anti-Semitism) can remain at the level of ideas and individual action, where it exists as a set of pejorative and negative ideas, discursive formations and behaviours, and while this affects the social structure, it does not shape or mould it. These are also the levels at which anti-Protestantism exists, at least in Ireland, and it tends to be motivated more by issues around Protestant politics than objections to Reformed theology.[3] Anti-Catholicism (like anti-Semitism) is at its most sociologically significant when it occurs at the third level (as anti-Semitism did, for example, in Nazi Germany[4]). In its extreme form, anti-Catholicism is a resource used to expedite goals, it forms a source of support and supplies material benefits to such an extent that the social structure is shaped and moulded by it. It thus becomes a major source of mobilisation in group conflict and in the regulation and control of group competition. Anti-Catholicism has been used in a two-fold manner in Northern Ireland: as a mobilisation resource to defend the socio-economic and political position of Protestants against opposition that threatens it; and as a rationalisation to justify and legitimise both that privileged position and any conflict with those who challenge or weaken it.

This explains its continued resonance. Anti-Catholicism survives in Northern Ireland when it has declined elsewhere, notably in Britain and the Irish Republic, nearest neighbours to Northern Ireland in the British Isles, because it helps to define group boundaries and plays a major sociological role in producing and rationalising political and economic inequality. Yet this is only part of the explanation for its saliency. There is a sociological dynamic which explains why it is 'received' so readily amongst its primary constituency. In some settings, anti-Catholicism becomes readily available and easily recognisable culturally as a resource for the purpose of social stratification and social closure because it fits seamlessly with society and its patterns of cleavage and conflicts. Without this seamlessness, there is no sociological dynamic to facilitate its reception amongst those who listen to it, believe it and who use it. In Northern Ireland, anti-Catholicism fits seamlessly with Northern Irish society for the following reasons. It has long historical roots in ethno-national traditions in Northern Ireland, going back to the original conflict between planters and Gaels and forming part of their ethnic myths; it has a legacy of efficacy and effectiveness in the past, providing many lessons of its effectiveness as a resource across time; anti-Catholicism is very consistent with the rendering of the Northern Irish society into the simple zero-sum game between two competing groups, which is the way the groups like to see the conflict, since gains for one can occur only at the other's expense; it fits the self-identities of the groups involved in this zero-sum conflict as religious groups, since religious labels are appropriated common-sensically to define the competition for power and privilege and group boundaries; moreover, the deployment of anti-Catholicism as a resource in structuring group relations fits with the high levels of religiosity in Northern Ireland and the value people place on religious belief in their sense of personal and national identity; and, finally, anti-Catholicism comes with its own immutable and in-built legitimation (God's scriptural injunction to oppose doctrinal error), which has a special cultural sanction in Northern Ireland because of the society's high religiosity. This seamlessness becomes a constraint for those people and groups which seek to move beyond sectarian politics. David Ervine, for example, said in interview that it is theology which keeps the conflict going in Northern Ireland because it treats it as a binary zero-sum:

> Sectarianism is a flower that's cultivated, nurtured, and owes its origins to historical circumstances and socio-political causes. I dislike use of the term because it suggests the conflict is about religion, when it's about politics. I prefer the term 'tribalism': religion is used to keep people in tribes. Tribalism is like piss down the leg, it initially gives a warm glow but it quickly goes cold. Some people use fear of the Pope and papal conspiracies in order to keep the problem as a two-party zero-sum conflict. Certain Unionists create tribalism, through creating fear, in order to keep people in their entrenched positions.

In short, anti-Catholicism resonates closely with the cultural milieu in Northern Ireland, in a way that 'race' does in Britain because of its imperial and colonial past;

anti-Catholicism is consistent with features of Northern Irish society. It is part of the ideological apparatus that constructs two mutually exclusive groups with opposed sets of interests and identities, and it forms part of the symbolic myths, rituals and language which reproduces and represents polarised and sectarian experiences and behaviour, even though in reality the differences between Catholics and Protestants are small. Therefore, anti-Catholicism operates as a sociological process only in a culturally demarcated and limited social context, although in such settings it possesses a distinctive sociological profile.

Historically, theological differences in Ireland obtained their saliency because they corresponded to all the major patterns of structural differentiation in plantation society, such as ethnic and cultural status, social class, ownership of property and land, economic wealth, employment, education, and political power. Colonisation proceeded on the basis of neutering the remnants of Gaelic and Catholic wealth and power by the ascendancy of Protestantism, linking this form of theology forever after with political loyalty, economic privilege, and cultural superiority. All the modes of differentiation in Irish society after the plantation coalesced around two polarities. The vanquished were Catholic, Gaelic-Irish, seen as savage and uncivilised, and were now economically dispossessed if not already poor; the planters were Protestant, Scots-English, saw themselves as culturally civilised, and were now economically privileged (see Ruane and Todd, 1996: 10–11). Anti-Catholicism thus easily stood as a representation of other conflicts and sets of interest. Anti-Catholicism, however, came with its own internal logic and justification, for as in as much as the planters had privileges it was because they had the true religion: Catholics were dispossessed and poor because they were not 'saved', being kept in bondage by their priests (see Bruce, 1994: 26–7). Anti-Catholicism remained important down the centuries because the patterns of differentiation in Northern Irish society have stayed essentially the same. Alternative lines of division are relatively weak in Northern Ireland (see ibid.: 28), with ethnicity, marked by religious difference, remaining as the only salient social cleavage. Modern industrial society in the North has not produced secularisation on a grand scale, and religious difference remains critical to many Protestants. As Bruce argued in relation to Free Presbyterians, 'being possessed of a strongly religious worldview, many Ulster Protestants explain a great deal of what happens to them in religious terms. They see the conflict in Ireland as a religious conflict. Their culture and their circumstances are mutually reinforcing' (Bruce, 1986: 244–5). However, the continued saliency of religion is only partly to be explained by the slow ravages of secularisation, with the commensurate high levels of religiosity in Northern Ireland. It also continues because religion stands in place for ethnic identity and thus represents the patterns of differentiation in an ethnically structured society. In the former respect anti-Catholicism continues as a throwback to Reformation debates about theology in a society still wedded to doctrinal conflicts because of its high religiosity; in the latter anti-Catholicism helps to define the boundaries of the groups involved in competition over power, wealth and status, it is mobilised to regulate and control that competition, and is used in social closure to protect the access of the Protestant ethnic group.

Anti-Catholicism has been deployed as a resource for ethnic mobilisation amongst Protestants in specific historical circumstances and events. Some of these have been theological, such as when Catholicism seemed to progress as a faith through church expansion, and when the Catholic Church became self-confident and articulate, notably, for example, during Cardinal Cullen's transformation of Irish Catholicism into a Roman ultramontanist form in the mid-nineteenth century, and during the early post-independence period in Eire when the Catholic Church became imperialist. Anti-Catholicism has also been mobilised in political events throughout Irish history, such as when the political interests of Protestants had to be defended during Catholic emancipation, Home Rule and partition, and when there was a desperately felt need for political unity, either as a result of notable instances of division, such as after the United Irishmen rebellion, or where in-group solidarity was recognised as important because of the threats to Union posed by out-groups, whether they be local Catholics, the Irish or the British. Durkheim's theory of religion, formulated at the beginning of the twentieth century from an analysis of pre-Christian religions, stresses the socially integrative functions of religious belief and this fits Ulster Protestant politics well. In times of political threat and instability, conservative evangelicalism acted as the sacred canopy, lending itself readily to anti-Catholicism because of the deep antipathy within conservative evangelicalism to the doctrine of the Catholic Church. Historians recognise this sociological truth. Hempton argues that evangelicalism drew together old adversarial religious traditions and different social classes under the banner of a shared anti-Catholicism (Hempton, 1996: 111), and he quotes another historian, David Miller: 'although antipopery had been an element of evangelicalism since Wesley, the movement's role in creating Protestant solidarity derived from more than a new way to stigmatise the ancient enemy. Evangelical emphasis offered these two churches [Episcopal and Presbyterian] a way out of the adversarial relationship in which they had been cast since the seventeenth century.' Anti-Catholicism thus built bridges between several camps within Protestantism, such as the different Reformed denominations, between clergy and laity, and the churches and voluntary associations, as Hempton emphasises (see ibid.: 112), but also between the urban and rural Protestant working class, and between them and the wealthy Protestant industrial and landowning elite. Church–state–society were in harmony as an ethos of godliness, good citizenship and political loyalty all worked together under the sacred canopy of an anti-Catholic conservative evangelical Protestantism, although this hegemony was never total given the small minority of theologically liberal Protestants and the yet smaller number of Protestant nationalists (on which, in the nineteenth century, see Loughlin, 1985; in the modern period, see Hyndman, 1996).

Economic circumstances have also provoked the mobilisation of Protestants by means of anti-Catholicism, especially when social closure was necessary to protect Protestant access to scarce resources, as occurred, for example, during Catholic threats to Protestant domination of the linen industry in the eighteenth century (which witnessed the formation of the Orange Order) and shipbuilding in the nineteenth. This also occurred when high levels of Protestant unemployment, notably during the 1930s, threatened their position as a labour aristocracy, and when non-sectarian forms of class mobilisation seemed to be successful in advancing the position of the Catholic working class. Sectarian riots can be closely tied to proselytising by the Catholic Church and political fears by Protestants, but also to the encroachment by Catholics into Protestant strongholds, whether jobs or territory, from which comes associated threats to scarce resources like housing, education and the 'social capital' arising from employment.

Mobilisation on the basis of anti-Catholicism during these events made reference to various features about Catholicism and Catholics, which illustrate the different dimensions of anti-Catholicism as a sociological process. There is a theological dimension, going back to the Reformation, with references to Catholic doctrine, especially as it concerns salvational truth, but there is also a cultural dimension, involving everyday discourse, imagery and values within Protestant popular culture. This anti-Catholic language can be called a discursive formation and it permeates deep within Northern Irish popular culture. Other dimensions to anti-Catholicism exist as well. There is a political dimension which involves defence of the Union, which Catholicism supposedly threatens, and an attack on Republicanism, which Catholicism is supposed to advance, even to the point of supporting terrorism. There is an economic dimension also, with the need for Protestant ascendancy and privilege to be protected, which involves references to Catholicism as allegedly endangering Ulster's wealth and prosperity because of its encouragement of sloth and laziness, and to Catholics as threatening jobs, housing and 'social capital'. Thus, anti-Catholicism can be classified according to the extent of its theological and political focus, giving different emphases in its articulation, as represented in Figure 1 (see Introduction, p. 4).

This serves to show that anti-Catholicism is not monolithic. Any sociological account of anti-Catholicism should describe its different forms and types, since they can articulate anti-Catholicism differently, leading on to other contrasts which help in the sociological description of the process. This study has shown that four modes exist, one of which is called the passive mode, which is an unsystematic and unformulated type of anti-Catholicism. Three forms of active anti-Catholicism exist, representing coherent systems with different sets of foundational ideas and forms of rhetoric, appealing to different primary constituencies, and with different consequences for establishing meaningful relationships with Catholics. These types are called covenantal, secular and Pharisaic modes. These modes can be plotted on two axes or continua – theological content (high to low) and political content (high to low), illustrating further differences that exist between the expressions of anti-Catholicism in Northern Ireland, as represented in Figure 5 (see Part II, introduction, p. 134). This description of the various modes of anti-Catholicism neatly captures the paradox of the process, in that it can be grounded in an interpretation of Scripture (covenantal and Pharisaic modes), which may (covenantal mode) or may not (Pharisaic mode) have political expression, and also be relatively devoid of theology and highly political (secular mode), emphasising an approach to politics much like one of the more theological modes (the covenantal). This reinforces the point that although these modes are empirical types, they do not exist in pure form in people's language and behaviour because there is overlap in the concerns of each mode and people articulate this cross-over in their own version of anti-Catholicism.

A description of the different modes of anti-Catholicism further highlights sociological features of the process, for underlying anti-Catholicism is a 'cognitive map' through which Catholic doctrine and practice are common-sensically understood and by means of which individual Catholics are classified as people. This is a very self-contained and closed map of the world because it is reinforced by a process of common-sense reasoning which ends up being immutable and resistant to change. Reasoning processes like distortion, deletion, denial and distancing are mutually reinforcing in their antipathy to Catholic theology and its practitioners and believers. But the significance of this process of common-sense reasoning extends beyond the immutability and self-containment it gives to common-sense knowledge. The process of common-sense reasoning elevates the anti-Catholic's common-sense notions about Catholicism and Catholics into intersubjective ideas shared with others, giving them the appearance of what social phenomenologists call 'factual reality', by which is meant the appearance of existing outside and beyond the individual's own everyday life-world. Thus, personal prejudices and biases become transformed because they appear to reflect a social reality shared with others. This transformation process further requires that the common-sense notions about Catholicism and Catholics, whether about theology, politics, life-style, or whatever, are socially disseminated and transmitted. Social dissemination amongst a group facilitates the sense that the common-sense notions are intersubjective and that they describe a social reality, but it also simultaneously reinforces the closed and self-contained character of these common-sense ideas by strengthening their immutability. The closed and self-contained character of the cognitive map of anti-Catholicism is reinforced by various religious and secular artefacts and behaviours which sustain and support anti-Catholicism. These range from the Bible version they read; the Church to which they belong and the ministers to whom they listen; the hymns which they sing; the other Christian groups and organisations with which they have fellowship; the secular newspapers they buy; the political parties and politicians they support; the marching organisations to which they belong; the area where they live; the places where they shop, send their children to school and spend their leisure; and their places of work, entertainment and pleasure. All these things assist in the social dissemination of common-sense notions and they involve sectarianised forms of social interaction which prevent or restrict contact with Catholics, ensuring that common-sense stereotypes, ideas, maxims and beliefs are not undercut by personal experience and are immune to empirical test in day-to-day life. The cognitive map of anti-Catholicism therefore continues to structure how anti-Catholics perceive, understand

and 'know' the Catholic Church and its members. This reinforces the anti-Catholic's belief that this common sense actually makes sense, so that it persists as the primary realm of relevance for understanding Catholicism and Catholics.

Another sociological feature of anti-Catholicism which is related to the cognitive map underlying it, is its bearing on the relationship between language and identity. Language plays a key functional role in anti-Catholicism over and above the pejorative descriptions it contains about Catholic theology and its believers. Language assists in transforming common-sense notions about Catholics and their faith into intersubjective categories partly because linguistic categories typify experiences and ideas, giving the impression that common-sense notions are shared, but also because language assists in the social dissemination and transmission of common-sense knowledge. Personal prejudices and biases against Catholics become a 'factual reality', thus appearing as a social reality beyond personal tastes, partly because of the intersubjective linguistic categories used in describing Catholic theology, the Catholic Church and individual Catholics. Yet language does more than describe: it represents and reproduces the world in which it operates. Critical linguists emphasise that language reflects ideological conflicts, and patterns of power and differentiation, so that anti-Catholic 'codes' and 'preconstructeds', such as 'No Surrender', 'Remember 1690', and 'not an inch', reproduce past patterns of power in Northern Ireland and reflect old conflicts in which Protestants were victorious. Language, however, does yet more interactive work, for it shapes as much as reflects some aspects of social reality, particularly group identities. Anti-Catholic language shapes how Catholics are perceived, so that talk about Catholicism is talk about identity. The language used in such talk is constitutive of the identity of the talker. Phrases like 'ye must be born again', 'Remember 1690', 'no Pope here', 'Home Rule is Rome rule', and 'No Surrender' both reflect and constitute a certain kind of Protestant identity. They are constitutive of a certain kind of Protestant identity because what it means to be Protestant, for certain group members, is never having to have surrendered, never being able to accept 'Rome rule', not accepting 'Popery', being 'born again' and so on, and letting 'insiders' and 'others' know this. Hence Rafferty's remark that 'deep and persistent intolerance, hatred is not too strong a word, of Catholicism' is 'the very touchstone of Northern Ireland Protestant identity' (Rafferty, 1994: 283–4). This is a mite too strong because anti-Catholicism is not the 'master status' of the identity of all Protestants in the North, and not all modes of anti-Catholicism involve an emotion as deep as hatred, but it describes well the identity mark of the more fundamentalist and conservative evangelical 'Bible Protestant'. However, while not typifying Protestantism generally, the anti-Catholic identity of this kind of Protestant, exemplifies, in extreme form, beliefs and values that in weaker versions are held by a far greater number of Protestants. This does not mean that Protestants have to lose their identity as Protestants in order for anti-Catholicism to diminish, merely change the constituents used to construct it.

For all these reasons, anti-Catholicism cannot be dismissed as 'not of major interest' (Jenkins, 1997: 112). While doctrinal and theological disputes are in themselves not sociologically fecund, sociology has an input into explaining why four-century-old theological conflicts remain pertinent in some limited social settings. As stressed here, ancient theological disputes still resonate because of high levels of religiosity, but the absence of secularisation is only part of a sociological account. In some settings, ancient religious differences are functional equivalents of other lines of differentiation. In this kind of social milieu, anti-Catholicism does important interactional work; it is one of the major resources which define group boundaries in Northern Ireland, and it helps to create and rationalise social closure, because it constitutes a significant part of the 'cultural stuff', as Jenkins himself puts it (1997), which comprises ethnicity in Northern Ireland.

The Sociological Decline of Anti-Catholicism in Britain

In as much as sociology can offer an account of the persistence of anti-Catholicism in Northern Ireland, it suggests an explanation for its demise elsewhere in Britain. In Scotland, the grounds for its decline in the twentieth century are clear (see Bruce, 1985b; Wallis and Bruce, 1986: 333–59). Protestantism in Scotland was more fragmented than in Ulster, so that attention was diverted away from sorting out relationships with Catholics into defining their position against each other. Thus, there was no equivalent to the social glue provided by conservative evangelicalism, so that Scottish Protestantism was not hegemonic. In Ulster, Protestantism is more cohesive, with unity around a conservative theological orthodoxy, while Scottish Presbyterians, for example, are liberal and more tolerant of doctrinal heterodoxy (Wallis and Bruce, 1986: 339). Fragmentation in Scottish Protestantism not only resides in regional and social differentiation within Protestantism (ibid.: 338), but also because there was no need felt for unity, since Catholics posed no threat. Catholics in Scotland were composed of ethnically Scottish Catholics, descendants of the Jacobean Highland Catholics, and the ethnically Irish Catholics, who were nineteenth-century economic migrants. Catholicism was thus a poor boundary marker for ethnicity and could not represent other conflicts. Moreover, the Irish Catholics were few in number and concentrated in one small part of Scotland. In this sense, there was no hegemony amongst Catholics either, divided as they were between the ethnically Scottish and ethnically Irish, and the Irish Catholics never established an exclusively Catholic political agenda, mostly working through the labour movement. Only claims of malevolent Catholic conspiracies emanating from Rome could manufacture a sense of threat, and the liberal inclination of Scottish Protestants made these unbelievable. Scottish society was also experiencing secularisation, with reduced levels of religiosity, a declining social role for the Church in politics and a reduction in the salience of religious affiliations within the social structure in the face of other processes of differentiation. Patterns of differentiation gave religious difference no resonance. In the absence of a pan-Scottish Protestantism and much saliency for religion, there was no specifically Protestant politics, no recognisable set of political or economic interests for Protestants, and no cultural stress on Protestantism as an ethnic boundary marker in the competition for scarce resources. When an exclusively Protestant politics existed in the twentieth century it fed much on Ulster's conflicts rather than Scotland's (Bruce, 1985b), and even this was killed by the Second World War, since Wallis and Bruce report that many activists in Protestant Action had their attitude towards Catholics change as a result of joint war service (Wallis and Bruce, 1986: 348–9), although these integrated forms of social interaction were greatly reinforced and extended by post-war major housing redevelopment and population relocation which broke up many of the old religiously structured communities and neighbourhoods (ibid.: 349). Residential segregation on religious lines continues, however, in Northern Ireland, which helps to maintain the saliency of religious difference as a social cleavage and ethnic boundary marker.

The sociological processes that make Scotland different from Ulster apply also to England. Historically, English society has been as anti-Catholic as Ulster, but it has waned as religious affiliation and commitment have diminished under the forces of secularisation. Catholicism has become less objectionable, if only because religion no longer provokes strong emotions. Thus, Paz (1992) argues that English anti-Catholicism, at its height in the Victorian period, has declined in the twentieth century along with the religious world view and high levels of religiosity which provoked it in the first place. Moreover, England (like Britain generally), has become a pluralist society, both in the sense that religious affiliations are more diverse, with an associated greater tolerance of diversity, and in terms of the diversity of social groups and possible boundary markers. Thus, even during the debates over Home Rule and partition at the beginning of the twentieth century, Ulster Protestants were bemoaning the apparent lack of a vigorous British anti-Catholicism, which they had been able to take for granted a quarter of a century before (see Hempton, 1996: 150), something which Walker attributes to the growth of religious pluralism in England (1989: 30). Religion lost its resonance as a social cleavage, therefore, not just because religion itself lost its social significance, for there was no longer a solid and simple binary zero-sum divide amidst all the competing religious affiliations. Catholicism pales in a religiously pluralist society, when it becomes just one denomination amongst others and when it confines itself to ministering to the Catholic community. Moreover, religious pluralism is normally associated with theological liberalism, or at least the reduced prominence for conservative orthodox positions amongst all competing ones, so that the market for anti-Catholic theology is restricted to the 'holy remnant', which itself grows smaller under the impulse of secularisation and liberalisation.

England is also a pluralist society in the sense that there are many kinds of social cleavage, diminishing the import of religion as an ethnic boundary marker. Ethnicity in Britain is not reflected in historic religious identities, as it once was. If 'ethnic honour' is still important to the English, the 'community of descent', as Weber put it, is not marked by religion but more by 'race' and national origin. Thus, what resistance there is to Irish Catholics in England, particularly noticeable in the modern period during the 1950s and since 'the troubles', is motivated more by anti-

Irish racism than anti-Catholicism, and it does not project on to English Catholics. But mobilisation by ethnicity (however defined or marked) competes with mobilisation by means of social class, and group mobilisation is diffused further by increasing post-modernist appeals to the environment or gender, complicating boundary markers and group membership. While Ulster has a simple binary divide, modern-day England is pluralistic in its social cleavages. Moreover, Protestantism does not have the functional role in forging social unity and national identity that it formerly had in Britain. If Protestantism was a social glue for Britain in the eighteenth century when the United Kingdom was first formed, as Colley (1992), amongst others, claims, it long ago lost this role. National myths are no longer religious, politics is not structured by theological allegiance, and sets of interests do not correspond to religious differences. Thus, even if one claims that anti-Catholicism at the level of ideas remains latent in English society, it does not occur there at the level of individual action or the social structure. Other lines of fissure at the structural level make anti-Catholicism irrelevant to the competition for scarce resources and pointless as a means of social closure. All of this marks Ulster in the late twentieth century as unique in the British Isles. The survival of anti-Catholicism in the US is thus puzzling, for at first sight it appears to undercut the sociological explanation of anti-Catholicism advanced here.

Anti-Catholicism in the US: Sociology or Theology?

A great deal of anti-Catholic literature that circulates in Northern Ireland is from North America. The depository of anti-Catholic literature known as the 'Vatican Bank' is located in the US, there are sites on the Internet from America which peddle anti-Catholicism, and perhaps the world's largest publisher of this kind of literature, Chick Publications, is based there, which specially tailors some of its publications to North American popular culture, by producing pocket-size comics. Paradoxically, however, the US is pluralistic in religious affiliations and in the range of social cleavages around which group mobilisation can occur. It is the epitome of the modern, and post-modern, industrial society in which secularisation has diminished the space for religion, and thus the saliency of religious differences, and it has a penchant for theological liberalism, as witnessed by the many dialogues between Reformed theologians and the Catholic Church that have occurred in the US. The Catholic Church is also perhaps at its most progressive and liberal in North America, blunting the edge of any remaining religious fissure. Sociologically, it appears most unlike Ulster and more like Britain. A sociological explanation of anti-Catholicism in Northern Ireland argues that anti-Catholicism survives primarily because it is a proxy at the structural level for other forms of conflict, rooted in economics, politics and 'social capital'. This gives an explanation of its relative demise in Britain, since the diffusion of patterns of differentiation in Britain causes religious affiliation to be a proxy for nothing other than faith in God as expressed in different interpretations of doctrine. The lines of fissure in Britain characterise the US as well.

Anti-Catholicism, in other words, ought, by this explanation, to have diminished in the US.

In an attempt to rescue a sociological explanation it could be argued that this description of patterns of differentiation in the US is inaccurate, and that anti-Catholicism survives in the US because it has remained a proxy for other sorts of conflicts, which have their base in the economic migration of Catholics from Ireland, Europe and the Spanish-speaking world. This results in competition over scarce resources and attempts at social closure through anti-Catholicism. There are three problems with this argument. First, some of the anti-Catholic literature is published in cities which have not yet received the wave of the most recent economic migrants from the Spanish-speaking world, although the effects of the much earlier Polish and Irish migration could remain as a distant remnant. Second, Catholicism is a poor boundary marker for economic migrant status given that many new immigrants are from parts of Asia and the Far East. Primarily, however, the articulations of anti-Catholicism in the North American literature make no reference whatsoever to these 'outsider' groups for whom Catholicism is supposed to be a marker. If the intent is to engage in social closure of otherwise marked groups by using the proxy of Catholicism, the attempt fails because no such groups are identified and no reference is made to scarce resources. The literature remains exclusively at the level of ideas without reference to social structural considerations, and even though the articulations are as much political as theological, the former concern is about the alleged world-wide political ambitions and conspiracies of the Catholic Church rather than narrow nation-state politics.

In this sense the US is like Britain in that anti-Catholicism remains at the level of ideas, rarely affecting individual action in the form of harassment of Catholics or discrimination against them, and never touching the level of the social structure (or certainly no longer doing so in the case of Britain). What differentiates Northern Ireland is the progression of anti-Catholicism to this third level. In using anti-Catholicism as a proxy for social structural conflicts, Northern Irish Protestants draw on North American literature at the level of ideas, importing the material in bulk and circulating it widely, but they give it a twist by using it functionally for social structural purposes and they add to it a local version in which the issues of social closure and ethnic boundary maintenance are overtly identified. The North American literature in Northern Ireland gets wrapped up in social structural concerns in a way that it does not in the US. What distinguishes the US from Britain is merely that anti-Catholicism at the level of ideas is overt rather than latent. It is so because there are fewer restrictions on freedom of speech in the US than in Britain and because there is a larger critical mass of conservative evangelicals in the US, which is partly the result of its larger churchgoing population overall and partly the growth of Christian fundamentalism and the Christian New Right in the US, which has not occurred in Britain (on the Christian New Right in the US, see: Bruce, 1988; Bruce et al., 1994; C. Hall, 1997). And it has remained important at the level of ideas in North America because, for a certain kind of Protestant, variously described as conservative evangelical, fundamentalist, Bible-believing, Christian New Right, and 'born again', theological doctrine is simply part of their self-identity as Christians.

This constitutes the irreducible religious dimension to anti-Catholicism (at least in its covenantal and Pharisaic modes): a 'holy remnant' remains locked in sixteenth-century theological disputes because their faith in God gives a personal preference for an ancient interpretation of doctrine. Sixteenth-century conflicts remain alive for them because of their version of Christianity and their choice of faith. They thus continue to serve as an audience for this material at the level of ideas, while some also show commitment to evangelising Catholics in order to 'save' them from damnation, for which this sort of literature has an added purpose (which is why Chick comics always end with a prayer which Catholics are supposed to say upon leaving the Catholic Church and obtaining 'true' salvation). The 'holy remnant' who believe such things is found throughout the White, Anglo-Saxon, Protestant world, which is why anti-Catholic literature at the level of ideas is published in Britain, Canada, South Africa, Australia and New Zealand, and is imported from these countries into Northern Ireland (see Figure 2 in the Introduction, p. 9), where it has been used for a much greater and broader social project, the purpose of which goes beyond theology to social stratification and social closure. This is the irreducible sociological dimension to anti-Catholicism. Religious bigotry is found throughout the world and in all faiths, and in some countries it expresses itself in anti-Catholicism, but what distinguishes Ulster Protestant bigots is not the level of religious bigotry but the sociological purpose to which it is put and the enactment of this project at the social structural level. This is what distinguishes anti-Catholicism from anti-Protestantism in Ireland.

Well, is Anti-Catholicism Scriptural?

Anti-Catholicism is a special form of sociological process because it comes with an in-built rationalisation and legitimacy that is unimpeachable, at least to Christians: it is sacred duty for Christians to reject Satan and oppose forms of false doctrine. The notion that anti-Catholicism is scriptural, and that loyalty to the one true God requires opposition to the Catholic Church, gives the process the same rationalisation as anti-Semitism and Islam-phobia. This study has attempted to show that anti-Catholicism has a sociological base and that *claims* that anti-Catholicism is scriptural have been used in a social project that was incidental to theology. However, this does not necessarily mean that it is unscriptural. Even right beliefs can be used for wrong purposes. Many Protestants, including some in Northern Ireland, would contend that Catholicism is unscriptural while baulking at the way in which theology has been used for secular purposes. This is particularly likely in the Pharisaic mode. The project to which others have put theology would not deter them from the view that anti-Catholicism is sanctioned by God; it is merely that some of the ways it is expressed are wrong – the claim itself is true. Are they right?

Christian sociologists, who are not expert theologians, need to tread warily in confronting this issue, yet as Christians, they are tempted to go where other sociologists might fear to tread. But since an answer to the question is implicit in the previous chapter, the argument of this book can be stated clearly and unambiguously in summary form. The claim that anti-Catholicism is scriptural is based on lies, half-truths, ancient prejudices and out-dated conspiracy theories. As discussed in Chapter 5, common-sense notions of theology amongst certain Protestants render doctrinal differences with Catholicism as more important than the larger areas of agreement over doctrine, overlook the different doctrinal positions of various Reformed denominations, and make no allowance for the radical shifts in Catholic doctrine, especially concerning the salvific role, since Vatican II. These days, anti-Catholicism is based on distorted notions of what the Catholic Church teaches and what Catholics are supposed to believe. Half-truths and lies help to support this distortion. This is not to say that Catholic doctrine and practice is wholly consistent with Scripture, no more than it is to claim that Reformed theology is either. But Catholic theology is not the anti-Christian doctrine it is caricatured as being, nor are its worship practices pagan. Anti-Catholicism is not, therefore, the way to deal with remaining areas of doctrinal disagreement, no more than anti-Protestantism is for differences with (or within) Reformed theology. It is a gross and calumnious distortion to claim that Catholicism in unchristian, and as part of the Church of Christ we should approach doctrinal differences in a spirit of love not hatred or rejection. But the distortion does not end there. Anti-Catholicism distorts Scripture, as Chapter 5 attempted to show. Anti-Catholics in the covenantal and Pharisaic modes seem more to avow historical continuity with sixteenth-century doctrine than show understanding of what Jesus or His Apostles actually said, and many Northern Irish believers in Him who said we should turn the other cheek seem unable to even extend a hand to their Catholic neighbours. Jesus says categorically that we should have the love of God in our hearts (John 5:42), even toward our enemies (Matthew 5:44). People who know Scripture, Jesus says, but reject what the author of Scripture preaches, will not receive honour from God (John 5:39–44). God wants His servants and children not only to say what He is like, but to be like Him; not only to say what He wants but to do and demonstrate His will; not only to declare what they think they should believe but to have a passion for the heart of God (for a similar point see Bickle, 1995: 92). Catholics clearly have a passion for the heart of God, but even if they did not, covenantal and Pharisaic type anti-Catholics are not being true to the heart of God by rejecting, harassing, intimidating, ostracising, ridiculing and caricaturing Catholics or their beliefs, who are as much His children as Protestants, made in His likeness. As John the Elder writes in the first of his epistles: 'whoever says that he is in the light, yet hates his brother is in darkness. Whoever loves his brother is in the light' (1 John 2:9–10).

The untrue claim that anti-Catholicism is scriptural constitutes, in sociological terms, a myth. In a study on South Africa, Leonard Thompson (1985) referred to the social function of myths, arguing that myths are tales told about the past to give credit to, or discredit, a regime, and that Afrikaners established a whole cluster of myths to support apartheid. Using this analogy, Bell (1990) looks at some of the myths within Loyalism in Northern Ireland. That anti-Catholicism is scripturally sanctioned is one of the myths of Ulster Protestantism generally. As understood in sociology and anthropology, myths are broader than Thompson suggested. They are false and fanciful stories and narratives that pattern social relationships between the subjects of the myth and those who reproduce it, registering either the subject's estrangement from or integration with the social group who hold to the myth (see, for example, Lincoln, 1989: 24). Some myths identify 'outsiders' in order to exclude them, others 'insiders' to include them; some groups feature themselves alone in the myth in order to socially integrate all group members. Myths thus involve narratives about the past in order to serve the interests of the present in defining social forms, social relationships and structural properties. In this way, they are socially integrative and exclusionary at the same time because myths address moral boundaries. They are also of practical value, in that myths can be used to supply precedents that help with solutions to present problems, and they provide models of appropriate behaviour in a host of situations, present and future, including struggles between antagonistic segments of society (see ibid.: 32). Myths therefore evoke sentiments about the past, present and future within an in-group, which assist in understanding social life and in shaping patterns of social action for that in-group, even though they are fanciful and false. Irrespective of their falsity, such myths become constitutive of society because they shape and mould how society is understood, which in turn affects the parameters of how people act. The claim that anti-Catholicism is scriptural is one such myth, whose purposes this book has hopefully illustrated. The myth has become constitutive of the way Ulster is defined for a certain type of Protestant, and it shapes how they perceive and relate to Catholics.

Persuading these sorts of Protestant that the claim is mythological, however, is difficult because the myth is so integrated into their world view and patterns of social interaction. To challenge it would require a complete reassessment of what passes for 'normality'. The everyday life-world and common-sense knowledge which sustain the myth and into which the myth is bound, would be threatened by the recognition that it is fanciful and mythological. Anti-Catholicism is 'normal' to these sorts of Protestant, and breaking through their notion of 'normality' will perhaps require the power of God rather than sociologists.

Postscript: A Better Way

Introduction

Protestantism is not innately anti-Catholic, and only specific social circumstances cause some Protestants in Northern Ireland to be so. Nor are all Protestants in Northern Ireland anti-Catholic; some are committed to developing positive relationships with Catholics and to healing communal divisions. There are several high-profile attempts to find a 'better way' for dealing with ancient theological conflicts and disputes, which display that some Protestants have a heart open to Catholics. These are in addition to the high-profile cross-community activities that take place in a secular context. Church-based initiatives include reconciliation and ecumenical groups, such as Faith and Friendship, the Lamb of God community, Corrymeela, Restoration Ministries, the Cornerstone Community, and Rostrevor Christian Renewal Centre; groups which confront conservative evangelicals with their responsibilities for peace in Northern Ireland, like the Evangelical Contribution on Northern Ireland (ECONI); and various initiatives which have involved Catholics and Protestants coming together to address issues of faith, theology, politics and sectarianism, such as the Inter-Church Group on Faith and Politics, the Irish Inter-Church Meeting on Sectarianism, and the Irish School of Ecumenics.

Together they have published an impressive amount of work which seeks to challenge sectarianism and find a 'better way', and many of these organisations and groups are responsible for pamphlets, magazines and booklets which point the direction forward. For example, ECONI has published *Faith in Ulster* (Thomson, 1996), *The Fractured Family* (Thomson, n.d.), and *Lion and Lamb*, amongst other things, the Inter-Church Group on Faith and Politics is responsible for publications like *Living the Kingdom* (1989), *Forgive Us Our Trespasses*, and *Remembering Our Past: 1690 and 1916*, and the Irish Inter-Church Meeting for pamphlets like *Sectarianism: A Discussion Document* (1993) and *Roots of Sectarianism in Ireland* (Liechty, 1993), these being the fruits of its large research project on sectarianism. Conferences on alternatives to sectarianism have been numerous, leading to publications like *Sectarianism* (Williams and Falconer, 1995); and inter-church forums are active, some of which have produced reports on their activities (see Morrow, 1997). In addition to high-profile activity, a considerable amount of cross-community work takes place at the local church level. Local churches have often sought to work together for the good of their neighbourhood, and churches from each tradition have opened themselves to members from the 'other side' and held joint activities, such as the Fitzroy-Clonard group and the Christian Fellowship Church's links with the Lamb of God community.

Some of the suggestions which appear in this Postscript thus replicate ideas and endorse themes that are now emerging widely as a 'better way' for dealing with doctrinal division. They are none the less worth restating, for it is appropriate to end this study of anti-Catholicism positively. The study has shown that fear of 'the other' is taught from the pulpits and in the writings of anti-Catholics. It is also transmitted through families, friends, and neighbours by means of common-sense articulations of anti-Catholicism. It is reinforced by sectarianised social norms which mitigate against conciliatory social contact between Protestant and Catholic individuals. It is fertilised by 'victim mentality' politics which stirs up fears of the end of the Union with Britain. The partisan local media often assist in this polarisation. Thoughts on a 'better way' therefore must address four realms: the realm of individuals, religion, politics, and the media.

The Realm of the Individual

Anti-Catholicism affects individuals, whether at the level of ideas, behaviour or the social structure, and mitigates against peaceful social relationships. The sectarian ghettoisation of where people live, work, and play is the context in which opportunities for social interaction with 'the other' are limited. Any social contact between 'divided' individuals that does take place has often been limited to confrontational contexts, for example, during contentious marches. Thus we suggest that anti-Catholicism (and anti-Protestantism) could be challenged by creating more opportunities for positive social interaction, including 'listening to each other's stories'.

It is well said by others before, that people in Northern Ireland need to learn something about themselves as much as other people. Addressing his fellow Protestants, with their 'precarious sense of belonging' in Ireland, the Rev. John Dunlop once wrote that they need to learn that they had developed a siege mentality to a degree that they had lost their spiritual freedom in Christ, that their victory in the 1690 meant dispossession and humiliation for their neighbours, that the Catholic community feels threatened, that they often come across to outsiders as intolerant and arrogant (1995: 61), that demands for justice for themselves must include justice for everyone, and that everyone is made in the image of God (ibid.: 121). Catholics also need to learn some things about Protestants: that Protestants feel their culture and tradition is threatened, that after nearly four hundred years, Protestants are not 'settlers', and that they will not, cannot, leave the North East corner of Ireland. All these things can be learned by telling and hearing each other's stories.

The end of apartheid in South Africa has exemplified the potential of this kind of interaction, and lessons can be learnt from this. Bishop Michael Cassidy, a key figure in the negotiations for peace in South Africa, has told of how people from across the political spectrum were given the opportunity to spend weekends away together. The agenda was simple: the participants were encouraged to tell each other their life stories. Debate, negotiation and criticism were all 'off limits'. This was a time to listen. At one such weekend, the leader of an extreme right-wing white minority party heard a black former prisoner at Robben Island tell of an incident in which a warder ordered him to dig a pit in the ground, get into it, and then bury himself up to his neck in it, so the warder could urinate in his face. This story cut through the propaganda which had for so long strengthened the divisions in South Africa. After hearing it, the white politician returned to his party and dissolved it. He had seen that the oppression of black people was not just a propaganda story made up by some terrorists. It was real. These weekends also gave black leaders the opportunity to hear the perspectives of their white opponents. Sharing truth instead of propaganda helped to create a context for meaningful negotiation.

Hearing each other's stories in Northern Ireland will enable people to get beyond the rhetorically constructed caricatures of 'the other', and go to the heart of the matter – that in Ulster, everyone suffers; in Ulster, everyone has a certain responsibility for the conflict; in Ulster, everyone fears someone else. The potential for good in hearing each other's stories is inestimable: people will see in each other what they have in common. Protestants will see that individual Catholics do not constitute the monolithic evil they have been taught to fear. This is the kind of social contact between individuals which is required to produce the context for a more just, equal, and peaceful society. But it cannot exist in a vacuum. The three other realms must work to afford individuals these opportunities. Some suggestions for these follow, and it is to the realm of religion that we now turn.

The Realm of Religion

Although the conflict engendered through the medium of anti-Catholicism is much more than a purely religious problem, the churches have a vital role to play in challenging the roots and consequences of anti-Catholicism. The churches could show leadership in four ways: facing the past, accepting responsibility for the future, creating conditions to engender trust between divided people, and addressing the socio-political norms which foster sectarianism. In facing the past, it is necessary to see that all sides in the conflict have some responsibility for it. It is also important to recognise that all sides have suffered because of the conflict. As the director of the Irish School of Ecumenics has said: 'some may bear more guilt than others, but [we must] ... face the reality that all are affected and all of us are responsible ... The churches have contributed to the building and cementing of sectarianism, now they need to collaborate in its dismantling' (G. Smyth, 1996: 53). The Irish Council of Churches suggests that Christian groups should 'examine [their] own tradition to see what particular responsibility it bears for what has happened'. The 'brokenness' must be named, faced, and acknowledged by those responsible for it. A former Moderator of the Presbyterian Church in Ireland, the Rev. John Dunlop, has suggested how this might be done:

in the past neither part of Ireland was successful in accommodating diversity ... As one considers the past, it seems to me impossible to take personal responsibility for something in which one was not implicated. I do not think, for example, that it is possible for John Major to take responsibility for British policy at the time of the Irish famine. However, what is possible, and what may be helpful, is to acknowledge that the community or nation, from which one is historically descended and within which one now belongs, did things which were wrong. As people frequently share some sense of pride in the past achievements of a community or nation, it not to be impossible to acknowledge some regret for past deficiencies. (Dunlop, 1996: 23)

To facilitate public acknowledgement of responsibility, leaders of the main Protestant churches could issue a joint statement of apology for any of the past actions of their churches which have in some way fostered anti-Catholicism. In 1966, the Presbyterian General Assembly passed a resolution encouraging Presbyterians 'humbly and frankly to acknowledge and ask forgiveness for any attitudes and actions towards our Roman Catholic fellow-countrymen which have been unworthy of our calling as followers of Jesus Christ'. Other similar actions could take place. For instance, the two anti-Catholic Articles in the Westminster Confession of Faith, and the declaration of the Ulster Covenant, are examples of Protestant Church actions which played a part in allowing division to foster, and these should be addressed as a means of fostering peaceful relationships. Victor Griffin, formerly Dean of St Patrick's Cathedral in Dublin, has argued that offensive references in various doctrinal statements constitute sniping and hardly endear people to the Christian faith – this applies to Catholic statements that Anglican orders are null and void, for example, and to the statement in the Anglican Thirty-Nine Articles that the Catholic mass is blasphemous, dangerous and deceitful (Griffin, 1996: 10; on changes in various doctrinal statements, see Inter-Church Council, 1993: 127–41). The Catholic position on mixed marriages could also be addressed. The churches need to speak out. The Methodist Church has said that

> silence has often been perceived as neutrality, but that is a delusion. Churches and theology are never politically neutral. Silence is always support for the status quo ... This is not about raking up the past and it's not about living in the past ... It's about the healing of memories, acknowledging the past, our sectarian contribution to the brokenness, division and suffering. Unless we name and own the past, there is no liberation to shape and build a new future. Only as we publicly acknowledge the pain of the past and our contribution to that pain, is there release of creative imagination to build peace and a new community. (McMaster, 1996: 34–5)

The Archbishop of Canterbury and Cardinal Daly have already made some conciliatory gestures similar to those suggested here. The Irish Council of Churches suggests that Christians 'be prepared to repent for what our tradition has done wrong and seek forgiveness'. It should be borne in mind that lack of action by many churches, as well as positive sectarian actions, had the effect of allowing the conflict to gain momentum. So it is not just what the churches did 'wrong' that must be faced; they must also consider what they neglected to do 'right'. There are signs from many church leaders that this is already happening. Kinahan (1995) says: 'so long as we Ulster Protestants refuse to respect or even hear the political and religious opinions of our Roman Catholic neighbours, there will be division and hatred in our land. It is my belief that ... this is totally antithetical to the gospel of Jesus Christ. Our present troubles are in no small measure caused by the refusal of Christians to take their faith seriously – in other words, by the refusal of Christians to be Christian.' After acknowledging the mistakes of the past, it is incumbent upon the churches to take responsibility for their role in the future. Perhaps the most important (and contentious) recommendations made by the Irish Council of Churches in this regard are to 'refuse to use politics or the State to sustain religious identity ... [and] seek as far as possible to remove, or at least mitigate, some of the adverse social consequences of theological or doctrinal differences'. The churches must take responsibility for dismantling anti-Catholicism and building peace. This includes articulating a theology of social engagement which underlines the Christian responsibility to be politically anti-sectarian, and to be so must be seen as mandated by the very nature of Christian faith. Churches must begin to see (and many already do) that engaging with the conflict here from an anti-sectarian perspective is not an optional 'ministry activity' for those who follow Christ. It is at the heart of the purpose of Christianity. Jesus Christ taught that his followers were to 'forcefully lay hold of the Kingdom of God' (Matthew 11:12), bringing justice and peace to society. All too often, the kind of contribution made to Irish society by the Christian Church has been the very opposite of that. This is not to say that all churches have made negative contributions to the conflict, but the hegemony of sectarianism is partly due to the fact that moderate opinion has been largely under-represented in the political realm. Churches which desire to be a part of peace-making should encourage their membership to be part of that change themselves. This means making informed decisions about politics, which will undermine the power-base of sectarian parties. There are parties on both sides of the debate over sovereignty which articulate a sectarian ethos, and there are other parties on both sides which articulate a pluralist ethos, embracing diversity. Churches should be involved in examining the political perspectives represented in Northern Ireland, and asking whether or not particular parties will foster peace, or feed division.

The division in Northern Ireland has been fostered by problems of perception; on both sides of the religious divide there are perceived doctrines which engender hostility between the two. Therefore, it is fundamental to any proposed solution to the division that people seek to understand and address the 'cores of reasonable concern' on the other side. To this end, churches need to examine their engagement with the conflict, and ask themselves what they can do to change circumstances. The Roman Catholic Church could engage in an exercise of articulating a defence against anti-Catholic rhetoric, and explaining what has changed in its doctrine in recent years, articulating what it believes in a more high-profile manner. For instance, the Roman Catholic doctrinal position on mixed marriages has changed to the effect that the Church no longer insists that the children of a mixed marriage be raised Catholic; the regulations surrounding the Eucharist with non-Catholics have been relaxed; perhaps most importantly, the Church no longer considers itself to be the 'only true Christian Church'. Protestant churches could show their support for this by stating publicly the level of doctrinal agreement between the main Protestant churches and the Vatican. A programme of education in which the non-covenantal Protestant denominations set out their basic principles of belief, alongside those of Roman Catholicism would go a long way towards removing many Protestant fears of the 'Catholic threat'.

It is also necessary that churches show leadership by involving church leaders in dialogue with each other, attempting to develop a public theology of reconciliation, being open and not ashamed to admit this, while creating opportunities for lay people to meet those in other denominations to 'share their stories'. Leaders and lay people alike should take the risk of meeting 'the others' for worship, or at least, attend other worship services without taking part, in an attempt to understand the reality of experience that exists on the other side. The Rev. Timothy Kinahan, a Church of Ireland minister, tells of going with a group of other Protestant leaders to a Novena. 'None of us Protestants felt happy with the theology that lay behind some of what went on, but none of us could deny that this was a real experience for those who took part, and that the prayers offered were deep and genuine. As our resident octogenarian Methodist said to me afterwards, "I can't condemn this now"' (Kinahan, 1995: 83). If, as the Methodist Church has said, 'there is a place in every local congregation and parish for a local parish reconciliation group', then local congregations should research the possibilities for this, and act accordingly. If leaders are seen to be taking these and other risks, trying to understand those different from themselves, building relationships with people in the other community, then the chances of such efforts succeeding among lay people increase. In the midst of all the practical attempts at dialogue, building trust, and engendering the conditions for reconciliation, what is most required is a spirit of generosity. Generosity to seek first to understand, then to be understood. Generosity to listen to those who feel hurt or isolated by us. Generosity to persevere when we see little or no hope of change. As Archbishop Desmond Tutu said: 'never be afraid to talk, because when people sit down and talk to each other they discover each other. Old obstacles seen in the light of a new relationship become less formidable and progress is made.'

Those Protestant churches which do not form part of the 'anti-Catholic' bloc can foster peace by supporting Catholic attempts at explaining doctrine, along with their own effort to articulate why they consider it acceptable to seek ecumenical goals. Unfortunately, most of such articulation has only reached a church audience, or worse, only church leaders. Something has to be done to disseminate it in the public arena. If this was creatively attempted, those people who subscribe to the three modes of anti-Catholicism would be isolated, and forced into the position of having to articulate their position in a way commensurate with the politics of peace-making, rather than the rhetoric of divisiveness.

The Political Realm

Politics in Ulster is sectarianised into three blocs. Unionism has traditionally articulated Protestant fears of a united Ireland, and this research has shown that these fears, to a great extent, can reflect in anti-Catholic beliefs. Political differences are still articulated in terms of religious nationalism – 'Protestant Unionism' versus 'Catholic nationalism'. Anything other than Unionism is conflated by Unionists as a Roman Catholic threat. The battle lines drawn during the Reformation may have become blurred elsewhere in the world, but, as is the case in many aspects of Northern Irish society, politics stays firmly rooted in the past. The more extreme, covenantal anti-Catholic political perspective, promoted by the DUP, explicitly articulates Unionism in terms of the sixteenth-century Reformation – the Pope is the antiChrist, Rome is the Whore of Babylon, the Republic of Ireland is a state in the clutches of Rome, IRA members are Catholics, and the threat to the Union is a Catholic one. Political articulations often remain ghettoised in the past, and one-issue politics, the issue of sovereignty, dominates. Parties are elected not on the basis of their social or economic policies, but on their constitutional stance. The battle lines drawn at the Reformation have disappeared in other societies, but in Ulster the fight against Catholicism rages on politically because theology stands for political and economic differences. Politics is so deeply rooted in historical sectarianism that socio-economic issues are always secondary to the question of sovereignty, which does not make for a mature democracy, and mitigates against equality, justice, and a healthy economy. It is clearly desirable that political loyalties and identities be extended beyond the single issue of the Union and political representatives should take a prominent role in de-escalating conflict by broadening the base of politics. This is already happening to some extent within Loyalism with the rise of the new Loyalist parties which are trying to mobilise on a non-sectarian basis, although they are meeting opposition from traditional Loyalism and old tribal loyalties. Such tribalism was described in an interview by David Ervine, from the PUP, as 'like piss down the leg – it initially gives a warm glow but it quickly goes cold'.

The Realm of the Media

The media has played an influential role in the transmission of anti-Catholicism, but it can also have a role in challenging anti-Catholicism. We recommend two simple things which journalists and broadcasters in Ulster can do to address this: identify the 'good things' that are being done in the name of reconciliation, and the 'bad things' done in the name of anti-Catholicism need to be faced and challenged in the media.

Conclusion

Choosing a 'better way' to deal with doctrinal disagreements requires, in the Rev. Ken Newell's view, 'the cross of the deepest choice'. That is, it involves a sacrifice. The difficult, sacrificial choice involved is that of giving up the security and comfort of old traditions, ancient ways of thinking, and familiar mind-sets. Peace asks more of people than hatred because peace requires people to change; all too often people see peace as requiring someone else to change rather than themselves. But peace is Northern Ireland requires that we ourselves change – that we release the bitterness, prejudice and bigotry which makes up our view of the world, that we let go of the painful memories and the years of resentment that are our preoccupation, and that we change our view of people and whole communities. Hanging on to the past, however, is easier because the past is what we are used to. However, there is no 'better way' in the past: peace requires courage and faith to break the vice-like hold of the past. Peace requires compromise, and compromise requires a break with ancient tradition and heritage. The 'better way' for all of us points in that direction.

Notes

Introduction

1. By social closure, sociologists mean the process by which groups protect their access to scarce socio-economic and political resources and close off access to less powerful groups.
2. Anti-Protestantism exists in Northern Ireland at the levels of ideas and behaviour, in much the same form as anti-Catholicism, but it has not permeated the social structure of Northern Irish society and thus does not exist at this level. This distinguishes it from anti-Catholicism. It is also the case that anti-Catholicism is more systematic, sustained and culturally embedded. Anti-Catholicism is a culturally sanctioned and legitimate resource available to Protestants, which has been mobilised politically and economically for long historical periods, distinguishing it further from the more occasional and ad hoc anti-Protestantism found amongst some Catholics. Anti-Protestantism is not a political, economic and cultural resource in the way that anti-Catholicism is.
3. Clearly, people saw the Pope as claiming infallibility long before the Catholic Church declared him so, which did not occur until the nineteenth century.

Chapter 1

1. Technically, it is only appropriate to refer to 'Britain' after English and Welsh union with Scotland in 1707, although Union itself reflected a long period before of English dominance.
2. British interests in Ireland changed back and forth, so they oscillated rather than made a unilinear progression toward the Catholic position.
3. Munster and Ulster were the two primary sites for the plantation. Informal colonisation took place elsewhere, but this was not a centrally planned plantation (Foster, 1988: 71).
4. The presence of Scots prior to the plantation feeds the twentieth-century myth that Ulster Protestants rather than Gaels were the original inhabitants of the province, and that the plantation was simply 'the great return'. This myth is popular amongst Loyalist paramilitary organisations, and appears in many articles in Loyalist magazines, since it offers a rationalisation for violence based on rights accorded to Ulster Protestants by means of original inhabitance.
5. While the tendency for the key social groups to define themselves in terms of opposition to each other began almost immediately with plantation, to begin with there was not a unified Protestant group, for while the Protestant denominations were united in their anti-Catholicism, they disagreed amongst themselves, and dissenters were subject to hostility from the Established Church, although not on the level of Catholics.
6. Thus, although the Presbyterian Church received quasi-state sanction by being financially supported by government, persecution persisted. The Church received this support on and off until disestablishment of the Church of Ireland in 1869.
7. The letter was a blatant attempt to stir up anti-Catholic feeling and bore little relation to reality. In 1682, for example, William Molyneux in Dublin collected together statistical accounts of Irish districts, and those from Ulster showed a quiescent and defeated Catholic population, little capable of massacre. The entry for the Armagh area said that the 'few Irish amongst us are very much reclaimed of their barbarous customs, the most

of them speaking English'. There were no Irish in Ballycarry, and Kilroot was 'all pres-
biterians and Scotch, not one natural Irish, nor papist' (quoted in Bardon, 1992: 149).

8. It is worth recalling that William's victory was also one for Parliament over absolutism,
and the new King William faced this as an early reality when the Irish Parliament
overturned his Limerick Treaty.

9. According to Bardon (1992: 170), the Catholic working class, unable to even contemplate
land purchase and expecting only the shortest lease, were hardly touched by the penal
laws. He does admit, however, like many others, that the penal code kept alive and vivid
the defeat, confiscation and subjugation it symbolised.

10. Episcopalianism had first to take a covenantal and conservative shift before pan-
Protestantism could emerge, and reform for Catholics become more threatening. This
did not occur until the nineteenth century.

11. The reasons behind the massive emigration of Ulster Scots lie elsewhere than in their
religious persecution. There was famine and disease in Ulster, as well as considerable
poverty as a result of rising rents. Poor harvests and bad weather affected farming in
Ulster severely at this time.

12. Thus ending the policy of English governments which sought to so denude the Catholic
Church of clergy that it would wither away.

13. The extent of Wesley's anti-Catholicism has been much debated. He is appropriated by
Protestant political clerics today, who are imbibed with anti-Catholicism, as one of their
pantheon. There are good grounds for this. Haydon (1993: 63–5), shows that early
Methodism had a dislike for Catholicism. Some of Charles Wesley's hymns demonstrate
this and John Wesley wrote supporting the penal laws. When John Wesley first went to
Ireland, he apparently took with him a history of the 1641 massacre, and in 1758 he wrote
in his diary that Catholics seemed to have changed little since then in their thirst for blood
(quoted in ibid.: 65). He was once attacked by a Catholic mob on an evangelistic mission
to Ireland and encountered some hostility from the Catholic clergy, but mostly he
restricted his activities to Protestant areas, showing little enthusiasm for converting Catholics
(on his missionary activity in Ireland, see Hempton, 1996; Hempton and Hill, 1992).
Yet, he was not consistent. The worst case of anti-Methodist violence occurred in Cork
and was from Protestants, and in his open letter to Catholics, for example, he was very
conciliatory, such that Burrows referred to 'Wesley the Catholic' and Haydon (1993: 17)
sees him as ecumenical. He set Methodism to be the friend to all and the enemy of none,
and modern-day Methodists in Northern Ireland lay great stress on the tolerant strain in
Methodism (see McMaster, 1996, 1997). As Montgomery (1993) argues, whatever anti-
Catholicism he may have had, he was always conciliatory and never doubted that
Catholics were nothing less than Christian.

Chapter 2

1. The bishops did not act uniformly on the extent to which they allowed fraternisation
with Protestant clergy. A parish priest in County Down was suspended in 1839 for
occasionally visiting his Protestant brethren (Rafferty, 1994: 118).

2. Liberal Protestants, in theological and political terms, were considered by other Protestants
as apostates, needful of conversion and correction, like Catholics.

3. Protestants eventually won so many concessions from the British government that the
system was no longer non-denominational but Protestant, and the Catholic Church set
up its own schools system. Ever since, Northern Ireland has been left with all the
misfortunes of segregated schools.

4. This is a point which Bruce recognises with respect to Paisley's evangelicalism in the
twentieth century, which he sees as arising out of a threat to a settled and secure Protestant

identity (for Bruce's claims about Paisley, see Bruce, 1986, 1994; see also Wallis et al., 1986).

5. A similarly rapid political shift, but one in the opposite direction, was evident in the Dutch Reform Church in South Africa, which went within the space of ten years from arguing that Scripture legitimised apartheid to a position of anti-racism. Positions of leadership within the Church were assumed by urban middle-class Afrikaners, from the 'enlightened' stance, wresting power away from the rural-based traditional conservatives. Power within the Ulster Synod from the 1820s fell into the hands of the conservatives under the leadership of Henry Cooke.

6. O'Connell even put up Protestants as pro-emancipation candidates supporting the Catholic Association, although not in the North.

7. Even stricter covenanters existed within the Reformed Presbyterian Church (on which, see Loughridge, 1984).

8. In later life, Cooke admitted that Catholicism was Christian, and he once attended a funeral at a Catholic church.

9. Thus is was that nearly a century before the great famine, some Protestant clergymen in Dublin were criticising Catholicism as injurious to industry, giving liberally to eating and drinking, and unwilling to work. See R. Woodford, *A Sermon Preached at Christ Church, Dublin on 13 May 1764* (quoted in Haydon, 1993: 4).

10. Cullen also insisted on Roman styles of dress, and priests around Dublin were required to wear soutanes and Roman hats.

11. Cullen wanted a specifically Catholic curriculum, which is why he favoured separate Catholic schools and objected to Catholics attending the new Queen's Colleges. Only a Catholic university could protect young Catholics.

12. He was not beyond being anti-Semitic either. He portrayed Jews as money-lenders who were fattening while Ireland starved, claiming that all Ireland's exports went to Jews in London.

13. Higgins's main contact with Cullen occurred before Cullen arrived in Ireland as bishop when Cullen was responsible for Irish matters in the Vatican. Higgins was an ardent supporter of Irish nationalism and gave himself the prefix 'O' to commemorate O'Connell.

14. Conservative evangelicals within the Church of Ireland and the Presbyterian Church were also in favour of reform of the Anglican Prayer Book because it was said to be 'Popish' and 'Romanist'. They wished it shorn of Catholic overtones, as they did other features of worship, like communion, which were alleged to be too Catholic (see Akenson, 1971: 303–4).

15. The 1848 incident is belittled by Kee as the battle of Widow MacCormack's cabbage garden (Kee, 1995: 103ff.) because it was so small scale but it was an important symbol of protest, both to later Irish Republicans, who would incorporate it into their pantheon, and to Protestants at the time.

16. One of the reasons why so much rioting took place on the streets in 1864 was because Edward Harland, shipbuilder and major employer, threatened to lay all men off if Catholic workers were victimised. By 1892, however, Catholic labour could be dispensed with, and a similar riot led to no such declaration in support of his Catholic workforce, who by this time comprised only about one in ten of the labour force.

17. It is worth noting that in this sermon Hanna also called on Protestants to defend themselves by military force if necessary, and he urged people to mobilise themselves into corps. The *Belfast Newsletter* carried an advertisement calling for tenders to supply 20,000 rifles before 1 June 1886.

18. This was in part a reference to franchise reform which opened up the vote to labourers and artisans, who used it to support landowners rather than farmers. As Walker notes (1989: 162), the beneficiaries of franchise reform were the landowners, not the farmers, for newly enfranchised labourers voted for landlord candidates rather than

representatives of the tenant farmers. Most labourers received better treatment from landlords than farmers. However, franchise reform also allowed the sectarian and anti-Catholic feelings of the Protestant working class to enter parliamentary politics, as candidates sought to appeal to this powerful section of the electorate.

19. There is some doubt that the marriage broke up under the advice of the priest for it was suspected at the time that the husband left of his own accord (see Liechty, 1993: 37).

Chapter 3

1.   There has been something like collective guilt by Unionists at abandoning Protestants in the South, which has led some Unionist politicians to aportion blame to a particular section of Unionism and to exaggerate the extent of the alleged annihilation of Protestants in the South. It is true that they are a cultural minority; that their population has decreased – in part through intermarriage, in part through migration North – and that they confronted a state which excluded them politically from positions of influence. But they have always been a very economically privileged minority, much like the English in South Africa or Jews in the US. For a review of the research on Protestants in the South which demonstrates this, see Whyte (1990: 150ff.).

2.   This was urged on the Church by Protestants and by English Catholics. An editorial in *The Tablet* on 4 December 1920 demanded that Cardinal Logue excommunicate all members of Sinn Fein. The Northern bishops in particular were against this (Rafferty, 1994: 206).

3.   To support his feeling that the Catholic Church showed Protestants like him little generosity in the early years in Northern Ireland, the Rev. John Dunlop cites the incident when the Catholic Church refused permission for members of the Irish government to attend the funeral of the Protestant former President of Ireland, Douglas Hyde, with the poor men having to sit outside the church in their cars (Dunlop, 1995: 113).

4.   The Free State government initially paid the salaries of some Catholic teachers who refused to recognise the new state, but this did not last long as the government became consumed in the civil war.

5.   The powers of the Act were described by G.B. Hanna, a liberal Unionist, as allowing the Ulster Home Secretary 'to do whatever he likes or let someone else do whatever he likes for him' (quoted in Farrell, 1976: 93). The Act was originally intended as an emergency measure, annually renewable, but it was made permanent in 1938. In 1963, when introducing draconian security legislation in the aftermath of the Sharpeville massacre, B.J. Vorster remarked that he 'would be willing to exchange all the legislation for one clause of the Northern Ireland Special Powers Act', which he intended as a put-down for his English-speaking critics.

6.   There is a claim that after the failed 1962 campaign by the IRA, which saw many volunteers stand down, it was incapable of reactivating itself for the terrorist campaign in 1968–9 and that the bombs were placed by the UVF in order to polarise the political situation and bring O'Neill down (see Farrell, 1976: 256). It was only after the deterioration of civil unrest in 1969–70 that the IRA resumed its terror campaign – before then the acronym had stood for, as commonly stated, 'I Ran Away'.

7.   Paisley and ordinary Free Presbyterians defend themselves by arguing that they are opposed to the Catholic Church rather than individual Catholics, that it is the system to which they are opposed not people (see Taylor, 1983: 102–3, 110; Cooke, 1996: 61). But this distinction is hardly maintained in discourse or action. As Cooke shows (1996: 62), describing Catholics as 'Popeheads' and 'incubators for Rome' hardly maintains the neat distinction, neither do the insults hurled at individual bishops, priests and nuns. It is hardly a distinction that Catholics in Northern Ireland recognise from their experience.

8. The Celtic church presents anti-Catholic Protestants with particular problems. St Patrick, therefore, could not be a Catholic. Paisley's *Protestant Telegraph* once said that he was a 'Biblical Protestant' and not a 'Papist priest', while most recently Clifford Smyth has claimed that the Celtic church was not Catholic (1996: 33).
9. As an illustration, the *Protestant Telegraph* wrote on 28 December 1968: 'Ulster is the last bastion of evangelical Protestantism; we must not let drop the torch of truth at this stage of the eternal conflict between truth and evil ... We are a special people, not of ourselves, but of our divine mission. Ulster arise and acknowledge your God.'
10. The sermon is recorded on tape and is entitled 'What is really going on at Harryville'.
11. The strategy gets its name from a Captain Boycott, who was land agent for an absentee landlord, who evicted three families over rent arrears and was ostracised by everyone in the neighbourhood, giving us the name 'boycott' (C. Smyth, 1996: 8).

Chapter 4

1. This will be discussed in much greater length in Chapter 5.
2. Some of the Old Testament prophecies which are popular in the covenantal mode, notably Jeremiah and Isaiah, look forward to the Messiah and indicate that the New Covenant will write God's laws on people's hearts. They use the phrase 'circumcision of the heart' to describe the contrast of the Old and New Covenants (see Jeremiah 4:4 for example). By this is meant that physical circumcision as a mark of the covenant with God, will be replaced with a spiritual one, where the mark of loyalty to God is carried by love in the heart.
3. The Protestant 'lads' were more heavily involved in a sectarian youth culture by virtue of their membership of the Orange flute bands, and more likely to engage in sectarian activity on the streets because of the masculine nature of much anti-Catholic intimidation. Thus Bell (1990) found that Protestant girls were more likely to be in relationships with Catholic boys across the sectarian divide.
4. The brutal murder of Tommy Morgan, a young and innocent Catholic teenager, near the village of Clough in the summer of 1997, his body left unrecognisable and identified only from dental records, was the responsibility of the LVF; those charged with his murder have entered the LVF compound in prison. In response to the murder, the largely Protestant villagers painted out all Loyalist murals and took down the bunting. The LVF ominously warned the painters, wiping out the red, white and blue, that the LVF knew who they were. In acts like this, one is hardly able to recognise the God that Billy Wright had supposedly converted to, and Pastor McClinton described Wright before his murder as having backslidden, knowing that he had walked away from the greatest friend (Jesus) he ever had, although McClinton still says that Wright was a committed born-again believer.

Chapter 5

1. Some Loyalists contend, however, that the Scots Irish were the first descendants, and thus that the plantation was a homecoming. This is another example of common-sense practical reasoning.
2. This is not to say that all those who favour this version are anti-Catholic, but anti-Catholics have a preference for the King James version based on the common-sense reasoning that it is a Protestant version, developed in a Protestant setting and used by God as a blessing to many Protestant revivals. This will be discussed later.
3. 'Brits out', 'RUC – SS', 'Free Derry', 'sniper's alley', and many more, are the 'pre-constructeds' and formulaic phrases of the anti-British discursive formation of Republicanism.

4. No one is arguing that all Protestants are anti-Catholic, nor that anti-Catholicism is constitutive of the identity of all Protestants. The claim is that anti-Catholicism is constitutive of the identity of those who happen to be anti-Catholic – it is the 'master status', as Weber put it, of anti-Catholic Protestants. It follows, therefore, that I am not arguing that Protestants need to change their identity before anti-Catholicism can disappear, merely that those Protestants who are anti-Catholic should construct their Protestantism by other means.

5. I am using the term 'conservative evangelical' here to describe a theologically conservative evangelical position, distinguishable from more liberal evangelical positions, some of whom could be ecumenical. This theological conservativism also tends to run with a conservative stance taken on political issues, as reflected in the political prelates like Cooke, Hanna, Paisley and McClinton.

6. In the evangelical tradition, certain people are recognised as being Spirit-filled because of the way the Holy Spirit has entered their lives, but this extends only to offices in as much as they would believe that the denomination as a whole has been specially blessed by the gift of the Spirit.

7. There is some uncertainty over whether the Apostle John, author of the Gospel, also wrote the three letters in the New Testament bearing that name, which have been attributed to John the Elder, who was a disciple of the Apostle (see Hunter, 1972: 178–9).

8. One other reason for the attraction of Paul's writings, especially his epistle to the Romans, is the stress he laid on obedience and loyalty to civil authorities and political rulers, a reassuring idea during moments of instability in late medieval Europe.

9. Contrasting Paul's statements on faith in Romans with his references to love in 1 Corinthians, Hunter (1972: 110) remarks that the former reveals Paul as the theologian, the latter the pastor.

10. Cooke notes that this letter was printed in full in the October 1983 issue of *The Revivalist*, Paisley's church magazine, but that it was not taken as a genuine expression of faith because Paisley's mind-set does not permit him to believe anything emanating from Rome (Cooke, 1996: 43).

11. There had also been a meeting in Lausanne between evangelicals and Catholics, which produced a joint report in 1984.

12. The Catholic notion of purgatory, describing a situation where salvation is uncertain and doubted, is replicated in Protestantism, at least as a practice if not a doctrinal belief, in that many Protestants are in a similar state of uncertainty and insecurity, knowing themselves saved but seeking reassurance from God that it is so. This 'Protestant purgatory', as Pastor Paul Reid once described it, tends to reflect in the same doubt about salvation as many Catholics who believe in purgatory, and in the same performance of 'good works' as a resolution to this existential anxiety. Anti-Catholics stress that there is no Biblical basis for belief in purgatory, and some Catholic theologians agree. McBrien's view, for example, is that there is no biblical basis (McBrien, 1994: 1166), but that it has become a practice that calls us internally to atone for our sin and by means of which we die and rise with Christ (ibid.: 1167). This makes it much like Protestant practices which resolve the existential anxiety by obtaining *reassurance* of salvation through good works.

13. The Vatican first sanctioned translations of the Bible in 1752, nearly one and a half centuries after the King James version, but by the end of the next century there were seventy-one Catholic vernacular Bibles (McManners, 1990: 351).

14. The following section is taken from Barkley (1967). Readers should also refer back to Chapter 4, where there is a discussion of interpretations of the Book of Revelation.

15. Gareth Higgins is separately undertaking research on the myth of the antiChrist in Northern Irish Protestant culture for a doctorate.

16. Given the frequency with which borders change, theology is clearly violated often.

17. Paisley has alluded to these remarks often in justifying his own harshness toward Catholicism.

Conclusion

1. Notions of national origin and native and settler mentality are reducible to religious difference.
2. In a new book, David Martin (1997) argues that religion can be a cause of conflict but only in as much as it constitutes one marker of social identity.
3. Rafferty (1994: 285) makes the point that Catholics tend not to define themselves in terms of their opposition to Protestants, in the way that certain Protestants do with respect to Catholicism. The latter tendency is likely to lead to greater antipathy because their identity is set up in terms of defiance and difference.
4. This is not to claim that anti-Catholicism in Ireland has ever attained the levels of barbarity witnessed in the Holocaust, although some Republicans would claim this. A similarity has been drawn between the 'great famine' and the genocide of the Holocaust, but this is not worth taking seriously (see Kennedy, 1997). There was, however, a strong element of racism in British policy during the famine.

Bibliography

Akenson, D.H. (1971), *The Church of Ireland* (New Haven, CT, Yale University Press).
—— (1988) *Small Differences: Irish Catholics and Irish Protestants* (Dublin, Gill and Macmillan).
—— (1992), *God's Peoples: Covenant and Land in South Africa, Israel and Ulster* (London, Cornell University Press).
Allen, T.W. (1994), *The Invention of the White Race* (London, Verso).
Arnstein, W.L. (1982), *Protestants Versus Catholics in Mid-Victorian England* (Columbia, Columbia University Press).
Ankerberg, J. and Weldon, J. (1994), *Protestants and Catholics: Do They Now Agree?* (Chattanooga, The Ankerberg Theological Research Institute).
Aughey, A. 1989, *Under Siege: Ulster Unionism and the Anglo-Irish Agreement* (Belfast, Blackstaff).
Bailie, W.D. (1981), 'The Reverend Samuel Barber 1738–1811', in J. Haire (ed.), *Challenge and Conflict: Essays on Irish Presbyterian History and Doctrine* (Belfast, Baird).
Bardon, J. (1992), *A History of Ulster* (Belfast, Blackstaff Press).
Barkley, J.M. (1959), *A Short History of the Presbyterian Church in Ireland* (Belfast, Publications Board of the Presbyterian Church in Ireland).
—— (1967), *The Anti-Christ* (Belfast, Presbyterian College).
—— (1981), 'The Presbyterian Minister in Eighteenth Century Ireland', in J. Haire (ed.), *Challenge and Conflict: Essays on Irish Presbyterian History and Doctrine* (Belfast, Baird).
Belfast Newsletter.
Belfast Telegraph.
Bell, D. (1990), *Acts of Union* (London, Macmillan).
Beresford, D. (1987), *Ten Dead Men* (London: Grafton).
Bickle, M. (1995), *Growing in the Prophetic* (Eastbourne, Kingsway Publications).
Blaney, R. (1996), *Presbyterians and the Irish Language* (Belfast, Ulster Historical Foundation).
Boal, F., Campbell, J. and Livingstone, D. (1991), '"The Protestant Mosaic": A Majority of Minorities', in P. Roche and B. Barton (eds), *The Northern Ireland Question: Myth and Reality* (Aldershot, Avebury).
Boettner, L. (nd), *The Mass* (Belfast, Evangelical Protestant Society).
Bowen, D. (1983), *Paul Cardinal Cullen and the Shaping of Modern Irish Catholicism* (Dublin, Gill and Macmillan).
Bowen, K. (1983), *Protestants in a Catholic State: A Privileged Minority* (Dublin, Gill and Macmillan).
Bowyer Bell, J. (1996) *Back to the Future* (Dublin, Poolbeg).
Boyd, A. (1969), *Holy War in Belfast* (Dublin, Pretani Press).
Breen, R (1996), 'Who Wants a United Ireland? Constitutional Preferences Among Catholics and Protestants', in R. Breen, P. Devine and L. Dowds (eds), *Social Attitudes in Northern Ireland: The Fifth Report*, (Belfast, Appletree Press).
Brewer, J.D. (1984), 'Competing Understandings of Common Sense Understanding', *British Journal of Sociology*, 35: 66–74.
—— (1990), *The Royal Irish Constabulary: An Oral History* (Belfast, Institute of Irish Studies).
—— (1991), *Inside the RUC: Routine Policing in a Divided Society* (Oxford, Clarendon Press).
—— (1992), 'Sectarianism and Racism and their Parallels and Differences', *Ethnic and Racial Studies*, 15: 352–64.

—— (1994), *Black and Blue: Policing in South Africa* (Oxford, Clarendon Press).

—— and Guelke, A., Hume, I., Moxon-Browne, E. and Wilford, R. (1988), *The Police, Public Order and the State* (London, Macmillan).

—— and Lockhart, B. and Rodgers, P. (1997), *Crime in Ireland 1945–95: 'Here be Dragons'* (Oxford, Clarendon Press).

Brown, T. (1981), *Ireland: A Social and Cultural History* (London, Fontana).

Bruce, S. (1985a), 'Puritan Perverts: Notes on Accusation', *The Sociological Review*, 33: 47–63.

—— (1985b), *No Pope of Rome* (Edinburgh, Mainstream).

—— (1985c), 'Authority and Fission: the Protestants' Divisions', *British Journal of Sociology*, 36:592–603.

—— (1986), *God Save Ulster!* (Oxford, Oxford University Press).

—— (1988), *The Rise and Fall of the New Christian Right* (Oxford, Oxford University Press).

—— (1994), *The Edge of the Union* (Oxford, Oxford University Press).

——, Kivisto, P. and Swatos, W. (1994), *The Rapture of Politics: The Christian Right as the United States Approaches the Year 2000* (New Brunswick, Transaction), published from the special edition of *Sociology of Religion*, 55: 3 (1994) on the New Right.

Buckland, P. (1981), *A History of Northern Ireland* (Dublin, Gill and Macmillan).

Campbell, A. (n.d.), *The Beast Has a Banner*.

Chadwick, O. (1990), 'Great Britain and Europe', in J. McManners (ed.), *The Oxford Illustrated History of Christianity* (Oxford, Oxford University Press).

Clayton, P. (1996), *Enemies and Passing Friends: Settler Ideologies in Twentieth-Century Ulster* (London, Pluto Press).

Clouse, R.G. (1980), 'Apocalyptic Interpretation of Roman Catholicism in Seventeenth-Century England', *Fides et Historia*, 13: 34–41.

Colley, L. (1992), *Britons: Forging the Nation 1707-1837* (New Haven, CT, Yale University Press).

Collinson, P. (1990), 'The Late Medieval Church and its Reformation', in J. McManners (ed.), *The Oxford Illustrated History of Christianity* (Oxford, Oxford University Press).

Combat.

Coogan, T. P. (1995), *The Troubles* (London, Hutchinson).

Cooke, D. (1996), *Persecuting Zeal: A Portrait of Ian Paisley* (Dingle, Brandon Book Publishers).

Corish, P. (1985), *The Irish Catholic Experience* (Dublin, Gill and Macmillan).

Cosgrove, B (1996), 'Intercommunion: A Change in the Requirements', *Ferns Diocesan Bulletin*, vol. 51: 4.

Curtis, L.P. (1971), *Apes and Angels: The Irishman in Victorian Caricature* (Washington: Smithsonian Institution Press).

Daly, Cathal (1983), *Coming Back Home* (Belfast, Blackstaff).

—— (1991), *Price of Peace* (Belfast: Blackstaff).

de Semlyen, M. (1993), *All Roads Lead to Rome?* (Gerrards Cross, Dorchester House Publications).

Devlin, Paddy (1981), *Yes We Have No Bananas* (Belfast, Blackstaff).

Dickson, D. (1987), *New Foundations: Ireland 1660–1800* (Dublin, Helicon).

Dunlop, J. (1995), *A Precarious Belonging: Presbyterians and the Conflict in Ireland* (Belfast, Blackstaff Press).

—— (1996), 'Brokenness, Forgiveness, Healing and Peace in Ireland: 3', in *Brokenness, Forgiveness, Healing and Peace in Ireland* (Belfast, St Anne's Cathedral).

Evangelical Contribution on Northern Ireland (1996), *Faith in Ulster* (Belfast, ECONI).

Fairclough, N. (1994), *Discourse and Social Change* (Cambridge, Polity Press).

Farrell, H. (n.d.), *Rome and the R.S.V.* (London, Trinitarian Bible Society).

Farrell, Michael (1976), *The Orange State* (London, Pluto Press).

—— (1978) *The Poor Law and the Workhouse in Belfast 1838–1948* (Belfast, Public Records Office of Northern Ireland).

Farrell, Monica (1986), *Why am I a Protestant Daddy?* (Belfast, Evangelical Protestant Society).

—— (n.d.), *The Protestant Question Box* (Belfast, Evangelical Protestant Society).

Fee, G.D. and Stuart, D. (1982), *How to Read the Bible for All It's Worth* (London, Scripture Union).

Fleming, G. (forthcoming), *McGinnis VC* (Belfast).

Ford, A. (1986), 'The Protestant Reformation in Ireland', in C. Brady and R. Gillespie (eds.), *Natives and Newcomers: Essays on the Making of Irish Colonial Society* (Dublin, Irish Academic Press).

Foster, R.F. (1988), *Modern Ireland 1600–1972* (London, Penguin).

Fulton, A.A. (1981), 'Church in Tension' in J. Haire (ed.), *Challenge and Conflict: Essays on Irish Presbyterian History and Doctrine* (Belfast, Baird).

Gailey, A. (1975), 'The Scots Element in North Irish Popular Culture', *Ethnologia Europaea*, 7: 2–22.

—— (1987), *Ireland and the Death of Kindness* (Cork, Cork University Press).

Garland, R. (1997), *Seeking a Political Accommodation: The Ulster Volunteer Force* (Belfast, Shankill Community Publication).

Gassmann, G. (1996), 'Lutheran-Catholic Agreement on Justification: A Historical Breakthrough', *Ecumenical Trends*, 25: 1–5.

General Synod of Ulster (nd), *Records of the General Synod of Ulster from 1691 to 1820* (Belfast, General Synod of Ulster).

Gibbon, P. (1975), *The Origins of Ulster Unionism* (Manchester, Manchester University Press).

Goldring, M. (1991), *Belfast: From Loyalty to Rebellion* (London, Laurence and Wishart).

Griffin, V. (1996), 'Brokenness, Forgiveness, Healing and Peace in Ireland: 1', in *Brokenness, Forgiveness, Healing and Peace in Ireland* (Belfast, St Anne's Cathedral).

Gumperz, J. (1982), *Language and Social Identity* (Cambridge, Cambridge University Press).

Hall, C. (1997), 'The Christian Left: Who Are They and How Are They Different from the Christian Right', *Journal for the Scientific Study of Religion*, 36: 46–79.

Hall, S. (1997), *Representation* (Milton Keynes, The Open University Press).

—— and du Gay, P. (1996), *Questions of Cultural Identity* (Milton Keynes, The Open University Press).

Harris, M. (1993), *The Catholic Church and the Foundation of the Northern Ireland State* (Cork, Cork University Press).

Haydon, C. (1993), *Anti-Catholicism in Eighteenth-Century England* (Manchester, Manchester University Press).

Hempton, D. (1980), 'The Methodist Crusade in Ireland 1795–1845', *Irish Historical Studies*, 22: 33–48.

—— (1986), 'Methodism in Irish Society 1770–1830', *Transactions of the Royal Historical Society*, 36: 117–42.

—— (1996), *Religion and Political Culture in Britain and Ireland* (Cambridge, Cambridge University Press).

—— and Hill, M. (1992), *Evangelical Protestantism in Ulster Society 1740–1890* (London, Routledge).

Hewitt, C. (1981), 'Catholic Grievances and Catholic Nationalism and Violence in Northern Ireland During the Civil Rights Period', *British Journal of Sociology*, 32: 362–80.

Hickman, M. (1995), *Religion, Class and Identity* (Aldershot, Avebury).

Hickson, M (1884), *Ireland in the Seventeenth Century or the Irish Massacres of 1641–2* (London, Longman Green).

Hill, C. (1971), *The Anti-Christ in Seventeenth-Century England* (Oxford, Oxford University Press).

Hoijer, H. (1967), 'The Sapir-Whorf Hypothesis', in R. Redfield and M. Singer (eds), *Language in Culture* (Chicago, University of Chicago Press).

Holmes, R.F.G. (1973), 'Eighteenth-Century Irish Presbyterian Radicalism and its Eclipse', *The Bulletin of the Presbyterian Historical Society of Ireland*, 3: 7–15.

—— (1981), 'Controversy and Schism in the Synod of Ulster in the 1820s', in J. Haire (ed.), *Challenge and Conflict: Essays on Irish Presbyterian History and Doctrine* (Belfast, Baird).

—— (1982), 'Ulster Presbyterians and Irish Nationalism', in S. Mews (ed.), *Religion and National Identity* (Oxford, Basil Blackwell).

—— (1983), 'Dr Henry Cooke: The Athanasius of Irish Presbyterianism', *Studies in Church History*, 20: 23–46.

—— (1985), *Our Irish Presbyterian Heritage* (Belfast, Presbyterian Church in Ireland).

—— (1997), 'Presbyterians and 1798', public lecture.

Hunter, A. (1972), *Introducing the New Testament* (London, SCM Press).

Hyndman, M. (1996), *Further Afield: Journeys From a Protestant Past* (Belfast, Beyond the Pale Publications).

Ing, P. (1984), *Straight to Catholics* (Kuala Lumpur, Catholic Research Centre).

Inter-Church Council (1993), *Sectarianism: A Discussion Document* (Belfast, Irish Inter-Church Meeting).

Inter-Church Group on Faith and Politics (1989), *Living the Kingdom* (Belfast, Inter-Church Group on Faith and Politics).

Irish News.

Irish Times.

Jackson, B. (1988), *Christian's Guide to Roman Catholicism* (Louisville, Kentucky, Christians Evangelising Catholics).

Jayyusi, L. (1984), *Categorization and the Moral Order* (London, Routledge).

Jenkins, R. (1997), *Rethinking Ethnicity* (London, Sage).

Johnston, P. (1997), 'Celebrating the Past?', *Lion and Lamb* (journal of the Evangelical Contribution on Northern Ireland), 11: 8–9.

Kee, R. (1995), *Ireland: A History* (London, Abacus).

Keenan, D. (1983), *The Catholic Church in Nineteenth-Century Ireland* (Dublin, Gill and Macmillan).

Kennaway, B. (1997), 'What is the Orange Order?', *Lion and Lamb*, 13: 8–9.

Kennedy, D. (1988), *The Widening Gulf* (Belfast, Blackstaff).

Kennedy, L. (1996), *Colonialism, Religion and Nationalism in Ireland* (Belfast, Institute of Irish Studies).

—— (1997), 'The Great Famine and the Jewish Holocaust Compared', paper to the American Conference for Irish Studies, Albany, NY, April.

Kinahan, T. (1995), *Where Do We Go From Here? Protestants and the Future of Northern Ireland* (Dublin, The Columba Press).

Larkin, E. (1972), 'The Devotional Revolution in Ireland, 1850–75', *The American Historical Review*, 77: 625–52.

—— (1980), *The Making of the Roman Catholic Church in Ireland 1850–60* (Chapel Hill, University of North Carolina Press).

Lecky, W.E.H. (1892), *A History of Ireland in the Eighteenth Century* (Chicago, University of Chicago Press, 1972).

Liechty, J. (1993), *Roots of Sectarianism in Ireland* (Belfast, Irish Inter-Church Meeting).

Lincoln, B (1989), *Discourse and the Construction of Society* (Oxford, Oxford University Press).

lo Bello, N. (1982), *The Vatican Papers*.

Loughlin, J. (1985), 'The Irish Protestant Home Rule Association and Nationalist Politics', *Irish Historical Studies*, 24: 341–60.

—— (1986), *Gladstone, Home Rule and the Irish Question* (Dublin, Gill and Macmillian).

Loughridge, A. (1984), *The Covenantors in Ireland* (Belfast, Cameron Press).

Loyalist News.

MacAtasney, G. (1997), *"The Dreadful Visitation" The Famine in Lurgan/Portadown* (Belfast, Beyond the Pale Publications).

MacIver, M.A. (1987), 'Ian Paisley and the Reformed Tradition', *Political Studies*, 35: 359–78.

McAuley, J. (1994), *The Politics of Identity* (Aldershot, Avebury).

McBrien, R.P. (1994), *Catholicism* (London, Geoffrey Chapman).

—— (1996), *Responses to 101 Questions on the Church* (London, Geoffrey Chapman).

McCarthy, D. (1997), 'Framework of Freedom', in 'Tolerance: Freedom of Religion and Belief', Supplement to *Fortnight*.

McDonagh, E. (1996), 'Brokenness, Forgiveness, Healing and Peace in Ireland: 2', in *Brokenness, Forgiveness, Healing and Peace in Ireland* (Belfast, St Anne's Cathedral).

McEvoy, K. and White, C. (forthcoming), 'Security Vetting in Northern Ireland: Loyalty, Redress and Citizenship', *Modern Law Review*.

McFlynn, F. J. (1981), '"Good Behaviour": Irish Catholics and the Jacobite Rising in 1745', *Eire-Ireland*, 16: 31–56.

MacIntosh, J.S. (n.d.), *Martin Luther* (Belfast, Evangelical Protestant Society).

McManners, J. (1990), 'Enlightenment: Secular and Christian', in J. McManners (ed.), *The Oxford Illustrated History of Christianity* (Oxford, Oxford University Press).

McMaster, J. (1996) 'Brokenness, Forgiveness, Healing and Peace in Ireland: 4', in *Brokenness, Forgiveness, Healing and Peace in Ireland* (Belfast, St Anne's Cathedral).

—— (1997) 'Friends of All and Enemies of None', in 'Tolerance: Freedom of Religion and Belief', Supplement to *Fortnight*.

McVeigh, R. (1995), 'Cherishing the Children of the Nation Unequally: Sectarianism in Ireland', in P. Clancy, S. Drudy, K. Lynch and L. O'Dowd (eds), *Irish Society: Sociological Perspectives* (Dublin, Institute of Public Administration).

Mallett, J (1997), *The Hidden Troubles* (Derry, Child Poverty Action Group (NI)).

Martin, D. (1997), *Does Christianity Cause War?* (Oxford, Clarendon Press).

Miles, R. (1982), *Racism and Migrant Labour* (London: Routledge).

Millar, J. (1973), *Popery and Politics in England 1660–1688* (Cambridge, Cambridge University Press).

Miller, D.W. (1975), 'Irish Catholicism and the Great Famine' *Journal of Social History*, 9: 81–98.

—— (1978a), *Queen's Rebels: Ulster Loyalism in Historical Perspective* (Dublin, Gill and Macmillan).

—— (1978b), 'Presbyterianism and "Modernization" in Ulster', *Past and Present*, 80: 66–90.

Moloney, E. and Pollack, A. (1986), *Paisley* (Dublin, Poolbeg Press).

Monaghan, P. (1997), 'What is an Evangelical Catholic?', *Lion and Lamb*, vol. 14: 11–12.

Montgomery, D.J. (1993), *Strangers No More? Evangelicalism, Anti-Catholicism and Evangelical Catholics* (Regent College, Vancouver).

Montgomery, J. (n.d.), *Spotlight on Romanism* (Belfast, Evangelical Protestant Society).

Morrow, D. (1997), *"It's Not Everyone You Could Tell That To"* (Belfast, Community Relations Council).

National Anti-Poverty Strategy (1997), *National Anti-Poverty Strategy* (Dublin, The Stationery Office).

Nelson, S. (1984), *Ulster's Uncertain Defenders* (Belfast, Appletree).

Newsletter.

Nic Ghiolla Phadraig, M. (1995), 'The Power of the Catholic Church in the Republic of Ireland', in Clancy, P., Drudy, S., Lynch, K., and O'Dowd, L. (eds), *Irish Society: Sociological Perspectives* (Dublin, Institute of Public Administration).

Norman, E.R. (1968), *Anti-Catholicism in Victorian England* (London, Allen and Unwin).

O'Connell, P.J. (1996), 'Sick Man or Tigress? The Labour Market in the Republic of Ireland', British Academy Symposium on Ireland: North and South, Nuffield College, Oxford, December.

O'Dowd, L. (1998), '"New Unionism", British Nationalism and the Prospects for a Negotiated Settlement in Northern Ireland', in Miller D. (ed.), *Rethinking Northern Ireland* (London, Longman).

O'Hearn, D. (1983), 'Catholic Grievances, Catholic Nationalism: A Comment', *British Journal of Sociology*, 34: 438–45.

O'Neill, T. (1969), *Ulster at the Crossroads* (London, Faber).

—— (1972), *Autobiography* (London, Hart-Davies).

Oppenheim, C. and Harkin, L. (1996) *Poverty: The Facts* (London, Child Poverty Action Group).

Paisley, I.K. (1958), *The 'Fifty-Nine' Revival* (Belfast, Martyrs Memorial Publications).

Patterson, H. (1980), *Class Conflict and Sectarianism: The Protestant Working Class and the Belfast Labour Movement 1868–1920* (Belfast, Blackstaff Press).

Paz, D.G. (1992), *Popular Anti-Catholicism in Mid-Victorian England* (Stanford, Stanford University Press).

Porter, J.L. (1871), *The Life and Times of Henry Cooke* (London, John Murray).

Porter, N. (1996), *Rethinking Unionism* (Belfast, Blackstaff Press).

Presbyterian Church in Ireland (1840–1850), *General Assembly of the Presbyterian Church in Ireland* (Belfast, Presbyterian Church in Ireland).

—— (1911–1915), *Minutes of the Proceedings of the General Assembly of the Presbyterian Church in Ireland* (Belfast, Presbyterian Church in Ireland).

—— (1921), *Minutes of the Proceedings of the General Assembly of the Presbyterian Church in Ireland* (Belfast, Presbyterian Church in Ireland).

—— (1969), *General Assembly Annual Reports* (Belfast, Presbyterian Church in Ireland).

—— (1986a), *General Assembly Annual Reports* (Belfast, Presbyterian Church in Ireland).

—— (1986b), *Minutes of the General Assembly and Directory of the Presbyterian Church in Ireland* (Belfast, Presbyterian Church in Ireland).

Protestant Telegraph (became the *New Protestant Telegraph*).

Rafferty, O.P. (1994), *Catholicism in Ulster 1603–1983: An Interpretative History* (Dublin, Gill and Macmillan).

Ramprakash, D. (1994), 'Poverty in the Countries of the EU', *Journal of European Social Policy*, 4: 117–28.

The Revivalist.

Rockwood, P.F. (1984), *Romanism and the Bible* (Bicester, Penfold Book and Bible House).

Roman Catholic Church (1994), *Catechism of the Roman Catholic Church* (Dublin, Veritas).

Ruane, J. and Todd, J. (1996), *The Dynamics of Conflict in Northern Ireland* (Cambridge, Cambridge University Press).

Shaw, J.J. (1888), *Mr Gladstone's Two Irish Policies: 1869 and 1886* (London, Ward).

Smith, M. (1995), *Fighting for Ireland?* (London, Routledge).

Smyth, C. (1996), *Boycott: An Examination of the Abuse and Persecution of Ulster Protestants and its Prophetic Significance* (Belfast, Inheritance Ministries).

Smyth, G. (1996), 'Brokenness, Forgiveness, Healing and Peace in Ireland: 5', in *Brokenness, Forgiveness, Healing and Peace in Ireland* (Belfast, St Anne's Cathedral).

Steele, E.D. (1975), 'Cardinal Cullen and Irish Nationality', *Irish Historical Studies*, 19: 8–16.

Stewart, A.T.Q. (1977), *The Narrow Ground: The Roots of Conflict in Ulster* (London, Faber and Faber).

Taylor, D. (1983), *The Lord's Battle: An Ethnographic and Social Study of Paisleyism in Northern Ireland* (Queen's University of Belfast, unpublished PhD thesis).

Thompson, J. (1981), 'The Westminster Confession', in J. Haire (ed.), *Challenge and Conflict: Essays in Irish Presbyterian History and Doctrine* (Belfast, Baird).

Thompson, L. (1985), *The Political Mythology of Apartheid* (New Haven, Yale University Press).

Thomson, A. (1996), *Faith in Ulster* (Belfast, ECONI).

—— (n.d.), *The Fractured Family* (Belfast, ECONI).

Todd, J. (1987), 'The Two Traditions in Unionist Political Culture', *Irish Political Studies* 2: 1–26.

Trew, K. (1996), 'National Identity', in R. Breen, P. Devine and L. Dowds (eds), *Social Attitudes in Northern Ireland: The Fifth Report* (Belfast, Appletree Press).

Ulster.

Ulster Bulwark.

Ulster Defence Association (1987), *Common Sense: Northern Ireland – An Agreed Process* (Belfast, Ulster Defence Association).

Vatican (1993), *Directory for the Application of Principles and Norms on Ecumenism* (Vatican City, Vatican Press).

Vaughan, W.E. (1984), *Landlords and Tenants in Ireland 1848–1904* (Dublin, Gill and Macmillan).

Vine, W.E. (1994), *The Origin and Rise of Ecclesiaticism and the Papal System* (Bicester, Penfold Book and Bible House).

Walker, B.M. (1989), *Ulster Politics: The Formative Years* (Belfast, Institute of Irish Studies).

Wallis, R. and Bruce, S. (1986), *Sociological Theory, Religion and Collective Action* (Belfast, Queen's University of Belfast).

—— Bruce, S. and Taylor, D. (1986), *No Surrender! Paisleyism and the Politics of Ethnic Identity in Northern Ireland* (Belfast, Department of Social Studies at Queen's University).

Whelan, K. (1996), *The Tree of Liberty* (Cork, Cork University Press).

Whyte, J. (1983), 'How Much Discrimation Was There Under The Unionist Regime 1921–68?', in Gallagher, T. and O'Connell, J. (eds), *Contemporary Irish Studies* (Manchester, Manchester University Press).

—— (1990), *Interpreting Northern Ireland* (Oxford, Clarendon Press).

Williams, T. and Falconer, A. (1995), *Sectarianism* (Dublin, Dominican Publications).

Wilson, S. (1984), 'The DUP' *Fortnight*, no. 201.

Wolffe, J. (1991), *The Protestant Crusade in Great Britain* (Oxford, Clarendon Press).

—— (1994), *God and Greater Britain* (London, Routledge).

Woodward, K. (1997) *Identity and Difference* (Milton Keynes, Open University Press).

Wright, F. (1973), 'Protestant Politics and Protestant Ideology', *European Journal of Sociology*, 14: 213–80.

Index